Parish Churches

Their *Architectural Development in England*

HUGH BRAUN

FABER AND FABER

London

*First published in 1970
by Faber and Faber Limited
24 Russell Square, London W.C.1
Printed in Great Britain by
W & J Mackay & Co Ltd, Chatham*

SBN 571 09045 1

To the
parochial church councils
who care for them

Contents

Illustrations

9

Illustrations

Illustrations

I

The Study of Old Churches

Our old parish churches, scattered in their profusion in every nook and corner of the land, have long been objects of interest as well as veneration. Everywhere one finds the village churches, some humble, others stately, and their counterparts the churches hidden about our densely populated cities. Finest of all are the large town churches, packed with monuments of past worthies, presenting their Gothic splendours as the central features of market towns, and surrounded by churchyards which join with the market-places to defy encroachment upon the ancient meeting-places of our urban communities.

To its parishioners their church is the shrine of their history, where their forefathers came in their day to be baptized and married, and around whose walls, their roles fulfilled, they have slept down the centuries in the midst of the scenes they knew.

But to the nation as a whole each parish church is a record of the country's past, a monument to the days of which as children we read in the history books. Kings and bishops pass, and straggling armies, here and there sad battles sweep up to its walls. As poverty and pestilence stalk by, the generations repair and enlarge their churches, adding stone upon stone and spanning across the walls with beams from parish coverts. Fire and decay destroy the village homes, but the parish church survives down the centuries as nucleus for each renaissance.

A national interest in the parish church as a subject for research developed as a reaction from two aspects of life at the close of the eighteenth century. One of these was the Industrial Revolution, the commercial and materialistic nature of which was beginning to irritate the intelligentsia of the period and recreate an interest in what was regarded as the romance of the Middle Ages.

The other factor was the rapidly increasing wealth and political power of the nation and a resulting chauvinistic dissatisfaction with the imported architecture of the Italian Renaissance. Horace Walpole's Gothic Revival, known from the name of his house as 'Strawberry Hill', was in reality a patriotic revolution.

The practical requirements of the new industrial architecture, however, encouraged the less romantic Humanist element among the savants to launch the far more serious Classical Revival which reached its heydey during the railway boom of the second quarter of the nineteenth century. It may well have been the excesses of this architecturally grim era which turned the Englishman's thoughts once more towards his national building style, the familiar Gothic of his parish churches.

The first person to write authoritatively upon the subject of what he called 'English' architecture was a Liverpool architect, Thomas Rickman. His book was published as early as 1817. It has formed the basis of all subsequent literature on the subject. It was he who divided English Gothic into three periods according to the lowering of the pitch of arches from 'lancet' to 'debased'.

It will be realized from this that, notwithstanding Rickman's practical knowledge as an architect, his consideration of historical architecture was based solely upon aesthetic grounds, an attitude which has unfortunately bedevilled all subsequent study and paved the way for the ever-increasing host of amateur architectural historians who are apt to treat all architecture not as building construction but as pictorial design.

Rickman's interest was academic. But the immense problems presented by the arrears of maintenance discernible in our great cathedral churches forced the leading architects of the day to begin a serious study of the 'Gothick'. One of the first to do so was Sir Gilbert Scott, who after an apprenticeship as a designer of workhouses in 1847 became appointed as architect to Ely Cathedral and subsequently to many others. It was in this fashion that the impressive era of Victorian Gothic came into being, architects great and small following the trend and interpreting the medieval as best they could, helped in no small degree by the romantic revival launched by the Pre-Raphaelites.

The revival of interest in matters medieval quite naturally brought about a reaction against the many drastic alterations made to the interiors of old parish churches since the Reformation. The resulting wave of 'church restorations' did a very great deal of damage to the buildings by removing genuine and often charming period features and replacing them with bogus and only half-understood 'Gothic' substitutes. Nevertheless such regrettable excursions had the effect of stimulating national interest in what had come to be accepted as our 'national' architecture.

As the architect of the period was too busily occupied with the practical responsibilities of his profession to devote much time to academic research, it was left to laymen to develop the study of English medieval architecture. In 1849 an Oxford bookseller, J. H. Parker, published a book which extended the work done by Rickman a generation earlier, introduced more detailed illustration to the public, but continued to discuss the aesthetic and delved no deeper into the constructional aspect of architecture. Parker's book went into a number of editions and until the end of the century he remained the authority.

When recalling the work of such men as these early explorers it becomes us to remember the transport problems they had to face. In Parker's day the railways were novelties represented by a few main lines, while Rickman had to rely entirely upon the horse. All the same, they managed to extend their studies over the countryside to provide them with sufficient material to establish a history of Gothic architecture acceptable to the profession, and to discover most of the more remarkable examples known to us today, a fact which in itself is truly remarkable.

While Parker was sufficiently broadminded to carry his researches into the sphere of medieval domestic architecture, the popular interest at the time was probably in the Gothic as represented by the great cathedral and abbey churches, and, more intimately, by one's own parish church. For the upper classes the period was one of expansion in ritual, away from the Methody chapel and towards the medieval splendour of vestments and scenic colour. Thus in addition to the pictorial aspect of architecture, the clergy in particular were becoming interested in the original ritual use of the medieval churches of this country.

An interest began to develop in the historical growth of the church plan. In the same way that elevational architecture had been examined from the pictorial aspect, the plan came to be investigated from the point of view of its accommodation. Although neither exercise was able to take into account any structural considerations, this amateur research continued to explore the church plan and authoritative statements began to appear from the pens of antiquaries.

In addition to a lack of architectural experience, the writers on architectural history were hampered by two other deficiencies. One of these was the ignorance of any country save his own which was then the birthright of every Englishman. The other was the Victorian bias against everything taught in childhood as unworthy of the Englishman's consideration.

Thus, apart from the subject countries of his Empire, the Englishman of the period could accept as significant only France and—for the aesthete—Italy. Holland and Germany were still barbarous. Spain had had the Inquisition and had sent an armada against us. And all had impossible hotels!

Ancient Constantinople was the capital of a country whose inhabitants were unspeakable. They were moreover heathen Mussulmen, foreigners of the worst kind against whom we had fought for centuries in the Crusades.

Latin was a respectable language, especially as, being dead, it was only used by the best-educated people. Greek was certainly respectable, but deviations from the Classical form employed by such people as the Byzantines could only be ignored.

When studying the history of architecture, that of the land of Homer could hardly have been disregarded. Nor could the achievements of Imperial Rome be passed over.

The difficulty presented itself of how to find a link which would bridge the Dark Ages and account for the eventual appearance of

1. The old wooden church at Stock in Essex

2. A little wooden church at West Hanningfield in Essex

an architectural style in this country. The only solution conceivable to the Victorian Englishman was that somehow there must be a direct connection spanning the thousand years between Imperial Rome and post-Conquest England. In other words, the architecture of the latter must be 'Romanesque'.

Thus by a stroke of the pen the glories of Byzantium are banished as though they had never existed.

Only fifteen years ago, the writer, visiting a London institute in which future architectural historians were being trained, and asking to see a book on Byzantine buildings, was told pityingly that the institute did not concern itself with *Oriental* architecture. Yet from the walls of many an English church the 'oriental' faces gaze down upon us today as from a Byzantine mosaic. Look at the great porch of Malmesbury in Wiltshire, or the tiny parish church of Kilpeck in Yorkshire, and you can see far Byzantium carved in English stone.

On page 241 of the *Larousse Encyclopedia of Byzantine and Medieval Art*, Professor Jean Hubert, discussing the Early Middle Ages, sets forth the situation with absolute clarity when he states 'Rome, five times conquered, was no more than a large city of ruins, its aqueducts in disrepair, its countryside a wasteland. The real capital was Byzantium, the only cultural centre . . . .'.

When the huge monastic churches came to be built, these adopted the elongated nave flanked by aisles and might thus be considered to be vaguely basilican. Nothing else about them was Roman. Their architecture was, as indeed one might have expected, entirely a development of the Byzantine. Away from these huge buildings, the rural churches probably followed more closely the compact plans of their more easterly prototypes.

The misleading term 'Romanesque' which has for some time past been applied to the architectural style which was being introduced into this country towards the close of the first millennium may owe its origin to the French, who call it, with still less reservation, 'Roman'.

Our own particular brand of 'Romanesque' has been still further bedevilled by having been divided into two halves on either side of the Norman Conquest, as though the whole of the country's building trade had been exterminated and replaced from the Continent in 1066.

The mistake is not due to the eighteenth-century antiquaries, who were patriotic enough to call all round-arched, pre-Gothick, buildings 'Saxon'. It is true that the enormous wealth looted from the English by the Church following the Conquest enabled it to rebuild all the great Anglo-Saxon minsters so that none remained to bear witness to pre-Conquest achievement. But the builders were still the same as before, and had their works been called at the time 'Norman' it would have been nothing more than a political trick.

It is now too late to restore the use of the word 'Saxon', so the writer has fallen back upon the use of the term 'pre-medieval' to designate the English Byzantine style which preceded the Gothic in this country.

English architectural historians have become accustomed to dividing their Gothic era into three phases—early, middle and late. Since Rickman's day they have been known by the slightly ludicrous names of Early English, Decorated and Perpendicular. Any subdivision of a country's architectural styles is apt to be invidious, for there are no sudden changes of style even where revolutionary influences irrupt from abroad. We shall find later that the middle and late periods of Gothic are apt to interweave more than might at first be supposed.

The movements accompanying the Crusades towards the end of the twelfth century hastened the development of the Gothic style in England. The intermediate period, however, called by architectural historians the Transitional, has not been separately dealt with in this book, nor has the rapid deterioration of English Gothic under first Spanish and then Dutch pressure been accorded more than passing notice as it began to develop through considerable confusion into the English Renaissance.

The thirteenth century, however, a period which saw the aesthetic zenith of the early, purer Gothic which is represented by Salisbury and the Yorkshire abbeys but never really had a chance of achieving a place in the architecture of the parish church, is nevertheless given its own chapter under the heading Early Medieval.

Rickman's two other periods, those not easily separable middle and late divisions which are perhaps styles rather than historical periods, have been joined together under the designation High Gothic. The whole arrangement is of course very arbitrary as, regional tastes apart, it may take several generations to change the face of a country's buildings.

Shakespeare has explained to us how a building is designed—first the plot, then the model. What he meant was that the plan comes first, then its elevational presentation. There are two aspects of any building, its lay-out and its appearance. Both are of interest to the architectural historian, and in a very old building the changes and additions to the plan and the recurring evidences of ever-changing fashion are both endless subjects for investigation.

This book follows the Shakespearian precept by dealing first with the growth of the parish church as a building designed to accommodate a congregation of persons engaged in worship and changing through the centuries as new factors influence the plan. Then, after some consideration of the constructional methods used, we examine the architectural forms deriving from these and the whims of aesthetic fancy by means of which each building displays its face to the countryside it adorns.

In planning, as in architectural expression, the nineteenth-century student of parish church architecture has hitherto devoted his attention towards trying to consolidate a firm link with Rome. Without pausing to consider the realities of the situation he has taken as prototype the Roman basilica, slipping without difficulty into the belief that there could be no other link possible. Had he ignored this preconceived notion and examined the plans of village churches more carefully, he would have found that the link was to be found very much closer at hand.

It is useless to study the plan of a building without going back in time to find out for what purpose it was designed. If one is withdrawing to some distance it is of no use to consider present-day arrangements as identical with those obtaining at the time the building was being planned.

Protestant England could not pretend to a history reaching back more than four centuries. Thus it was important to take the study of the English church plan back over that distance and pick it up at the period just preceding the Reformation. In other words, one had to examine it not only from the point of view of a Roman Catholic, but a Roman Catholic of medieval days.

The difficulty is at once apparent. For the Victorian church, of whatever denomination, packed with pewing and comfortably be-hassocked, bears no resemblance whatsoever to the bare, absolutely unfurnished building of medieval days.

Nor could anyone familiar only with the Anglican parish service, read by a priest seated throughout it just beyond the chancel arch, imagine the same chancel being solely occupied by a priest stationed at a distant altar, far away from his congregation at the end of an empty chancel.

Anyone examining the situation by trying to adopt the viewpoint of a nineteenth-century Roman Catholic would probably have got no further than trying to equate it with an experience of a Mass attended in some church in France or Italy. For here he would have encountered the open 'Baroque' plan and a service still impossible to transfer to an English parish church of the Middle Ages with its long lonely chancel and its spreading transepts from which no one could have seen anything of what was taking place at the altar.

Confronted with this problem of trying to discover just how these churches were used, the writer has studied a number of recommended authorities but has utterly failed to discover any contemporary account of instructions issued to parish priests to assist them in regulating the performance of their rustic services, nor indeed any suggestions as to how these were organized with regard to the buildings themselves.

A vast amount of research has been undertaken and voluminous literature published on the nature of the 'Roman-Frankish' ritual employed during the performance of the Mass in a great church of what we would call our Anglo-Saxon period. All writers agree that even such highly organized worship followed a great variety of interpretations. By the Middle Ages there were in England at least five 'Uses'—of Sarum, York, Bangor, Hereford and Lincoln.

And all these were designed for celebrating the Mass in a monastic choir, a long clear room having the altar at one end and fixed stalls at the other, and could hardly have been transferred to a parish church, administered by a single priest standing before a congregation crowding into a seatless hall, a rustic flock attending to the words of a pastor, far removed in every way from professionals assisting at an organized ritual.

When chancels were short Byzantine annexes and the altar was close at hand one could perhaps visualize the Mass performed as in the 'open' Roman Catholic churches of the present day. But the elongation of chancels which came about during the thirteenth century and the consequent removal of the altar fifty feet or so away from the congregation—where it remained until the Reformation—suggests that more of the service may have taken place at the chancel arch as in the Byzantine ritual, a possibility which is emphasized by the continued use of the transept in English parish church planning.

It appears that in Anglo-Saxon days there was a prelude to the service known as the 'Fore-Mass'; perhaps this took place at the chancel arch.

The writer has talked with priests, Catholic as well as Anglican, who find no difficulty in contemplating the possibility that the scene during Mass in an Anglo-Saxon parish church may not have appeared so very different from the more 'homely' service one sees today in the churches of Orthodoxy.

After all, the church vestments used today in an English church are Byzantine garments, and the Roman Church has never abandoned the use of the Greek appeal 'Kyrie eleison'—Lord, have mercy upon us.

To have talked in this fashion to a Victorian Protestant would have seemed to him the height of impertinence. Orthodoxy would have seemed to him a greater heresy than the Roman, and, in view of its geographical situation, little better than Mohammedanism. The life of Byzantium was known to have been notably immoral. Orthodoxy was the religion of the barbarous Muscovite.

The unravelling of the true history of the English parish-church plan requires the co-operation of two persons, the architect and the ecclesiastic. More than a century has passed since the day of the

Oxford bookseller, and our horizons have extended far beyond his. Yet no attempt has been made by historians to re-examine the tentative theories of Parker's day and reconsider the 'Romanesque' attitude towards English ecclesiastical origins. The writer hopes that this may now be done, and a more reasoned investigation undertaken.

When examining medieval ecclesiastical architecture it is essential to keep in mind the wide gulf separating the 'great' church from its poor parochial relation. At the turn of the millennium the monastic churches were quite enormous, while the parish churches were architecturally almost negligible. The great cathedral city such as Exeter, or the abbey town such as Wilton, had its inhabited area divided, like the countryside about it, into small and densely-packed areas each with its parish church, completely dominated by the great churches towering above them. So they remained throughout the Middle Ages.

But as time went on and market-towns developed independently of the ecclesiastical centres, the single parish church of a township which had hitherto known only a small population might have had to be developed with each generation as its congregation increased, until at the height of the medieval period it might have reached a scale where it could at least vie with many of the lesser monastic churches. Such large town churches might become multi-aisled and extend their transepts to an inordinate length. They would become cluttered with the tombs of rich merchants, and those who perhaps could not achieve right of interment among the noble families whose sepulchres lined some neighbouring minster.

But it is not with these great town churches that the following pages are concerned, rather with the smaller, more intimate buildings found in the country parishes.

2

Early Churches

The church as we have known it for many centuries is a building designed for the congregational worship of a unique God, omnipresent but at all times invisible. Christianity as a religion has been in existence for less than two millennia. But the buildings it uses for worship can trace their origins much further back in history, into the dim distances of the pagan eras of antiquity.

It was difficult for primitive men to feel much confidence in an invisible God whose lineaments they could not conceive. The deity they worshipped and at times appealed to had to be represented by some sculptured figure from which they could form some impression of a real personage and not merely a wisp of cloud or a borrowed voice. The statue had to be established in a becoming setting and attended by a retinue of priests. In this we find the beginnings of religious architecture, the provision of a house for the god.

The shrines of an even dimmer antiquity notwithstanding, the origins of our architecture may be said to stem from the Classical Age of Greece which produced such temples as the Parthenon at Athens. The temple of that day was a rectangular building the roof of which was supported upon sturdy columns of the 'Doric' Order within which light stone partitions surrounded the actual apartment inhabited by the god in the form of a votive statue.

From its primitive beginnings in Bronze Age Greece, temple architecture developed into a style having as its ordinance the 'Corinthian' Order, in which the slender column was crowned by a lovely capital, the 'bell' of which was ornamented by leaves of the acanthus fern, lapping it in tiers and springing out at each angle to form a 'volute' resembling a frond beginning to uncurl. Upon this Order was based the magnificent Hellenistic temple architecture which attended the birth of the Roman Empire.

Great builders though they were, the Roman engineers had no real architectural style of their own and displayed their wisdom by adapting the Hellenistic style to their own large secular buildings constructed in purely practical fashion of brick and concrete. With such sophisticated materials, however, they were able to develop the arcuated form of construction, new to the world of architecture. As Roman taste developed, the arch came to be employed not only as a structural device but as a feature to be displayed in elevations, either singly or as part of an arcade.

The principal ceremony connected with pagan worship was the sacrifice upon an altar, often accompanied by fire. Such altars had inevitably to be set up in the open air, so that the congregations attending upon the sacrifice were without shelter.

The altar was situated before the entrance façade of the temple, so that the statue representing the god was, if not actually visible, at least imaginable to the assembled worshippers. The line passing between the altar and the statue constituted an axis or orientation governing the lay-out of the temple enclosure.

The heyday of the Hellenistic era came at the beginning of the first century A.D. when the Western world was beginning to drift away from paganism, with the monotheistic religions—Judaism and, later, Christianity—bringing the curtain down upon the obsolescent architecture of Classical days. The huge temples of the period were being surrounded by spacious enclosures of ornamental walling designed as scenic architecture on a magnificent scale. The temple of Apollo at Didyma in Asia Minor had its congregational area before the altar laid out in this fashion as a sort of open-air nave, perhaps the first attempt to create an architectural area, not for the accommodation of the god, but for those who were engaged in worship. This fine achievement appeared, however, at the very end of the pagan Hellenistic era so that instead of launching a type of structure which might have soared to unimaginable heights, the Didymaean adventure followed the old gods into oblivion.

During the Imperial Roman period the stage was reached at which worshippers frequented the temple itself to view the votive statue. It therefore became desirable to endow this with a special architectural setting instead of merely placing it in the centre of the apartment.

The old gods of Babylonia had always been set in a niche formed in a wall, as though appearing in a doorway to receive the petitions of their suppliants. The statues were, however, quite small and in no way compared with the huge creations of the Hellenistic world.

One of the most remarkable features of historical architecture is the apse. At first glance it appears to be an incomplete building of which one half is missing. Its external appearance, as a somewhat clumsy bulge, is incidental to its internal function, which is to invite one to inspect some feature to which it forms a setting. In effect a horizontal arch, it may perhaps have had its origin as a revetment to earthwork, as would be necessary, for instance, when providing an entrance façade to a tumulus. The concave façade of the 'long barrow' is a feature well known to the archaeologist. The trilithons of Stonehenge, tomb of the sun, are arranged in a horseshoe formation which would seem to be analagous to an apse. It is possible that the introduction of the apse into the Roman temple as a setting for the cult statue may derive from some such prehistoric origin.

As the Roman engineers developed their new arcuated designs they discovered the tunnel vault and, eventually, the dome. By forming a semicircular recess and covering it with a half-dome they perfected the apse. Lofty apses or 'exedrae' were set in the architectural walling enclosing the wide courts of the Hellenistic temples where they made attractive settings as 'nymphaea' for fountains. Eventually they were brought inside the temple itself to provide an impressive background for the cult statue, setting it, not just in a doorway, but in a cavernous home.

From this period the apse became the recognized terminal feature for a religious building. In addition, the sophisticated

Romans provided an apse at the end of their hall of justice so as to introduce an atmosphere of awe surrounding the magistrates seated around its wall. These justice halls, and indeed any large building of exceptional merit, were designated by the Greek word 'basilica', this meaning, simply, a hall fit for a king. No other architectural period has produced an expression of this sort simply denoting the superlative in architectural excellence. The term 'basilica', therefore, has always remained in use to denote a building of incomparable majesty. To this day, the Baroque cathedral of St. Peter at Rome is called 'basilica'.

Contemporary with the Hellenistic temples were the synagogues of the Jews, the first people to worship an invisible god who needed no representation in sculptured form. Their buildings were designed from the first to accommodate their worshippers under cover. Although not large in area, they were planned to be as commodious as possible. Short rectangles in form, their lines were those of the lesser or provincial Roman basilica planned as a central structure with its walling carried on Classical columns and surrounded on all sides by an aisle with a lean-to roof. (Fig. 1.)

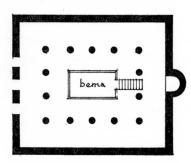

Fig. 1
Plan of early Synagogue
Based on that of the small provincial 'basilica'. A tall central structure carried on columns and surrounded by an aisle. A miniature apse enclosed by doors to provide a cupboard containing the sacred scrolls which are brought to a raised platform, the *bema*, to be read to the surrounding congregation.

The apse was there, but reduced in scale so as to form a cupboard closed by doors which when opened disclosed instead of a statue the scrolls of the Mosaic law, the whole feature designed more on the lines of the Babylonian cult niche rather than the large Roman apse or exedra. An interesting piece of furnishing was the raised platform provided in the centre of the synagogue to which the scrolls were brought for reading to the congregation. On the same platform a trained choir led the liturgy.

Christian worship was intended from the start to be conducted under cover, as befitted a religion opposed to 'pagan' ceremonial in which the sacrifice was attended in the open air.

The basic action in the Christian form of worship was the communal enjoyment of a sacramental meal, such, indeed, as could have been taken in an ordinary home.

Such research as has been found possible into the arrangements for Christian worship in the very early days has indicated that no recognized form of church existed and that the early Christians gathered in ordinary houses to affirm their creed, celebrate their Mystery, and say their prayers in as inconspicuous a fashion as possible. While large gatherings are known to have taken place in the underground caverns outside Rome, the church was not yet a recognizable building.

Thus with the sudden flight of the old gods from the Rome of Constantine in the first half of the fourth century, the architects of the imperial city found themselves completely taken by surprise.

Above three holy sites in Bethlehem and Jerusalem the emperor erected charming little memorial temples, basilicas in miniature. It is to the design of these buildings which, small though they might be, were intended to represent monumental architecture in its highest form, that we owe the origins of Christian church design; but Constantine's three temples were nothing more than monuments and could in no wise accommodate a host of worshippers.

The problems set by congregational worship on an imperial scale were new to architectural experience and the Roman architects were faced with having to design and build covered accommodation, without loss of time, to meet the new demand.

The buildings they ran up were very large, but of the flimsiest construction. They consisted of a long central structure covered with a simple roof and having its walls carried on rows of columns, sometimes salvaged second-hand from destroyed temples. Wide aisles flanked the central 'nave'. Their size and special dignity entitled them to be called 'basilica' but architecturally they were negligible when compared with their mighty Imperial predecessors. (Fig. 2.)

The apse was there, recalling both the pagan statue and the ring of dignified magistrates now replaced by clerics. Before it was set the raised platform of the Jews, also used to seat a choir. In the chord of the apse was the altar upon which was performed the Christian Mystery.

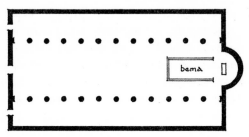

Fig. 2 *Plan of Christian 'Basilica'*
The type of church erected in the Rome of Constantine for Christian worship. A wide nave flanked by wide aisles beyond rows of columns. Covered with light timber roofs. An apse to accommodate the seats of the clergy. In the chord of the apse, the altar; before this the raised *bema* upon which a choir sang and the scriptures were read to the congregation.

Such were the great churches of Constantine's Rome before he moved his capital to the shores of the Bosphorus. It was in these vast bare barns that the Roman Church was established and in which it had to maintain its dignity for centuries to come while Christian architects were covering Europe with some of the most magnificent buildings the world had ever seen.

For soon the imperial city, seat of the Popes and headquarters of the Latin Church, was to decline into a ghost town, having to wait patiently for a thousand years until an architectural Renaissance could restore to it its lost glories.

Meanwhile the churches of both the Latin and Greek rites spread throughout Europe, North Africa and the Near East.

Christianity is believed to have reached Britain by way of Gaul during the third century. Early in the next, bishops are recorded as established in such cities as London, York and Lincoln. Of this period the only known remains of a church are those at Calleva, now Silchester in Hampshire, where the building appears to have been designed as a miniature reproduction of a Roman basilica.

Detached from Roman Britain and preserved from its eventual fate, Ireland is believed to have been originally converted by missionary monks making the long journey along the southern shores of the Mediterranean. Thus during the fifth century, when Christianity was becoming submerged in the stress of heathen invasion, Ireland was developing as the seat of a Celtic Church which was to maintain Christian worship in these islands throughout the Dark Ages closing in upon them.

The Celtic Church appears to have been based upon monastic settlements of humble huts surrounding chapels which were originally simple rectangles but later seem to have been provided with small square chancels. In due course the Celtic Church was able to establish itself to some degree in Britain, but none of its original churches has come down to us.

The Roman rural temple in this country was a small square room surrounded by a veranda, a feature common to all Romano-British domestic buildings and possibly introduced into the temple plan to serve as a rustic version of the Classical peristyle. It seems possible that some of these structures—perhaps even some of the larger ones in the cities—may have been preserved undamaged by subsequent invaders of the country.

When St. Augustine undertook his missionary expedition to Britain at the close of the sixth century, he appears to have been anxious to avoid any disrespect towards existing native customs. He erected several very well-built churches along the south-east coasts which were simple rectangular rooms with an apse at the end and had the remaining three sides surrounded with pillared verandas or porticos. The churches were lofty and must in their day have been most impressive even though they could hardly have stood up, architecturally speaking, to their predecessors the pagan temples in the Roman cities amongst the ruins of which they were built.

A handful of these churches of St. Augustine survived the Dark Ages and are with us today, the most notable example being that at Bradwell in Essex. But their provenance was too restricted for them to have had any influence on the future of English church design. In the simplicity of their plan, however, they must have accorded well enough with the taste of the Celtic Church which remained the only form in which Christianity held on to these islands during the period of the Dark Ages.

Such hold as the Latin Church retained in this country was due to the security of its tenure in Ireland. This was the Celtic Church, established in primitive monastic settlements each with a small chapel or oratory. Its Rite was 'Latin', and its culture strongly Celtic.

During the Dark Ages the Celtic Church in England had dwindled to two main sites. In the north-east the sea-girt rock of Lindisfarne and in the south-west the Isle of Avalon hidden in the Somerset marshes remained strongholds of Christianity surrounded by pagan England. While its buildings may have been too insignificant to be counted as architecture, the Celtic Church continued to maintain its spiritual links with the city of the Popes and by doing so assured the continuity of the Latin Rite in this country.

3

The Byzantine Church

The transfer by Constantine of the capital of the Roman Empire from Rome to Byzantium resulted not only in the building of a great new city on virtually a clear site, but the founding of a new metropolis provided from its inception with an entirely new state religion. As an architectural revolution it was unparalleled in history.

The known world was covered with the temples to a long-established pantheon, architecturally the most magnificent examples of contemporary culture. And all now suddenly become obsolete.

In their place, the votaries of the Hellenistic and Roman world were demanding an entirely new type of building—a Christian church.

In essence, the requirements of the plan were simple enough. What was wanted was a large building capable of accommodating a large congregation under cover.

The hastily-erected 'basilicas' of Rome had been but temporary expedients fulfilling this requirement. But architecturally they were contemptible successors to the glorious temple groups of the Hellenistic Age all of which were still very much in evidence.

Thus it was demanded of the architects of the day that they should apply their skill in designing, not only large buildings for Christian worship, but structures presented in such a fashion that they should represent the crowning architectural achievements of their Age.

The temples of the pagan era had relied for their effect upon row after row of tall columns crowned by masses of rich sculpture. But these costly features, no longer structural but become purely ornamental, had now been banished to the interiors of buildings. Here, in reduced condition, they were being employed to carry walling and by opening up the lower parts of this to enable the floor areas of buildings to be extended into lateral or circumambient aisles.

The early basilicas had been covered with open timber roofs. The latest structural discovery, however, was the vaulted ceiling of stone or concrete which had been developed into a truly monumental architectural feature, the dome.

It was the dome which came to be adopted by the architects of Byzantium as the architectural indication of a church.

A place of worship is usually aligned upon a sacred axis, as Christian churches are aligned upon Jerusalem. But a dome is unsuited as a form of roofing for a building having a pronounced axis; thus the Byzantine churches tended towards more centralized plans, concentrating worshippers into a compact area rather than forcing them to extend away from the altar as in the Roman basilicas.

With such a demanding form of roofing, the domed churches were unable to expand laterally to cover a wide area. But externally their architecture had produced something missing from major structures since the days of the Pyramids, an impression of which the principal element was a vertical one. From this time onwards, the Greek architects—and they were Greeks rather than Romans— no longer concentrated upon the Hellenistic passion for spreading their compositions over vast areas but exercised their structural capabilities in raising them ever higher towards the heavens. This established the form of the Christian church as a lofty structure piling up towards a central crowning feature.

In Rome itself, Ravenna, and other towns of Latinism the basilican halls continued to be built out of the ruins of paganism. But in the Byzantine regions in which a new world culture was taking root, the church form in process of development was adopting the compact centralized plan.

The feature continued from basilican architecture was the use

3. The stone tower-nave of Barton-on-Humber church in Lincolnshire

4. The turriform church at Breamore in Hampshire

of columns to support walling and the lateral expansion of a main structure by means of aisles. And by employing heavy masses of stonework, legacy from the imperial engineers of Rome, in place of the slender columns of the past, the Byzantines were able to lift their structures to a considerable height before crowning them with the desired dome.

An innovation introduced by the Byzantine architects was the division of the aisles into two stories: the vaulted floors—again a Roman device—of the galleries being carried upon a lesser arcade springing from turned columns of Classical type. This 'duplex' principle of alternating heavy piers and slender columns plays a large part in Byzantine ordinance and may be found echoed even in some English parish churches of the twelfth century displaying in their aisle arcades pillars alternating with piers.

But architectural detailing apart, the spirit of Byzantine church architecture was undoubtedly born in the three little memorial temples erected by Constantine over the holy sites in Bethlehem and Jerusalem. These little shrines, most venerated in all Christendom, were not aligned in the normal fashion upon a sacred axis but were actually focused upon the shrine itself and could thus concentrate upon an effect, not of length or breadth, but of verticality.

The three memorial temples were not, however, quite the first of their kind. Circular temples were not uncommon in the Hellenistic world. And the last great temple of all, which bade farewell to all the gods of Olympus, was the mighty dome of the Roman Pantheon, perhaps after all the real progenitor of the churches of Christendom.

But away from Jerusalem the alignment upon the city as a sacred axis had to be maintained. Thus in its final form the Christian Church, even the cathedral in Constantinople itself, had to adopt this axis and abandon the perfect circular plan. Nevertheless the vertical element remained, announced without any chance of misapprehension by the dome, great or small, crowning every Byzantine church.

Thus the structural nucleus of every Byzantine church is a central turriform structure with four semicircular—later to become pointed—arches rising from four tall and massive piers. The tower rises high enough above the surrounding roofs to carry a low dome, usually with a ring of small windows round its base, and often covered with a low-pitched conical roof. (Fig. 3.)

The visible part of the central nucleus becomes circular or octagonal to help carry the dome. The ring of small windows lighting the 'crossing' below is the origin of the English lantern tower.

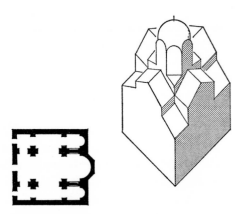

Fig. 3   *Byzantine Church*
A tall building centralized upon a crossing covered by a dome, four short projections supporting this to give a cruciform plan. The whole enclosed within a square. Often two-storied beyond the cruciform portion. Of no great extent when compared with the 'basilican' church, but structurally and aesthetically a building of far greater architectural merit.

The four arches of the crossing lead into four short but tall projections covered with low-pitched roofs which abut against the side of the tower. The cruciform mass thus produced is common to the normal Byzantine church.

The complete circular plan of Constantine's three buildings which had a central feature surrounded by an aisle was retained for special buildings only. Charlemagne's palace chapel at Aachen was so designed—it remains to this day. An early church at St.

Augustine's abbey at Canterbury was of the same form. The Knights Templar retained it throughout their history in recognition of their special interest in Jerusalem. A number of their churches remain to this day, notably the Temple in London.

But the standard plan of the Byzantine church was the central tower surrounded by four short 'wings'.

While Rome remained the political capital of the Latin Church —the liturgical language of which continued, however, to be Greek in some regions as late as the sixth century—Byzantine power and culture ignored it to spread its far more powerful influence into Western Europe. As the Holy Roman emperors shifted their interest away from Italy into the Rhineland, the Western empire, while accepting the Pope of Rome as its spiritual head, was in every other respect a western counterpart to Byzantium and followed the fashion set by the great metropolis.

In architecture, however, the western regions could not compete. They could not raise a dome. So while subscribing to the principle of building churches round and up to a central feature, they had to translate the dome into a tall timber roof. Thus the central domed nucleus of the Eastern Byzantine church is represented in the contemporary West by a towered nucleus capped with a timber steeple. (Fig. 4.)

The building materials of the ancient world were stone and brick. The West had field-stone for rubble walling but as yet no freestone for mason-work. The craft of brickmaking had almost entirely vanished with the Legions.

But the forests of the West could produce quantities of good building timber. So it was towards this material that its architects turned for the construction of important buildings. Western Byzantine timber architecture has so far attracted the attention of few students, but in Scandinavia, Central Europe and Russia there are well-known examples which have managed to avoid the conflagrations of the passing centuries.

The churches of the middle of the first millennium in Western Europe were planned mainly in accordance with the structural requirements of raising a building which would show itself above the humbler roofs about it and to some extent hold its own amongst the trees, hills and other natural features in the immediate neighbourhood. Such buildings would of necessity be much cluttered up with structural elements connected with this desire for height.

Where materials permitted they had an eastern apse. Where not, they compromised with a square recess.

In their simplest form they were a single square tower. The first development would be the addition of the four 'wings' supporting the nucleus. Lastly would come the addition of aisles filling in the four corners.

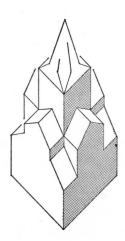

Fig. 4
Western Byzantine
Sketch based upon the ninth-century church of Germigny-des-Prés near Poitiers, but omitting its apsidal terminations. Plan similar to Eastern Byzantine but central feature raised to form a tower. A timber 'broach' is indicated to suggest original form of tower roof.

At the present time there has been no research into how these churches were used. The Orthodox congregations pressed upon the entrance to the apse indicated by the screen or iconostasis. Possibly the Western churches were utilized in much the same manner.

In the Greek church of today the priest stands before the iconostasis while the congregation gather round him, taking turns to hold his heavy missal and joining far more intimately in the service than a Western congregation seated sedately in its pews could do today.

It may be that in the early days of the Latin Church in this country the same kind of intimacy prevailed in the humble seat-less village churches.

4

The Anglo-Saxons

By the second half of the first millennium Rome, seat of the Popes and religious capital of the 'Frankish' Church, had become a ghost-town of imperial memories haunting mile after mile of ruins already overgrown. Culturally it had ceased to exist. Byzantium, now Constantinople, was the capital of a rich empire, founded upon Christianity, and covering with its churches the whole of the Ancient World and all south-eastern Europe. In the Rhineland the Western Emperors adopted Christianity to the extent that they called themselves 'Holy' and 'Roman'. But such culture as they had assimilated was derived from Constantinople, not from the ruins of Classical Rome.

The Eastern and Western Churches each employed its own Rite. The latter had several of these. During the fourth century when the 'Roman' emperors were still in Italy the 'Gallic' Rite is thought to have been carried thence to Africa and onwards to these islands, there to establish the 'Celtic' Church which continued to be the acceptable form of worship until the middle of the seventh century.

The Celtic Church, based for practical purposes in the security of the Irish zone, was probably an 'official' church, patronized by the nobility and centred upon monastic settlements. It was administered by bishops of native origin but maintaining loyal though tenuous contact with Rome. Scattered about Britain within the Celtic orbit were the monastic houses, later to become harassed and destroyed by various Continental invaders. Lack of resources would have precluded the erection of churches for ordinary folk.

The missionary expedition of St. Augustine was an isolated incident, and the pressure from the East forced the British Church to retreat into its two strongholds of Lindisfarne and Avalon. Nevertheless when Christianity finally became established in the Anglo-Saxon England of the seventh century, it was in accordance with the Latin Rite and under the aegis of the Celtic Church that it did so.

For practical purposes, however, Anglo-Saxon England was an appendage of Western Byzantinism, a culture which had progressed along different lines from that which had founded the Celtic Church some three centuries earlier. In Western Europe the form of the Latin Rite in use was the 'Gallican' and it was in the 'Roman-Frankish' form of this that the ritual employed in Anglo-Saxon England came to be established.

During the latter part of the eighth century, church organization had come to be sufficiently well established for the country to be divided into dioceses. But parish development probably followed at a very leisurely pace. The Heptarchy was an uneasy confederation and it was not until 829 that a central government came into being. It may have been well into the tenth century before the parochial organization of England became an established fact.

But by this time Anglo-Saxon England had become a country in its own right. On the perimeter of the sphere of Western Byzantinism, it was particularly free to develop along its own lines as befitted an island nation. Thus, the Danish attacks notwithstanding, the country's monastic houses developed and in doing so provided architectural leadership, until by the tenth century their churches had attained a high degree of architecture. And in their shadow the parish churches at last began to rise.

At the end of the tenth century Archbishop Dunstan was classifying churches as head-minsters, middling-minsters, and lesser-minsters. It sounds as though all these classes represented churches of monastic origin; the term may, however, have been in general use for all churches. A fourth class, churches with no burial ground, he calls field-churches.

The first buildings in which village worship took place may well have been domestic structures as in the early days of Christianity.

But when proper churches came to be built, they would most probably have been founded on the Byzantine model, in its Western form, this of course very far removed from its Constantinople origins.

In architecture there are two primary dimensions, length and breadth. If a roof be needed to protect occupants from climatic conditions, and the third dimension be thus incorporated, this need be no larger than required to enable those below it to stand upright. To increase the vertical element in a building is to approach the monumental.

With this element becoming the primary factor in the design of the Christian church it can be appreciated that, however extensive the plan of a church might be, it was essential that it should be seen to rise above all surrounding structures.

In Eastern Byzantium it was the dome; in the West it was the tower with the steepled roof. Thus we can be fairly certain that the first real parish churches to be built in this country—perhaps in the middle of the ninth century—would have either been very simple structures on the Celtic plan or designed as turriform naves with a small excrescence on the east to contain the altar. (Fig. 7d.) And humble though they might be, their religious status would at once have been advertised by virtue of their height.

The area of the turriform nave would have been governed structurally by the walling material available, in particular the lengths of timbers available for spanning the roof. With posted construction, a timber tower could easily have been surrounded by an aisle in imitation of a large Byzantine church. (Figs. 5 and 6. Plate 1.) The outer walling of such an aisle could be of timber framing or of stone. In some cases the aisle wall could have attained the height of a tower in its own right, with the posted structure remaining concealed within.

A stone-walled building, however, could not have been expanded by means of aisles, as the local builders of those days would have lacked the skill to carry the walling above openings by systems of arches carried on pillars. Thus the only way to extend the accommodation of early stone buildings was to build on adjuncts of stone or timber and make openings through the nave

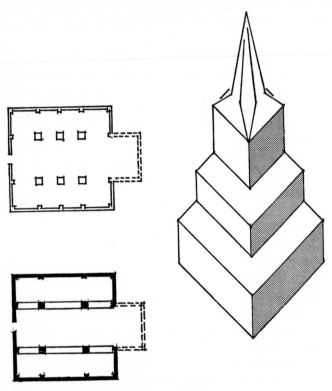

Fig. 5 *Early Timber Church in England*
Based upon a square tower carried upon four great posts but occasionally six as at Blackmore in Essex, upon which building the sketch is based. Surrounded, as in its prototype sketched in Fig. 4, by an aisle. No chancels now remain, as most of the surviving timber churches have been preserved only to serve as bell-towers at the west end of later stone naves. It will be noted that there is an intermediate stage forming a lean-to carried upon the aisle roof which may serve to indicate the system upon which the elaborate timber steeples of contemporary great churches were assembled.

walls to effect connection with each. As the early builders seem to have been unable to turn arches of any but very small spans, such openings would have been very narrow; they could, however, have been quite high.

The side walls of the nave being only half the distance from the altar of that at the west end, the most useful situations for such adjuncts were in those side walls. Thus the lateral 'wing' came to be an established feature of the stone turriform church, joining with the chancel—and perhaps a western extension as well—to imitate the cruciform mass of the contemporary Byzantine church. (Fig. 7*a*. Plate 4.)

There are many indications that the east wall of the nave with the chancel entrance there situated was the focus of the nave plan. The nave of an early church at North Elmham in Norfolk actually runs north and south so that the apse is set in a long east wall. (Fig. 8.) In larger and later churches, such as that at Milborne Port in Dorset, the 'transept' arches of what has become a central tower are set tight up to the east wall so that this runs almost unbroken from the end of one transept to the other.

The majority of turriform naves were probably extended westward by means of a 'wing' on this side so as to produce the Byzantine effect of a cruciform pile of structures supporting a central feature. (Fig. 7. Plate 2.)

It will be seen that all these turriform churches set out on a centralized plan, whatever their system of construction, were purely Byzantine in concept and owed nothing to the long 'basilican' plan originating in the Rome of Constantine.

But the Byzantine plan never made any headway in the old Hellenistic regions of Syria and the North African littoral. Those areas of Christendom remained loyal to the Roman basilica, building wide churches with their naves flanked by Classical columns or Roman arches and covered with timber roofs, low-pitched in the Classical fashion.

North Africa in particular was a region which would have nothing to do with the centralized plan which it would clearly have regarded as 'un-basilical', possibly 'oriental', and certainly barbarous. And it was by way of these regions that the Celtic Church found its way to Britain.

When the Dark Ages came to an end with the spread of Christianity through Anglo-Saxon England during the eighth century, the Celtic Church had two bases from which to expand. Of these the Northumbrian, in the Anglian sphere, would have been by far the most accessible to Continental civilization. Hence it is along our eastern littoral, from Northumbria to the East Saxon border, that we find the earliest churches. These followed, however, the Celtic plan of nave and chancel, both raised in height to monumental degree. (Fig. 13.) By the end of the millennium the Celtic Church form had taken over all the eastern dioceses of Durham, York, Lincoln and Elmham in East Anglia.

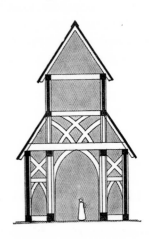

Fig. 6
Section through a 'four-poster' church
Showing the four posts carried on their sleeper foundations and the manner in which they are braced together by curved struts and braces. The surrounding aisle can also be seen.

In Saxon Wessex, however, progress from the Glastonbury base seems to have been much slower. There is no evidence that the Celtic Church plan made any headway at all. It seems probable that Wessex had to wait until the ninth century at the earliest before any kind of parish church plan became accepted, and that when it did, the model was not the Celtic, but the Byzantine plan, emanating from the Rhineland, which came to be adopted.

A building of extraordinary interest is the church which appears to have been built by St. Aldhelm at the beginning of the eighth century at Bradford-on-Avon in Wiltshire. It is built of stone and must have been one of the first stone buildings to be erected since Roman days. The walling is extremely primitive and owes nothing to mason-craft. Its plan comprises a rectangular nave set east and west with a small chancel projecting from its east wall. It displays the proper element of height but there is no sign of any tower.

Thus it is basically a Roman type of church of Celtic origin. But on each side of the nave a small 'wing' projects to introduce a cruciform element into the plan which must certainly represent Byzantine influence.

Perhaps the best-known example of the Western Byzantine type of church—though unfortunately rebuilt—remaining today is that at Germigny-des-Prés near Orleans dating from about the year 810. It has a towered nucleus flanked by the typical four short arms which are in this case extended by apses in their end walls. The exterior illustrates the Byzantine device of piling up a system of features towards a central climax, in this case the central tower, the focus of the interior being the space surrounded by the four great piers of the crossing below. (See Fig. 4.)

Scattered about Western Europe are small square or circular buildings called today 'baptisteries' which are in fact almost certainly early churches supplanted by later buildings and relegated to their present use. Ecclesiologists have become so accustomed to regarding an axial plan as essential to a church that they cannot conceive a church as having a centralized form unless it should be a building of the Templars, with whom it was inevitable.

Even as late as the twelfth century a great Byzantine church such as that of St. Mark at Venice was being followed by another, lavishly be-domed, at Périgueux. During the previous century, however, the octagonal central tower had become the crowning feature of the Western great church.

An early record of exceptional importance is that giving an account of the erection in 878 by Alfred the Great of a church at Athelney in Somerset—ancient Avalon—as a memorial of his victory over the Danes. The description of the building states clearly that it was founded upon four great piers and goes on to say that it was the first to be built upon this plan. This gives a date for the introduction of the standard Byzantine plan into this country.

This was however an important church. The parish church would not have been raised upon piers and arches. The central nucleus would have had to be content with narrow arched openings leading into the adjacent 'wings' and chancel.

When such early adjuncts to an ancient church were retained into the medieval period the arches leading into them had to be widened.

Western adjuncts are not always present to complete the cruciform arrangement. When these are eventually built they are often larger than the others and may have a wide arch joining them to

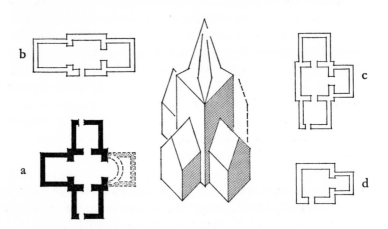

Fig. 7 *Stone tower-nave*
 The 'turriform' type of church, representing the Western Byzantine style in England. Various types of plan are shown. (a) is represented by Netheravon in Wiltshire, (b) by Barton-on-Humber in Lincolnshire, (c) by Hemyock in Devon, (d) by Barnack in Northamptonshire. No chancels remain today; they may have been square or apsidal. Various ways in which the tower might be roofed are shown in Fig. 23. See also Plates 23 and 24.

the central area. That at Netheravon in Wiltshire is an impressive example now lacking its 'west nave'.

 Fig. 7 illustrates the various ways in which the tower-nave could be extended in order to increase accommodation. The completely cruciform plan, as at Breamore in Hampshire, is shown at 7*a*. The 'axial' arrangement is shown in 7*b*: the church at Barton-upon-Humber in Lincolnshire would appear to have been on this plan, which survives into the twelfth century. The nave with wings only, may be seen illustrated in 7*c*. Hemyock church in Devonshire may have been of this class which is seen without its tower at North Elmham in Norfolk. (Fig. 8.) There must also have been churches consisting of a nave only, as in 7*d*; such still exist on the Continent. No chancels attached to turriform naves now remain. They may have been apses or square-ended, long or short as suggested in the illustration.

Discussion of this type of plan cannot, however, be complete without an examination of the twelfth-century 'axial' plans with central towers some of which may be found to have originated as turriform naves still retaining original chancels. (See Fig. 10, also Plate 8.)

It seems strange to find a Christian church properly orientated as regards its apse but with its architectural axis running north and south, defying not only Roman usage but the much nearer Celtic association. Such churches may however have been uncommon. There can be no doubt that the route of future development was indicated by the 'west nave'.

The 'Romanizing' of parish church plans and the abolition of the obstructive turriform nucleus eventually led to the western arch being omitted and the whole nave being covered with one roof passing from west to east.

This is in fact the stage reached by the parish church plan at the end of the first millennium. Rectangular nave and chancel are set out on the simple 'Celtic' plan. But the transverse element west of the chancel arch is not abandoned, the two 'wings' remaining to form what may be called the 'pseudo-cruciform' plan. (Fig. 9. Plates 5 and 6.)

In many an old church we may discover the remains of an arch which once led into an early wing. Sometimes such arches have been enlarged. Often some variation in the eastern arch of a medieval arcade may recall a vanished wing. Frequently the wing itself has been rebuilt as an expanded end to a later aisle. (Figs. 15, 16, 17.)

While there is no doubt that the plans of the eleventh century on the whole indicate that the designers of the English parish church were abandoning the Byzantine form and turning towards the long Roman plan, there are plenty of indications that the

Fig. 8   *Elmham Church*
>   This remarkable building of which remains exist at
>   North Elmham in Norfolk, is believed to be of
>   eleventh-century date. Its nave runs north and south
>   (compare Fig. 7c) with the apse in the east wall
>   and a 'west nave' flanked by miniature aisles
>   to balance this and complete the cruciform plan.
>   As it seems probable that some kind of central feature
>   would have existed, the sketch indicates a wooden steeple.

transept was to be retained and that a cruciform or pseudo-cruciform plan had come to stay. During the twelfth and thirteenth centuries some of the smallest churches will be found to have sprouted some kind of broadening-out at one or both sides of the east end of the nave.

As late as the fifteenth century the aisle-less pseudo-cruciform plan with a western bell-tower is still normal practice for parish church builders, clearly indicating the desire to concentrate the accommodation upon the chancel arch. (Fig. 17*b*.)

Returning to the eleventh century, there can be no doubt as to the Byzantine affinities of Anglo-Saxon England. The prestige of

46

Constantinople was such that many of the survivors of Harold's army enlisted in the forces of the Emperor of the East, preferring to do this rather than undertake the much shorter journey to join their cousins in the Rhineland.

There may well have been plenty of eleventh-century church builders who were continuing to build turriform naves, in stone as well as timber. And some of these stone naves which were raised above adequate arches may today be central towers.

In the Western Byzantine world every building had to be covered with a high-pitched roof to shed snow and prevent its blowing into the shingled covering. And most square buildings, such as those of turriform character, had to be covered with something in the nature of a timber steeple. Thus the steeple must have become as common an architectural feature in the West as the dome with its low conical cap was in the East.

The central lantern tower, derived from the Byzantine dome with its ring of small windows, had become firmly established as an appropriate and indeed desirable crowning feature of the great monastic church set out on the long Roman plan.

In order to be able to appreciate the importance of stylistic pressures upon the church architects of the period it is necessary to recall the vast extent of the Empire of Holy Church. For today the great minsters which for so long loomed over the land are gone. St. Edmundsbury, once the largest church in the world, is represented by a shapeless mass of masonry, Evesham by a single small archway. Mitred Cirencester is as though it had never been. And in addition to such huge establishments there were scores of smaller ones, the priories, their sites all gone back to cattle-pastures. All these places had their churches, each with its central tower rising above its choir.

While it would seem most unlikely that either the finances or the architectural potential of the parish would have enabled it to emulate the ordinance, internal or external, of a neighbouring priory church, it would seem quite likely that an enterprising township might like to have gone as far as raising a parish church with a central tower rising above transepts, the whole in rubble stone instead of expensive masonry. Cruciform parish churches are found in close association, as in Wessex. And, stylistic pressures apart, there can be little doubt as to the aesthetic appeal of the central tower as a crowning feature to any church, large or small, once the Byzantines had introduced this feature as the external symbol of a religious edifice.

In some cases existing turriform naves provided the nucleus of

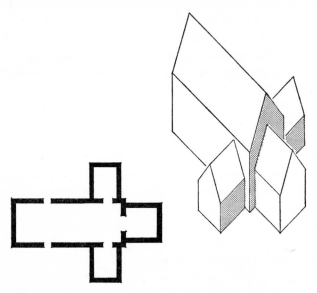

Fig. 9 *Pseudo-cruciform church*
The type of plan developed from that shown in Fig. 7*a* by
dispensing with the turriform nucleus and combining its
area with that of the 'west nave'. The lateral wings remain;
the arches leading to them are often very narrow. This type
of church plan was common during the eleventh and twelfth
centuries. See also Plates 5 and 6.

a central tower. And there are known examples of a pseudo-cruciform church being converted to cruciform by the erection of a central tower at the east end of the nave between the wings. (See Fig. 12*a*.) Careful examination and detailed measurement can sometimes produce surprising results.

The thirteenth century was the period for central tower developments in the parish church plan. It should be noted that the central towers of parish churches were rarely lantern towers such as had been raised over the crossings of great churches to light them. The parish church tower was simply a bell-tower, usually with only its belfry stage rising above the roof. The ringing-floor would be contrived immediately below the belfry, sometimes projecting downwards into the church. Thus the crossing arches of parish churches, especially in the case of early towers, are often quite low, similar to those in aisle arcades.

During the twelfth century one finds small churches which seem to combine both types of plan by setting a central tower between nave and chancel but dispensing with wings. This type of plan is called by antiquaries the 'axial'. (Fig. 10. Plate 8.)

It should be emphasized that during the eleventh century the plans of the parish church and the minster had been developing along entirely different lines. The great monastic churches had been expanding their monumental plans on a vast and extravagant scale, rivalling each other in their lengths until they had become the largest edifices in the world of their day. Though begun as compact centralized structures of Byzantine form, for a century past they had been reaching eastwards in emulation of the basilican type of church. They had built new eastern terminals to their choirs, incorporating a transept with a lantern tower over the crossing.

It was not until the end of the twelfth century that some of their flimsy lanterns, most of which fell through ignorance of structural design, were to soar anew above their crossings as lofty central towers, restoring to the great church of the Middle Ages the focal feature abandoned through over-concentration upon planning extent. Thus it may be to the development of the central towers of parish churches that we owe the beginnings of Lincoln or Canterbury.

While the cruciform village church is limited in its distribution to certain areas, it is the western bell-tower, rising through the centuries towards great architectural glories, which is the crowning feature of by far the majority of English parish churches.

The origin of the western bell-tower is interesting. When the great abbey churches of the tenth century were beginning to expand eastwards from their original Byzantine turriform beginnings, these remained as western towers. Their retention was inevitable, as the new lanterns over the crossings were too light in construction to be able to carry bells. As the fashion for spreading frontispieces, twin-towered, took over the development of the western façade of the great church, most of the great west towers were swept away, that of Ely remaining as one of the latest and

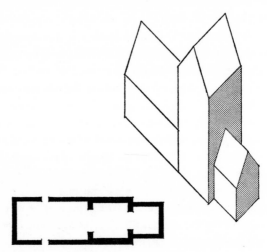

Fig. 10 *Church with 'axial' tower*
A twelfth-century type of plan probably developed
from that shown in Fig. 7*b*. Various alternative
types of tower-roofs are shown in Fig. 23. See also
Plate 8.

most magnificent. But the western bell-tower had by this time come to be established as a standard feature in any parish church which was able to afford such a luxury.

Extension eastwards from one of the tall early churches was a practice also followed by the parish churches. Stone turriform naves can be found now serving as bell-towers. Some of the early timber churches of Essex remain at the ends of later naves. (Plates I and 2.) Sometimes the tower framework was incorporated within the west end of a stone nave. Some examples of timber framing carrying bells above the west end of a nave. hitherto believed to be late medieval, will be found in fact to be earlier than the walling about them, this often of the thirteenth century. Late towers raised within the west ends of naves may represent a rebuilding of a timber predecessor.

Where naves attached to the eastern side of an early timber church have been subsequently extended with aisles it will be found that their arcades have half-bays at their western ends indicating where the aisles have been extended there to absorb the eastern aisle of the timber church.

One of the most interesting examples of the development of a medieval church from a turriform ancestor may be seen at South Brent in Devonshire where at the west end of the large nave is the original tower standing upon all four arches and retaining its southern wing.

The Byzantine church began by having no chancel other than the Classical apse containing the altar. The cathedral at Constantinople lacked any kind of chancel. But by the seventh century the development of the ordinary 'four-poster' plan resulted in the creation of an aisle, east of the crossing, the centre bay of which provided a short chancel preceding the apse. Thus the sanctuary became as long as it was broad.

To both the Eastern and Western churches, the apse remained the only acceptable termination. The Celtic Church, however, never seems to have subscribed to the Classical plan in this respect, possibly because the construction and roofing of an apse would have been beyond its capabilities. Thus it had become understood from the start in this country that the square-ended chancel could be accepted instead of the traditional apse. As most of the Anglo-Saxon parish churches were of timber construction, unsuited to circular planning, the normal timber-framed chancel was square on plan. The masonry apse, however, continues well into the twelfth century in the parish church, as may be seen in fine form at Steetley in Derbyshire. (See also Plate 6.) Notwithstanding Continental insistence upon the traditional form, however, England retained the square end to its chancels, supported by the choirs of the great churches.

An interesting variant of the normal semicircular apse is the polygonal one with three sides, a common Byzantine form, which from its incidence in this country might be called the 'Mercian apse'. That at Wing in Buckinghamshire is a well-known example from the eleventh century in which each face is ornamented with an arch in low relief clearly indicating its Byzantine origins. The polygonal apse actually continues in use right into the Gothic era and thus outlasts the older form. Externally it appears most attractive but it was possibly inconveniently planned.

The strongest support to the square-ended plan came from the twelfth-century Cistercians, who seem to have regarded it as a manifestation of austerity and a kind of visible protest against the contemporary Benedictine terminal feature of a great apse surrounded by an aisle. Not to be thought of as inferior designers, the Cistercians would on occasion employ the eastern aisle in connection with the square-ended presbytery, a pleasant example of the growing individuality of the English church-builder.

This was despite the powerful pressures emanating from the Continent which must have borne heavily upon the great establishments.

The parish churches, however, free from such influences, were able to develop even more independently.

5

Medieval Churches

The eleventh century saw the consolidation of the English Church under the aegis of a host of rich and powerful monasteries which absorbed virtually the whole of the Anglo-Saxon building potential and converted this to its use. Building mystique was derived from Western Byzantinism with its political headquarters in the Rhineland. Scandinavian influences had endowed the Anglo-Saxon style with many and varied forms of lavish ornament, all of which continued in use notwithstanding the change in supervision consequent on the change of ownership. It is probably quite wrong to attribute this ornament to the appearance of the Normans, who came to this country not to civilize but to seize. It is true that one finds certain forms of Classical ornament appearing after the Conquest but such would probably have drifted over from the Continent in the normal course of progress.

It is doubtful whether any Continental influences affected to any large extent the actual building craftsman. It was probably contributions by travelled amateurs which played the greater part in introducing new ideas into architecture. Among these would have been, in course of time, those who had taken part in the then spectacular expeditions to the Crusades, visiting on the way many parts of Europe, the Eastern Byzantine world, and the ancient lands of Hellenism. Such travellers, besides encountering undreamed-of architectural marvels, would have been able to appreciate for the first time the Roman church in regions nearer its heart-land, and compare its manifestations with corresponding

English versions. It was probably the Crusading expeditions which finally brought about the end of Byzantine England.

The twelfth—Crusading—century was the period which saw the transition from Anglo-Saxon to medieval England. The parish church nave settled down to its final rectangular form, elevated as high as possible but no longer turriform. The early-medieval nave was usually about twenty feet wide and perhaps sixty feet long for the normal parish church. Two doors were set facing each other at a point about two-fifths or three-eighths of the length of the nave from its western end.

While in these days many north doors have been blocked up to defeat the north wind, in medieval days they were important for processions, especially that held on Palm Sunday when the congregation left the nave by the north door. The procession passed round the east end of the church and halted at the churchyard cross which was usually somewhere on the south side of the church. The procession should properly speaking have re-entered the church by its west door. But English climatic conditions did not favour west doors. Not until the late-medieval bell-towers were being added to the west ends of naves did the west door come to be accepted. Processions used therefore to re-enter the church by the south door.

The south or sunny side of the church was usually its entrance front. In some situations, however, the position of the village—or perhaps the manor house—might determine otherwise.

The nomenclature of the adjuncts to a church have become muddled in the course of translation from the Latin. The pillared 'veranda' surrounding the little church of St. Augustine's day was called a *porticus*, which is of course simply 'portico'. If the outer side of a *porticus* became wholly or in part built up as a solid wall it still retained its designation, which was confusing as the built-up part no longer served as a porch. A structure projecting at right angles to the main building was called an *ala* or 'wing'. With the provision of openings leading out of the nave into a *porticus* this appendage began to share with the wing the same designation of *ala*. Hence the modern word 'aisle'.

Except in small churches where the parish may have failed to expand its population, the nave seldom omitted to develop its plan

as the Middle Ages approached. Perhaps the most striking introduction into the form of the twelfth-century parish church was the
arcade of semicircular—later pointed—arches carried upon a series
of either piers or pillars beyond which the width of a nave could be
increased by perhaps even half as much again. Single arches had
long been used in parish churches, especially at the entrances to
chancels, but a series of arches each supporting its neighbour was a
feature only employed hitherto in the greater buildings. The
embellishment of these arcades, in particular the capitals crowning
their supports, was to provide carvers with pleasurable exercises
for centuries to come. (Plate 10.)

Those who would assign to the English medieval church plan a
'basilican' origin see evidence of this in aisled construction. But
this is a basic architectural device found even in the most primitive
timber buildings and is an obvious method of widening a plan.
The great West Mercian churches of Gloucester, Tewkesbury, and
vanished Pershore, lined with gigantic circular piers, would seem
to illustrate crude attempts to copy the basilican model, but such
structures belong to a sphere far removed from that of the contemporary parish church.

Architectural students know that in order to achieve a stable
elevation one's interest should be directed to a central opening
rather than a solid support. The medieval church designers seem
to have developed this rule of design to the extent that they avoided
central openings in lateral treatments to which attention was not
to be diverted. Certainly most church arcades, whatever their
length, are usually set in an even number of bays. In parish churches
the number is usually four, in very small naves, two. In the great
churches the arrangement may be due to the use of the duplex bay
in which piers and pillars alternate, but this would be unlikely to
affect the parish church.

The first aisles were always very narrow, usually less than eight
feet wide. The reason for this was that they had to be roofed by
extending the nave roof downwards to cover them before its eaves
came too near the ground to allow for windows in the aisle walls.
(Fig. 14.)

The addition of side-aisles to the nave indicates the first stage towards extending the accommodation of the basic parish church plan. This by the end of the twelfth century had established itself in two main sizes. The larger parish churches were either pseudo-cruciform with lateral wings near the east end of the nave (Fig. 9), or, less frequently, fully cruciform with a central tower. (Fig. 11.) Such churches could easily be enlarged by the addition of aisles to the nave.

The small parish church was usually on the 'Celtic' plan of small nave and chancel (Plate 7)—the former probably too short for widening, so that the building would either survive the centuries unaltered, as at Barfreston in Kent, or be pulled down entirely and rebuilt. The churches with 'axial' towers (Fig. 10)—relics probably of early turriform types—could have their naves widened by aisles or even extended lengthwise away from the tower. For the western bell-tower, which was to be so common a feature in the years to come, was then a rarity and any existing towers would have been too valuable to lose.

The belfries of that period, where no central tower existed, would probably have been timber turrets, either carried on heavy tie-beams spanning the nave or perhaps a wing, or supported by timber posts from within the building in the fashion of an early timber church.

The chancels of churches prior to the end of the twelfth century were either apses or square-ended adjuncts of little projection. But this was about to be changed.

The eastern arms of the great minsters had not originally been given any great projection, for the monastic choir had been sited at the eastern end of the long nave and had the lofty crossing immediately to the east of this so that a short presbytery was all that was needed to give internal dignity to the monks' part of the building. But the fashion was appearing for longer eastern arms to augment the dignity of this part of the building and give a better balance externally to the greatly-extended naves.

It may have been partly due to the increased length of the choir of the great church that the thirteenth century saw the chancels of parish churches similarly extended.

But the functions of the two structures were in fact entirely different. The monastic choir had become a spacious apartment, enclosed by screens to form a church on its own. At the west end were the fixed stalls of the community; at the opposite end, separated from them by a wide area of pavement, was the high altar. But the long parish chancels were simply long empty halls with the altar at the east end and the chancel arch at the west. The only occupant of such an apartment would presumably have been the priest, celebrating the ritual of the Mass at the altar, far away from his congregation except when they actually drew near to communicate.

There seems to be no explanation for the sudden elongation of the medieval chancel, nor any description as to just how it was utilized with regard to the congregation. But from the beginning of the thirteenth century onwards the long chancel was a permanent part of every English parish church and it remained so for more than three centuries. Common to all sizes of churches, they were well-designed structures lit at first by lancet windows and later by fine traceried ones. Each had its own 'priest's door' in its south wall.

It will be found that many of these extravagant chancels were added originally to parish churches having some connection with a rich monastic house. Such chancels may have appeared during the course of an architectural competition between a number of such establishments having responsibilities for churches in neighbouring parishes.

But a desire for architectural dignity, especially in comparison with the eastern arm of the great church, could account for only one aspect of the innovation. Was there a change in parish church ritual requiring a longer chancel? Conversely, how did the new situation affect the conduct of the services? There seems to be no literature throwing light on the matter, the service books of the Middle Ages being concerned with the scene in the minster choir.

It may be that the chancel extension was intended to enhance the dignity of the altar by removing it farther away from the laity. The revised prayer book of 1552 envisages the communicants separating themselves from the main body of the congregation by approaching the altar, men on one side, women on the other. Is this perhaps a recognition of a practice to be continued from medieval days, the entry into the chancel only of those actually communicating? The Reformed prayer book of course refers to the altar as being in the 'body' of the church, *or* in the chancel.

Bearing in mind that the chancels of the Middle Ages, like the naves to which they were attached, were entirely empty of furniture, and not packed with seating as today, it is possible to imagine the parish chancel capable of comparison with the contemporary monastic choir without, of course, the latter's seating arrangements. Thus one might see the parish chancel as a spacious apartment designed to welcome the communicants when their time came to approach the altar. A hint of this is given when one discovers that the eastern faces of the chancel screens are often as elaborately decorated as those facing the nave.

In default of explanations connected with ritual one must take account of the fact that intra-mural sepulture must have been a greatly appreciated status symbol during the Middle Ages when the eastern arms of the great minsters were being lengthened partly so as to provide more space for the interment of important personages. Thus it is conceivable that the chancels of parish churches were extended to provide places of sepulture higher up the social scale than could be achieved by those whose relics were assigned to the nave.

While the long chancel remained as such throughout the Middle Ages, by the end of the fourteenth century its enclosed character was disappearing as it first became aisled and found itself absorbed into the wide spaces of the 'hall' church (Fig. 19), with the chancel arch finally abolished and only lines of screenwork remaining, as in the choirs of the great churches, to indicate its sanctity.

A feature of the English parish church plan hitherto ignored by historians is the concern of its builders to provide as great a width as possible immediately at the entrance to the chancel, by means of lateral transepts, suggesting the possibility that more of the parish service was being conducted at the entrance to the chancel than, as today, at the altar itself.

When trying to discover the development of the church plan

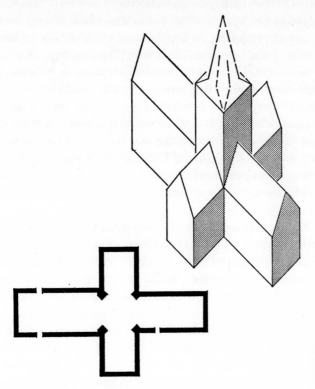

Fig. 11 *Early medieval cruciform plan*
A thirteenth-century plan having affinities with the early
turriform church but architecturally probably an attempt to
emulate the form of the smaller monastic church. The transepts
sometimes have small eastern transepts.

there are two methods to employ. The best clue is to note in what
style an entirely new church was being planned and in what fashion
it differs from its predecessors. The other method of approach is
to note in what fashion existing churches were being altered at the
time and thus discover what new features were considered desirable to bring old churches up to date.

One type of church aimed at by the designers of the thirteenth
century is quite clearly discoverable. This is the cruciform plan

with a long chancel and a bell-tower above the crossing between a pair of proper transepts. Such churches sometimes have wide naves roofed in one span without aisles. The whole arrangement seems to aim at producing an architectural effect similar to that of the church of a minor monastic house. (Plate 11, Fig. 11.)

When considering this possibility it must be remembered that there were at the time scores of such buildings now virtually entirely disappeared, to serve as models for enterprising builders of parish churches. It is to be noted that many of these churches have chapels contrived in the east walls of their transepts, as at Amesbury in Wiltshire and Uffington in Berkshire (Plate 11), and that such chapels form a usual feature of the monastic transept, which needed a good supply of side altars whereas the parish church did not.

A not uncommon practice during the thirteenth century was to utilize existing wings as a basis for conversion to a cruciform plan. Sometimes a central tower was built up inside the east end of the nave—a reversal of the process by which the pseudo-cruciform plan had been developed. But a more common arrangement, where the nave was aisle-less and the wing arches remained, was to retain these for the lateral arches and throw transverse arches across the building to complete the crossing. (See Fig. 12a.)

To increase the accommodation of an existing small church three methods could be employed. A simple method was to throw out one or two wings at the east end of an aisle-less nave. Alternatively arcades could be cut through the whole of a side wall, or both of these, and an aisle or aisles built.

But the most effective way was to remove the existing chancel and build on a complete new east end with a crossing supporting a central tower, commodious transepts, and one of the new long chancels. (Fig. 12b. Plate 12.)

Naves were sometimes lengthened westward, but such extensions were uncommon, possibly because development of the accommodation away from the altar would not have been popular, and also because there might be a belfry of some sort existing at this point. Widening was clearly the device aimed at during enlargement.

A widening of early narrow aisles presented a problem in that this would probably require a reconstruction of the whole roof of the nave. If a roofing material such as lead, which only requires a flat pitch, could be used on the aisle roofs a major re-roofing might have been avoided, but normally the walls of the nave would

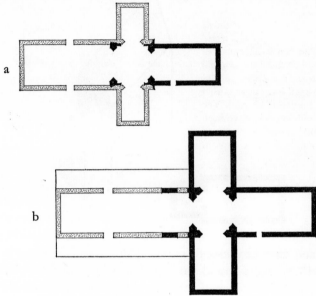

Fig. 12 *Thirteenth-century improvements*
Showing attempts to convert the pseudo-cruciform plan to true cruciform. (a) shows a tower constructed between the original 'wings' by throwing two transverse arches across the nave on either side of these. (b) shows the wings abandoned and a complete new east end added with a central tower set between large transepts. The long thirteenth-century chancel is shown.

have had to be raised to take up the extra height of the widened aisle roof. As a widening of the aisles meant thrusting the natural lighting of the nave farther away from it, the 'lantern' system of lighting was introduced by the formation of a row of windows above the lateral roofs, a device known as the 'clearstory' which by the middle of the Gothic period was to become a standard feature of all the aisled structures. (Fig. 14, Plate 17.)

The 'Celtic' plan of nave with small chancel attached to it went out of fashion during the thirteenth century. Thenceforth the really small parish church is set out in the same fashion as the chapel of a palace or castle. This is a simple rectangle incorporating

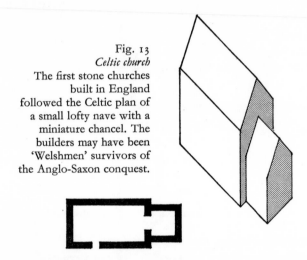

Fig. 13
Celtic church
The first stone churches built in England followed the Celtic plan of a small lofty nave with a miniature chancel. The builders may have been 'Welshmen' survivors of the Anglo-Saxon conquest.

nave and chancel under one roof. The internal division, if one existed originally, would have been achieved by some kind of timber partition. None of these, however, have survived, having been replaced at some later period by an ordinary rood-screen. Comparatively few of these small and humble parish churches would have survived into the era of the High Gothic.

At this time very many of the old parish churches of the country had become too small for their congregations, notwithstanding constant accretions which had muddled their original plans to a degree unworthy of a monumental building. Thus by the end of the fourteenth century the country was swept by a rebuilding programme which removed great numbers of old parish churches and replaced them by others of what had become a standard pattern.

The large parish church in the wool-rich market town would continue to vie with its monastic rival by adopting a complete cruciform plan with a fine central bell-tower. Village churches already planned cruciform would have been loth to abandon their towers but it is on record that some preferred to clear them away as obstructions and build anew at the west end, in what had become the accepted position for the bell-tower.

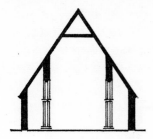
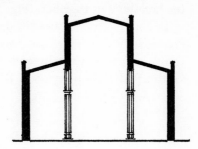

Fig. 14. *Development of aisles*
Early aisles were narrow so that the nave roof could be extended to cover them. With the reduction of roof-pitch following the introduction of lead, the aisles became wider, and were covered with lean-to roofs abutting against a nave raised to accommodate a tier of clearstory windows on either side.

Rebuilt from the ground up, the standard parish church plan of the late-medieval period can be found in possibly half the parish churches in England. In the West it is ubiquitous. The nave is clearstoried and has wide aisles. Four bays is the common arrangement but five sometimes occur, possibly a relic of some eastern arrangement of transeptal nature existing in the old church and retained for convenience in the rebuilding, which would presumably have been carried out piecemeal so that the church could remain in use throughout. The eastern end of each aisle is almost invariably widened out in pseudo-transeptal form. In the second bay from the west a two-storied porch projects to indicate the southern entrance. The chancel is probably three bays long and lit by large windows; the arch leading into it is now as wide as possible. At the west end of the nave a tall arch leads into the lower part of the bell-tower and the 'processional' doorway in its west wall. Such was the fully-developed parish church plan which served until the end of the medieval period. (Fig. 15.)

These were of course the fully developed churches. The smaller parish church was in effect a perpetuation of the 'Celtic' plan with a broad aisle-less nave and a chancel of medium length, compromising between the long thirteenth-century type and the short twelfth-century form. But all these churches would have been provided with a western bell-tower costing as much as the rest of the building put together. (Fig. 17*a*.)

In the absence of documentation, the chronology of parish church architecture is of necessity vague. While the major churches can be assigned to the thirteenth, fourteenth and fifteenth centuries, Gothic parish churches really fall into two categories, the first of

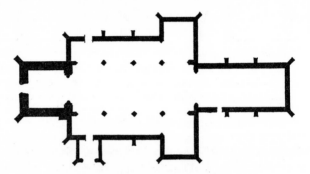

Fig. 15 *Plan of typical fifteenth-century parish church*
Note the nave, four bays and the vestigial
'wings' at the eastern ends of the wide aisles.
The long chancel is retained from early medieval
times. The western bell-tower has become
obligatory.

which, the early medieval, finds its designers aiming at emulating the form of the smaller monastic church.

The problem of the structural maintenance of the medieval parish church is one which must not be overlooked. The twelfth and early thirteenth centuries covered the initial period of development. Thereafter, the parochial establishment having been completed and accommodated in good buildings, a century seemed to have elapsed during which these were allowed to deteriorate without provision for maintenance while the greater churches continued to absorb most of the country's building potential. Contemporary reports on parish churches during the first half of the fourteenth century often indicate an almost incredible amount of dilapidation, such as major churches lacking a chancel roof. It was not until the improvement in the country's finances with the coming of the wool boom that the parish churches were taken in hand, by which time very many may well have been past economic repair. This may have been the main reason for the nation-wide rebuilding programme which inaugurated the era of the High Gothic with its host of magnificent parish churches entirely re-placing ancient predecessors.

The era of the High Gothic covers the fourteenth and fifteenth centuries, but only in respect of the greater churches. What was happening to parish churches during the first half of the fourteenth century is not clear, but it may be assumed that the Black Death put an end to whatever it was until the last quarter of the century. By this time the parish church in its final form was being developed, reaching its full flood of rebuilding during the next century. It is thus simpler to refer to this class of church as being of fifteenth-century type, even though it may in fact belong to the latter part of the previous century. As the architectural period continues up to the collapse of the Medieval Church towards the middle of the sixteenth century some of the buildings referred to as being of fifteenth-century type may well be in fact sixteenth-century foundations.

In each period of its history the church plan becomes stabilized to an agreed standard in regard to its essentials. It then goes on to expand in various directions to provide for contingencies associ-ated with changes in fashion.

Possibly one reason for the vast size of the English monastic churches was their popularity as places for the burial of important personages. While their choirs were usually reserved for prelates, naves, aisles and transepts became filled with the country's squires and nobility. The tombs themselves, some of which were raised biers with arcaded sides and surmounted by a portrait effigy, were becoming notable architectural embellishments in the great buildings.

With the burial place was often associated a chapel in which prayers might be said in perpetuity for the soul of the deceased.

The chantry chapel too became a lovely architectural feature within the great church.

In default of interment within some minster, a rural nobleman might like to prepare a tomb for himself in the parish church he and his family attended. The ends of transepts are often provided with low arched recesses for such interments. Some of the altars now represented by their piscinae may have been employed for the use of the chantry priest.

But it would seem unlikely that a medieval squire would have been permitted to appropriate part of the accommodation of the church for use as a place of sepulture to be filled with family tombs. It would be necessary for him to provide an addition to the building for this purpose. An obvious site for this would be found beside the chancel, probably on its north side so as not to interfere with access to it. The walls of a chancel being comparatively low, the provision of an aisle to it would present a roofing problem. Either the roof of the aisle would have to be pitched very flat, or it would have to be provided with its own independent roof with a gutter between this and the chancel roof, both of which schemes would involve the use of lead.

The dignity of the east end of a parish church would have been greatly enhanced by the addition of aisles to its chancel. Within, the building would benefit from the more spacious eastern terminal probably furnished with fine tombs or even chantry chapels. But externally the aisle would have introduced a structural revolution by flanking one gable with another, an innovation only possible by the construction of a wide lead gutter to carry away melting snow. This discovery was to have wide-reaching results.

The use of lead having enabled roof-pitches to be reduced considerably, some of the old narrow-aisled naves had their arcades removed and a wide-span roof thrown across from one aisle wall to the other, thus increasing the accommodation and removing a number of obstructions with the one operation.

The fourteenth century was the period of nave-widening. Hitherto the nave had been as it were an ante-room to the chancel, but now it began to assume a greater importance resulting from an innovation in the form of the church service.

The change was due to the introduction of the Mendicant Orders into this country. These travelling friars specialized in the preaching of sermons. Their own churches were provided with exceptionally wide naves for the accommodation of large con-

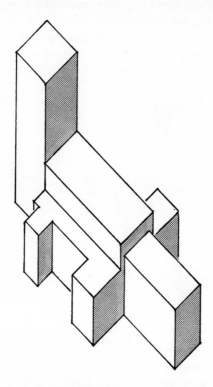

Fig. 16 *Sketch of typical fifteenth-century parish church*
See also Plate 14.

gregations gathered to listen. Unlike the older Orders, the friars contented themselves with eastern arms to their churches which were comparatively humble and in general form resembled large editions of the chancel of the parish church, the stalls being at the west end by the entrance arch. The excessive length of the old monastic nave was a disadvantage when listening to a sermon, and the friars built their naves short and as wide as possible. The old

clerestoried nave with its comparatively narrow aisles being unsuitable, the wide 'auditoria' of the friars were constructed on the
'three-gable' principle with the side aisles as wide as the centre
nave itself and the whole magnificent structure lined with lofty
traceried windows, thus creating a spacious hall, airy and well-lit,
very different from the cramped naves of earlier days.

The new arrangement was undoubtedly Continental in origin.
At this time a number of large parish churches, especially in

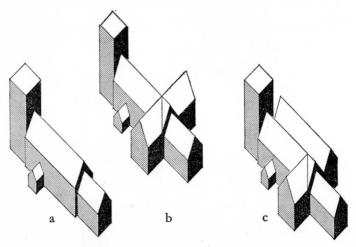

Fig. 17 *Types of fifteenth-century churches*
(a) Simple church of nave and chancel, derived from early
Celtic church. (b) Development of the early pseudo-cruciform
plan but with no lateral arches and transept of equal height to
nave. (c) Composite plan having aisle on one flank of nave and
a wing or transept on the other. Roofs are shown high-pitched
for covering with tiles. The western bell-tower is obligatory.

Germany and the Low Countries, were being designed on an
entirely different system from that obtaining in this country. The
buildings were set out as complete rectangles with a wide apse
embracing the whole width of the building with its aisles. The
arcades were very tall and the whole church was ceiled at the same
level, under a tall western roof. These churches are called by
Continental antiquaries 'hall churches' and this designation has
come to be applied to the triple-naved churches met everywhere

in the south-west of England and representing the final form of the English Gothic parish church.

The planning arrangement of the hall church had been made possible by the new device of roofing each portion of the plan with its own pitched roof. (Fig. 18.) A development of this principle was the reintroduction of the 'pseudo-cruciform' plan on an enlarged scale, with large transepts of the same width as the nave, all three roofs being of the same height and thus easily joined together without the intervention of a central tower. (Fig. 17*b*.) The hall churches had of course no clearstory.

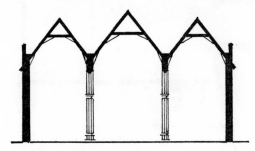

Fig. 18 *Section through 'hall' church*
Nave and aisles of almost equal width and
each covered with its own independent roof.
The nave has no clearstory. See Plate 16.

The principle of building with independent roofs made it possible to plan churches unhampered by earlier formalities which had regulated their lay-outs. A medium-sized church could now have a single aisle to its nave, with perhaps a solitary 'wing' balancing it on the other side. (Fig. 17*c*.) It is noticeable how the popularity of the projecting 'wing' as an aesthetic feature of the elevation continues (Plate 14.); thus such compromise plans seem to provide for the aisle to be on the north and the wing on the south or entrance front.

Planning with independent roofs, in 'hall church' style and without clearstories, is most common with the late Gothic churches of the south-west, with their pitched roofs, and less common with the lead-roofed buildings, such as those of East Anglia. (Fig. 20. Plate 16.)

Internally the English hall churches appear as plain rectangles with the chancel indicated by a screened enclosure, its western or 'rood' screen usually being carried for the whole width of the church so as to enable its loft to be reached by a stair formed in the aisle wall. There is no structural division between nave and chancel. (Fig. 19.)

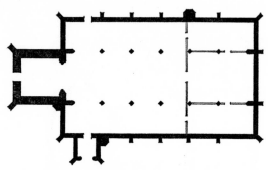

Fig. 19 *Plan of 'hall' church*
The building has become one single
rectangle, its chancel having been formed
by enclosing it within screens. The west tower
is sometimes absorbed within the rectangle
by carrying the aisles beside it.

This planning by means of screens, long the normal practice in the great churches where pillars and arches were structural features supporting the roofs and were not necessarily intended to be regarded as related to the accommodation, enabled the screen-makers of the monastic choirs to transfer their attention to the chancel of the parish church. The results were spectacular, with elaborate tracery maintaining vision through the screen and above it miniature vaulting systems carrying the overhead gallery or loft. (Plate 22.)

Most of the larger urban monasteries provided, usually to the north-west of the monastic church away from the cloister, a parish church for the use of the townspeople. The naves of the great churches themselves were open to the public except in the case of the Cistercian houses where they were used by the lay-brethren.

At the Dissolution, most of the great churches were swept away. Rarely, as at Christchurch in Hampshire, a monastic church was suffered to remain intact as a parish church. Nearly always, the choir at least was destroyed, that of Pershore Abbey, now a parish

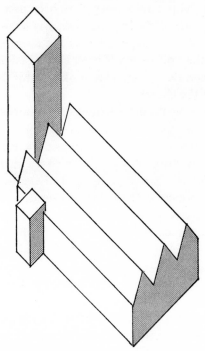

Fig. 20 *Sketch of 'hall' church*
This type of church is common
throughout the West Country.
See Plate 16.

church, being a notable exception. Sometimes a monastic nave, as at Dunstable in Bedfordshire or the towering fragment at Malmesbury in Wiltshire, was retained as a parish church. Or just an aisle, as at Little Dunmow in Essex, might remain in parochial use as a memorial of a great church of other days.

There were quite a number of small monastic houses which actually shared their churches with parishioners. The planning arrangement is uncertain and requires investigation. The monastic portions of such churches have of course for the most part been removed, leaving here and there a tantalizing arch or a wall-fragment to encourage speculation. The monastic choir would presumably have been at the east end, possibly beside the parish chancel. But a large transept may have been used for the purpose. Possibly only one of the two chancels may have been orientated. In any case the monastic portion of the church must have been accessible to the cloister or whatever comprised the living quarters of the community. So one may look for this on the customary south side of the church.

The 'professional' congregations of the monastic choirs, forced to long periods of worship by night as well as by day, had to be provided with fixed seating. The naves of parish churches had no seating but were bare halls about which the rustic congregations ebbed and flowed. Not until the end of the fourteenth century, when the introduction of the lengthy sermon changed the situation, did the parish churches turn towards the provision of fixed seating for their congregations, thus completely changing the appearance of parish church naves towards their present-day arrangement.

6

The Reformation

In 1539, when the work of obliterating the magnificent series of monastic churches was begun, the parish priests must have been concerned as to what the fate of their own churches was to be. Would their status be enhanced by the removal of such massive competition, or would the next step in the religious upheaval be the destruction of parish churches also? Contemporary writers have calculated that there were at the time some 46,000 parish churches in the countries forming the English realm. The Reformation was certain to affect them very considerably but in what fashion no one could be certain.

But the breach with Rome turned out to be a political rather than a religious revolution. The Dissolution of the Monasteries, establishments regarded both as enclaves of fifth-columnists and as parasitical to the economy of the country, had no counterpart in the parishes. The King made it clear that he had no wish to change religious practices, and demanded only that he be regarded thenceforth as the head of the English Church in place of the Italian Pope. The services in the parish churches continued as before in the care of their parish priests, still supervised, under the King, by the same diocesan bishops now increased in numbers to fill the huge gaps in the ecclesiastical hierarchy resulting from the monastic Dissolution.

In illustration of the continuance of the old order one may cite the existence of a beautiful screen erected at the entrance to the chancel of Washfield church in Devon. Although as late as 1624, nearly a century after the Reformation, this lovely feature is entirely in the medieval tradition except for the fact that instead of the 'Popish' Rood one finds the royal coat of arms.

The inevitable loss of prestige suffered by the whole of the English priesthood during the sixteenth century, however, was bound to exert a creeping effect upon the sanctity of the long medieval chancels which had for so long been its special preserves. So it comes about that the eastern end of the church, once its most important element, began to suffer the loss of the whole of its ancient dignity.

Almost simultaneously with the religious revolution carried out by Henry VIII, the reactionary anti-Reformation movement introduced by the Jesuits began to spread through the Continent from Italy outwards. This clever Order was too wise to ignore altogether the grievances underlying the now powerful forces opposing some of the more objectionable aspects of the medieval Church.

It seems probable that one of these objections may have been the existence of the long chancel which had carried the altar, and presumably the priest, much too far away from the congregation trying to take part in the service. Thus it is to the Jesuits we owe the abandoning of the long chancel altogether and the refashioning of the east ends of churches on the 'Baroque' plan with a short sanctuary and flanking transepts, a reversion, in fact, to the original Byzantine concept. This plan has been followed ever since in Roman Catholic churches.

Nothing of the sort was done, however, in this country. The Acts of Uniformity of 1549–52, though clearly envisaging the eventual abandoning of the chancel altogether, describe the altar as being set 'in the body of the church' *or* in the chancel, thus permitting retention of the latter if so desired. It is however clear that the trend was to omit the chancel from liturgical arrangements and reduce the church to the nave only. And as the spacious preaching nave had for more than a century become the primary concern of the church architects, the loss of the long chancel seems to have been readily accepted by most of them. Any new churches of the Elizabethan / Jacobean period are planned as simple rectangles with the altar against the east wall.

But with the rapidly expanding new class of lay magnates the parish churches were coming under fresh influences and developing a new significance as establishments the control of which had been removed from Holy Church and handed over to the King and his ruling class.

The monastic churches had sunk into piles of ruin burying in their fall the memorials of the emblazoned past. Thus the parish churches had become the only surviving places of sepulture for the new lords of the countryside.

Ample precedence already existed for using the eastern ends of parish churches for this purpose. And from the chancel aisles it was but a short step to encroachment upon the chancel itself, no longer protected from desecration by the power of Holy Church. The Elizabethan Age was one of great affluence displaying itself in wondrous raiment. The ponderous tombs of the period which began to clutter up the old chancels made full use of the space provided for sculptural extravagances.

The Dissolution of the huge monastic houses and the consequent cessation of all their activities released upon the country the whole of the monastic maintenance organization—which meant in fact a very large part of the building potential of the country—and diverted this to the provision of mansions and farmhouses for the new landowners. This transformation of the purpose of English architecture from the ecclesiastical to the domestic resulted in an architectural revolution as well as a religious one. This fact combined with the enormous stylistic revolution spreading through the Continent was to complicate the lives of the English architects for several generations.

The new architectural style entering the country from Europe bore no resemblance to the native Gothic which had for so long dominated English architecture. Gables, buttresses, pinnacles, traceried windows, battlements, carved grotesques—all these fripperies were being banished into history. The pointed arch gave place to the semicircular one and the detail attempted was based on the austere forms of the Italian Renaissance or as near to it as the isolated English architects could get. There was of necessity a 'Gothic overlap' which lasted into the middle of the seventeenth century and the churches of this period are interesting for their curious mixture of detail. But the plain rectangular buildings now being planned were best suited to the new architecture and by the latter part of the century the Gothic had disappeared altogether. The western bell-tower, however, a feature of the medieval plan, continued in use but with an elevation presented in Renaissance style.

With the approach of the eighteenth century the accommodation of the parish churches, the new ones painfully small by medieval standards, the medieval ones themselves drastically curtailed through the re-siting of the sanctuary at the east end of the nave, found their pew-space inadequate for their congregations. In order to increase the accommodation without building additions to the structure, the churches were provided with upper galleries in the manner of the contemporary theatre. These galleried churches are the 'auditoria' recommended by Wren for the rebuilding of the London parish churches after the Fire.

The plan of the post-Reformation sanctuary in the Anglican Church was very simple. The altar was set hard up against the east wall of the building with a small rectangular railed space before it from which the clergyman conducted the communion ceremony. Close by this was the pulpit, now an important part of the church furniture; pressing close upon it was the pewing. Galleries flanked the building, and with the introduction of the pipe-organ into the parish church during the eighteenth century to accompany the hymn-singing, these were accommodated in western galleries, often in the base of the tower. The organs were flanked by tiered seating for their choirs. In many small village churches the place of the organ was taken by a village orchestra of fiddle, flute and serpent.

Having suffered the closure or complete loss of their chancels, the naves of the medieval churches had now to undergo severe transformations to bring them into line with contemporary planning. Worst of the accretions were the galleries, their supporting beams cutting into the ancient stonework of pillars and being driven across the delicate tracery of windows.

When one deplores the drastic 'restorations' of the mid-nineteenth century one must pause to consider what the old churches must have looked like immediately after the galleries had been taken down and the scars and mutilations revealed in all their shame. The devoted church restorer of today, archaeologically-minded, would have done his utmost to preserve every vestige of antiquity. But in those days the equally conscientious architect would have been driven by horror at the mutilations to clear everything away and rebuild it tidily in his best Gothic.

As the eighteenth century turned into the nineteenth the rise of Nonconformity began to fill the villages with small and cheap editions of the Protestant auditoria. The over-all similarity between the churches of the two cults was sooner or later bound to create a demand for revision of the Anglican design in order to create a decent distinction. Anti-industrialism allied with neo-medievalism produced a remarkably speedy reaction towards the restoration of the church plan of the Middle Ages with the long chancel restored to favour, to serve as an immediate distinction that the building was a church and not a chapel.

The new or restored chancels, however, in no way resembled their medieval predecessors. There was no return to the old mystique, to the dim cavern of the past. The new chancels were cheerful apartments lined with seating, simulating the old monastic choirs, for the accommodation of the singing men and boys lately stimulating the efforts of the congregation from the elevation of a gallery at the west end of the nave.

Regrettable in the extreme as spoiling the lines and fenestration of many a fine old chancel was the custom of affixing to it 'vestries' in which the Protestant clergyman and his choir could don their laundered surplices. Worse still was the addition of a large and lofty 'organ chamber' to accommodate—and stifle—the instrument removed from the gallery.

It was a sad period for the old churches. Many which had come to be regarded as hopelessly de-medievalized were ruthlessly swept away and rebuilt, as were many humble village churches the architecture of which was regarded as substandard. And so many were restored not simply by removing unsightly accretions but by the removal of all post-Reformation features, many of them probably charmingly executed, and replacing them with bogus medieval substitutes designed by architects having but a superficial acquaintance with the style they were trying to imitate.

As with all revivals, design was based upon illustrated textbooks. For the English Gothic there were the publications of Parker and his imitators. Stylization was divided rigidly into the three accepted periods—Early English, Decorated and Perpendicular. Stylistic architecture had come to be regarded as so individualistic that each was regarded as an entirely separate style with an ordinance, and even sculptured detail, assigned to it for acceptance without question by the architect. Clients fancying a particular period would expect the architects to give them what they wanted. All this resulted in an utterly non-medieval rigidity of expression which banished sensitivity and has resulted in the bad reputation suffered by Victorian Gothic at the present time.

With the present century, during the first quarter of which there were a number of church architects who had outgrown the brashness of the Victorian period and were designing attractive churches which owed nothing to 'style' but were sympathetically English medieval in feeling, church architecture seemed to be likely to enjoy a revival. But many factors, the invention of the motor car amongst others, were drawing the old congregations away from their parish churches towards a lighter-hearted Sunday away from home.

With congregations declining in numbers and the clergy finding it difficult to fill their chancels with choristers, some church architects, notably the late Randoll Blacking, sought to reintroduce the Baroque plan by reserving the chancel as a morning chapel and bringing the parish altar west of the rood screen. In churches thus replanned one can once more appreciate the aesthetic, as well as the practical, value of the broad effect created by a long transverse wall forming an extended back-cloth to the altar instead of tucking it away at the end of a long chancel. And over the screen or reredos a distant view of the old east window still preserves something of an atmosphere of mystery.

From the point of view of the ritualist the arrangement has much to commend it. The traditional Elizabethan nave of the Reformed Church, with its altar at the east end, is pleasantly recalled. There is some resemblance to the monastic arrangement of high altar and nave altar. And in essence it is a return to the Orthodox plan of a nave shared by priest and congregation for the 'family' service but with a chancel reserved for actual Communion.

With architecture today in a state of chaos and all innovation equated automatically with improvement, the demand for change at any price was bound to affect the Christian Church. The Roman Catholics have decided to improve still further on the Baroque plan by abandoning that orientation which has throughout history been a basic factor of the plan of the religious building, or for that matter even of the theatre. In future the altar is to be brought into the centre of the building, from the perimeter of which the congregation can observe, as in a circus tent, the new liturgical performance. The Anglican Church, no longer, alas, willing to preserve its independence of thought, is following suit.

It is not only in respect of its planning that the English parish church is losing its ancient position as a building of architectural note. The waywardness of so much of modern church design will do irretrievable damage to the history of ecclesiastical architecture. The plea that modern trends represent reaction from revivalism is valid. That they represent 'contemporary' architecture, however, is specious.

For there is no such thing today as 'contemporary' architecture. At any historical period, and in any country, 'contemporary' architectural style is displayed in the form of variations upon a basic ordinance, framed by the leaders of the craft and accepted by all its practitioners. Only in variations of interpretation, as by detailing, may the architect display his individuality. For without the acceptance of a basic ordinance, any architecture will dissolve into chaos, history will come to a halt, and development cease for lack of an organization relying upon continuity.

7

The Masons

Architecture is primarily building. Thus it helps one to study architecture if one can appreciate the methods of building and the structural problems involved.

The medieval builder was not the head of a building firm as today. He was a craftsman, sometimes a carpenter or 'wright', more often a mason, who relied upon sawyers for his timber or quarrymen for his stone. From time to time he had to find specialists such as smiths, plumbers, or glaziers to add their particular contribution to the building.

During the Middle Ages only the more affluent could afford to pay a builder. The Church and the nobles built minsters and castles. The poor man had to raise his house himself 'of poles and thatch at every lane end'.

There were no architects. The greater structures had men of exceptional genius to design them. Small buildings were set out and detailed in contemporary local fashion.

The Anglo-Saxon building tradition was a timber one. The only word in their vocabulary to indicate building of any description was 'to timber'. The builders were thus the 'wrights', later known as carpenters from the Latin, but in truth the highly-skilled craftsmen we know today as 'joiners'.

Building in timber is an affair of posts set at intervals and joined at their tops by beams. In order to set out the plan of a building in an orderly fashion it was necessary to employ a system of measurement. The unit used was the rod or pole—later called the perch—of sixteen feet, still used by countrymen today when discussing their gardens.

The length of the village pole was arrived at by stopping sixteen grown men as they entered the church porch on a Sunday and making them place their right feet one behind the other. A pole cut to this length became the standard unit for the village. A cord of pole length folded twice became the yard. Firewood is still cut in lengths of four feet and called 'cordwood'.

Later on, variations of the yard—the ell and cloth-yard—came into use. When the yard became shortened to three feet the pole became sixteen and a half feet or five and a half yards. From this revised yard the furlong, mile and acre are derived.

Another ancient measure, long employed by mariners and miners, was the fathom, during the Middle Ages also used for the measurement of buildings.

By twice folding a cord of four feet the foot could be reproduced. Below this were inches, but what these were in early medieval times is now a mystery. The writer has often examined the courses of stone in a building to try to discover from differences in height what units were marked on the iron squares of the masons, but has failed to solve the problem.

Building contracts were in use during medieval days. Their language passed from Latin to French during the fourteenth century, English taking over about 1400. Work was measured by the rod or perch, varying from sixteen to twenty-four feet through intermediate stages, demonstrating the lack of any co-ordination of units of length throughout the country in medieval times.

The early builders could not calculate. Illiteracy apart, it must be remembered that until the end of the sixteenth century when arabic numerals reached us through Spain, the simplest sum, even ordinary addition, could not have been resolved without using counters on a chequer-board. At the beginning of the last century this was still in use, to add up parish accounts still being kept in roman numerals.

Measurements had to be kept as simple as possible. It is doubtful whether planners were aware of the 3:4:5 proportion for setting out a right angle. So rectangles were probably corrected by matching diagonals.

It is noticeable that when the long chancels were added to old naves during the thirteenth century builders who blocked up the chancel arch before sighting the axis of the new chancel often went astray.

The pole and its derivatives can be discovered everywhere in medieval buildings. A twenty-foot main span with eight-foot aisles is common in early days. But the variations of the pole are legion. Lincoln Cathedral and the Tower of London were set out using a pole of eighteen feet.

The span of the roof governs all building down the ages. But the system of planning longitudinally in a series of bays is a legacy of building with timber posts. This practice continues to assert itself upon the whole of English medieval architecture, being constantly expressed on the faces of masonry walling in the form of shallow pilasters and, later, projecting buttresses, separating the bays in which the main windows are sited.

Sleeper foundations or sills are essential for the support of timber posts, to prevent their pushing down into the ground. This sleeper foundation was known as the 'tablement' from the Latin word for plank. The medieval builders knew nothing of the principle of spreading footings over the ground to reduce the pressure per square inch on the soil, nor did they sink their foundations below ground level to avoid frost damaging the soft lime mortar, yet only in rubble walls where the flat stones are not large enough to stand on their own do we find much trouble today.

It was unusual to attempt to level the site for a medieval building; the builders preferred to pack up the lower part of the walling until they reached a level 'tablement' which in stone building became the plinth.

The craft of stone buildings, as opposed to that of skilled masonry, has been followed since prehistoric times. It originated from clearing the stones lying about land to be ploughed and moving them to the edges of the field to be heaped there in some kind of rough wall.

The first step in clearing would be to remove the large boulders —called in the West Country 'moor-stone'. These could be roughly shaped by hammering and built up, first into field walls and eventually into the walling of buildings. This is the kind of walling which can be found in the little church at Bradford-on-Avon in Wiltshire considered to have been built by St. Aldhelm at the beginning of the eighth century. From this technique develops the type of walling known as 'random rubble' which, properly faced-up and with the individual stones reduced from their original 'Cyclopean' scale, is frequently met with in pre-medieval days.

In most of the limestone regions—the Cotswolds, for example —the good freestone is overlaid by shallow strata, pieces of which break away and lie about on the surface as 'field-stone'. This may be seen everywhere used for field walls. When laid 'dry', without mortar, the proper system to employ is that known as 'herring-bone'. The stones are laid in rough courses eight inches or so in height, not flat on their bed but diagonally, each alternate course sloping in the opposite direction so that the whole locks together. This style of walling may be found in many ancient churches. A more sophisticated method of using this type of stone is to hammer it into shapes which can be laid in normal courses as 'coursed rubble', but this needs mortar to keep the stones from falling out of the wall.

All this kind of walling is known as rubble walling and is not masonry. Much of the walling of our parish churches is of this kind, worked not by freemasons but by wallers or 'nobblers' using hammers.

As long as mortar is available for bedding the stones a perfectly good wall can be made of the various kinds of rubble stones. But the limitations of such a wall would soon be found. Apart from the properly 'dressed' stone needed for lining openings, unless similar stones could be found for stiffening any angles of the building these would soon weaken and fall away. Where the building site was close to the remains of a Roman building bricks from this could be salvaged and used to strengthen the angles of rubble walling. Stones squared by the Romans may also have been dug up and used.

Thus good 'quoins' or angle stones are essential to the stability of a wall. In rural areas it was probably the desperate need for procuring these which first encouraged local builders to learn how to cut stone instead of just hammering it into shape. And from such beginnings they may have learned the principles governing the construction of a masonry wall.

Any wall is set out with two faces; the space between these is filled with a 'core' of 'spalls' or chips left over from the shaping. In a rubble wall there is little difference between the three portions. Towards the middle of the medieval period the core was of stones so carefully laid that the thicknesses of walls could be considerably reduced. In masonry the theory is to lay the stone so that it will take up a position in the wall similar to that which it occupied in the quarry. Thus it is hoped it will stay there for ever.

Each stone has a 'face' to show to the world. It has two 'beds', to lie on and to carry the stone above it. The face of the stone is squared-up on either side to meet its neighbours. The rest of the stone, its 'tail', is buried in the wall.

True 'freestone' is limestone. Its best quarries lie along a line sweeping round from Northamptonshire through Somerset into Devon. Lincolnshire also has fine freestone. There are also some lovely local stones such as those of Ham Hill in Somerset and those of Horsham in Sussex which are no longer used. Colour in a stone is due to impurities and affects its durability, but faint tints such as are found in Chilmark stone in Wiltshire add greatly to its interest, each stone varying slightly from its neighbours and the whole constantly changing between damp and drying out. The most perfect stone, Portland, is constant in colour and apt to be rather grim in consequence.

While true freestone is always a limestone, there are other building stones which are geologically speaking sandstones, or as the medieval builders called them, 'gritstones'. They are usually highly coloured and have comparatively poor wearing qualities compared with the freestones, but can be very attractive to look at. Derbyshire and the West Midlands are sandstone areas, also Devonshire.

The presence of stone quarries played a major part in the development of English medieval architecture. Wherever they happened to be founded, the great monastic houses were usually able to assure themselves of a plentiful supply of freestone and assemble a team of craftsmen to work upon it. As time

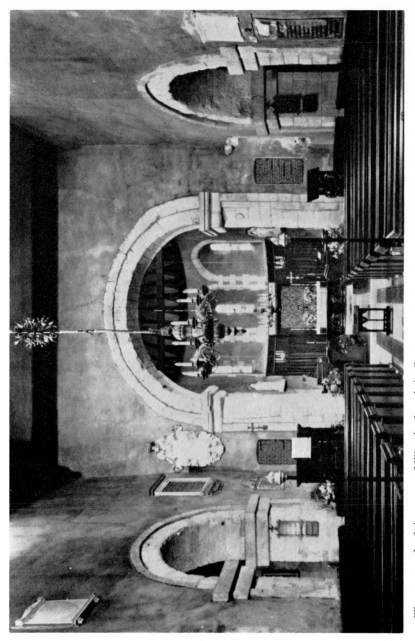

5. The east end of the nave of Worth church in Sussex

6. The south wing and apsidal chancel of Worth church in Sussex

went on and their maintenance teams became established in their lodges, these became a source of inspiration to the whole district and were able to no small extent to influence its architectural development.

Extensive quarry areas such as existed along the limestone belt could also provide their own sources of masonry mystique as masons and quarrymen came and went between lodge and quarry. In this connection it is sad to note that while a mason can be taught his craft in a school, the lore of the quarrymen is bound to the soil and can only be passed on from father to apprentice—if not to son—*at the quarry face*. Once closed, a quarry can never be reopened.

The combination of a rich monastic house with a stone-producing area such as the Benedictine Abbey of Gloucester hard up against the Cotswold oölite, could produce something in the nature of an Architectural School. Glastonbury in Somerset, similarly favoured, must have done the same in its region and may well have provided the inspiration and designing skill which produced the lovely series of parish church towers in that county.

Even the rural Cistercians, breaking away from their early austerity to the extent of raising gracious churches in the valleys of Yorkshire, were able to make their early Gothic architecture a style of great beauty which continued into the era of the High Gothic as a notable School creating a series of fine parish churches.

In the absence of adequate supplies of local stone, however, the great monasteries seem to have been less able to affect local architecture. Thus the enormously rich abbey of St. Edmundsbury in Suffolk played a small part in improving the local style until the very end of the medieval period when it may have helped with the design of the late Gothic churches of East Anglia. Even these are notable for the spectacular carpentry of the roofs rather than the excellence of their masonry.

It must have been difficult in medieval days to transport stone to a stoneless region. So monasteries, with their huge building complexes to maintain, may have been somewhat greedy for free-stone and unwilling to spare enough for the parish churches. It may well be that it is not until the building and maintenance programmes of the monasteries were slowing down that we find parish church architecture really coming into its own.

Certainly it is not in the surviving great churches—with the possible exception of the last of all, Bath Abbey—that we find the latest phase of the High Gothic at its most perfect, but in the parish church, often serving quite a small village yet possessing a large and beautifully-designed building complete with soaring bell-tower.

Vanished now into history are nearly all the quarries of England whence grew her lovely medieval architecture. For every one still open there are a hundred represented by an acre or two of tumbled turf or a thicket of brambles. The great quarries of Barnack in Lincolnshire which gave birth to the greatest buildings of the Age are known today as the 'Hills and Holes'.

The freestone was hacked out of the quarry in huge lumps and broken down into manageable sizes. It was then put on a heavy block of stone called a 'banker' for the mason to work on it. The Classical tool for working stone is the two-handed axe, double-headed for balance and very thick and heavy. Until the end of the twelfth century it was the only tool available for dressing stone and the uneven diagonal slashes it left on the faces of the small stones of the period are easily recognized today. (Plate 32a.)

The carvers who ornamented the timber buildings, however, used chisels for carving their motifs. These tools, which were struck with a wooden mallet or 'mell', were probably little more than a quarter of an inch wide, as are their successors today. Towards the end of the twelfth century a new type of chisel came into use. It had a blade about three inches or so wide and after about 1180 comes into use for dressing the face of a stone after it had left the axe. During the thirteenth century the 'bolster', as it was called, was used with great care. The stones had now become about twice as long as their height and the tooling was run absolutely vertical and so neatly that each stroke joined exactly with that below it. (Plate 32b.)

After the end of the century, however, the masons speeded their work up, holding the bolster diagonally and dressing the faces of the now much larger stones as quickly as possible without the refinement enjoyed by their predecessors. (Plate 32c.)

The mason at his banker was protected from the weather by a lean-to roof set against a wall. This was his 'lodge'. He cut his stones true with the aid of an L-shaped iron called a 'square', on which his inches were marked. To strike the curves of mouldings or tracery he had his 'compass'—which we should call today 'dividers'. A feature of many old buildings is the series of geometrical figures 'doodled' on old walls by jokers who got hold of the mason's compasses during his absence from his lodge.

Each mason had his own sign-manual or 'mark' to indicate the stones prepared by him. Such marks were not intended to show on the wall-face and are usually found on a bed.

With the change in roof design brought about by the use of lead, the whole 'eaves' system which since the beginning had formed the traditional way of bringing a roof out over the wall it was protecting underwent a complete change. Lead was unsuited to eaves construction, so these were abandoned and the foot of the roof concealed behind a parapet (Fig. 22) behind which was a lead gutter discharging through spouts or 'gargoyles'. The thin parapet walls needed special stones having no 'tail' but squared-up on both faces. This kind of stone is known as 'ashlar'. When both faces are neatly dressed as for a parapet it was known as 'perpeyn' ashlar.

By the end of the fourteenth century a new use was found for ashlar. It could be used for facing walls built of rubble, much in the same way as one uses concrete blocks today. One can always tell ashlar by the regularity of the stones—in the mid-fifteenth century eighteen inches by a foot high was a standard size—and by the absence of proper quoins, for the edges of the blocks, six inches or so thick, can be seen at each angle.

From this period, masonry began to deteriorate in favour of applied ashlar until masonry walling began to disappear altogether and mason-work is seen only at quoins to rubble or brick walling. At the time of the reaction against brick-faced buildings which is found at the end of the eighteenth century, a new vogue for ashlar facing appears in all good buildings.

In medieval days the majority of the stones cut by the masons were facing stones or quoins. When an opening was reached, however, its lining stones had to be worked into the coursing, and the wedge-shaped 'voussoirs' cut to turn its head. Among other special stones needed were the 'serches' cut with extra-wide tails for lining the wells of newel stairs. The 'jambs' and arched head of an opening could either be simply-cut stones or could be ornamented with lines of mouldings carried round the lining and greatly adding to the mason's problems as each stone had to fit exactly with its neighbours without a break in the profile of the moulding.

The stone bracket or 'corbel' is an ubiquitous feature of medieval architecture. It is provided as a projection from the wall-face to carry anything from the end of a timber beam to the end of a heavy arcade. During the fourteenth century small openings were spanned by a flat stone lintel having its ends supported by a pair of opposed corbels. This is called by antiquaries the 'Edwardian' or 'Caernarvon' arch as it may be seen in a number of door-heads in that castle. Small timber-framed openings are sometimes lined with a similar feature, their jambs curving inwards and then cut back vertically to meet the lintel. The fronts of Gothic porches frequently display this timber version of the Edwardian arch.

The advantage of the lintel is that it needs no centering. Its disadvantage is that unless it is very deep a very slight movement of the building may crack it, for stone has no tensile strength. It was the experience of the Byzantine builders in the earthquake-ridden regions of Anatolia and Syria which taught them to use lintels in conjunction with arches over them. Thus if the lintel cracked the arch would keep the wall over it safe. During the twelfth century the system, probably noted during Crusading expeditions, was used to great effect in the doorway of the English parish church. The lintel made it easier to fit the door, for round-headed doors are liable to jam against the inner side of the arch unless it should be raised or made segmental as was done in some cases to prevent this. The semicircular 'tympanum' between lintel and arch became a site for sculptural decoration. (Plate 29.)

As experts in arcuated construction the medieval builders were always loth to trust stone lintels and made full use of the principle of the 'relieving arch'. Most flat-topped windows, such as are found during the High Gothic era, have these arches built into the wall over them.

Even mason-builders seem never to have lost sight of the timber origins of the English building trade. The curious lines of long stones ornamenting some of the stone tower-naves, held in position by short stones here and there set deep into the wall, recall timber construction in a remarkably emphatic form, translated with not inconsiderable difficulty into a crude stone technique.

The stone plank or 'table', from the Latin word meaning plank, is found everywhere in medieval masonry. Most buildings had the lower part of their walling built up to a common level and marked with a 'tablement' with its edge bevelled off to produce a plinth above which the wall was reduced slightly in thickness. All building heights were measured above the tablement.

Tablements—called today 'water-tables'—were set in projecting lines immediately above the junction of a roof with a wall so as to keep stormwater from running down the wall-face straight into the building. 'Table-stones' were used to form the internal sills of windows. 'Bench table-stones' provided the lines of stone benches sometimes found lining the sides of a medieval church The 'string-course' used for horizontal punctuation is formed of the same stone 'planks' and was known in the Middle Ages as a tablement.

Students of Classical architecture will recall that the Doric frieze of the Parthenon is formed of a series of 'metopes', carved in relief and separated by vertical 'triglyphs' which are reproductions in stone of the ends of the rafters. Above this frieze is seen the spreading cornice representing the eaves in architectural form. The eaves of the early buildings in this country had no such enrichment. Below them, however, is frequently seen a tablement projecting from the wall and carried by a series of corbels often carved into grotesques. In such 'corbel-tables' the corbels may represent the ends of the rafters converted, like the Doric triglyphs, to architectural use. (Fig. 22.)

The corbel-table was obviously a popular architectural expression and continued in use even after eaves had been abolished in favour of gutters concealed behind parapets. As it was an advantage to bring the parapet as far forward as possible to allow for a wide gutter, so the corbel-table was retained to carry the projection. During the early-medieval period the tablement was replaced by a miniature arcade of trefoiled arches springing from corbel to corbel.

From early parapets with their coping-stones is developed the battlement imitating the military device with its embrasures or 'vents' separated in the ornamental form by 'merlons', 'crests' or 'cops'.

Stone-carving was probably executed on the scaffolding, to avoid damage to it while it was being set in position. The mason would leave a rough lump called a 'boasting' as a basis for the intended carving.

As architect to the building, the mason would be responsible for explaining to the client by means of models the nature of certain complicated features. He might, for his own instruction, make small-scale models in stone of part of the building where the modelling became complicated. The writer has seen a Maltese mason make a model of a complete pier with the springing of its arches, with all the mouldings worked in, all to about one-twentieth full-size.

Such mouldings would be designed by the mason and cut out of a piece of lead sheet or board to form a 'template' or profile capable of being applied to each stone so that the moulding would pass round the opening without any awkward joints. It is believed that Gothic architecture was carried about the country by journeymen masons 'borrowing' such templates or even models.

All architectural detail such as window tracery would be set out by the mason on boards. Everything would have to be drawn full-size and each stone laid on it and worked to fit its part in the design before being sent up to the walling mason or 'setter' for fixing it in its assigned place.

As nowadays, prefabrication was not uncommon, quarries having their own lodges capable of supplying ready-made such simple features as doorways and even traceried windows of moderate size. Great Continental quarries such as those of Caen continued to supply such features right through the medieval period.

Window tracery was set into an opening the frame of which was lined with dressed stonework often embellished with mouldings of the period. The stones of the lining were each carefully bonded in with the walling material and were in fact laid together with this. Thus an inserted feature may at once be detected by breaks in the coursing between wall and lining. The tracery of windows was made separately and fixed into the lining without being bonded into it.

The opening though the wall, the 'reveal', usually splayed internally to increase the light, was also lined with masonry. In the inner face of the wall was the 'scoinson' arch, also formed in dressed stone. The inner edge of the scoinson arch was sometimes softened with a roll moulding passing round it. Sometimes this internal arch was converted into a feature in its own right, as at Bampton in Oxfordshire, by throwing out cusps and making its silhouette foliated.

At first windows were set in line with the outer wall face with a wide 'rere-arch' to carry the core of the wall. But during the High Gothic period the windows were set into the thickness of the wall where they helped to carry the core over. This reduced the inner splay and enabled the masons to elaborate the external elevation of the window with more moulding. The principal feature of the outer splay was a wide shallow hollow known as a 'casement 'moulding.

The elaborate Gothic mouldings which at first seem so complicated are in reality composed of a series of profiles which are individually quite simply cut. There are two basic forms, the roll formed by flanking an edge or 'arris' with grooves or 'quirks', and the plain chamfer. If the original arris is left on the stone instead of rounding it into a roll it becomes a 'bowtell'. Hollows are produced simply by deepening quirks and scooping them out between the rolls, multiplied to enrich the series. (Fig. 24.) The front of a roll can be varied by having a small flat 'fillet' left on it, with the sides of the roll worked up to it in a double curve or 'ogee'.

The above are the basic mouldings which produce the rich profiles of the early-medieval period. During the High Gothic era, when the carpenter was beginning to vie with the mason in his contribution to architecture, the forms of moulding based on the chamfer came into use. These are much broader in effect and lack the richly undercut rolls of the thirteenth century. The chamfers are either flat, hollowed like a shallow casement moulding, or wavy. In pillars the attached shaft is used to cover the flat portions between the chamfers. (Fig. 25.)

The turning of large columns was an operation playing no part in Gothic architecture, circular pillars being built up in 'drums' as in Classical days. The same principle was followed when forming slender shafts or colonettes by working a section of each with each course of stone. But in order to turn the Purbeck marble and other detached shafts of the thirteenth century it was necessary to construct a stone-lathe.

The writer, when advising upon the rebuilding of the buildings of Valetta after the last war, had a stone-lathe built for him by his master mason, Montebello. Its principle feature was a huge stone fly-wheel some four feet in diameter and having a hub, rim, and spokes all cut out of the solid and resembling an early wheel window. This heavy piece of machinery was mounted upon a sturdy wooden frame and turned upon an iron rod cranked at either end to form a handle.

The long square stone to be turned was held between two L-shaped spikes fixed into two masses of stone called 'logs'. A rope was twisted round the stone, taken to the wheel, and tightened into a groove cut in its rim.

The operation of a stone-lathe is sheer drama. First the master mason and his assistant had to apply themselves to the cranks and get the great wheel spinning faster and faster until it was whizzing round at an incredible rate. With the assistant standing well clear, the master mason took up a heavy chisel set in a long wooden handle nearly a yard long and approached the spinning stone. At the outset the bombardment of flying spalls appeared dangerous to a degree but by persistence he wore the stone down to a roughly circular form after which he was able to apply himself deftly to the

7. A small church of primitive type at Heath in Shropshire

8. A church with an 'axial' tower at Iffley in Oxfordshire

delicate task of completing the column without making a mistake which would have wrecked an expensive piece of stone some five feet long and a foot in diameter.

The Maltese stone-lathe was probably constructed in a tradition handed down from Byzantine, if not from Imperial Roman, times. Its form indicates the kind of machinery which the combined efforts of the carpenter and smith were able to bring to the assistance of the masons.

The mason could not turn an arch without the help of the carpenter who had to construct the timber 'centering' for him. When extending a building, however, the cutting of an opening in a wall was simplified for the medieval builder by his rigid attention to the principle of 'bonding' which requires that in each course of masonry a vertical joint shall be as close as possible to the centre of the stones above and below. If this principle is followed, a hole cut through a wall will only let the walling above collapse until the bonding takes over and the top of the opening becomes triangular. The smaller the length of stone used in comparison with the height of the courses, the steeper will be the sides of the triangle and the stronger the resulting support.

It is possible that in early medieval days, when arches were acutely pointed, openings may have simply been knocked out in this way and subsequently lined with dressed masonry picking up the wall over. The change to long shallow stones would however have made this rather a dangerous practice, so one can imagine instead the slotting of the wall to accommodate the new respond or pillar and the subsequent turning of the arch stone by stone, working up to the apex and using the remains of the old wall as the centering. Building an arch in 'orders' would have been very helpful as such arches only need centering for their lowermost order.

Cutting openings in a rough wall of random or even coursed rubble with its bonding rather sketchily arranged, must have been a difficult operation and would have needed the introduction of short lengths of timber known as 'needles' thrust through the wall and supported at either end by vertical 'shores'. The better the walling, the fewer the needles required to hold up the structure while the opening below was being cut and lined.

Some parts of England, notably East Anglia, have as their field-stone flint, lying in great nodules capable of being broken in halves to provide two faces and a long tail which can be built into a wall. An ingenious system of using flint is to lay ordinary masoned wall-stones at intervals with flints between them, each course set out so that its opposite faces alternate the treatment. The next course is laid to be exactly the opposite of that below. The result is a chequer-board of flint and freestone. This is a useful method of using second-hand stone and is found everywhere after the Dissolution of the monastic houses and their subsequent wrecking.

The wool-rich parishes of East Anglia, too far removed from quarry areas to be able to build their large churches in masonry, imported small quantities of good quality freestone and worked this into fretted patterns similar to that used for the pierced parapets of the period. With this fretwork they built their wall-faces, backing them with flint rubble and filling in the interstices of the tracery with neatly squared flintwork. This is called 'flushwork'.

If one pauses to consider the large number of Gothic churches still remaining, adds to this a possible equivalent amount of material destroyed at the Dissolution, and then reflects upon the extremely elaborate nature of Gothic design, one may well wonder where all the skilled designers came from. The answer is probably that there was a great deal of copying of major elements and all individuality was left to the detailing introduced by the mason after his own special taste. One can imagine the medieval 'client' pointing out some feature which took his fancy and asking for something like it, with variations as in some other building, and so on. Contracts are in existence to indicate that the copying of the towers of parish churches, for example, was a not uncommon practice.

The general running-down of the magnificent medieval mason-craft following the decline of the great monasteries towards the sunset of the Middle Ages must have had the result of putting masons out of employment and reducing the intake to the lodges. Such innovations as the introduction of the 'ashlar' principle of *facing*, instead of building, with stone, point to the decline of interest in the great medieval craft, emphasized by the general coarsening of ornament and the retreat from the Gothic arch. Carpentry was achieving marvels in the roofs of parish churches, but the only contribution to the mason-craft of the Gothic twilight was the glorious fan-vaulting which could only be afforded by the most affluent communities. (Plate 30.)

Building in general was becoming less of an art. Speed of construction was being taken into consideration. A standardized form of building material, easy to make, transport and lay, and enabling building to be executed without the services of the highly-skilled and expensive freemason, was becoming popular. So into the sphere of building enters the 'red mason' with his pile of bricks.

The craft of brick-making was well understood by the Romans and most of their building in this country was carried out in this material. Even when building in rubble, bricks were used for quoins, for lining openings, and in the lacing courses, several bricks in depth, which were built into rubble walls to strengthen them. Salvaged Roman bricks, an inch and a half or so in thickness, were greatly sought after by the Anglo-Saxon builders for quoins and dressings.

From the early-medieval period onwards, bricks from the stoneless Low Countries were imported into East Anglia which was equally ill-provided. During the fourteenth century a region having good building stone but lacking stone suitable for paving slabs, might import such bricks—known as 'Flanders' or 'Holland' tiles—for flooring its churches.

The actual 'wall-tile' for building, about two inches thick, was being made in this country where suitable clay existed by the second quarter of the fifteenth century, but had been imported for use in East Anglian walls at least a century before this. By the end of the fifteenth century brick had come to be regarded as a suitable material for use in the best class of building, and was already being shown as a facing and not merely used for the core of the wall. Such bricks are known today as 'Tudor' bricks. They are encountered everywhere during the sixteenth century, especially during the Elizabethan Age.

During the seventeenth century when brick was becoming the universal English building material, about two and a half inches was the standard thickness, and by the eighteenth century it had settled down to the standard two and five-eighths of the present day. Peculiar to the Georgian era is the use of over-burnt 'headers' or 'chuffs' arranged in diaper patterns in the brick bonding. During the nineteenth century one sometimes finds three-inch bricks, especially in the industrial Midlands.

It took a long time for the bricklayers to discover how to bond their brickwork. At first they used them just as coursed rubble, maintaining the bonding principle as far as possible but employing no bonding plan. During the Tudor period, it is obvious, they were afraid that their 'stretcher' bricks would fall out, so they employed plenty of 'headers' to tie them in. The core of the wall was laid anyhow.

With the seventeenth century brickwork became so thoroughly studied that a proper system of bonding came into use. This was the 'English' bond which employed alternate courses of headers and stretchers neatly laid and properly interlocking in their courses and presenting an orderly appearance on the wall face. By the next century, however, the Dutch had taught us the proper way to lay bricks and introduced us to the 'Flemish' bond in which each course alternated headers with stretchers and changed step with those on either side of it. This is the established bond for this country which has been employed ever since.

No walling, whether of stone or brick, can be laid securely without beds of mortar. The manufacture of this requires lime, produced by burning the waste of limestone quarries. The quicklime mixed with sand forms mortar, which is not only essential for bedding the face stones of a masonry wall but desirable for consolidating the core of rough pieces of stone often thrown in anyhow where no one could see them. Buckets or cauldrons were needed to bring the mortar to the building course.

Transport of stone to the site could be by pony-back or by sled. It is interesting to watch stone sizes increasing as transport becomes more efficient with the passage of the centuries.

Scaffolding was essential for access to building work. The holes for the 'putlogs', the timbers carrying the scaffold planks and passing from wall to pole, can be seen everywhere in medieval buildings, generally as neat little square holes filled after the scaffolding had been struck. The pulley-wheel was used to lift materials to the scaffold, where the 'setters' laid the stones sent up to them by the banker mason working below.

8

Carpenters and Others

As one travels through the western counties, especially Devon or Cornwall, one cannot but remark upon the paucity of really old buildings. Church after church displays the soaring western bell-tower and the spacious fenestration of the High Gothic. It is true that freestone is almost entirely lacking in those regions west of the Exe, but so it is from East Anglia. And field-stone for walling is to be had for the taking and the local 'nobblers' and even the stonemasons seem to have had little difficulty in working even the grim granite to their requirements.

The deficiency may have been in that regular forest timber which since Anglo-Saxon times has been the basic building material, if not for walling, then for roofing. The heart of England provided an inexhaustible supply of this until a greedy iron industry began to denude it for fuel. But in the West, hammered by winds for so much of the year, timber trees seem to have been harder to come by and carpentry a trade far less common than that of granite-hewer. Thus it may simply have been the difficulty of roofing large buildings which delayed the development of medieval architecture in the West.

Oak, and by the fourteenth century elm, were the principal building timbers. For several centuries now we have employed imported softwoods for the purpose and even such hardwood as we may use for special purposes is brought to us from far countries. Thus our native woodland industry has long passed into history and it would be difficult to discover anything about it today. There must have been many hundreds of saw-pits in and

about the great forests of the Middle Ages, each with its heavy
bench and pair of sawyers, 'top-dog' and 'under-dog'—the latter
always smothered in sawdust—hauling the heavy saws to and fro
along the great trees. But the sawyer, like his colleague the quarryman, has been forgotten while the memories of inspired masons
and carpenters linger down the centuries among the stones and
beams of the great buildings they raised.

Like the contemporary mason, the early 'house-wright' executed his work with what today would be considered very clumsy
tools. After the felling axe had dropped, topped and lopped the
tree, and the sawyer had squared-up the logs into beams, these
were not taken into a 'shop' and put on to a bench but worked on
the ground as they lay with swinging strokes of the axe.

Where a sawpit was not available the wright squared-up his
logs by standing on them and attacking them with an all-purpose
tool called a 'twybill', a double-headed axe having one side turned
to serve as an adze. Fashioned in coarser mould, the West-
Country 'toobell' is still in use as a kind of mattock for working
amongst roots and boulders.

One of the interesting features of medieval carpentry is the way
in which the tapering nature of a tree is accepted as fundamental
to the design. No attempt was made to keep an even width of
timber throughout the length of a rafter, though exposed beams
were usually kept even for aesthetic reasons.

A common size for rafters was six by five inches tapering to five
by four. They were of course always laid flat until the end of the
seventeenth century.

Posts were set upside down so that the thick root-end could be
mortised to provide seatings for the several beams the posts had
to carry. These posts were known as 'teazle-posts' from some
resemblance to the plant.

Only the heart of the wood was used, the sap-wood being
axed away, possibly so as to discourage boring insects. It is the
'chamfering-off' of the edges of the beam to remove the last
vestiges of sap-wood which is so typical of medieval carpentry and
which forms one of the origins of the Gothic moulding.

The light, long-bladed axe was deftly wielded when cutting the mortices and tenons, and the augur or 'wimble'—from which 'gimlet'—bored the holes for the pegs holding the joints together.

Planks were massive timbers eighteen inches wide and six inches thick. They were used in belfry floors to stop the clappers of bells from hurtling down upon the heads of the ringers. Boards were of the same width as planks but about one and a half inches thick. During the fifteenth century when elaborate screenwork was being produced in large quantities, imported oak called 'Eastland' or 'ostrich' boards were used for this, Continental timber being apparently better seasoned than ours was.

The early timber buildings of this country were founded upon posts set in rows opposing each other in pairs at bay intervals, the space between the rows representing the span of the roof. Two lines of sleepers formed the foundations. In the tall churches these were beams about two feet square, but in normal buildings they were planks laid flat on a low wall of rubble stone. The timber foundation was called a 'tablement' from the Latin word for plank. The rubble underneath it allowed it to be levelled-up and at the same time kept it dry. In a stone building, the tablement became a stone plinth with its edge bevelled back so that the wall could be given an aesthetic foundation as well as a structural one.

From the sleeper foundation rose the posts, stepped upon it as masts on a keel, joined together as they rose by systems of curved struts and braces, the sweeping curves softening the aesthetic rigidity of the lines and enabling use to be made of curved pieces of timber. (Fig. 6.)

Ubiquitous are the curved 'saltires' which sweep across from post to post, their form probably deriving from the shape of the wooden packsaddles which carried most of the loads of the day. The double curve of the ogee, perpetuated in stone beneath the central tower of Wells Cathedral, must have developed from the graceful profiles of the timber prototypes.

After the hardwood logs had been sawn into squared timbers at the saw-pit, the round-faced boards resulting from this operation were adzed down at their ends and fitted into horizontal sills and heads to form partitions or 'bratticing' for the external walling.

9. The twelfth-century nave of Whaplode church in Lincolnshire

10. A richly-ornamented arcade of the twelfth century at Stapleford in Wiltshire

The church at Greensted in Essex is still walled with bratticing of this description.

After the age of timber-building had given place to that of building in stone, the carpenter's primary task became to provide a roof. The principle of early roof construction was very simple, each roof consisting of a series of 'couples', pairs of rafters 'halved' and pinned together at the apex and set close together along the line of the building. There was no ridge piece. In order to give some sense of triangulation to each couple and prevent its collapse when the roof-covering was applied, a short horizontal timber called a 'collar' joined the rafters rather more than half-way up.

At the top of the wall, a heavy timber called the 'wall-plate' was laid flat on the masonry, in the manner of a tablement, to carry the rafter-feet. The plate was solidly bedded-down on the wall-top so that it would not slide off and imperil the stability of the roof. But often the outward thrust of the roof was so powerful that it could actually begin to topple the walls and force them to lean outwards. To check this the carpenters set massive beams called 'tie-beams' across from side to side to tie the opposing plates together and thus complete the triangulation of the roof.

But the tie-beam was aesthetically an unattractive feature as it cut across the building and spoilt its internal form. The great halls of the Anglo-Saxons were formed of lines of wide timber arches called 'crucks', each arch being constructed in the same way as a roofing 'couple' but the rafters being massive curved timbers rising direct from the ground without any walling. The interior effect of such a building is that of a long pointed tunnel. This is very probably the effect sought after in all English roofs even after they had been raised upon walls. It is in essence the form of the Gothic interior.

Tie-beams passing across this tunnel-like space would undoubtedly have ruined the effect. So the carpenters, the nature of whose material would have made them much more familiar with the principles governing statics than the more pedestrian mason, discovered ways of making the roof more stable without resource to the primitive tie. They had from early times discovered the principle of triangulation and during the early-medieval period were developing it in their roofs by adding extra braces from the collar down towards the rafter-feet to stiffen each couple and reduce the risk of its spreading. This began to introduce a curved outline into the roof which by the selection of curved timbers for the strutting could be smoothed down into the desired tunnel-like effect. In this way the medieval 'cradle-roof' came into being.

It is noticeable that while in the well-timbered parts of England the cradle roofs gave way to the magnificent low-pitched roofs of the High Gothic, in the West, where large timbers to construct the great trusses were difficult to obtain, and slate could be used for covering instead of lead, cradle roofs formed out of the curved western timber continued to the end of the Middle Ages. (Plate 21.)

But it was the gradual development upon the tie-beam which led to the introduction of the carpenters' finest contribution to English medieval architecture, the elaborate roofs of the fifteenth century which attained their finest form in East Anglia.

Although the tie-beam began as a device for tying the sides of the roof together, by the High Gothic era it had come to be accepted that it could be used as a base for actually propping up the roof in the centre. From this time the tie-beam became the basic feature of a device called a 'truss', set across the span at bay or half-bay intervals and used to prop up the roof by means of a series of timbers set, for the first time, longitudinally from one end of the building to the other. The uppermost of these timbers was the ridge against which the rafters leaned, no longer joined in 'couples' but each one an independent timber. Between ridge and plate were 'purlins' passing from truss to truss and carrying the rafters in the centre of their span. (Plate 19.)

The development of the High Gothic roof is expressed by the variations in the design of the roof-truss. These variations are innumerable both in respect of the systems of timbering used and the forms of decoration subsequently applied. The lowering of the roof pitch and the pressure of the lead covered on the flat-laid rafters made it necessary to increase the amount of timber needed to carry its covering.

Anyone who visits the churches in a region such as East Anglia one cannot but be impressed by the versatility and independence of thought displayed by the carpenters as each worked out his own system of roof truss independently of his neighbours. A number of devices can be seen, each used in a slightly different manner and augmented by the introduction of non-structural timbers, finally completed by magnificent carving.

Basic to the simple roof truss are the central 'king-post' and the pair of 'queen-posts', carrying the large 'principal rafters' between which pass the purlins. Sometimes a wide timber arch fills the truss instead of a system of vertical members. And as the ends of the tie-beam are often stiffened by timber brackets passing down the wall, the tie-beam carrying an arch sometimes has its middle portion omitted and only its bracket-supported ends retained. Such curtailed beams are called 'hammer-beams'.

Until the very end of the medieval period, when the pitched roof had vanished and been replaced by the lead flat, the tie-beam was never a readily acceptable feature of the church interior. The arched truss carried by a pair of hammer-beams began to open up the roof once again. Eventually the two hammer-beams were provided with another pair above them and the width of the arched truss reduced. In its final form the hammer-beam truss came to be built up in its entirety with these curious devices. (Plate 20.)

It is a curious fact that the excellent joinery technique and superb craftsmanship of the carved screenwork of the South-West is nowhere matched in its roofs. The roof-truss is almost unknown in that region; the old system of 'close-coupled' rafters continues in use to the end of the medieval period. But the 'cradle-roofs' of the West cover wide spans, over aisles as well as nave, and contributed in no small part to the development of the 'hall' church. (Plate 21.) Longitudinal timbers resembling purlins were used to strap each couple to its neighbour, carved bosses being provided to mask junctions between members.

The timber architecture of a country is bound to be affected by the nature of its material. England's timber is hardwood, capable of producing curved as well as straight members. The fact that the Gothic arch, constructed in stone, is less liable to spread and collapse than the Classical semicircular form, was probably discovered during the adventurous days of the twelfth century; but the Anglo-Saxon 'cruck' of two curved timbers, depicted on the Bayeux Tapestry and still to be met with in our villages today, is a Gothic arch and may have had a good deal more to do with the development of medieval English architecture than can nowadays be determined.

The earliest crucks were pairs of curved timbers used so as to form walls and roof in one piece without facing the problems resulting from trying to balance rafters on the tops of walls. At first the crucks were set close together to be used as rafters but during the later Middle Ages they were set at bay distance to form trusses and carry purlins. Originally the crucks were formed of bowed timbers but at the end of the medieval period bent timbers, giving more headroom, took the place of the old curved profiles. From an association of the angled truss and the wall was developed an open type of roof displaying the truss in its least obstructive silhouette. The cruck principle, used to the full in the Midlands but seldom seen in the West, appears to have given birth to an interesting form of open roof, its trusses formed of specially selected angled timbers, in a number of High Gothic roofs to be seen in East Anglia.

The 'saltire' or diagonal cross formed of two struts crossing, was nearly always formed of two serpentine timbers, so that these met in a silhouette of 'ogee' form finishing in a sharp point. It is interesting to note that the French equivalent of 'Gothic' is 'Ogival', thus giving recognition to a feature which is certainly not of masonry origin as representing the most magnificent masonry style the world has ever seen.

In order to support the centre of the purlins midway between the trusses, and at the same time brace the roof longitudinally against wind pressure on the gable ends, systems of 'wind-braces' were introduced along the sides of the roof. These were formed out of arched or serpentine timbers. They add greatly to the elaboration of the High Gothic roof, and in a simple form are met with everywhere in the roofs of the mid-sixteenth century, being retained at the ends of roofs for a century after this.

The roof of the High Gothic era began as a soaring piece of carpentry determined to uphold the Gothic tradition. But the demands of a lead covering, difficult to stop from creeping down a steep pitch, forced the eventual abandoning of the traditional form.

As the roof-pitch sank towards the flat, dignity was restored by raising walls and increasing the size of the fenestration. The truss disappeared and was replaced by a massive tie-beam having just enough rise in the middle to retain a small degree of pitch in the roof. Thus in its final form the roof became a fine timber ceiling (Plate 18.), a panelling of tie-beams and purlins, often elaborately ornamented and with long brackets carried from the ends of the tie-beams down the lofty walls of the nave or its clearstory. (Plate 20.) Such coverings could not compete in magnificence with the trussed and hammer-beamed roofs of recent years, but the effect of the whole interior, albeit reduced to an austerity of detail, continued to appear spacious and dignified by virtue of its impressive proportions.

At the end of the medieval period the parish church had become an edifice of simple proportions, lofty in the Gothic tradition, and covered by a flat roof which showed beneath as an attractively carpentered timber ceiling. One might have supposed that the Dissolution of the monasteries would have released material and enabled the parish churches to launch out into even finer architectural adventures. What happened, however, was that the whole of the building industry went over to building great halls for lay magnates and ignored church building as belonging to an obsolete social order. It also happened, however, that some parish churches were able to expand here and there by salvaging some fine timber roof from a monastic house in course of demolition. Such may still be discovered today.

Parishes needing lead for roofing repairs might find that the enormous tonnage salvaged from the monasteries had all been assigned to lay people for their new mansions. Thenceforth the tendency is to go back to high-pitched roofs which could be covered with the clay tiles now coming into more general use.

The church roofs of Elizabethan and Jacobean days are often quite interesting. A great many exist which have not been replaced by sham-Gothic cradle roofs during nineteenth-century restorations. They are all built on the truss principle. Both kinds of pitch may be found, the high for tiles, the low for lead. The trusses carrying the former still display, in simplified form, the old devices of wide arches and even hammer-beams. The low-pitch trusses have king-posts and queen-posts, often indicating their post-medieval date by employing shapes for these suggestive of the Renaissance baluster. Nearly all the roofs of this period make full use of the strange 'square-onion' drops, usually pierced, possibly a pathetic attempt to recapture something of the lovely pendants of fifteenth-century fan-vaulting which the plasterers of the period had already introduced into their domestic ceilings.

The roofs of our parish churches have suffered far more seriously than the walls supporting them. During the comfort-loving eighteenth century many medieval roofs lacking in any particular aesthetic charm were ceiled-in with lath and plaster.

While we are fortunate in that so many of our magnificent High Gothic church roofs still survive notwithstanding the encouragement given to the spread of the death-watch beetle by the change-over from oil lamps to electric lighting, still more of the lesser roofs, deemed not so worthy of retention, were swept away during the age of restorations. Most of the roofs which replaced them have gone back to the early-medieval pitches indicated on tower walls by the remains of water-tables. The type of roof most favoured by the nineteenth-century restorer was the open cradle form.

The plaster ceiling was not a feature of medieval architecture, though boarded 'wainscot' was often provided over the altar to keep dirt from the roof from falling upon it. The final elimination of the roof-truss under the lead-covered roofs of the fifteenth century had created the situation that the underside of the roof, like that of the 'solar' floor, had become a ceiling. The very great skill of the contemporary carpenters enabled them to make the late-Gothic ceiling a thing of outstanding merit. (Plate 18.)

The original incitement of the medieval carpenter towards aesthetic achievement was the conversion of the structural roof into an object of beauty in its own right. Centuries were to elapse before even a start could be made. Meanwhile the jumble of rough 'couples' formed but a rustic heaven when viewed from below. Thus the early architects were trying where possible to conceal it behind some kind of ceiling.

In the Age of the Mason the ceiling was a stone one. It first consisted of a system of stone tunnels running along the building with lateral ones crossing this at each bay. The amount of timber centering required to turn these vaults was very considerable. A scaffolding had to be erected and each stone held up by its individual prop until its particular ring of 'voussoirs' had been completed and the whole arch would stand.

By the twelfth century the principle of building arches in 'orders' had been extended to cover vault construction. Each 'groin' where the various tunnels intersected was set out as an arched rib built up on the usual timber centering. Between the skeleton thus provided each section of the vault could be turned independently and with greater ease than before. During the High Gothic era the number of ribs increased and the masons began to devise patterns to be set out in a reticulation of tracery sometimes even foliated like that of windows.

Vaulting, however, really belongs to the architecture of the great churches. A very expensive item, it is seldom found in parish churches except in some chancels and under the wooden floors of towers and the muniment rooms over porches, the 'stone solars' of the medieval builder.

The latest development of vaulting, in which it becomes a richly panelled ceiling springing in cones from each point of support and displaying the most enterprising pendants suspended in space between its sweeping spans, is only occasionally met with in unexpectedly beautiful side chapels contributed by some wool magnate of the fifteenth or sixteenth century. (Plate 30.)

Whether of boarded wainscot or stone vaulting, the ceiling of churches prior to their being covered with lead must have been a valuable asset. Early churches would have undoubtedly been covered with thatch of marsh-reed—the straw of those days would probably have been too short for the purpose. There are still some thatched churches remaining in East Anglia suggesting that all the original churches of the region may have been so covered.

The best buildings of pre-medieval England were covered with shingles. Salisbury Cathedral was designed to be so roofed and remained so until the middle of the thirteenth century. Shingles were narrow boards, today about two feet long, and probably then of oak. The bottom edge of each was rounded so as to direct storm-water passing down it away from the joint beneath. This produced a curious fish-scale appearance to the buildings which may clearly be seen in the Bayeux Tapestry. The original roof of the twelfth-century church of Kilmersdon in Somerset was carried on an exceptionally fine corbel-table supported on large and elaborately-carved corbels, between which the roof covering was repeated in stone to form a frieze passing round the building. The shingles depicted are four inches wide and laid to a gauge of six inches.

We do not know whether the shingles were fixed to battens as they are today. It seems possible that the roof was first boarded over to provide a ceiling below. The Bayeux Tapestry makes it clear that the 'bratticed' sides of timber buildings had the boarding hung with shingles.

The use of certain types of stone which could be saturated with water and left to a frost to split into tiles was known in Roman Britain. Many of these may have been salvaged from the ruins by the Anglo-Saxons. And the technique of manufacture must have been passed on to the medieval builder, for stone tiles were in use in many parts of England right through the Middle Ages and indeed right up to the present day.

Clay roofing tiles were being made in England as early as the thirteenth century and were being used in some districts for covering the high-pitched medieval roofs with something more durable than shingles. The manufacture of such tiles was however limited to such areas as could find suitable clay. The supply seems never to have been anywhere near up to the demand.

In addition to the frost-riven tiles of fissile stone there are the ancient slates of Westmorland and Cornwall, true slate-stones which make the finest roofing materials and moreover display lovely colours. At the end of the eighteenth century the grim grey slates of North Wales began to spread over the country. Their weatherproofing qualities make them the most watertight of this

11. The thirteenth-century cruciform church at Uffington in Berkshire

12. A thirteenth-century crossing at Amesbury in Wiltshire

type of covering and they will last as long as their nailing can be kept from rusting. And their appearance, not so far removed in colour from the grey of lead, made them acceptable to the church architects of the Victorian era.

The builders of the High Gothic were particularly fortunate in that this country produced most of Europe's lead. The effect of this on our architecture is very noticeable. Continental architects continued to build the tall Gothic roofs to the very end of the medieval era, maintaining to the end of the Middle Ages the soaring effect of their buildings. In England, however, the use of lead brought the roof-pitch down towards the flat, and with it the form of the late-Gothic arch. A parallel example of the effect of materials upon architectural aesthetics may be found in Spain, where the low-pitch roof of interlocking 'Roman' tiles enabled the architects to build with depressed arches as in England. During the early sixteenth century we can detect a curious sympathy between the two countries in respect of their architectural affinities—in England the four-centred arch, in Spain the three-centred.

Although we do not hear anything of the medieval plumber, as we do of his more expressive colleagues the mason and carpenter, his craft has always been a highly-skilled one and his contribution to our medieval architecture, albeit from what might be called the industrial angle, of the utmost significance to its development. Medieval lead was very heavy and had to be melted down in great cauldrons, probably on the building site, and there cast into sheets in wooden trays made up by the carpenter and covered with sand. The writer has employed such a plumber who worked in this fashion, stripping the old lead from a roof, melting it down, recasting it, and re-laying it on the roof, all without leaving the churchyard.

The actual laying of the sheets is a skilled operation. The sheets are lapped horizontally like tiles but their edges have to be cunningly folded together after a fashion known only to the plumber.

Everything connected with the laying of lead is a specialized operation, for lead should not be nailed or it will tear. Its coefficient of expansion is so high that it is always on the move creeping to and fro. The replacement of the early projecting eaves with lead gutters set behind a parapet forced the plumbers to develop their special skill in laying their remarkable material until they had reached a degree of efficiency almost forgotten today.

The lead 'flashing' used today to cover the junction of leadwork with a wall was not used in medieval times, the practice being to divert the stormwater running down the wall-face with a projecting stone 'water-table'. The sites of these now cut back to the wall-face give the clue to many a vanished roof.

England has always been fortunate in the possession of good supplies of metallic ores which could easily be extracted by open-cast mining. Much of the lead used in the Roman Empire came from Mendip; the lead mines of medieval Derbyshire supplied much of Europe. The Forest of Dean and the Sussex Weald provided England with all the iron it needed.

In the days before the Factory Age most villages had a blacksmith. The amount of ironwork used in the medieval village was minute by modern standards, but everything there was had to be his concern. And with the spirit of the age of craftsmanship affecting all tradesmen, the smith would if desired mould his practical rods and bars into interesting shapes for the greater glory of his craft. Thus magnificent church ironwork, especially in the ornamentation of the church door, may be found from Anglo-Saxon days, in addition to the humble 'hooks and bands' upon which every door had to be hung. The smith had to fashion the 'ferramenti' of stanchions and saddle-bars to which the leaded glazing of the windows was secured. And every nail used in the construction had to be hand-wrought by him.

A great deal of the ornamental ironwork of the medieval period is still in existence unaffected by the rust of possibly as much as a thousand years. This seems incredible having regard to our climate. It may be due to the fact that the medieval iron was smelted with charcoal instead of mined coal.

In a climate such as that of England the weakest point in the design of any building is the potential leakage to rain and wind represented by its windows. Thus all early windows were kept as small as possible. For quite apart from the areas presented by large windows to the elements, anything closing the opening would have to be made of perishable materials. Thus where the quarries permitted, a common form of window used in belfries is formed of thin stone slabs pierced with foliated openings.

Primitive windows, if they were closed at any time, used wooden shutters for the purpose. They were not hinged but were wedged into a rebate cut into the outer edge of the window such as can still be seen in many a pre-medieval window. During the last stand of the Saxon army at Hastings their shield wall was made of hastily collected shutters.

Oiled linen fixed into a wooden frame was employed as 'glazing' in small windows well into the medieval period, even in churches.

The glass of medieval days was made with great difficulty from the outer portions of blown sheets and set as a mosaic of diamond-shaped 'quarries' fixed together with a network of delicate grooved strips hand-tooled by patient plumbers and known as 'calms'—pronounced 'cames'. The painting and firing of pictorial glass came into the province of the glazier whose methods may have shared something of the experience of the contemporary potter.

During the twelfth century painted glass was reserved for the great churches. It does not appear in the parish church until the High Gothic era. In early days, heraldry provided the most popular form of expression.

> 'Wide windows y-wrought . . .
> Shining with shapen shields . . .'

The floors of humble churches may have been of beaten earth, sealed, perhaps, with the blood of oxen. For only in certain parts of England can one find stone suitable for splitting into the comparatively thin slabs required for paving. In the West, huge slabs of slate were available, but it is only in the stone regions of Somerset and Yorkshire that true paving stones could be discovered. Many churches may have been floored with water-worn cobbles from stream beds or old alluvial areas of geological days.

Since the ninth century the ecclesiastical authorities had insisted upon the kneeling position for confronting the more sacred phases of the Mass. Hence many church floors may have been carpeted with rushes. There was of course no fixed seating until the fifteenth century. Prior to this the congregation had stood or moved slowly about the building when not actually kneeling.

The altar would have always been raised upon a 'foot-pace' similar to the dais raising the high-table above the rush-strewn 'marsh' of the contemporary great hall.

Special tiles were being made for this purpose by the thirteenth century. They were usually yellowish in tone and were decorated with the tri-lobate 'stiff-leaf' motif of the period, later with beasts and heraldic shields. Highly glazed to preserve their surface, they are today known as 'encaustic' tiles, but in medieval days simply as 'painted' tiles. They were often set out in groups of four; borders too were manufactured. A number of monastic houses, notably Chertsey Abbey in Surrey, had factories for making these tiles. During the nineteenth century vast quantities of them, known as 'Minton' tiles, were made in the interest of church restoration. Thousands of grave-slabs were levered up from the floors of medieval chancels and replaced with Minton tiles.

For the paving of the main body of the church imported bricks could be used. 'Flanders tiles' and 'Holland tiles' had come into use by the fourteenth century, probably brought back as ballast in ships carrying wool to the Low Countries from the great East Anglian ports now vanished beneath the waves.

It should be remembered that the interiors of churches were places of sepulture for local notabilities. This must have caused frequent disturbances to the church paving which must in consequence have seldom presented a level appearance. When fixed seating came in during the fifteenth century interment would presumably have been thereafter restricted as far as possible to the open spaces between the blocks of seats.

As early as the twelfth century the walls of churches were being decorated with paint. By the end of the medieval period much of the wall-painting is of a high order; but nothing is known of the artists who contributed it as well as probably a still greater amount of painted pictures once ornamenting the walls of the great churches now vanished for ever. Much 'superstitious' painting must have been obliterated during the seventeenth century when the white-washing of church interiors was in vogue.

9

Pre-Medieval Architecture

To the Anglo-Saxon, building was an incomprehensible trade. There was no word for it. All construction was known as 'timbering'. Boat-building they understood, and the stepping of a mast on its keel. When raising a tall building they first laid sleepers on the ground and then erected posts on the foundation thus assured. Such a rapid system of building, far quicker than the raising of a wall by placing stone upon stone, was ideally suited to the erection of a church which needed at all costs to achieve the monumental element of height. Raise four tall posts and a tower was well under way.

As workers in wood the Anglo-Saxons were familiar with the principles of joinery technique and thus could provide their timber towers with the struts and braces necessary to assure their rigidity. (Fig. 6.) For covering they had two methods of using the by-products of their timbering. Oak shingles could be used as in later tile-hanging to provide a waterproof sheathing. Or a sturdy wall standing up in its own right could be formed with the rounded planks sawn in the pits from the squaring of the great posts and beams, framed into horizontal timbers at sill and head.

A few of their timber churches of late date have been preserved to serve as bell-towers at the west end of later stone naves (Plate 1), connection with which has resulted in the loss of their eastern aisles and their chancels. In addition to these almost perfect tower-churches, the remains of many more are probably to be found enclosed within the western ends of later stone naves, having been retained to carry bells. Hundreds must have disappeared without trace, burnt by Danes or in later conflagrations, or simply pulled down for shame at their rusticity. They have however their memorials in stone towers such as those of Barton-upon-Humber (Plate 3) in Lincolnshire or Barnack and Earls Barton in Northamptonshire. The so-called 'long-and-short' work at the angles of early stone churches is clearly intended to represent timber posts, each separate vertical stone having, however, to be held in position by a horizontal one 'bonded' into the wall.

An early stone tower such as that of Earls Barton is of the greatest interest as it indicates the elaboration of the contemporary wooden structure. Cross-bracing or 'saltires' are shown, and even timber arches—recalling the wooden 'stave-churches' at Urnes and Borgund in Norway. Short stone 'headers' are built in here and there as required to tie in the long stone 'timbers'. The system is of course purely decorative. It may be partly nostalgic, partly in the nature of an apology for a lack of proper architecture with which to embellish a building of such importance.

When one recalls that early Anglo-Saxon England built entirely in timber and that perhaps from the eighth century onwards they were actually constructing churches in that material, it is indeed tragic that the whole of that early timber architecture has been lost to us. During the following century the forays of the Danes across England resulted in church-burning on an extensive scale and much of the original work must have vanished at that time. But following the pacification of the invaders at the end of the ninth century church building would presumably have recommenced on an extensive scale. Thus we might have hoped that at least a few tenth-century examples of Anglo-Saxon timber architecture could have been preserved.

Such buildings as remain, however, are probably two centuries later. Complete ones—save for their chancels—form a group in Essex. They are timber parish churches on the 'four-poster' plan. The great church at Blackmore, however, is believed to be of monastic origin. Its nave is two bays in length, on the Byzantine 'duplex' plan. (Fig. 5.) Above this reaches an impressive network of timbering crossing and criss-crossing on its way towards the belfry stage high over the centre of the church. It was aisled about, but the eastern aisle was removed when a twelfth-century stone nave was added. This great timber church is possibly itself of mid-twelfth century date, but only by subjecting its timber to the modern radiological test could one obtain a closer dating and even then the factor of error could cover more than a century.

It was not until recent years that the true nature of these remarkable turriform churches, Anglo-Saxondom's tribute to Byzantine architecture, came to be realized. For some reason they were regarded as bell-towers added during the fifteenth century to the stone naves. But scientific investigation of the timbers of Nave-stock church in Essex, carried out by Mr. C. A. Hewett, confirmed the writer's view as to the real date of the structures by indicating the year 1193 with an allowance for error of sixty years each way. The preservation of the Essex group of churches is undoubtedly due to the difficulty of obtaining stone for bell-towers in this part of the country. Others, however, may be discovered elsewhere, absorbed by the stone walling of a thirteenth-century nave.

One can learn a great deal from a study of these remarkable buildings. One is struck most forcibly by the pure Gothic of their elevational form due to the use of the wooden 'cruck' or timber arch everywhere in the design. We know that the pointed arch had entered into Eastern Byzantine architecture as early as the seventh century and must have often been encountered by Crusading travellers; and it is clear that the Gothic arch is far more stable structurally than the primitive form. That Gothic as a *timber* style was in existence as early as the eleventh century is indicated by the illustration in the Bayeux Tapestry of the Confessor's hall at Westminster.

Passing from Anglo-Saxon timberwork to their efforts as builders in stone we find the picture shrinks considerably, for their work is primitive and appears to lack any stylistic influence at the level of the parish church. One may even wonder whether the ordinary Anglo-Saxon builder ever really learned to build in stone at all until a date well after his conversion to Christianity.

It must surely now be accepted that Anglo-Saxon England was not in fact destroyed at the Norman Conquest. And recent ethno-graphical research has suggested that the Anglo-Saxon settlement itself did not automatically eject the indigenous inhabitants and that for a long time to come the 'Welshmen', as they were called, continued to play a large part in the social life of the country. It is even suggested today that cranial measurements and so forth indicate the average Englishman is far more Celt than Teuton.

So the possibility exists that the men who raised the early stone churches for the first Anglo-Saxons who were received into the Celtic Church of their day were in fact themselves Celts, building in the same primitive rubble style as was employed in contemporary Ireland.

The churches they would have built would have been of the utmost simplicity, having but a nave and a chancel. (Fig. 13.) This type of plan survived in hundreds of small parish churches right through the glorious days of the twelfth century and indeed right through the Middle Ages, always recalling the Celtic, not the Byzantine, origins of the English Church. (Plate 7.)

While for ritual purposes the Celtic plan of nave and chancel was all that was actually required architecturally such structures must have been very unsatisfying. The great minsters were showing what could be done to raise a church towards the clouds by means of towers. And when one realizes that every tower had to be roofed in steeple-fashion it at once becomes apparent that the architectural brilliance of those days has gone without recall.

Four types of towers were to be found. There were original turriform structures of Western Byzantine form, some of them still serving their original purpose and others attached to the western ends of expanding churches. In the minsters were those central lantern towers, lightly-constructed upward projections of the walling providing a tier of windows lighting the choirs below. A number of stone turriform tower-naves of the Barnack type must have been in existence as well as scores of timber towers such as was to be seen later at Blackmore. In addition to all these structures there were the slender Byzantine bell-towers which we can see today all along the eastern side of England from Durham through the East Riding to Lincolnshire and East Anglia. These towers look impressive enough under their medieval lead flats.

13. A richly moulded arcade of the early-mediaeval period at Stoke Golding in Leicestershire

14. A fully-developed High Gothic church at Lowick in Northamptonshire

What must the countryside have looked like when every tower was steeple-crowned?

Although the bell-tower at the west end of the nave is in by far the majority of cases an addition of the fourteenth or fifteenth century it would seem very likely that the England of the eleventh twelfth and thirteenth centuries was a many-steepled land and this not only by reason of the great host of monastic houses whose countless towers have toppled into the dust.

It may be that the continued existence of such an apparently inexplicable structure as the axially-planned church of the twelfth century with its central tower but no transepts is simply due to the need for incorporating a tower into the design. And while a bell-tower of the Anglian type can carry a bell but is no use for accommodating a congregation, a central tower can serve both purposes.

It is also possible that the type of church-plan represented by the remains at Barton-upon-Humber in Lincolnshire which has a chancel and west nave but no wings (see Fig. 7*b*) may have been quite common in eleventh-century England and that the axial church is thus simply its twelfth-century successor.

Returning to the early stone churches of England and their possibly very primitive character there can be no doubt that although timber was the national building material at the time, there was ample field-stone available for the raising of a simple stone-walled structure such as a primitive 'Celtic' church. If lime could not be obtained for making mortar—and one can imagine that the monasteries were very probably monopolizing supplies of this expensively-produced substance—the stones could be laid 'herringbone' and and thus prevented from falling out of the wall.

In this or any other form of stone building the real problem was how to secure the angles of the building. Here the ruins of Roman towns may have provided the solution. One can imagine the search for cut stones and salvaged bricks to be used for the essential 'quoins' of the structure.

Apart from primitive doors and windows only one important architectural feature was needed, the doorway leading from the nave into the chancel. The building style being basically arcuated, the opening would have to have an arched head. During the development of church-building in stone one can follow the gradual widening of the chancel arch from the first narrow openings lined with massive stones to the more spacious features more daintily formed in architectural style with properly masoned stonework.

The next most important feature architecturally was the entrance door. The uncertainty with which the early builders tackled arch construction is indicated by the way in which they would avoid it by using a triangular door-head formed of two lintels leaning against each other. (See Plate 3.) Yet even by the eleventh century the influence of Byzantine architectural contacts led them to adopt the combined arch-and-lintel construction with the semicircular 'tympanum' for spanning narrow openings.

To the early builder in stone the turning of an arch upon its wooden centering must have been a considerable feat. And as he attempted wider spans, his ignorance of the principles of abutment would have constantly led him into situations when his new arch began to let him down. Many a chancel arch of the twelfth century —and later—looks alarmingly unstable today, having been steadily collapsing until some late medieval-builder at last saved the situation by adding a buttress.

During the eleventh century the principle of centering an arch in expanding 'orders' saved some of the centering and lightened the appearance of the finished arch. Finally the introduction of ornament in the way of roll-mouldings to soften the edges of the orders began to pave the way for the richly-moulded arches of the Gothic era.

The 'imposts' from which an arch sprang were important to the design. Early imposts, like the soffits of the arches they carried, were plain stone faces. But with the ordered arch came the half-shaft passing up the centre of the impost to carry the lowermost order (see background in Plate 9.)—a Byzantine device used in connection with the 'duplex' system of employing small arches carried on columns within the span of great arches supported by heavy piers. Sometimes there was a pair of such shafts set side by side. All have caps of some description, either the formal 'cubical' type or crudely-carved where the architecture was unsophisticated and the carvers enterprising.

In those early days, carving was an alternative to a sophisticated architectural ordinance. The latter is clearly illustrated by plain arches rising from square imposts with embellishment restricted to neat rolls worked on the edges. When carved caps appear one knows that local enthusiasm has replaced architectural supervision.

This is in fact the key to that fascinating period in the history of architecture, the twelfth century in England. For the great monastic houses not only monopolized the building trade but the architectural 'profession' as well. The minsters were set out and detailed in accordance with an accepted ordinance. The parish churches 'did it themselves' making up for lack of sophisticated knowledge by taking full advantage of the versatility and enthusiasm of the amateur. It is to this charming quality of the vernacular in Anglo-Saxon church building that we owe the wonderful riches of the 'Norman' doorway with its limitless range of motifs. No other western historical style can equal this for exuberance.

It was during the twelfth century that the style reached its zenith. Beginning with the two doorways, the entrance doorway and that leading into the chancel, the riot of sculpture spread over arcades and even wall-faces, in almost oriental profusion. The church of Elkstone in Gloucestershire is an example of one of the liveliest of these sculptors' playgrounds.

None of this detail is architectural. For such is usually restricted to the great churches. The Byzantine wall-arcade is an example of this staider form of ornament, which may however still be seized upon by the sculptors for embellishment according to their peculiar taste.

A great deal of architectural embellishment is of the form known as 'aedicular'—the repetition of a structural feature in miniature for ornamental purposes. The 'blind arcade' is an example frequently met with in all periods of medieval architecture, formed in or in front of a plain wall-face and often providing a framing for a range of small windows. The miniature arcade occurs everywhere as a wall-decoration, either as a dado or imitating one of the upper galleries found in Eastern Byzantine churches. Another aedicular device is the flanking of windows with tiny reproductions of columns with cap and base. (Plate 8.)

The beginnings of architecture in England were the result of the colonization of the country by Benedictine monks from the Continent. Eastern Mercia was the original Benedictine sphere of operations, and the Barnack quarries in Northamptonshire its first source of building stone. In this connection it is of interest to note that three of the most elaborate stone tower-naves surviving today, Barnack, Earls Barton, and Barton-upon-Humber (Plate 3), are grouped together at this north-eastern end of the freestone belt.

It is tempting to suggest that the stone tower-nave may have originated there and spread south-westwards along the stone areas. The writer has noticed them at North Leigh in Oxfordshire, Netheravon in Wiltshire, and Hemyock in Devon.

The western arch at Netheravon is a very elaborate one. Hemyock has lateral arches only, which is of interest as the planner of the church at North Elmham in Norfolk actually regarded the north-south axis as the more important and his nave runs across the building, which in this case, however, has no central feature. The church at Breamore in Hampshire (Plate 4) with its large turriform nave is quite close to the stone belt.

The 'Anglian' architectural style which developed with the original Benedictine areas in eastern Mercia is almost pure Byzantine and used the massive square pier with angle rolls or shafts as its characteristic supporting member for aisle arcades. This might be called the 'Doric' of Anglo-Saxon architecture—indeed the cubical cap it employs upon its shafting is actually a derivative of the Greek Doric capital.

At one time there must have been a great many parish churches lined with arcades founded upon the heavy Anglian piers. (Plate 9.) The obstructive nature of the supports, however, resulted in nearly all these arcades being subsequently remodelled with lighter pillars in the Gothic style. In many churches though, the old Anglian responds remain as mementos of the original design.

The Anglian style spread throughout the eastern parts of the country and into Wessex. But at the close of the eleventh century a new monastic immigration began to take root in Western Mercia beside the heart of the stone belt where it formed the Cotswolds. It was the Burgundian Cluniacs, a wealthy Order which aimed at rivalling the Benedictines with their building programmes. With them the Cluniacs brought the first sophisticated architectural style.

It will be recalled that the principal feature of Classical architecture was the circular column, first drum-built then turned on a lathe, and always provided with a sculptured capital. It was these columns which had lined the original basilicas of Rome, and in Latin eyes must have represented the only supporting features acceptable in a Christian church, the massive piers of the Byzantines being regarded as crude and barbarous.

At the close of the eleventh century, the Cluniac monks began to set about the introduction of the circular pillar as a rival intended to oust the Anglian pier. While the turning of a column required the construction of a stone lathe, circular pillars could be built up in masonry or even in drums if the pillar was small in diameter. Thus during the twelfth century a Western type of circular pillar —perhaps the only true 'Romanesque' feature in English architecture—came into general use in the parish churches of the period. (Plate 10.)

The finest of the Byzantine churches were provided with upper stories set between the great piers, the floors of these galleries being carried upon small columns. This association of pier and column—the last in Western Byzantine architecture represented by a circular pillar—resulted in the 'duplex' bay system in which pier and pillar alternate, an effect which may sometimes be detected in the aisle arcades of twelfth-century parish churches.

The Anglo-Saxons employed only the simplest forms of architectural embellishment. The most common form is the edge-roll, used both to soften the edges of arch orders and the angles of the piers supporting them.

In vertical situations the edge-roll becomes virtually a slender colonette and as such needed a cap and a base.

Here the Classical Orders came under review for the purpose. The spreading Doric capitals known to students of such temples as the Parthenon were unsuited for use in confined situations such as the head of an edge-roll or a 'nook-shaft'. If on the other hand one should find a Doric capital with one angle broken off and should be tempted to break off the other three to adjust the balance, the residue would have very little projection beyond the shaft and would thus be quite suitable in a confined situation. Finished at the top with a suitable moulded strip these 'cubical' caps were adopted for completing the fully-developed shafts passing up the angles and filling the recesses of the ordered Byzantine piers. Immature moulded bases finished the shafts off at the bottom. The piers, like all walling of the period, rose from a simple chamfered plinth.

Such simple treatments completed the interior ordinance of the Anglian church of the eleventh century. But the new 'Romanesque' elements beginning to filter into the westerly districts required a different treatment.

The secondary columns which had supported the galleries of the major Byzantine churches had required spreading capitals which would provide a sound seating for the wide soffits of the arches springing from them. The architects, stronger here on the constructional side than on the aesthetic, produced a curious travesty of the Doric capital which is known as the 'cushion' capital and resembles nothing so much as one of these domestic objects split in half.

It was some form of the cushion capital which crowned the circular pillars of the Western style in England. As the twelfth century wore on it developed its own regional peculiarities. By association with the equally curious cubical capital it developed the system of convexities forming the 'coniferous' capital, while the Corinthian inspired the concave variation known as the 'scalloped'. Under the influence of the Crusades this began to sprout odd-looking 'volutes' at its angles until it eventually began to take upon itself some of the attributes of the Corinthian capital itself, the most beautiful architectural feature the world has ever seen and which could hardly have failed to enchant anyone who had ventured into Hellenistic lands.

A device which penetrated down from the great churches was that of vaulting. This was only used in parish churches where the walling was low and the building lacked aisles. Chancels were the part of the twelfth-century church most frequently vaulted. Ribbed vaulting was used, the heavy ribs being carried down upon imposts similar to those supporting main arches. The ribs themselves often lent themselves to the same elaborate ornamentation as the other arched members of the system.

While according full admiration to the building achievements of the twelfth century, it is necessary to recall that these were the result of a prodigal use of materials employed with an almost complete absence of the most elementary knowledge of static engineering. Simple stresses in buildings were beyond the comprehension of those who made them. As experienced timber-workers they were familiar with the spread of roofs and the effect of this on any walling upon which a roof might be raised. They could secure the timbers with braces, but the use of abutment to prevent the overturning of a wall was beyond their comprehension. They could strut up a timber wall, but never discovered how to turn a wooden strut into a stone buttress.

The arch was a mystery to them. They knew it had to be turned on a timber centering but had not the remotest idea of the forces waiting to destroy the arch as soon as the centering was struck. With supreme faith they performed immense labours in raising the huge crossing piers of their minsters. Again and again these collapsed under pressure from the surrounding arcades. But the builders never understood why. Even as late as 1225 they had not discovered where the fault lay, as the distorted crossing piers of Salisbury Cathedral demonstrate to this day.

The low arcades of the parish churches carried little load and have survived without misfortune. But as chancel arches widened and absorbed more and more of their abutment the weight of the gable over began to squash the arch and spread the imposts until many collapsed. And the buttress—as an *abutment*—does not in fact reach the parish churches until the era of the High Gothic.

So the buttress in its familiar Gothic form was not a feature of the pre-medieval church. Yet they were not by any means lacking in external punctuation.

The Anglo-Saxon builders—and that includes those of the trade who continued operations after the Norman Conquest—would have had their architectural approach to any building coloured by hereditary familiarity with timber techniques, in particular the basic ordinance of bay design as represented by the row of posts forming the long side of a building. As a stone building has no posts, the temptation would be to indicate the bays by some masonry feature externally. Internally, of course, pillars supporting an aisle arcade would automatically establish a masonry bay ordinance. The early masons recorded this on the external wall-faces by applying vertical stone projections or pilasters as it were recalling the posts of a timber building.

These pilasters played an important part in the elevation of the twelfth-century church. Often they had their angles softened by the edge-rolls of the period. Sometimes the slender shafts thus produced had their own small cubical caps and primitive bases.

At the angles of the building the pilasters might be paired, with perhaps an extra nook-shaft between them. But the most common arrangement was a square projection known as a 'clasping pilaster'. (Plate 8.)

The ordinance which became established at this period for the exterior of the parish church is of the utmost simplicity. The bays are indicated by the pilasters, but these reach neither the ground nor the eaves, being set on the plinth and merging into the 'corbel-table' above, all three features having the same projection from the wall-face to facilitate the union. In the centre of each bay is a window.

While some churches had quite large windows filled with glazing, the windows of the pre-medieval parish church were generally very small and had their interiors widely splayed so as to diffuse as much light as possible. They are always set high up in the walling, probably so as to collect as little stormwater as possible. And as the walls of early naves were usually extravagantly high in themselves in order to emphasize the dignity of the building, they seem to us today to be very high indeed.

One may often find traces of small round-headed arches showing above a Gothic nave arcade. These are not, as might have been supposed, the remains of an earlier clearstory, but simply vestigia of the original windows of a pre-medieval nave.

15. The High Gothic chancel at Walpole St. Peter in Norfolk

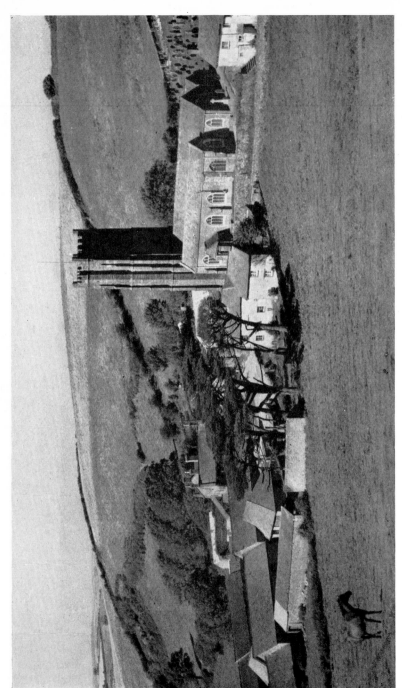

16. A West-country hall-church at Chivelstone in Devon

The window most typical of Byzantine architecture is the *bifora* with its two small arched heads divided by a squat colonette carrying a rectangular slab set at right angles to the wall-face. It was incapable of being glazed and is met with for the most part in belfries. (Plate 3, also 6.)

Punctuation is an important factor in all elevational architecture. It tidies up the elevation by establishing an ordinance, without which the building may appear as an ill-considered assortment of odd features. Vertical punctuation disciplines an elevation by sorting it out into orderly compartments and replacing confusion with a pleasant rhythm. (Plate 6.) This is the function of the bay as used not for constructional purposes but as an aesthetic device. Vertical punctuation is of course achieved by the pilasters, later becoming buttresses.

Horizontal punctuation is primarily concerned with maintaining a sense of stability. The tablement or plinth is of course a primary example of this. The impressive ordinance of the corbel-table performs the same function for the upper part of the building by disciplining the eaves of what might be a somewhat rustic roof. The other function of horizontal punctuation is the linking together of what might otherwise be isolated features, especially windows. Horizontal lines joining the sills of windows stabilize an elevation.

Any arcuated style is apt to produce a restless effect through the constant rise and fall of the series of arches covering it. The value of horizontal punctuation here is its use to join together the arches at their springing lines, a device which at the same time stabilizes the individual arches themselves. (See Plate 11.)

The complete medieval window usually incorporates a projecting moulding called a 'drip-stone' which passes round the arch and throws off stormwater coming down the wall-face above which might continue down the glazing. These moulded drip-stones play a significant part in medieval architecture aesthetically as well as practically, as they are frequently carried across from window to window as 'string-courses' and thus form an important item in the horizontal punctuation of an elevation.

The string-course is of the utmost value internally for it plays a number of parts. As a drip-stone passing round the arcades it prevents condensation from dropping on the heads of the congregation. (Plate 10.) But its most important function is to serve as an 'impost moulding' marking the top of a pier or impost and indicating the springing line of its arch. As it does this it may be extended along the wall, as it was externally, to link one springing line with another. When joining the sills of windows together it provides horizontal punctuation to the interior of a building.

All these 'tablements' or moulded stone planks which may seem so insignificant compared with the major architectural features of a building play in fact a very important part in Gothic design. In each period their mouldings are more or less standard; thus they can give important clues to the dating of a building. The pre-medieval profile was square at the top but had its underside chamfered away. (Fig. 27*a*.)

The principal architectural feature of the pre-medieval parish church was its doorways. Of these the most important was the entrance to the chancel. At first this was simply an arched opening, but the extraordinary development of vernacular carving during the twelfth century completely transformed this most significant feature into a portal of barbaric splendour unparalleled in any other historical architectural period.

The doorway into the church was a miniature of the chancel arch and probably served as the original model for the greater feature. The 'arch-and-lintel' combination developed in earthquake ridden Syria and brought over at the time of the Crusades introduces the semicircular 'tympanum' as a site for pictorial carving. (Plate 29.)

The development of the elaborate arches grows out of their construction in a series of expanding orders. The imposts of the chancel arches and the jambs of the entrance doors are similarly ordered to match those of the arch. Sometimes the sides of the openings are carved with the same abandon as the arches, but more often the shaft with its cap and base is used instead.

One of the aesthetic delights of the study of architecture is the investigation of the aesthetic expressions common in each individual generation. While today the architect seems determined to be different from his colleagues and painfully striving to devise new methods of expression, his predecessor during the great days of English architecture worked with the national team, accepted the general lines of any particular type of treatment, and within these limitations demonstrated his skill and inventiveness.

Each period has had its own sign-manual in respect of running ornament. The ancient Greek fret is an example, and so too are the lovely sweeping vine-scrolls of the heyday of the Hellenistic which architects could not bear to allow to disappear but carried along with the centuries through the Byzantines and into Anglo-Saxon England.

Our own pre-medieval sign-manual is the ubiquitous zigzag or 'chevron'. Clearly of wood-carving origin, it must have been developed from taking two opposing swings of an axe at the edge of the timber to remove what woodsmen call a 'kerf' and then continuing all along the edge of the timber until the whole edge had become serrated. It is less a carver's device than a lumberman's. During the twelfth century the zigzag develops every conceivable kind of variation and begins to achieve the systems of rolls and deep hollows associated with the Gothic mouldings of the next century. It becomes altogether lively and not without charm. (Plate 10.)

The heavy angle-rolls with which the early masons relieved the crudeness of their jambs and arch orders began to expand into moulding systems which for the most part consisted of convex members. Occasionally broad shallow hollows appear, but nothing approaching the deep channels of the early-medieval period. And should a hollow appear, the carvers seem to have been constrained to fill it in at intervals with punctuation in the form of little pyramids or 'nail-heads'.

Part of the charm of Anglo-Saxon carving lies in its irresponsibility. This is particularly noticeable in connection with the voussoirs of which an arch is composed. No attempt was made to keep each stone equal in size. Thus the angles of the zigzag were all different, though set out to the same template so that they would meet at the joints. This casualness presumably originated with the grotesque schools of carving which produced beak-heads and similar motifs needing no system of continuity. (Plate 29.)

It is strange that any art historian could ever have regarded an architectural style which makes such a feature of the grotesque as 'Romanesque'. Surely the writhing dragon is a product of North-Western Europe and can have no counterpart in the folk-lore of Italy.

How welcome are the Anglo-Saxon dragons into the architecture of our land! And how homely seems the vigorous human element displayed by the caricatures ranged along a corbel-table! Childish, perhaps, but after all they represent the childhood of our architecture.

Early Medieval Architecture

For many decades past, architectural historians have been concerned to divide their subject into stylistic periods. They encounter the difficulty that such divisions are anything but clearly delineated. For styles not only merge into each other but change and interchange amongst periods and between regions. The early antiquaries employed a simple yardstick for separating the 'Saxon' and the 'Gothic' in the change of the shape of the arch from semicircular to pointed. They still, however, had to try to explain such anomalies as the appearance of zigzag ornament along a pointed arch, or a semicircular arch which unaccountably rose above graceful Gothic shafting. So they set aside the tremendous twelfth century as a period of 'Transition'.

Actually the change of the arch silhouette, though due to structural reasons, was of less architectural significance than the changes in the church plan and the abandoning of the old pseudo-Classical forms of the capitals which marked the end of the so-called 'Transitional' period and indicated the end of Byzantinism and the beginnings of a national English style later to develop into magnificent architecture and produce buildings of superlative beauty.

The troubled reign of King John, with its tale of quarrelling armies straggling from siege to siege of antiquated fortresses, may be said to mark, approximately, the end of the early or Byzantine period of English architecture.

The long reign of Henry III was ahead. The previous century had experienced the Anarchy, followed by the turbulent reign of

Henry II during which barons and bishops had been building sturdily and had left their sign-manual on glorious minster as well as massive donjon. It had seen the Crusades, and many an English journey to Outremer and the cradle lands of the East. And thus contact with its origins must have done much to help perfect the architecture of the great Anglo-Saxon churches and their humbler brethren in the parishes.

But the Crusades had at the same time brought about a complete reorientation of England's Continental associations. Until the end of the eleventh century the link had been with the Teutonic lands, the Benedictines, and Byzantium. But colonization by Burgundian Cluny had fostered the Latin influence and started a centripetal swing focused on Rome which the Crusades had greatly strengthened. During the twelfth century England's long association with Teutonic, Byzantine, Germany was to weaken to extinction, to be replaced by a strong cultural contact with 'Romanesque' France, even to its language taking the place of English as the speech of the intelligentsia as well as of the new nobility.

With the coming of the thirteenth century refinement came to English architecture. The replacement of the axe as a finishing tool by the driven bolster revolutionized masonry technique and paved the way for an elaboration of architectural ornament worked on the banker and not left to the enterprise of the enthusiastic but undisciplined sculptor. Stones were better cut and walling more carefully laid with proper attention being paid to the strength of the core, so that walling could be less massive and openings more generous. The tooling marks were neatly aligned over the faces of the stones, and the whole presentation was clearly intended as a rejection of earlier barbarous effects.

The change from the Classical form of arch to the form which was later designated by the derisory adjective 'Gothic' is one of the most dramatic incidents in architectural history. That the latter is structurally more reliable is indisputable, and from this point of view alone it must have been more than acceptable to the illiterate successors of the great empires. Initially it was undoubtedly regarded as aesthetically barbarous. One might almost imagine that the Renaissance movement was started as a holy war for its extermination. Yet for a few generations it formed the basic element in what is probably the most beautiful architectural style the world has ever seen.

A great many students of architecture have been speculating upon the origins of Gothic architecture, as represented by the distribution of the pointed arch.

Once a more liberal and experimental type of architecture had superseded the established ordinance governing Imperial Roman architecture, the more reliable type of arch was bound to replace the simpler form. By the middle of the first millennium, the eastern parts of the Byzantine Empire which had absorbed the great Hellenistic culture had adopted it. The Omayyids, Moslem heirs to the Byzantines, took it up, and the lands of Outremer in which the Crusaders operated had changed to it well before their day.

Gothic architecture is in reality an abstract sensation—an urge to build, not vastly as in the days of the great empires, but as close as possible to the clouds. Its greatest achievements are triumphs of faith over ignorance. It employed the pointed arch because it had 'arrived'—that it happens to suit a vertical style is possibly quite fortuitous.

Its forms are not derived from masonry. For this produces massiveness. The lightness of Gothic architecture seems to indicate a structural system based upon carpentry. But its aesthetic spirit seems to link it with the forest glades of Western Europe, glories the Ancient World had never known.

The architectural style used by the designers of the great churches of the Anglo-Saxons had been a degenerate form of a noble style developed far away in a great empire. And it is difficult to appreciate today that the huge minsters raised by the Anglo-Saxons were actually the greatest buildings of their age. And their architecture died with them. It was not possible to bring them into line with the architecture of medieval England. They had either to remain as they were or be pulled down and rebuilt from the ground up.

The English Gothic marched more or less in step with that of the Ile de France. But magnificent though our efforts might be, they fell hopelessly behind the Continental achievements. Lincoln Minster is a beautiful thing, but Beauvais or Le Mans can look down upon it. In magnitude, England's supremacy had been surrendered.

But for beauty of style the English Gothic can hold its own. Not only at Lincoln and in a host of glorious churches now vanished except for forlorn fragments, but in the humble arcades of many a village church, allowing its rustic congregation a glimpse of surpassing loveliness. (Plate 13.)

The underlying difference between the early-medieval building and its predecessor is due to the excellence of its masonry work which enabled it to attempt a lightness of form which was the antithesis of the massiveness that marked the Byzantine. This light-handedness is all the more remarkable in view of the ignorance of structural engineering which plagued the builders. It seems essential to credit them with a perfect faith in their efforts to build to the greater glory of God. And when one realizes that the whole of the building potential of the age was absorbed in this work to the exclusion of improvements to living conditions, one can begin to realize a little of the inspiration behind medieval Christendom.

The ancient Greeks, the Romans, and the Byzantines, were mathematicians, and the two last civilizations produced capable engineers. Yet their buildings were massive and employed a wide factor of safety to achieve moderate heights. The English builder of the Middle Ages, lacking the slightest knowledge of engineering, would raise a lantern tower on tall piers which he had watched as they leaned inwards, watched again as they leaned outwards. When the tower began to break up he would pull it down and build it higher, finishing it off with a spire of stone until he had taken it over four hundred feet into the air. He could have had no idea whatever of the load per square inch he was placing on the bases of the piers. Did the masons as they piled stone upon stone ever consider for a moment that each one might be the last they would ever lay? Had they done so, would Gothic architecture have ever been?

Gothic architecture owes its effect to two factors, the grace of

17. The stately East Anglian church of Lavenham in Suffolk

18. A spacious High-Gothic aisle at Thaxted in Essex

its construction and the richness of its ornament. As in all architectural styles this is of two kinds. One is the carved ornament applied to completed stonework and woodwork by artists. This has no structural function. The other is the true architectural detail by which structural features are moulded aesthetically to disguise their purely structural application. This is the higher function of the mason.

Peculiar to Gothic architecture is the running moulding, the origins and development of which will be discussed in Chapter 15. With the plainly ordered arch of Classical times submerged for good beneath this Gothic richness, any such Classical remnants as circular pillars or Corinthian capitals must have seemed anachronisms. An early modification of the circular pillar was the addition to it of four slender shafts, which helped it to equate more easily with the moulded arch above. At first these shafts were detached, turned on a lathe and secured to the pillar by built-in collars. But the cruciform plan soon became homogeneous, with the four shafts formed together with the stones of the pillar. This in various guises became the standard parish church pillar for the remainder of the medieval period. With the development of mouldings those of the arch and pillar sometimes matched each other. In the richest examples the springing line was indicated by small caps breaking the lines of the more salient members passing up the column.

As the old capitals disappeared, and the mouldings of arches and the pillars supporting them became closer in outline, two methods of marking the springing line are found. One is the presence of the small caps referred to above. The other is the introduction of an impost moulding, sometimes quite elaborately carved, passing round the whole perimeter of the pillar. The versatility of the medieval builder is, however, also indicated by the frequent use of a continuous treatment passing along pillar and arch with a complete disregard for indicating the change between the two.

We have noted that the pre-medieval string-course was a crudely-shaped member having a square top surface and a chamfered lower edge. The early medieval was always a round 'bull-nose' or 'torus'. In the richest work it was deeply undercut. A narrow version used in both pre- and early-medieval architecture and continuing throughout the medieval period below the bells of caps is the 'astragal' retained from Classical times to mark the junction of capital and shaft. A Gothic impost moulding often consists of an upper 'torus', a carved bell, and an astragal below to contain this.

The carvings on capitals, though possibly derived from those on the Classical imposts, were soon to be completely Anglicized, the acanthus which formed the basic motif of those early days being replaced by other leaves presumably of English origin. The trilobate 'stiff-leaf' clover possibly represented the Trinity. Found everywhere during the thirteenth century, it later becomes replaced by less rigid, more naturalistic foliage.

Pillar bases were restricted to the simple chamfered plinth, except where colonettes or other special members called for individual bases to complete them. The model for the pre-medieval and early-medieval base was the Classical form having two torus mouldings separated by a concavity. Pre-medieval bases were shyly moulded, but with the moulding development which characterized the thirteenth century the Classical form was revived with a vengeance, the intermediate 'cavetto' becoming a channel so deep that it is called a 'water-holding' base.

While the buttress, as such, had still not become a part of the exterior ordinance of the medieval church, the pre-medieval pilaster had grown outwards from the wall until it had begun to resemble one. The aisles of Salisbury Cathedral were vaulted and there must have been a considerable strain upon the light walls. The buttresses, however, although part of the aesthetic design, were not built with the walls but added afterwards as ornament.

This introduction of a buttress-like feature is, however, an architectural event of the greatest significance. Byzantine architects, in common with those of all previous building styles, had limited their elevational treatments to a display of flat surfaces only broken by features of quite small projection. The presentation of anything of a protuberant nature was a development new to elevational architecture.

The significance was twofold. Firstly by emphasizing the bay it established the general lines of the architectural style to come. Above all it gave an assurance that Gothic architecture was to become a style which concentrated upon the vertical element in its punctuation and developed this as the very essence of its aesthetic appeal.

Forgetting for the moment that these features were eventually to project at right angles from the wall and become Gothic buttresses, and accepting them for the moment merely as punctuation devices with breadth and projection about equal, we can see that their appearance began to transform the whole of the exterior ordinance of the parish church. The determination with which the rhythm of the bay was maintained is indicated by the presence of a 'buttress' in the centre of the west wall of the thirteenth-century nave, having a window on either side of it instead of a central west window such as one would have found during the next century when the High Gothic style had become fully established and sophisticated designing was replacing primitive empiricism.

The west doorway is Byzantine in origin and is common during the twelfth century where it carries on the tradition of central feature to an entrance façade. It disappears during the thirteenth century as attention becomes drawn to its unsuitability in the English climate. The High Gothic restores it to its original status, regardless of whether or not a bell-tower is acting as a kind of porch for it.

Continuing the normal practice followed in bay design, windows were set in the middle of these. Few church naves or their aisles can still show windows of the thirteenth century as these were still very small, only differing from the pre-medieval window in that they had become slightly taller and had a pointed head. Thus most of these windows have since their introduction been replaced by more spacious ones displaying the tracery of the High Gothic era.

Development progressed, however, to the extent that windows became grouped in pairs. This is of importance as it was by closer grouping and reducing the amount of stonework separating the pair that the mullion was eventually discovered, a device which was to transform fenestration and pave the way to the traceried glories which play such a large part in Gothic architecture.

The place where early-medieval windows may usually be found today is lining the long chancels of the thirteenth century. Possibly the dim lighting they produced was helpful to the atmosphere required of a medieval chancel. The east wall was almost invariably lit by a triple group of lancet windows with the centre light higher than its fellows. These have nearly all been removed and replaced by larger windows. (Often, however, they may be found reinstated in a new position, in an aisle or the east wall of a transept.)

The cross-section of the early-medieval nave differed little from that of its predecessor where aisles were included in the design either originally or by enlargement. The aisles themselves were still quite narrow so that they could be gathered in within the compass of one wide roof. The clearstory does not really descend from the great church to the parish church until the era of the High Gothic when such features became common to all. (See Fig. 14.)

Between the twelfth and thirteenth centuries there came about a considerable change in carved ornament. All the earlier wood-carving crudities disappeared and were replaced by an attempted stylization which was tentative and unenterprising. This is possibly due to the monopolization of the more able artists by the monasteries which at the time were absorbing practically every craft concerned in building. Here and there, however, we find a parish church displaying really beautiful carving on capitals in an arcade. But generally speaking there is nothing in the early-medieval period to approach even remotely the enrichment of doorways and chancel arches one finds in the humblest churches during the twelfth century. (Plate 29.)

Something wonderful had been lost, leaving a void. That something was the glorious swan-song of a vigorous art become, alas, in contemporary eyes barbaric.

What happened to them all, that race of natural artists from whose skimming chisels grew the breath-taking chancel arch of Rutland's Tickencote? Did they really apply themselves to a study of other models until they could produce such entirely different forms as one finds during the thirteenth century? What one fears is that this carving emanates from schools founded and instructed by the monastic Orders, and that the feeble carving one finds in contemporary parish churches represents attempts by the remnant of the grand old carvers of Anglo-Saxondom to try to copy the new forms that were quite beyond their comprehension.

So passed the era of English Byzantine which in its day had given the world its greatest buildings. By the end of the thirteenth century the mason-craft of England had achieved establishment. From Barnack to Beer the quarrymen of the freestone belt had assured the country of its supply of walling material. Spreading forests were still there for the roofing.

Cistercian colonization of the wilder regions of the North and West had done for them what the Benedictines had done for Mercia a century or two earlier. The South was keeping going with chalk and flint and imported materials, still far behind Yorkshire and the Midlands in everything connected with architecture, its Continental links quite unable to help it to overcome the basic shortage of essential materials.

England was riding on the sheep's back. The parishes were flourishing. The country was ready, under the aegis of Holy Church, for two centuries of High Gothic.

II

High Gothic

===

The era of High Gothic reaches from the last quarter of the thirteenth century across the first half of the sixteenth, the whole a period of the noblest architecture. Its complexity is only now beginning to be understood. It comprises those periods called by Rickman 'Decorated' and 'Perpendicular'. But this devoted architect, together with most of his successors, was working solely on stylistic grounds and failed to appreciate the difference between aesthetic style and historical period. In point of fact both of his styles, marked as they are by curvilinear and rectilinear window tracery, interlock throughout the period in accordance with local taste and structural requirements.

It is nevertheless possible to detect two divisions of the High Gothic period, which one might call Middle and Late Medieval, separated by the Black Death at the middle of the fourteenth century which destroyed half the population and must have brought an end to architecture on the grand scale for a generation. Prior to this catastrophe one finds exuberance, after it a loss of charm and a kind of hardening into austerity. Yet even the four-centred arch, assumed to represent the sign-manual of the fifteenth century, may be found associated with the normal Gothic arch, representing not period, but current taste.

The first or Mid-Gothic period was one of church-building on the monumental scale, mainly under monastic patronage. Its second half was the era of the parish church, funds for which were becoming diverted from the monasteries towards the expanding finances of the wool trade.

Thus for a start we have building on two scales, one emanating from the highly organized workshops of the great monastic houses, the other recruited locally in the parishes from journeymen and what might be called 'local builders'. Hitherto these men had been tradesmen of indifferent skill, not even the leavings of first-class establishments. But now church-building had become the province of properly trained and experienced men. Once it had only been possible to employ such craftsmen for important features such as arches, doorways and windows. Now the whole church was being built by professionals.

Nevertheless such 'local builders' lacked the contacts available to the large monastic workshops. Thus local style is much more noticeable in the parishes than it would be among the great church buildings.

It is this regionalism in parish church architecture which is still confusing students and making it virtually impossible to detach one period from another. A century and a half ago, Rickman was able to detect the difference between what he called 'Decorated' and the more austere 'Perpendicular'. Styles they certainly were, but as periods they cannot be so clearly established. Broadly speaking the graceful tracery of the 'Decorated' window preceded the panelled ordinance of the 'Perpendicular' but in actual fact both appear in important buildings at the very beginning of the High Gothic era and features of both styles may be found inextricably mixed together in parish churches of the fourteenth century. Thus it becomes hopeless to try to dogmatize about dates on stylistic grounds only.

Nevertheless both these manifestations have come to be accepted as *styles* for a century and a half; thus it is possible for them to be kept separate up to a point. But it must always be remembered that, unlike the pre-medieval and the early Gothic, they more than just overlapped, they actually intermingled, not for half a century, but for two.

The principal element which differentiates the early medieval from its succeeding periods is the use of lead for roofs. Most of Europe's supply of this material came from England, so that even the parish church could make use of it.

The true English roof, built of timbers and designed for a hard climate, was very steeply pitched to reduce the danger of its spreading or even collapsing under a load of snow. Originally thatched or sheathed with shingles, it was adequately watertight and could protect the timber buildings from deterioration. But such roofs, one of the basic elements from which Gothic architecture was created, suffered from lack of permanency.

Lead began to appear on the great churches during the late thirteenth century. Its introduction brought about a revolution in English architectural style. On a steep pitch it gives endless trouble as its weight causes it to slip down; its high coefficient of expansion makes it subject to continual 'creep'. Properly laid, however, it has the great advantage of needing hardly any pitch at all to keep out the weather and gives far less trouble from the two properties noted above.

Thus the High Gothic is based not on high roofs but on high walls carrying roofs which may at times be barely visible. The bottom of the roof suffered at the same time vital changes, for the high-pitched roof is carried out in wide eaves over which the stormwater falls clear of the walls and windows, while the lead roof is finished at the bottom with a lead gutter set behind a parapet and discharging through long spoutings. In this way the parapet came to be an integral feature of the High Gothic building, concealing behind it even more of the once all-important roof. (Fig. 22.)

The great church of the Ile de France had replaced the lofty Byzantine nucleus with a building raised as high as possible above the ground throughout its whole length, thus setting the pace for future Gothic buildings throughout Europe. The English church was far from aiming at anything of like scale. Bearing in mind that the village home of the period was a hovel owing nothing to the builder, it was very easy to raise the parish church to a height sufficient to enable it to soar above such pathetic structures. Thus stylistic factors changing the elevational form of the great contemporary abbey or cathedral have no bearing on that of the parish church.

The towering nave of a great church could double the width of its bays and still span them with a tall Gothic arch. But if a

19. An elaborate High-Gothic roof at Somerton in Somerset

20. The hammer-beam roof of March church in Cambridgeshire

parish church were to do the same with, say, its chancel arch this would look ridiculous with a tall arch on comparatively stumpy columns. So with the increased spans coming into use the arches themselves came to pe pitched lower, a modification conveniently conforming with the lowering of the roof, now lead covered.

The early parish churches had been, each in its parish, of a magnificence most spectacular when compared with its architectural surroundings, though as nothing when compared with the great churches of the monks. For its particular purpose, however, it may well have been much too small and cluttered-up to accommodate all its parishioners. So the aim of the parish church builders of the High Gothic era must have been to provide more spacious buildings, still far removed in point of scale from the greater churches but still displaying a vertical element proportionate to their plans so that every aspect of dignity could be maintained. And for a crowning feature there would be the soaring bell-tower at the west end.

Internally, much of the archaic atmosphere of mystery had been banished from the chancel by the widening of its entrance arch. Privacy however was soon to be partly restored by the provision of a chancel screen.

The most noticeable improvement in the parish church was the enlargement of its windows. The development of the mullion which followed the coupling of windows during the thirteenth century had resulted in a multiplicity of lights and the consequent need for devising some system of carrying the glazing into the arched head of the window. It was in the course of solving this problem that the masons devised the technique of tracery, the innumerable variations in which bestow such glamour upon the churches of the High Gothic. The development of tracery design is undoubtedly due to the masons' experiments with the 'compasses'—which we should call today 'dividers'—on pieces of board available in the lodges. The stonework of medieval buildings is covered with examples of 'doodling', especially in geometric designs and rosettes, scratched into the stone.

The lines of mullions could be carried up into sub-arches concentric with the main arch. Or their direction could be changed every so often so as to form a reticulation. Each change of direction produced an 'ogee' form, the shape which provides French architects with their name for Gothic architecture. It may have been the French who invented the 'foliations' in which the lobes or 'foils' are separated from each other by projecting teeth or 'cusps'. One type of foliation displays a rounded foil attached to a long tail, called a 'flamme'. The popularity of this feature during a certain period in France gave a name to the style known as 'Flamboyant'.

One of the delights of Gothic is the silhouette which gives the whole style its French designation of 'Ogival'. Probably derived in part at least from the wavy cross-braces of timber architecture and encountered everywhere when following the flowing lines of tracery, the lively ogee is peculiar to the Gothic and creates one of the most opulent silhouettes in architectural history. In aedicular form, as for example when used above niches and completed with a crocketed finial, it provides a notable crowning motif unparalleled in any other architectural style.

Improvements in the natural lighting of parish churches during the High Gothic era were almost universal and resulted in the replacement of many of the earlier pre- and early-medieval windows. Sometimes, however, such improvements were restricted to the provision of new large windows at the most important point in the church, the neighbourhood of the chancel arch. Such windows may be seen at the east end of the nave or, where this is aisled, at the west end of the chancel. If there is a solitary window it will be on the south side.

The French builders who since the thirteenth century had been raising their towering churches, must have acquired a much wider experience of building statics and the means of combating them than was known to us here. Calculation was of course impossible, but the general nature of the forces involved in the destruction of an arch, and the means of opposing this, must have been appreciated by them. By the fourteenth century the device of the flying buttress was being employed by English builders. But it was still only just being realized that the principle of top-loading a buttress to provide a counterpoise against a lateral thrust could add greatly to the defence against the arch. It was this discovery which not only encouraged them to raise their central towers but also enabled them to check the creeping collapse which had for so long been threatening the early crossings and the lanterns above them.

In parish churches the buttress comes into its own during the fourteenth century. At the angles of buildings it henceforth adopts a diagonal stance so as to appear to be checking any possibility of the angle coming away through the loosening of its quoin-stones. In masonry of any quality whatsoever the risk was very small. But the diagonal buttress becomes a standard item of ordinance for the remainder of the medieval period. (See, however, Chapter 8.)

With the buttress was associated the pinnacle which provided its top-load and also served as an ornamental finial. And with the

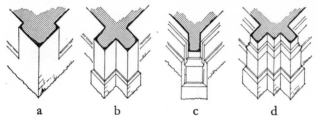

Fig. 21 *Buttresses*
    (a) The 'clasping pilaster' seen at the angles of twelfth-century buildings. (b) The thirteenth-century arrangement. (c) The 'French buttress' found throughout the High Gothic period. (d) A fifteenth-century arrangement.

pinnacle is also associated the parapet, the crowning feature of the wall which had superseded the eaves of earlier days. The early-medieval parapet retained the corbel-table and employed it to bring the parapet forward and allow for a wider gutter behind it. The later parapet replaced the corbel-table with a string-course which was usually of a cornice-like form and enabled the parapet to be advanced as before if required.

By perhaps the year 1400 the elevational appearance of the well-masoned Gothic parish church had settled down to a recognized ordinance, based, of course, on the bay. This seems to have varied from twelve to sixteen feet in width, indicated by buttresses passing up the elevation, divided in two or three places by receding set-offs, and either dying into the string-course below the parapet or carried up through it to end in a pinnacle.

The lower part of the wall is given a standardized plinth treatment. The lowest member of this is the 'tablement' forming the base of the building and may be simply a plain chamfered plinth. After a couple of feet or so of plain stonework the main plinth moulding appears. This is a curious ogee-shaped projection hanging down in a not very attractive fashion. It seems difficult to equate this with the 'pedestal' ordinance found in Classical ordinance but there seems to be no other possible origin for this curious triple arrangement. The Classical form of pedestal is crowned by a cornice—a clumsy projection upon which even the ugly Gothic ogee is an improvement.

At the wall-top, where this changes to become the parapet, there is always a string-course, usually a wide 'cove', which is the

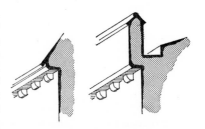

Fig. 22
Eaves and Parapet
The original function of the
'corbel-table' was to fill in under
the eaves of a high-pitched roof.
It was retained beneath the parapet
of a low-pitched lead roof to bring
the parapet forward and increase
the width of the lead gutter behind.

Gothic equivalent of the Classical cornice. This is an important feature as it indicates the level of the vital gutter which collects the stormwater from the roof. The spoutings or gargoyles are set out along the line of this string-course.

The parapet may be flush with the wall or may take advantage of the coved string-course to project slightly. In humbler work the parapet may have a straight 'saddle-back' coping, but the most common arrangement is the battlement, often supported aesthetically by the pinnacles separating the bays.

Within the area enclosed between the buttresses, the heavy plinth, and the parapet is the large traceried window of the High Gothic era. This usually has a 'drip-stone' passing round the arch to prevent stormwater running down the wall-face above from continuing down the glazing. Sometimes these drip-stones rise from carved 'stops' at the springing line, but often this line is carried across between the buttresses in the form of a string-course.

Even the smallest parish church endeavoured to build for itself a bell-tower, almost invariably at the west end. It might be very plain, with no angle buttresses—indicating that such were regarded as ornamental but not essential. By the High Gothic period it would be parapeted and very probably have pinnacles at the angles. The most important element in the tower was its belfry stage, now carrying a ring of bells, perhaps as many as eight. The belfry windows would be treated as architectural features. Below the belfry was usually a ringing-floor, lit by a small window on each face.

The lower part of the tower formed part of the accommodation of the church with which it was connected by a tall arch. At the base of the tower there was usually a west door, not intended to be a normal entrance to the church but for the re-entry into the building of the Palm Sunday procession. The west doorway was usually treated architecturally so as to give an effect of a façade. Normal doorways were seldom so treated, but during the High Gothic era the front of the south porch was nearly always embellished to form a frontispiece.

The effect of the west tower of the English parish church relies upon the fact that it may be seen to rise from the ground. It is axiomatic in architectural design that every tower must do this if it is to achieve its full status. Imagine the effect of Canterbury's Angel Tower standing in magnificent isolation instead of rising above a clutter of roofs which absorb half its height!

The appeal of the central tower—seen in so many of the thirteenth-century parish churches—is partly that it carries on the old Byzantine tradition of providing a crowning feature to a great building, and partly due to its being the 'status-symbol' expected of a great church. And there can be no wonder at the appearance during the High Gothic era of such glorious parish churches as Yorkshire's Hedon or Patrington. But such were enormously expensive productions and are exceptional. The average village church could produce something equally impressive in height by building a western tower, a fact which is demonstrated by so many villages in Devon and Somerset.

The tradition of the timber 'broach' is continued with the High Gothic spire of timber or stone but the feature is surrounded by a parapet, often ornamental and sometimes provided with angle treatments based on tall pinnacles and perhaps flying buttresses. Some of the more elaborate tower-tops were adjusted to form elaborate stone 'lanterns'. (Plates 14 and 28.)

Records tell us that there were once many more parish spires than we see today. They were expensive items to raise, and once the elements had brought about such injury to a spire that it had become unsafe, a change in the fortunes of the parish might have made its replacement impossible. The same can be said of our cathedrals, a number of which have lost their spires. Add to these the spires of vanished abbeys and one can imagine the English landscape of the fourteenth and fifteenth centuries alive with Gothic steeples. (This subject is elaborated in Chapter 14.)

The great enemy of a spire is lightning. The lightning conductor is a modern invention. Even in these days the writer has seen more than one stone spire riven by a strike. A timber broach would have speedily been transformed into a beacon. Should this have happened after the thirteenth century the broach would almost certainly have been replaced by a simple flat lead roof.

While externally the churches of the High Gothic era had become architecturally excellent due to the accumulated skill of centuries of mason-craft, their interiors, although not very much more spacious and lofty, had lost much of the charm of earlier days and as time went on began to approach austerity. The semi-barbaric mouldings which had rioted with such enthusiasm over the arches had been pruned down to basic forms which now appeared coarse. Most of the sculptural ornament which graced the fourteenth century had vanished by the next. But the coldness of the masonry was being used as a foil to the splendid efforts of the carpentry.

It has been explained earlier how the interior of the roof had become an architectural feature of the highest quality and how the roof itself had been in some cases so much reduced in pitch that its almost flat underside now formed a magnificent panelled ceiling. (Plate 18.)

The carpentry of the ancient 'wrights' had relied for aesthetic embellishment upon the use of curved timbers. The new carpentry was what we call today 'joinery' which relies basically upon the framing together of straight timbers to form various types of panelling. This class of Gothic 'carpentry' may be seen on the grand scale in the ceilings of the period.

But the introduction of the 'parclose' screen as a system of partitioning enclosing the chancel and its chapels, brought the carpenters in touch with a highly refined branch of their craft. During the fourteenth century many stone screens were erected having tracery similar to that seen in the windows. But such had very wide openings and failed to provide the privacy needed. Hence the introduction of church woodwork on a furniture scale. (Plate 22.)

All such work relies basically upon a system of panelling. Whatever refinements in the way of mouldings and carving may be added subsequently, screenwork is framed together in panels. The rectangular panel was a form foreign to Gothic aesthetics, but under pressure from the carpenters it had to be accepted. The masons introduced it as a wall-ornament. And of course it found its way everywhere into the tracery of the window-head. The foliations were still as prominent as ever, but the window-lights had their arched heads flattened considerably to suit both the panelling and the current form of the main arches of the building.

A feature of the High Gothic era is the square-headed window. These were not large, but, appearing as they did as early as the fourteenth century, seemed to indicate the eventual fate of Gothic architecture and its sweeping arches. The arch developed from the necessity of spanning large openings with small stones, but the development of window tracery enabled the masons to carry a series of stones laid flat across the heads of the mullions. It will be noticed that in doing so they were greatly helped by the use of the ogee arch. The drip-stone covering the top of the window was of course flat at the top, the first appearance of the 'label-mould' which was soon to be employed everywhere in domestic architecture and continues in use in the masonry regions until the end of the seventeenth century.

The flat-topped opening, and the rectangular frame to which it led, become an important feature in the masonry work of the High Gothic. In doorways especially, the frame is found enclosing the arched opening. The triangular areas or 'spandrels' between the haunches of the arch and the frame become sites for carving, either foliated panels or heraldic shields.

Within these High Gothic frames one can watch the arch changing. In the majority of cases it retains the 'equilateral' form of the Gothic arch, but it is often four-centred or, in some of the more opulent examples, the three-centred 'Spanish' arch.

The Gothic was not a style which appreciated the façade. Even the west fronts of the great churches were designed with little understanding of the principles governing the creation of a 'frontispiece'. There were two towers, and between them a west window with a gable over it. Most of the English west fronts look unbalanced and top-heavy, that of Wells cathedral being the exception. In the parish churches the architectural façade is met with only at entrance doors, where some attempt is often made to achieve cooperation between the west window and the doorway below it. The most determined effects are usually those achieved by the large south porches with their chambers over them. Churches and great halls were probably at this time pooling their design experiences.

Gothic architecture, based as it was upon individualism and never properly organized, never succeeded in attaining perfection as an architectural style. Its creations remained assemblages of features—ranges of buildings with here and there a tower—gathered together with none of the architect's regard for composition as a whole. Gothic design never really developed beyond the bay, perfection in itself but only an architectural sample, incomplete and incapable of being assembled with others to form a considered entity. Plans were never adjusted, as in highly developed architecture, to enable an architect to build up a fine three-dimensional presentation. Gothic employed no textbooks: its success does

21. A West-country cradle-roof at St. Endellion in Cornwall

22. The rood-screen at Manaton church in Devon

indeed lie in its lack of such sophistry. It is thus essentially a primitive style, incapable of being assimilated into an advanced civilization—a product of an illiterate, ignorant culture sand-wiched between the Ancient Wisdoms and their renaissance.

The lack of a means of communication between ourselves and the Middle Ages is quite profound. Even as late as the end of the medieval period we are still in the dark as to how the church services were organized. We know from the buildings themselves that the long chancel still remained, and that its obscurity, relieved for a time by the widening of the chancel arch, had now been restored behind the richly-carpentered rood-screen. The nave was basically still a great hall thronged with congregations attending upon the priest in his chancel.

What we do know is that the popularity of the parish sermon had introduced a new element into the service. It may be a result of this that fixed seating at last began to appear in the naves.

This was the biggest revolution the parish church had known. It is impossible to over-stress the importance of the change and its effect upon the architectural appearance of the interior of the building.

Hitherto the naves had been great empty halls. One might almost have called them architectural barns. But now they had become seated auditoria, in the style of a theatre—something quite new in architectural history.

The loss to the proportions of the building was catastrophic. One only has to enter a cathedral nave whence its chairs have been removed to appreciate this. And the lesser proportions of the parish church made the situation worse. The new screenwork became half-submerged in the sea of seating.

It may have been due to the introduction of church seating that we owe the raising of the pillars of the arcades on what amounts to the Gothic equivalent of a pedestal, a rather more refined version of the exterior plinth arrangement. It would be interesting to dis-cover which of the two treatments was devised first.

The provision of fixed seating also had the result of finally obliterating any record in the church plan of the use of the nave by the congregation during the earlier seat-less days. With the seats in the transepts, however, facing inwards, it still seems difficult to appreciate what part the elongated medieval chancel played in the service if most of this was performed by the priest at the altar.

As we watch the Middle Ages drawing to their close we are forced to accept the fact that the whole era, with its many magnificent architectural creations, is unlikely ever to emerge with clarity from the native mists which still enshroud that curiously inarticulate period in our history. To attempt to understand it seems at times as difficult as to try to appreciate the mind behind Stonehenge. We can only reach a general impression of the approach towards an architectural ordinance, but with parish church architecture represented by a collection of individual items, each in itself utterly charming and each contributing to cheerful confusion, their tale is not easy to unravel. And when an ordinance at last begins to appear, it produces dignified external presentations behind which bleak interiors seem to mourn the livelier fantasies of the early days.

The Gothic fervour had evaporated. And the friendly dragons which had teased our Anglo-Saxon ancestors had long ago returned to their misty homes taking with them so much of the ancient splendour of barbarism.

12

Renaissance and After

The revolution of 1534 during which a stroke of the pen extinguished the main inspiration behind English architecture and brought about its virtual collapse, can have few parallels in architectural history. Parish church architecture of the period had reached a high degree of perfection by producing spacious well-lit buildings beautifully furnished and crowned by soaring bell-towers of superlative beauty. (Plate 28.) The last of these had been built.

With the disintegration of Holy Church in England, during the sixteenth century, the building trade shifted its allegiance towards the erection of mansions to house the heirs of the monastic lands. Few churches were built and fewer enlarged. A century and a half was to elapse before an interest in church building began to reappear, and that in a very restricted form. During the interregnum architecture in this country disintegrated into a state of chaos, suffering a series of influences which increased confusion rather than leading to a real revival in the art of church design.

These influences notwithstanding, the Gothic tradition continued in some strength. During what is known as the 'Gothic Overlap' which carried on throughout the seventeenth century, the main lines of buildings developed away from the medieval while details and ornament remained much as before but on a reduced scale owing to loss of patronage.

The broadening of plans continued, with a reduction in height away from Gothic extravagances. Main arches were Classically semicircular, but windows were more domestic in form and adopted the Renaissance square shape, the retention of mullions enabling the flat lintel-stones to be carried without fear of collapse. Gothic cusping, omitted from domestic windows by the middle of the sixteenth century, remained in churches for another hundred years.

At the end of Elizabeth's reign Renaissance motifs were appearing in parish church doorways, brought over in most ill-digested form via Spain and the Netherlands, the last sending over its quota of refugees from religious persecution. Curious distortions notwithstanding, one cannot fail to notice the arrival of small flanking pilasters with their Classical caps and bases, linked above the doorway by some attempt at the Classical 'entablature' of architrave, frieze and cornice. These doorways of the beginning of the seventeenth century are first found in mansions, whence they transfer themselves to parish churches, often getting themselves mixed up with debased forms of the Gothic arch in an attempt to become ecclesiastical.

It was sub-Renaissance features of this description which were being introduced into existing churches during the seventeenth century. The architecture of the period was basically domestic, and this fact makes itself clear. Even the transomed window, designed to enable the lower lights to be opened as casements, may be encountered in some places. For while no doubt a great many small medieval churches were abandoned as redundant during the seventeenth century, those which remained in use were still kept in good order and repair.

There was, of course, a great deal of mutilation, owing to a general architectural indifference. Windows, for example, might lose their tracery. Maintenance would have been limited to essentials, with neither money nor skill available for the fal-lals of 'Romish' architecture. While most of the work of this period was swept away during the restorations of the mid-nineteenth century, some of it still remains in poor and isolated parishes. It is perhaps a pity that we have lost with it what might have been some quite charming manifestations of Renaissance vernacular.

At the beginning of the seventeenth century the Italian Renaissance in its authoritative form was beginning to reach this country by way of printed textbooks. These were used first of all to help with the design of large houses, later with smaller ones. Not until the next century with its 'Georgian' architecture do we find such sophisticated features as windows designed on the aedicular principle, with surrounds and pedimented tops, appearing in the parish church. Even then, the style is either found in the towns or in parishes where the squire or parson had some special interest in architecture or could obtain the services of one of the few professional architects of the day.

The English parish church of the seventeenth century relied upon brick for its walling. Its windows were possibly as large as those of its High Gothic predecessor but, having no mullions, had to be covered with a semicircular arch. The only tribute to architectural style would be the springing lines marked by square impost blocks and the crown of the arch locked by a keystone.

The construction of a square-headed opening without support from mullions was a problem the Renaissance builder solved by devising the 'flat arch' which employs voussoirs but works them to a flat soffit. With the aid of this method of spanning a window opening, the Renaissance style was able to develop unimpeded by constructional problems.

It is surprising to discover how many old arcades, some of them pre-medieval, were rebuilt during the seventeenth century, the remains of the earlier responds giving the game away. Within the village church the pillars became rough imitations of the Classical form with very primitive copies of the Tuscan or Roman Doric capitals crowning them. Ordered arches came to an end with the medieval period; the soffits of the future were invariably flat.

Brick was the material commonly used for the village churches of the seventeenth century, even the openings being lined with this material. Stone was however often used for quoins. From the seventeenth century onwards most interiors of churches were plastered.

Most churches after the middle of the century were covered with roofs of low pitch, and their gable ends were often worked up with moulded cornices to form a triangular 'pediment'. Both methods of finishing the bottom of the roof were used. Eaves were supported underneath with some kind of large cornice, often a wide 'cove'. Parapets concealing lead gutters were quite plain with a flat coping instead of the medieval 'saddle back'. The Gothic cove was often succeeded by a small Classical cornice at the same level.

The sturdy bell-tower continued in favour. It was quite plain, its angles unbuttressed, and displayed a simple arched window in its belfry stage. The angles of its parapet were capped with urns or obelisks instead of pinnacles.

As North-Western Europe's contribution to Byzantine architecture had been the steeple, the same was its retort to the tower tops of the Baroque. As a country England seems always to have been addicted to the 'whispering spire'; even the Reformation seems to have been unable to break it of the habit. The Renaissance steeple was an interesting essay in architectural ingenuity, being in effect a diminishing pile of aedicules, every stage a little Classical temple, and crowned by an obelisk, the Renaissance retort to the Gothic pinnacle. During the eighteenth century even village churches produced such features, probably inspired by a squire with an interest in architecture.

The Georgian era, during which the part of patron of architecture, once the role of the medieval abbot, had been taken over by the farming squire, was the time for the full establishment of the English Renaissance style. It is necessary, if one is to make a study of post-Reformation parish churches, to familiarize oneself with the ordinance of the Italian Renaissance as devised and published by its great architects like Vignola.

The style was derived from that of Imperial Rome, building with arches but presenting its elevations in the only architectural style its engineers knew, that of the Hellenistic world. The basis of this was the Classical Orders, reduced in Roman architecture to a modified form of Doric for general use and the glorious Corinthian for special effects. Each Order had two main parts, the column—sometimes attached to a wall as a flat 'pilaster'—and the entablature which it carried. The column was divided into base, shaft and capital, the entablature into architrave, frieze, and cornice. Each Order had rigidly established proportions.

It was the ignorance of these which at first contributed to the charm of the post-Reformation parish churches. The style reached this country fourth-hand. From its source in Italy it flowed to Spain as the Baroque, whence it emigrated to the Low countries and became inextricably muddled and mixed with various Gothic elements until it became practically a style of its own. Thence through commercial contacts and the troubles of Protestant refugees it reached the English countryside.

Only by research into authoritative Renaissance publications and comparison of some element with its English variant can one begin to appreciate the parish church architecture of the seventeenth century. Even by the time of Wren, English Renaissance architecture was still a style of its own.

But by the eighteenth century, however, not only had the textbook triumphed, but under the Georgians English architects had developed a fine native style, so that the newly-built parish church of the period could be regarded as an unexceptionable contribution to the architecture of the Renaissance.

The most outstanding feature of post-medieval architecture is the cornice, unknown to the Gothic world which had substituted for it the corbel-table. This relic of Hellenistic days has three parts of which the most important is the square 'corona'; below this is the 'bed-mould' and above it another moulding called the 'cymatium'. Cornices may be found crowning the building itself and aedicular features such as the surrounds of doorways and windows.

Although the cornice should properly speaking be supported by a frieze and architrave to form a Classical 'entablature', one most frequently finds it in this country on its own. The Classical architrave, however, is frequently used as a *surround* to openings such as those of windows; again a feature having no counterpart in Gothic architecture.

A medieval feature, which although not forming a part of Renaissance ordinance had nevertheless to be used where required, was the buttress. Buttresses dating from post-medieval times can often be found attached to old parish churches, having been added to check the thrust of an arch or the toppling of a wall threatened by a spreading roof. They are generally of brickwork, the nature and bonding of which will often give the clue to their date.

Vertical punctuation was still being employed in post-medieval days, being effected by Classical pilasters having proper bases and capitals. In the richer churches the pilaster was used extensively for interior punctuation—a device unknown to the medieval designer except as applied to the whole of a wall surface—especially to help carry the heavy cornices which helped to transfer something of the exterior elevation into the treatment within the building.

The Renaissance architects reintroduced the apse, employing it as of old to be a setting for the altar. It was in this part of the church that the English reaction to the dreariness of the Reformation seems to be particularly emphasized, both by the architectural elaboration of the apse itself and the richness of the Baroque reredos which it often incorporated.

For its greater glory the Renaissance incorporated into its neo-Roman architecture the Byzantine dome, raising it upon a tall drum and setting it up to be not only the focus of the church plan but also the crowning glory of the building. Here and there the dome finds its way, under Georgian patronage, into the English parish church.

Every architectural period has its own peculiar feature acting as a kind of sign-manual to the period and appearing in no other. The Early Renaissance in England is marked by the baluster, the stumpy, vase-shaped colonette which is found everywhere in balustrades, lightening these in similar fashion to the pierced parapets of the High Gothic. Unknown in Classical or Gothic days, it is the Baroque contribution to the Renaissance, and first appears in quaint forms cut out of boards in the balustrading of Elizabethan times.

Finials have always been an important feature of architectural elevations, breaking into what might be a too-rigid skyline and adding a spice of gaiety to the silhouette. In Gothic days it was the pinnacle with its climbing crockets. The Renaissance architects employed the bare pyramid for the same purpose. Another feature encountered everywhere during the eighteenth century, not only

23. A post-Reformation church at Wolverton in Hampshire

24. A post-Reformation interior at North Runcton church in Norfolk

on funerary monuments but as architectural finials, was the Classical urn, perhaps less suited, by reason of its rather top-heavy silhouette, than the tapering obelisk but clearly regarded as more refined than the obelisk and generally replacing it during the eighteenth century as an angle finial.

The changes in the interior of the English parish church between the medieval and the Renaissance are very marked. Architecture, originally intended to be employed on the exterior of the building for public display, began to be transferred to the interior of the building for the delectation of the congregation. In this connection it has to be remembered that a feature such as an aisle arcade, much though it may delight us today, was introduced as a structural necessity and ornamented only as an afterthought.

But the most noticeable change would have been the clear evidence that henceforth the congregation was aiming at attending communal worship in as much comfort as possible. With the introduction of fixed seating during the fifteenth century the first steps towards eliminating the primitive austerity of religious practices had been taken. Thenceforth the development of church seating makes a steady progress towards the cosy 'horse-boxes' of a hundred years ago which were to be swept away with such determination by the doubtless horrified 'restorers' of the middle of the nineteenth century.

Some way had to be found of excluding draughts descending from the open roofs of the unheated buildings. With this in mind the practice of what was until recently called 'under-drawing' was developed. Wall-plaster, which requires a prodigal use of expensive quicklime, was rarely used during the Middle Ages. But occasional lime-washing must have eventually produced a similar finish and certainly enabled the walls to be painted. Roofs were open to the underside of their covering, though boarding known as 'wainscot' was often fixed to the underside of the rafters in the bay over the altar to keep droppings away from it. Sometimes these boarded ceilings were treated architecturally with miniature vaulting ribs and carved bosses at intersections in the form of a canopy.

Contrary to general belief, plaster will not adhere to wood. It requires a system of thin laths round which it is 'keyed' by the skill of the plasterer who with a sweep of his trowel flicks the material between and behind the lathing. This is a highly skilled craft and does not appear in this country until the sixteenth century. Moulded plaster ceilings, however, developed rapidly and by the beginning of the next century had reached a very high degree of art which was deriving its motifs partly from the contemporary vernacular Renaissance and partly from the lovely forms seen in that fan vaulting which was the High Gothic's greatest achievement.

But such magnificence apart, the introduction of the plaster ceiling was an important innovation in all buildings including churches. (Plate 24.) During the eighteenth century in particular, a large number of the old open roofs were 'under-drawn', their plaster all having to be torn down and the roofs opened up again when the 'restorers' got at them. With the Classical Revival of the second quarter of the nineteenth century, when flat ceilings were the vogue, even ancient churches had flat ceilings thrown across them.

In parenthesis it should be noted that the open cradle roofs of Western churches, with their patterns of slender ribs meeting carved bosses at the intersections, are quite suitable for plastering and indeed probably have been so treated from pre-Reformation days.

We have seen how unpopular the brick elevation had been to the late eighteenth century-observer and the attempts which had been made to conceal it behind 'ashlar' stonework. Such treatment, however, was costly and could not have been employed by the custodians of the village churches.

Lime plaster used externally will not stand up to the weather. The nodules of 'Roman' cement, however, can be burnt to form a substance which mixed with an aggregate will produce a waterproof 'rendering'.

This form of rendering became acceptable as a decent covering for brickwork or old rubble walling. The aggregate used was collected from the sides of the water-bound 'macadam' turnpikes of the era, now, alas, no longer available to the architect restorer trying to patch old Roman cement renderings which have parted company with the walling behind them.

The writer cannot at this point forbear to comment upon the modern practice of covering church walls with Portland cement rendering. The colour is most unsightly and will never weather, as the old renderings could, by growing algae. Even the addition of 'pebble-dash' to improve the texture produces but a poor substitute for the fine old work. And cement can never be removed from stonework and will destroy its face *for ever*. It is greatly to be hoped that this practice, which in particular is ruining a number of ancient bell-towers, will be abandoned before our countryside becomes covered with cement church towers. The writer has enlarged upon this problem in Chapter 19.

Although it is preceded by the Late-Georgian reaction towards the medieval, the Classic Revival of the second decade of the nineteenth century is best considered in conjunction with the Renaissance, as it was based, in effect, upon a wish to reform the Baroque excesses of the High Renaissance and force it back into the austere rigidity of its original Classical derivatives.

Appearing about 1840, its influence may be detected by rather coarse Classical mouldings and an absence of ornament other than frets, keys and similar geometrical devices. The Greek Doric Order of the Parthenon appears in heavy porticos, a poor successor to the charming portals of Georgian days. Unlike the modified Roman of the Renaissance, the Greek Revival remained utterly pagan and was never absorbed into English church architecture.

The romantic revival of the Gothic style which came about in the latter part of the eighteenth century found a building trade utterly unable to cope with it. The Gothic mason had long since departed with his lodge into history. With most of his quarries weed-grown the art of the quarryman had been largely forgotten. Smoking brick-kilns provided the country's building material, a substance virtually unknown to the medieval church-builder.

But the 'carpenters', now 'joiners', were as good and better, than ever, and able to turn their hand to anything. So the first Gothic Revival was in part a Carpenters' Gothic. Then there was the new craft of the plasterer, with his armatures of 'stick and rag', to help with the detail. The old Gothic sturdiness, born of structural necessity, was not repeated. Only the beauty was retained, to be utilized as a stage architecture—the 'Romantick Gothick' of Strawberry Hill.

Is there a lesson still to be learned from the lovely 'Gothick' of the Regency which the visitor to an old parish church may some day be privileged to encounter? It seems impossible to deny that it was in essence retrogressive in that it represented an architectural style which had in process of time risen to a zenith and thence not so much to a final disappearance as to a submergence beneath a torrent which had set impassable obstacles in the path of its future progress. Had it not been thus, one must always wonder how our national architecture might have developed as it disembarrassed itself from lingering archaisms of medievalism and its obsolescent building practices.

Fearful was the blight of ugliness which drove the rediscovered Gothick from our pleasant land, to return again unrecognizable as revivalism in its most sterile form, unintelligent sophistry lacking the lightest touch of tenderness. For even in the original, the stateliness of the loveliest medieval building is something awe-inspiring—infinitely remote. The dainty playfulness of the Regency Gothic must surely go straight to the heart. Why did it pass, like the mayfly, in the span of a summer's day in the architecture of our land?

Some of the charm of the Georgian Gothic was even allowed to stray into the little Nonconformist chapels of the period, but soon after the beginning of the nineteenth century the majority of these had rejected such frivolities and settled down into an almost featureless form seeming to call attention to the miseries of the early industrial era. Such dreariness being inacceptable to the parish churchman, however, Gothic forms began more and more to represent the appropriate Anglican architecture.

This somewhat pathetic period in church architecture is not without interest in that one can detect the devotion underlying the work performed at the time. There were only a very few architects available to design Gothic churches. Even the best architects were still inexperienced in the style, and the churches built by the Ecclesiastical Commissioners were desperately lacking in charm. But it was 'Commissioners' Gothic' which set the pace for the eventual Victorian Gothic Revival. And although its architects studied their 'styles' with devotion, few succeeded in breaking away from the grimness of its beginnings. Only such inspired men as Pearson or Gilbert Scott the younger, who could on occasion break through the bonds of copyism, succeeded in creating really fine churches capable of being compared with those of the past.

Much more interesting is the rustic 'do-it-yourself' style known as 'Churchwardens' Gothic'. This made no pretence of erudition and dispensed both with architects and skilled builders. What was however clearly displayed was a sympathy with the 'national' style and a determination to get back into it and away from the uglier manifestations of the brick Renaissance. The brick remained, but the arches went back again to Gothic forms. There was no stone available, nor were there masons to work it, but tracery there had to be, so this was indicated in joinery, generally simply by a pair of pine mullions. Rough and even ludicrous it might be—but it was Gothic.

The growing interest in the 'national style', which Thomas Rickman had committed to print, was making it clear to the architectural profession that Gothic was to be the only suitable form of architectural presentation for churches.

Unlike its light-hearted Georgian predecessor, Victorian Gothic was a serious affair, constructed in stone and with all its details properly studied and reproduced in unexceptionable form. Rickman's three divisions of the style were accepted without question, and no deviations from the published ordinances of each were countenanced. This is undoubtedly the principal reason for the dullness of the churches of the period, for the charm of the medieval parish church lies in its ever-changing moods as each generation laid a light hand upon it.

With the Gothic Revival came the Gothic Restorations. We shall never know what our losses during that period were. For our parish churches they probably equalled in aesthetic and archaeological damage the destruction of the monasteries. The interiors of churches were relentlessly stripped of everything accumulated during the past three centuries as the re-medievalizing process went on. What was perhaps worse was the way in which whole buildings lost their character beneath an overlay of flint and stone and even brickwork, making them look as though they had just been built. In this craze for a most un-medieval tidiness all external wall-faces disappeared—for ever . . .

. . . and with them vanished for ever the patina of the centuries.

13

Some Features of a Church

The essential parts of a church are its nave and chancel. To the enlargement of the congregational area are given the aisles and the wings or transepts. The bell-tower, central, western, flanking or detached, is an important, but not essential, part of the parish church.

The transept or, in its humbler form, the wing is an almost universal feature of all but the humblest churches (Plate 14) and is provided to increase the width of the building at a point immediately before the entrance to the chancel. These lateral projections may be prominent, with a pitched roof, or may be a short length of aisle with a lean-to roof. Sometimes they form the base of a bell-tower. During the early-medieval period transepts flanking a central tower were popular as giving the parish church something of the distinction of a minster. At this period they often have one or two shallow chapels projecting from their eastern walls to accommodate altars to some favourite saints. Though these chapels disappeared during the High Gothic era the eastern walls of transepts still had altars set against them here and there, their piscinae remaining to remind us.

A distinction should be drawn between the transept of the great church, which is a structure set athwart the main axis of the building at a 'crossing', and the 'wing' of the parish church which is an extrusion from the side of the nave in order to increase its width, the widening in every case occurring immediately west of the entrance to the chancel. The transept or wing continues in use to the very end of the medieval period, and is often found breaking out of the rectangle of the hall church. The greatest possible width at this point appears to have been the ultimate aim of the builders of parish churches at the time of the Reformation.

During the twelfth and thirteenth centuries the end walls of transepts were often used for the interment of important lay folk, broad low recesses being constructed in the walling for the display of effigies. After the Reformation the transepts of parish churches were often converted into family mausolea and, cut off from their naves by screenwork, no longer appear to add their projection to the width of the building.

The crossing, if one exists, is always an impressive part of any church. (Plate 12.) During the pre-medieval period the arches carrying the four walls were designed and built separately, with their responds projecting well into the building. But by the early-medieval period each corner of the crossing was being properly designed with a crossing pier built as an entity to carry the arches on either side of it, a much less obstructive arrangement.

Externally, the most impressive part of any church is its bell-tower. Attempting a rough survey of the distribution of medieval bell-towers in England, one can omit the very humble parish churches which clearly could never have afforded the cost of one. Churches of cruciform or 'axial' plan can also be omitted as these had towers which formed part of the building and were not provided to be purely bell-towers. The same can be said of all old tower-naves retained.

If one excepts all these special types of churches and concentrates upon the normal western tower typical of the English parish church, one finds very few that are earlier than the fourteenth or fifteenth century.

Of these normal examples, perhaps half are the result of a complete rebuilding of an early church which had thus entirely vanished (one would however have expected that such an expensive item as a bell-tower, had one existed, would have been retained).

The remaining towers have been added to existing churches by removing the west gable of the nave and building there a tower with a tall arch leading into the church.

One wonders what arrangements for bell-hanging were available before the new tower was built. Some of these may have replaced early timber naves retained for the sake of their belfries. But from remaining examples it seems most probable that the belfry of the early-medieval church was a small construction of timber or stone attached to the west gable. Early-medieval roofs were insufficiently stable for them to take the load of a bell. One often sees at the west end of the nave of a small church a beam carried upon posts and stiffened by curved struts, to serve as a support for a timber bell-turret carried partly upon the beam and partly upon the west gable.

Many tower-less churches still have stone bell-cotes, some of them single, others double. Some are charming little turrets with pyramidal coverings. The central 'buttress' passing up the west gable of the thirteenth-century church would have helped to carry the turret. (See Plate 7.)

The examples one finds today are all on small churches, but one can conceive that similar turrets may well have served as belfries on quite large buildings until such time as the enormous cost of a proper tower, having a whole ring of bells, could be accumulated.

Similar turrets can be found on the east gable of the nave to carry the 'sanctus' bell rung during Mass at the Elevation of the Host.

Of great importance was the church porch, not only as a place for the doffing of headgear, but as a public meeting-place which played an important part in the social life of the medieval parish. The early porches were simply roofed areas before the church door, its protection to the interior of the building being, however, incomplete as it never had an outer door and thus did not act as a proper air-lock.

The church porch possibly owes its origin to a similar adjunct set before the great hall of the manor house to protect its occupants to some small degree from draughts every time the main door was opened. Architectural tradition requires that an entrance feature, which plays an important role in advertising the dignity of the building to which it gives access, should be accorded special treatment. (Plate 17.)

It may well be that the medieval porch developed along domestic rather than ecclesiastical lines. We can see, however, that it came to be given the monumental dimension of height, being raised to two stories, the upper serving traditionally as a depository for important records best kept, away from rising damp, on an upper floor.

In parish churches the 'solar' was either carried on timber joists wrought on their undersides to form an attractive ceiling, or else constructed as a 'stone solar' upon ribbed vaulting.

The church entrance thus developed into a fine two-storied frontispiece having an ornamental outer arch with often a good traceried window over it. The porch parapets were often carried up over the entrance to form a parapeted gable often with crenellations and pinnacles to match the rest of the building. The wide outer arch would, as abutment was now understood, require sturdy angle buttresses to support it, and these would be carried up towards pinnacles. Various types of panelled devices might be employed to cover areas of walling left between features.

Within, the porch might become an apartment of considerable charm. It might have seats flanking it for use during conferences, official or merely social. Corbels carrying ceiling beams or vaulting ribs might be attractively carved, the system extended to bosses marking the junctions of joists or vaulting ribs. At the back of this fine ante-room would be the entrance door of the church, probably itself a feature of architectural magnificence.

Probably few visitors to an ancient church pause to take note of the entrance door itself which may often be contemporary with the opening in which it hangs. Medieval doors are formed of two thicknesses of boarding, the outer vertical, the inner horizontal, the two thicknesses being clamped together with rows of heavy hand-made nails clenched on the inside. Hinges were straps fixed to the boarding and turned into loops swinging on hooks built into the stonework of the jambs.

During the pre- and early-medieval period the straps were elongated and carried across the boarding to give the door additional strength. They were wrought into strange shapes of writhing dragons, later into conventional scrolls with 'stiff-leaf' and similar forms of terminal. Those at Haddiscoe in Suffolk are notable examples of the medieval smith's artistic ability.

This kind of ironwork went out at the end of the early-medieval period, as the door of the High Gothic era had its outer boarding covered with strips of moulded wood applied in the form of tracery and matching the tracery in the church windows. Many of these doors remain today as fine examples of Gothic woodwork.

A lot of the door furniture of the village churches is of considerable antiquity. Many an old iron draw-handle remains today which is possibly as old as the original church, having been transferred from door to door as each wore out.

After the main buildings of the church, its next most prominent features are its buttresses. Originally non-structural, they developed from the pilasters affixed to pre-medieval walls to recall the posts of timber structures and provide vertical punctuation at these points. (Plates 6 and 7.)

These pilasters were gradually extended outwards from the wall and during the early-medieval period their projection about equalled their width. (Plate 11.)

In pre-medieval buildings the pilasters adjoining the angles of the building were either kept separate or were joined together solidly to form a 'clasping pilaster' embracing the angle. As pilasters were often embellished with slender shafts up either side, the angle of the clasping pilaster was frequently provided with this feature. (Plates 7 and 8.) During the twelfth century, buildings lacking pilaster treatment were frequently provided with angles reinforced by double quoins to give them added strength in view of the weakness of the mortar used.

With the development of the true buttress during the thirteenth century as a definite projection from the wall-face, the angles of the building were augmented by pairs of these which were in fact merely prolongations of the walls themselves. These buttresses set at right angles to each other are characteristic of the early-medieval period and—with a reservation to be noted later—disappear entirely thereafter. (See Fig. 21.)

The standard angle buttress of the High Gothic—comprising

the fourteenth and fifteenth centuries—is the diagonal one called by English builders the 'French buttress' and thus presumably an importation from the Continent. At the end of the Gothic period, however, there is a return to the early-medieval pair, modified, however, in that a portion of the angle of the building itself is left between them.

Thirteenth-century buttresses were finished off with gablets. Although the principle of applying top weight upon an abutment to counteract a side thrust was not appreciated in this country until the High Gothic era, one finds here and there buttresses capped with rough pyramids resembling embryo pinnacles. During the High Gothic era, the pinnacle in its most elaborate forms, covered with 'crockets' and finished with a finial, frequently tops the buttress of the period, joining with a pierced and crenellated parapet to form a coronary system round the top of the walling.

What would Gothic architecture be without the pinnacle? The spire and the pinnacle—the latter being the aedicular offspring of the former—are both peculiar to the Gothic style.

To recapitulate the theory behind the buttress and the essential factor in its design, it is easiest to recognize it as a portion of the wall set at right angles to the main wall-face to counteract a thrust upon the wall from some internal force. As this force lessens with the height, buttresses are reduced in projection, by means of 'set-offs' as they rise. Where not required to carry ornamental finials, or to support a counterpoise, they normally die out into the wall at the height of the string-course which indicates the top of the wall and the beginning of its parapet.

The flying buttress, a half-arch carrying a thrust from a wall over to an isolated buttress, is not often found in parish church architecture, but examples are seen serving an ornamental purpose at the angles of spires, pretending to support these from the angles of the tower. (Plate 14.) Flying buttresses always need a pinnacle as counterpoise.

The stone stair enclosed in an octagonal turret is a common feature in the medieval parish church. There was usually one leading to the ringing-floor of the tower, often carried right up the belfry and the leads. (Plate 16.) During the High Gothic era of elaborate rood-screens with 'lofts' over, all these had to be reached by stone stairs. Many of these were contrived in older walling and at times seriously weakened the abutments of the chancel arch. Where possible, new stairs were built attached to an outside wall, that of an aisle for example, leading to the end of an extended screen. Such stairs might be continued to the ringing-floor of a central tower. As the porch stair gave access to the southern leads one generally finds the rood stair on the north side of the church, carried up to the leads there.

Some parish churches were provided with a sacristy, usually on the north side of the chancel, the priest's door being on the south side. It is a small room, lit only by narrow windows, often vaulted over as its purpose was that of a strong-room. Sometimes there is a chamber over for the priest.

A crypt is rarely found in a parish church, but such were sometimes built at transept-end to provide a bone-hole. In towns and where the soil was hard for digging graves, these could be used several times over provided their contents were decently transferred to a consecrated building.

To be found in many churches is the so-called 'low side window'. It is a small window having its sill well below the normal level, always situated near the west end of the chancel and generally on its south side. The fact that the purpose of these windows has never been explained is a measure of the lack of research undertaken into the ecclesiological aspect of the English parish church. The writer has discussed the problem with Continental priests and has been told that it is a normal feature of old parish churches and is an opening originally provided for donations, in particular 'oil for the lamps'.

Among odd openings found within the medieval church are the 'squints', mostly obliquely pierced, beside the chancel arch, enabling persons who might find themselves crowded into a corner there to catch a glimpse of the altar.

An important feature of the sanctuary is its 'piscina', the stone sink, usually cut into the sill of a low niche, but sometimes carried clear of the wall on a short colonette, provided to accept the water with which the sacred vessels were washed after Mass. Piscinae may be found in other parts of a church, in a transept or the end of an aisle. They always indicate the site of a vanished altar and are usually on the south side of this.

Stone seats were sometimes provided at the sides of a church, along the aisle walls. No other permanent seating was provided except in the sanctuary, where one may often find elaborate stalls formed in the masonry, surrounded with carved ornament in the style of large niches. These are the 'sedilia' provided as seats for clerics. They are usually arranged in ascending stages towards the east. They generally form an elaborate architectural composition and often incorporate the piscina in its niche.

Another niche found in the sanctuary is the 'aumbry', a cupboard in which the sacred vessels are kept before Mass. The aumbry is usually on the north side of the altar.

On this side, too, may sometimes be found an elaborate niche designed as a tomb. This is the Easter Sepulchre, provided to accommodate the sacred elements during this period. Sometimes an actual tomb was set there and designed to incorporate a niche for use at Eastertide.

With intra-mural interment a normal practice, the chancel was the most favoured situation for sepulture. In the small parish chancel there was no room for the 'altar' tombs erected in the great churches; thus monuments had to take the form of features set in a wall. The southern wall being occupied by the sedilia and the chancel doorway itself, the least encumbered one was that opposite; thus the northern wall of the chancel, near its east end, was usually the site for the tomb of its builder.

A feature similar to the piscina but always found at the church door is the 'stoup' for holy water into which persons entering the building dip their fingers.

A 'chantry' is a prayer offered up for the soul of someone who has died. Bequests to finance such were common in many parishes. The proprietary 'chantry chapels' founded in the great churches for the chantry priests are found only in the large parish churches in the market towns. But there were many places in a village church—a chancel aisle or a transept-end—appropriated as mortuary areas for important families. Altars in such situations could be used for the offering-up of chantries.

There are no indications that the early-medieval church had a chancel-screen. The introduction of this was probably an attempt to restore to the chancel something of the seclusion it had enjoyed since Anglo-Saxon days and before chancel arches were widened during the early-medieval period. There are some stone chancel-screens of fourteenth-century date remaining in parish churches, some of which are in their original position while others have been removed into a transept arch to enclose a family chapel.

The elaborate wooden screens of the last Gothic period completely cut off the chancel from the nave with a partition having its upper part pierced for restricted vision but still of suffi-cient solidity to confer an atmosphere of privacy upon the most sacred part of the building. (Plate 22.) Chancels flanked by aisles also had the openings into these closed by screens, the whole arrangement being derived without doubt from that of the screened choirs of the monastic churches.

Chapels lying beside chancels were also screened at their west ends, usually in line with the chancel-screen itself, so that a con-tinuous line of elaborate timberwork might reach across the church at its old focus of interest, the line passing across the front of the chancel arch.

The chancel-screen itself was crowned by a crucifix or 'rood' and thus became the 'rood-screen'. As candles were lit before the rood and these required attention, the screen had to be capped with a narrow gallery or 'rood-loft' to provide access. (Plate 22.) The stairs formed in the wall to reach the rood-loft usually remain to this day even though screen and loft may have vanished long ago.

The rood-lofts of the fifteenth century are carried out over their screens on aedicular representations of stone vaulting, always richly laced with ribs and sometimes approaching the 'fan' variety. The whole feature was designed to form a frontispiece, similar to the Byzantine 'iconostasis' of long ago, displaying before the eyes of the congregation a vision of beauty denied them in their every-day lives and preparing them for the mysteries associated with the dimly-seen altar. The resemblance to the iconostasis is heightened by the dado of painted saints filling the lower parts of the chancel-screen.

During the fifteenth century, when the English parish church reached the zenith of its architectural excellence, the rood-screen with loft and access stairs seems to have been as obligatory a feature as the western bell-tower.

The roofs of parish churches were probably not always maintained to perfection. Thus one frequently finds the bay over the altar provided with a ceiling, often elaborately ornamented, to protect it from droppings. As the rood-screen came into general use, the same kind of ceiling was often provided in the half-bay immediately to the west of this so as to protect this magnificent architectural feature and the rood above it.

There are indications that in some parish churches the upper part of the chancel arch was blocked by a boarded 'tympanum', possibly painted, acting as a back-cloth to the rood and completing the seclusion of the chancel. Those tympana which exist are believed to be post-Reformation, but in view of the attitude to both the rood and the chancel itself at this period this seems most unlikely.

The carved stone 'reredos' which is set into the east wall of the chancel to act as a back-cloth to the altar is but seldom found in medieval parish churches, though a great number were added during the last century.

The particular feature introduced by the reforming element which attained its most significant form during the Commonwealth was the altar rail, a wooden balustrade of typical Renaissance design fencing off the altar and restoring to it something of the dignity lost to it with the rejection of the rood-screen. Some of these seventeenth-century altar rails, a great number of which have fortunately been retained to this day, afford excellent examples of the joinery of their period.

One of the great differences between the medieval churches and the 'Reformed' ones of today is the elimination of statuary from their interior architecture except that associated with their monuments. In the ancient parish church the tall niche is a frequent feature of the eastern walls of chancels, aisles and transepts. They were provided as settings for the statues of favourite saints, but most of their occupants were destroyed by the Puritans of the seventeenth century.

The niche is a Gothic example of that favourite architectural device, the aedicule, which is a miniature reproduction, for the purposes of ornament, of some larger feature actually forming part of the structure. The Gothic niche is usually flanked by little buttresses ending in pinnacles and over it is a charming composition suggesting an elaborate gable end complete with finial. Within this may be a dainty foliated arch partly concealing miniature vaulting covering the head of the niche. The whole feature is usually founded upon a small corbel that once carried the statue itself and the miniature architecture by which it was flanked.

Gothic Architecture was the product of the craftsman developing his own details upon a series of familiar elements accepted by his contemporaries as forming a basic ordinance. The only assemblage of such elements being the vertical bay, the elevational design of a major building remained nothing more than a row of these. By the sixteenth century, however, the south side of a parish church having had forced upon it the special dignity of displaying an entrance front, we find this joining with the contemporary great hall in utilizing such features as the two-storied porch, projecting wings, stair turrets and details such as buttresses, niches, and a battlemented parapet, to introduce for the first time in this country the elaborate architectural façade.

14

Towers

=====

The tower as such is not a part of the church plan for accommodating a priest and his congregation. It serves two functions, one practical, the other psychological.

Christians are called to church by the ringing of a bell, a tower being provided to raise this above surrounding obstructions, hills, trees and houses, so that its sound can be carried about the parish.

Moslems are called to prayer by the voice of the muezzin. The writer was once asked by the priest of a Byzantine Christian village near Irbid in Jordan to design a church and was anxious to make certain that nothing essential was omitted from the design. The priest told him 'The Moslems hate bells—so we must have a tower with a bell in it.'

The architectural significance of a tower, however, lies in that it supplies its church with the element of monumentalism, the dimension of which is height. Probably costing as much as the rest of the church put together, it raises the building above everything else about it. To this day it overtops the village. How much more must it have done so when the village homes were mere hovels.

It is of interest to try to imagine what might have been the architectural landscape of England during the twelfth century. The principal edifices would have been the great monastic churches, their elaborate steeples towering over all. After them would come the sinister keep-towers of the castles, their pitched roofs barely visible above protecting parapets. Above the humble roofs of each village or township would rise the walls of its parish church, either of stone or timber, crowned in each case by a bell-turret or the steepled roof of a tower. During the next century the central towers would be rising above the village churches, each capped by its lofty timber broach dominating still further the village beneath.

By the end of the fourteenth century most of the churches would be building a tall west tower, lead-covered and no longer needing a spire to emphasize its height, though in many cases the traditional monumental form might have been retained.

A large building is not necessarily monumental. For monumental architecture must display the element of height. The Byzantine church architects appreciated this. All their churches are lofty, their elevations leading up to the central dome. The early French cathedrals were of immense height so that the buildings themselves towered above the roofs of the city encompassing each. The Anglo-Saxon minsters were very large buildings but even as their architecture advanced they never attained the height of the great Continental churches of the thirteenth century. It is to this characteristic of the English great churches that we may owe the development of the church tower to the degree of splendour it achieved in this country.

The bell-tower has existed in this country since before the Norman Conquest. But at this time their scarcity was such that a landowner whose church possessed one was entitled to the rank of Thane.

The monastic developments of the ninth century began the expansion of the great churches along their axis to a new focal point where transepts joined the main structure. With the addition of aisles to all four arms, the lighting of the 'crossing' presented a problem. As the nave was lit by its clearstory, this was carried up over the transept roof to perform the same duty for the crossing. Thus in the heart of the building we find a low tower or 'lantern', similar in principle to the lighting arrangements under the Byzantine domes but having windows all round it which matched those in the adjoining clearstories. Contemporary illustrations suggest that some of the first timber steeples erected over these early crossings may have incorporated a ring of windows at the base.

The lantern tower is not however a bell-tower and was of too light a construction to have stood up to the swinging of bells. Those lantern towers which survived the destructive forces inherent to their construction were sometimes subsequently raised by a belfry story. But most churches with lantern towers had to build a separate bell-tower close by, as at Chichester or Salisbury.

Most of the early great churches had expanded eastwards from the original turriform nuclei and some of these may have remained, as they may be seen to do in the German cathedrals, as western adjuncts to the completed church. Such structures would have had belfries built into them and thus would continue to serve as bell-towers for the enlarged church. It is clear that well into the twelfth century the bell-tower of the great English church was at its west end. The cathedrals of Winchester and Old Sarum had them, flanked by their original transepts. The sole survivor, one of the world's most beautiful towers, may be seen at the west end of what is now the cathedral church of Ely.

The two types of church plan which had developed by the time of the Norman Conquest, the 'Celtic' type with nave and chancel (Fig. 13) and the Byzantine type with the turriform nave (Fig. 7), have been described in Chapter 4. The latter had a ready-made place in which to hang its bell, the other had no tower at all.

Only a very small tower is needed to carry a bell. The Byzantine campanile is a slender structure having no resemblance to the Gothic bell-tower of medieval England. We may find a series of such structures which have been added to early churches all down the Anglican littoral from Durham to the East Saxon border, each with the primitive Byzantine *bifora* in its belfry stage. North of the Wash they are square stone structures, typically Byzantine, southwards in East Anglia they are of flint, circular in plan for lack of stone for quoins. (See also Plate 27.)

Although the parish bell-tower hardly appears at all in permanent form until the fourteenth century, many old timber naves may have been retained to carry the bells. (Plate 1.) Some had stone naves built on to them, others incorporated the posted structure within the new stone walls. Some stone bell-towers have been built up inside the west and of an early nave, perhaps on the site of an early timber tower.

The twelfth and thirteenth centuries saw the foundation of a number of small monastic houses in the English countryside, each with its church of nave, transepts, choir and central tower. Practically all of them have disappeared today but when they were standing they must have produced a very strong influence on the church-builders of the locality. With such examples before them, it is no wonder that many designers of thirteenth-century parish churches adopted the cruciform plan with the central tower (Fig. 11 and Plate 11), as often as not with an aisle-less nave. The small church with the central tower but no transepts, common in the twelfth century, indicates the desire to introduce the feature wherever possible. (Fig. 10 and Plate 8.)

In addition to the church and minster towers which covered twelfth-century England there were scores of castle towers, massive fortified houses of a type never before known in architectural history. Limited to England and the Norman Empire, these massive structures, three stories in height, were covered with pitched roofs concealed behind high parapet walls to prevent their being shattered or burnt by artillery. Larger towers had two roofs side by side to reduce their height, a very early use of the internal lead gutter.

Architecturally their exterior ordinance was clearly defined by large clasping pilasters at each angle. Larger towers had one or more pilasters between these emphasizing the essential bay design. Some of the later towers reduced the wide Byzantine pilasters to a narrow form having greater projection, embryo buttresses of early-medieval type.

Neither the twelfth nor thirteenth century saw much building of bell-towers to parish churches. The tall Byzantine campanile seems never to have spread westward from the Anglian littoral into the rest of England. Here and there, however, one finds very large and massively-built towers at the ends of parochial naves, clearly intended to serve the dual purpose of extra accommodation and bell-tower, perhaps in the same way as the axial towers. These towers, which appear to be of early thirteenth-century date, all have the intermediate 'buttress' in the middle of the side walls in the style of the contemporary domestic tower.

When examining old churches it is of interest not only to discover what new types of church came to be introduced with each changing fashion, but also how existing churches were 'modernized' to bring them into line with the current fashion. For example at the close of the twelfth century a number of pseudo-cruciform churches had central towers built at the east end of the nave between the early wings so as to convert them to the fashionable cruciform type. (Fig. 12a.) It is usually easy to tell whether a central tower is part of the original design or not, for if it is not one cannot fail to notice the confusion which has been caused inside the church by trying to fit in a stair to the ringing floor. Had the tower been planned from the start access to this would have been incorporated into the design so as not to obstruct the church below.

On the other hand, there are indications—and records—that as time went on the central tower not only lost its popularity with the congregation but was actually pulled down so as to free the most important part of the nave from the obstructions created by the crossing piers. Apart from this, however, it is doubtful whether a stone tower, once erected, would have ever been pulled down and replaced. We may therefore consider the possibility that our losses of western towers of early date will have been negligible.

It is impossible to overstress the essential monumentalism of the bell-tower, costing possibly as much as the rest of the building put together and serving only to carry bells. The spirit that raised the towers of English churches is identical with that behind the great temples of dynastic Egypt: the erection of a monumental structure to advertise the glories of religion. The accommodation provided by the ground story of a west tower was of little value as it was so far away from the centre of interest at the opposite end of the building. It is for this reason that we find a not inconsiderable number of transeptal towers the ground stories of which added considerably to the accommodation just at the point where it was most needed. Another saving in cost was to set the tower over the porch to the nave door. This however gave the church a somewhat larger porch than it might have needed.

Detached bell-towers, in the fashion set by many of the great

churches, are not uncommon in parish churches also. The beautiful
thirteenth-century example at West Walton in Suffolk is well
known.

Towers were not covered with flat lead roofs until the High
Gothic era. Before that time there were several methods of roofing
a tower.

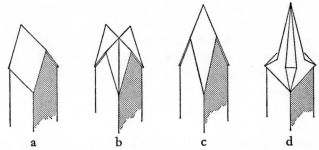

Fig. 23 *Early tower roofs*
    Some types of tower roofs which preceded the lead flats
    commonly seen today. (a) The saddle-back which is simply a
    pitched roof. (b) The cruciform roof which may be seen at
    Hinton Charterhouse in Somerset. (c) The Rhenish 'helm' roof
    of which the only surviving English example is at Sompting
    in Sussex. (d) The broach, of which many examples remain.
    Copied in stone it becomes the Northamptonshire type of spire
    and from it is derived all forms of this feature.

A simple but not very subtle method was to provide two opposing walls, usually the north and south, with gables and then roof
it as any other building. (Fig. 23a.) Towers on a rectangular plan
suggest a roof of this sort. A 'saddle-back' roof, as it was called,
may be seen on Sarratt church in Hertfordshire.

The standard Rhenish tower-top was the 'helm' which was built
up on four gables with timbers joining their summits to form a
diagonal square carrying rafters meeting to form a spire-like roof
having four diamond-shaped planes. (Fig. 23c.) There must at one
time have been many helm-roofs in England, but their only survivor is at Sompting in Sussex.

It is doubtful whether it would have been possible to build an
ordinary pyramidal roof at a period when ridge-pieces, and therefore in all probability hip-rafters, were unknown.

It seems most probable that the tower roof of early days was set up with rafters set at a very steep angle like the poles of an Indian tepee. And it is of interest to note that this kind of structure is favoured by timber builders, some of the early timber towers having their posts set sloping inwards at quite a considerable angle.

Subsequent developments indicate that the top of the tower was converted into an octagon by having beams set across its angles. Upon this base the rafters would have been set up at a steep angle to form a spire or 'broach'—meaning a spit—exerting no outward pressure and thus requiring no transverse ties.

Four triangular spaces were left at the angles of the tower and these were covered with low lean-to 'roofs'. The whole structure was covered with shingles and capped with a lead 'poll'. A number of these timber broaches remain to illustrate what must have been the commonest form of covering to the top of an early tower. (Plate 25.)

Contemporary illustrations of great English churches—on seals for example, or in the Bayeux Tapestry—suggest that the broach may sometimes have formed the central core of a steeple of considerable elaboration, with a surround of lean-to roofs raised upon timber wall-frames to provide tiers of windows for lighting the church below. During the thirteenth century the enormous central tower of St. Albans Abbey, even in those days as high as it is today, was crowned by an elaborate octagonal steeple. The staggeringly beautiful towers of Lincoln once had spires on them.

So it is not inconceivable that many of our pre-medieval parish churches may have been crowned by timber steeples displaying a degree of elaboration impossible nowadays to imagine. In this connection it is of interest that during the whole of the Middle Ages the word 'tower' was only used to designate the military structure. The church tower was always called the 'steeple', as though this feature had become inseparable from the form.

An indication of one type of feature may be found in most of the stone spires which replaced the timber ones. This is the dormer window. It is not a medieval type of window at all and does not appear serving this purpose until after the end of the Gothic era in England. The Renaissance dormer is much wider than the kind

25. A timber broach at Bury in Sussex

26. A stone broach at Slawston in Leicestershire

seen on the sides of the stone spires and is formed by cutting several rafters and 'trimming' them to form the opening. The prototypes of the spire-dormers must have been fitted in between the rafters; they are indeed very narrow with acute little gables. (Plate 26.)

The form of the base of the broach, like all other medieval roofing-forms, changed with the introduction of lead. The small roofs round the base were omitted and the space left at each angle covered with a lead flat. The corbel-table associated with all early eaves was often retained, but it would in future carry a parapet in the same way as elsewhere in the church.

In order to carry a dome upon a square tower it is necessary first to convert the square into an octagon. This can be done by throwing diagonal arches called 'squinches' across the angles. The device was well known throughout Byzantine architecture. The towers of the early Rhenish cathedrals were generally converted into octagons as soon as they had cleared the roofs, in readiness for the timber steeple.

By replacing their timber angle-beams with squinch arches the English masons could begin to copy the timber broach in stone. At first the stone forms imitated their predecessors, sometimes throwing out spur roofs at the angles but with these rising ever more steeply and sweeping up in the lines of the spire. A great number of these stone 'broaches' were built in Northamptonshire with its good freestone and many skilful masons. A study of these structures might enable one gradually to work up a knowledge of those earlier timber steeples many of the details of which may have been copied in stone.

These tall stone roofs are really rather remarkable achievements, with their eaves and corbel-tables all worked out in amenable stone. With the coming of lead the spire changed by dispensing with its angle features and surrounding itself with the usual parapet. Opportunities for angle treatments were seized with the usual enthusiasm of the medieval mason, until the High Gothic spire became one of the great features of historical architecture.

Most towers had built-in staircases leading to their ringing-floors. The later ones carried their stairs up to the leads. They were nearly always worked into an angle, usually an eastern one, of the thick walling, with a slight projection as required, but a series of Devon towers make a special feature of the stair turret by projecting it from the middle of a side wall. That the stair turret was regarded as an architectural feature of importance is shown by the fact that it is usually found on the south, or entrance, front. (Plate 16.)

Before the era of lead roofs the tower stair would have ended at the ringing floor. The existence of a short stair thus probably indicates that the tower was originally roofed with a timber broach.

By the end of the Gothic era the great towers have a turret at each angle, replacing the angle buttresses which had been the normal angle-feature of the tall tower. Such turrets rose high above the parapet and were often capped with little ogee domes.

When considering the problems facing the primitive builder one should remember that while the erection of a timber structure poses no very great difficulty, a request for it to be lifted up and set upon a wall is quite another matter. The 'close-couple' roofs of early days, brought up from a safe anchorage on the ground and perched upon the tops of walls, were far from stable, and to expect them to carry any weight such as a bell would have been unrealistic. Thus any timber bell-turret of those days would have had to be carried either on posts rising from the ground or on tie-beams passing across the building at plate level.

During the High Gothic era, in regions such as Somerset, blessed with fine freestone and a notable masonry school—probably based on the great abbey of Glastonbury—tower design reached considerable aesthetic heights. The development of tower architecture can be followed, in this region and others similarly engaged, in the same way as the student of today can be taught the elements of architectural design in any type of building.

A tower is aesthetically the most important structure to face an architect. It cannot be hid. However thoroughly an indifferent architect's elevations can hide themselves within the streets of a town, his tower rises visible to all. Yet nowadays as often as not a tower has become merely a pile of identical stories heaped up until a halt is called.

The medieval architects took the elevational presentations of their towers very seriously indeed. Mere height alone was not enough. The ground story being part of the church, it had to display the west window with a door below this for processions. These two features were often combined to provide a fine façade to the building.

The basic elements of the tower proper, that is to say the portion which rises above the roof of the main structure, are the two stories connected with the ringing of the bells. In the beginning we find just the small window lighting the ringing-floor and over it the larger one allowing the sound of the bells to ring out over the countryside. In low towers the ringing-floor may be kept low down within the roof level of the nave so that only the belfry rises above this.

As the outward indication of the bells within, the belfry windows always form the elevational focus of the deisgn. At first a simple Byzantine *bifora* (Plate 3) this is followed by a pair of lancets; eventually the belfry window becomes traceried to match the rest of the windows in the church.

We have noticed a tendency for large thirteenth-century towers to have their elevations divided into two bays by a medieval strip or embryo buttress. This practice continued into the High Gothic period, being followed where the masons were embarking on an elaborate elevation incorporating a buttressed treatment. Reaching the belfry story the medial strip or buttress split this into two portions with a window in each, thus greatly adding to the elaboration of the crowning story.

But all architectural students know that the central feature of an elevation should be an opening rather than a solid obstruction. Thus the last stage in tower design was to divide the elevation vertically into, not two, but three parts, resulting in a belfry stage with twelve windows ranged around it, a treatment providing a basis for considerable architectural embellishment.

Much of the architectural effect was produced by the buttresses. The normal form of the High Gothic angle-buttress projected diagonally but later towers, especially in the West Country, returned to a variation of the early form by setting the buttresses in pairs, leaving, however, a portion of the angle of the tower between them. (Plate 17.) Panelling spread over the blank spaces of walling and the vertical elements of this joined with the medial buttresses to accentuate the soaring effect. The pinnacles growing out of the summits of the buttresses and joined by lengths of pierced parapet helped to create a lively skyline. At the zenith of the High Gothic era, the tall towers of the English churches must have been among the finest achievements of their age. (Plate 28.)

Much of the glory of the tall tower vanished from church architecture with the passing of the Middle Ages. But the church tower—now always at the west end—continued to be accepted as an essential part of the building. It soon lost its unnecessary and aesthetically anachronistic buttresses. Its parapet became plain, with possibly urns or obelisks capping the angles. Its windows became simple round-headed openings in the style of the period. More often than not it was built of a pleasant brick, perhaps with stone quoins and a touch of stone here and there at windows or doorways. (Plate 23.) The English steeple was recalled in many ingenious Renaissance forms.

What would the countryside of England be without its church towers? They seem everywhere, peering shyly over the tops of great trees or soaring high above them. It is though they were mounting guard over the fields about them.

On many occasions they must have served as watch towers, especially during time of war. We can think of the mail-clad nobles of the Wars of the Roses struggling up the winding stairs to peer out from the leads in search of the sheen of enemy armour.

How many of our towers may have played host to Cromwell, Fairfax, Prince Rupert, or star-crossed Majesty itself? Reflect on the missions of accoutred colonels, attended by perspiring troopers, climbing up these rural observation posts, forever planning new battlefields.

The high bells did not always peal out so merrily.

There were times when the tenor was called upon to mourn.

15

Architectural Details

═══

As was explained at the outset, architectural history has for the past century and a half been studied in terms of aesthetic expression. Although Thomas Rickman was an architect, he was less concerned with the churches he was studying as buildings than as examples of an architectural style the aesthetic forms of which were at his time becoming of great interest to the élite. His successors have for the most part adopted the same approach and a very great many books, some of them elaborately illustrated, have been produced carrying on his work. But as very few of the writers have been architects they have been unable to study parish churches as buildings comparable in their way with houses or factories.

Yet architecture is composed of three elements, as Sir Henry Wootton and Sir Christopher Wren, at the beginning and end of the seventeenth century respectively, have both pointed out. First comes the purpose of the building and the efficiency with which it fulfils this. Then there is the form of its construction which will ensure its stability. And then, and not always lastly, is its ability to delight the eye with its dignity and charm. Indeed it is not really the architecture so much as its embellishment, which particularly delights the ordinary man.

The system of architectural ornament which sets the Gothic apart from all other styles is the moulding. The Classical architects formed their columns strictly in accordance with a recognized Order. The moulded Gothic pillar would have shocked their orderly minds by its infinite variety. Heavily-moulded 'architraves', also rigidly following an accepted ordinance, could be converted by the Roman architects for use in framing an opening. But no Classical moulding ever marred the plain soffit of the arch until its bleakness came to be softened by panelling.

Either through ignorance, or simply because they would have considered it barbaric, the Romans made no use of the 'ordered' arch constructed in expanding rings and thus economizing in timber 'centering'. This was left to the more practical and ingenious Byzantines.

But the elevational presentation of the ordered arch can appear rather crude and unattractive unless some kind of treatment should be given to the series of hard edges passing along each order. To this is possibly due the invention of the Gothic moulding.

It must have been the timber-builders who first employed the chamfer, the adzing away of the edge of the beam to convert a right angle into two obtuse ones. The principle of the chamfer was to play a large part in the later development of the moulding.

The medieval mason, however, approached his material from a different direction. His system was to take a chisel and cut a groove, called a 'quirk', on either side of the angle and work the stone between these quirks to form a 'roll'. (Fig. 24.) This is the second source of the Gothic moulding and that which brought it to its greatest achievements.

The first rolls, used by the pre-medieval masons, were six or eight inches across or more in the larger buildings. When they were used up the imposts of openings they could become worked up into colonettes with caps and bases. Above them the soffits of the arches were generally still flat, but sometimes had edge-rolls also. An ordered arch of this early period might have a half-shaft run up the face of the impost to meet it.

Once the orders began to creep into the arch soffits and be repeated in their imposts, rolls called 'nook-shafts' became formed to fill in the re-entrant angles as well as the salient ones. We can see the beginnings of the system of Gothic mouldings.

During the early-medieval period this developed with great rapidity. The rolls became more slender, the quirks expanded into deep channels. Rolls became triple, the hollows between them deeply undercut. Soon the actual arch orders became invisible, submerged, as had been intended from the start, in a riot of mouldings. (Plate 13.) Some rolls were pointed like a keel, others had little flat ribs running down them. Some had their sections moulded to 'ogee' forms.

This was the period of the Cistercian colonization of Yorkshire. Their great tower-less churches, denied carved ornament, worked out their own scheme of non-representational ornament in the form of richly-moulded arches.

A good deal of the early-medieval moulding mystique rubbed off on the parish churches. On the whole, however, their treatment of orders inclined towards the humble chamfer. (Fig. 25.) Coarseness was somehow avoided, and the small scale of the architecture

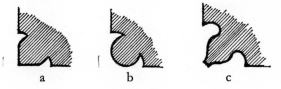

Fig. 24 *Development of masons' mouldings*
      (a) The initial 'quirks' forming the 'bowtell'. (b) The
      completed 'roll'. (c) By working up the section,
      undercutting and shaping, the complete profile of the
      Early Gothic period is achieved.

was probably less suited to the opulence displayed by the great churches. The chamfer continued in use right through the High Gothic, sometimes tending towards concavities or even quite broad hollows. But parish church architecture on the whole did not attempt the wilder extravagances of moulding systems.

Piers supporting arcades began as blocks of walling left between the openings. The Anglian pier of the pre-medieval period usually had rolls or colonettes at the angles and a single impost moulding marking the springing line. A half-shaft was sometimes added to carry an ordered arch.

The circular pillar came in at the end of the eleventh century as a rough copy of the Classical column. It continued into the early-medieval period by which time it had attached to itself four slender shafts to make it cruciform on plan. (Fig. 26.)

But a circular pillar, even if provided with a wide square capital, is hopelessly ill-adapted to carry an arched structure over. Despite encouragement from Continental Gothic influences, by the end of the thirteenth century it had vanished for good in favour of the traditional cruciform pillar with simply chamfered edges. This is almost certainly of timber origin and designed to fit in with the similarly chamfered struts and braces connecting with the timber posts as they rose. (Figs. 25 and 26.) In masonry a springing line would be marked by an impost moulding.

The attached shaft, however, retained some influence, appearing against or as a projection from the pillar, varying its own projec-

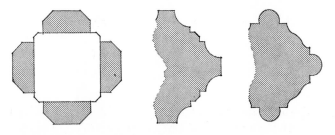

Fig. 25 *Mouldings derived from carpentry*
The timber posts of the early buildings are joined by lateral struts or braces having their edges 'chamfered' free of sapwood. As a refinement, these chamfers are hollowed out. As the section develops, the simple hollows adopt a wavy profile, while slender shafts are added to improve the appearance of the flat faces of the four projections. These are the parish church mouldings.

tion from half- to three-quarter round. In the former case the impost moulding might pass round the profile of the pillar. The bolder shafts would probably have their own caps.

The pre-medieval capitals, the 'coniferous' and other variations on the Corinthianesque, and the early Byzantine cubical caps, have been dealt with elsewhere in this book. The purely Gothic cap—there were no large 'capitals' in Gothic architecture—was a somewhat complicated feature which never achieved a proper ordinance and unless smothered in carving is seen as a rather ugly piece of design.

27. 'And little lost Down-churches praise The Lord who made the hills'
Southease, Sussex

28. 'Boston . . . Boston . . .
    Thou hast naught to boast on . . .
    But a great church, with a tall steeple . . .'

Its top member, the 'impost moulding', is a repetition of the form of the string-course of its particular period. Below this comes a curiously coarse kind of 'abacus'. Below this again is the 'bell' of the cap, a vague hollow cone of indeterminate profile. Separating bell and shaft is the 'astragal' or necking, the traditional member employed in all columnar architecture at this point.

The base of the pillar was derived from the 'Attic base', the Classical model from which all such features had sprung. This base had two roll mouldings separated by a hollow or 'cavetto'. The Anglo-Saxon base was of slight projection with its members hardly differentiated, but the bases to the later circular pillars spread themselves to match the capitals over and often had small 'spurs' filling in the angle between base and column. In these bases the hollow member became so deeply excavated that it began to collect condensation down the walls. These 'water-holding' bases were therefore abandoned by filling up the hollow with a third roll. The form of the impost moulding changed to match, becoming less undercut at the end of the thirteenth century and finally changing to the triple roll.

The development of the parish church pillar from the early-medieval through the High Gothic may best be described as a progression from the fully-moulded pillar with a continuous capping towards a 'cruciform' pillar with miniature caps to its four attached shafts. In any case the real finish to the pillar is the impost moulding marking the springing line of the arch.

The complete impost moulding as seen capping a pillar or respond is a combination of moulding and cap. Its upper member is the normal moulding which forms the string-course of the period. Below this comes a wide hollow acting as a sort of 'bell' to the feature ; this is sometimes carved. Below this the impost is completed by a small roll or 'astragal'. All these Gothic cap mouldings, never managed with the same skill as those running with the arch, appear wretched without the attentions of the carver who could fill the bell with foliage, as during the fourteenth century. (Plate 13.)

Arches were sometimes allowed to run their mouldings right down into the pillars without any indication of the springing line.

In single arches where the span was small, projecting responds particularly obstructive and the wall massive enough to take any thrust from the arch, as in the case of a tower arch, the arch orders were allowed to die away into the respond—the 'discontinuous impost'. Another way of avoiding obstructive responds was to let the arch spring from a corbel.

It is only from within a great church that one can receive the full impact of the richness of Gothic mouldings. But most old parish churches, even the humblest, will usually display an example or two of that other most characteristic aspect of Gothic architecture, the traceried window.

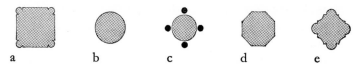

Fig. 26 *Pier and Pillars*
> (a) The heavy 'Anglian' pier of the eleventh century with its angle-rolls, derived from the Byzantine. (b) The plain circular 'Romanesque' pillar of the twelfth century, most common in the South and West. (c) The early Gothic pillar with attached shafts. (d) Plain octagonal pillars are common to Gothic parish churches of all periods. (e) The 'cruciform' pillar of the High Gothic.

Owing to our climate, the smallest aperture in the walling affects the comfort of those within the building to a degree far greater than in warmer countries in which architecture had been born and developed prior to its appearance in Western Europe.

In the small parish church of pre-medieval days the little windows are few and are often set so high up in the walling that they could not have been reached even to shutter them. They would not have been glazed, and had no drip-stones to prevent their collecting stormwater running down the wall-face over them. So they were set as high as possible to reduce the amount of this and perhaps find some protection from the overhang of the eaves.

Medieval glass was cast in diamond-shaped 'quarries' set in lead 'calms' and the panel sprung into grooves cut into the stonework. These grooves were set into a flat area of stone surround representing the exact sight opening of the window. In order to allow as much light as possible to reach the interior of the building this flat area was kept as small as might be and the stonework splayed away on both sides so as to expand the size of the actual opening as quickly as possible.

When it appeared, the mullion adopted the same system of chamfers, keeping as narrow a front as possible to the light. At first the chamfers were flat but they soon became concave, remaining so until the end of the medieval period. During the latter part of the sixteenth century the mullion became convex, to continue in that form as long as the feature survived.

During the early-medieval period, when the 'lancet' windows had been set in pairs with masonry forming embryo mullions separating them, it became the practice to extend this masonry upwards and provide there a quatrefoil light, the whole design being incorporated within the internal arched head of the window opening. In this way was invented the system of filling a window opening with bar tracery.

It was the multiplicity of patterns available to the ingenious mason with his 'compasses' which enabled him to raise the High Gothic to a degree of aesthetic excellence that has allowed it to become one of the great historical architectural styles. The introduction of the triangular 'cusp', which enabled the heads of all windows to be foliated, greatly added to the liveliness of the designs.

The heads of the windows could be varied in a number of ways. The shapes could be steeply pointed or depressed. An ogee head could be used. The drip-stones could be covered with crockets. Major mullions could be treated as aedicular buttresses. Running ornament could be spread over the stonework as fancy dictated. For as dressed masonry turned out by a mason of the highest skill, and unfettered by any rigid ordinance, there was no limit to the aesthetic possibilities offered by a large Gothic window.

There were the two main schools of tracery, the curvilinear and the rectilinear. The former was best suited to tall openings, the latter to broader ones. In the normal course of events, windows became wider, their arches correspondingly lower in pitch, and their tracery tending more and more towards the rectilinear. But there is no doubt that the two styles were interchangeable, appear in the same buildings at the same period, and were more dependent upon circumstances and taste than upon historical period.

Tracery spread from the windows of the High Gothic all over the structure. It covered wall-faces and intruded itself into vaulting. It developed its own systems of 'orders'—primary, secondary and so forth—as its complications increased. The major orders of tracery produced small rolls to their mullions and bars. In large treatments such as the Somerset bell-towers the elaboration of the members grew until each had a series of mouldings almost going back to the riches of early Gothic days. One may well ponder on what might have been the end of such brilliant excursions into masonry if progress had been allowed to take its course.

But parish church architecture quickly collapsed at the Reformation, the skill of centuries has in an instant of time to be thrown on the scrap heap while the disorganized remnants of medieval freemasonry strive to assimilate a new ordinance and try it out on a new type of building. It is only in special features such as arcades, which adopt Classical forms, and windows which are larger than the domestic, that the details of the Renaissance church differ from those of the mansion of the period.

16

Ornament

═══

All architectural styles employ ornament, sometimes purely for embellishment, more frequently with some architectural purpose in view, such as to emphasize some particular feature or to disguise some defect or awkwardness in its character.

The most interesting type of ornament is that which is purely architectural, such as the moulded arch or its imposts, of the form of columnar architecture's most important feature, the capital.

The legendary origin of the Corinthian capital is always worth recalling. Of the sculptor of ancient Corinth who placed upon the grave of his infant daughter a basket containing her toys, with a flat stone on top to keep out the rain. And how, returning later, he found that the acanthus fern he had planted on the grave had climbed the sides of the basket and curled under the stone in a manner which he was able to capture and perpetuate for ever as the Corinthian capital.

His capital formed the crowning glory of the mighty temples of Hellenistic days and spread through Rome and Byzantium to our shores. Even in its most primitive forms its spirit seems to haunt in particular the churches of the twelfth and thirteenth centuries, linking rustic England with the seas Odysseus sailed.

Prior to the introduction of the first 'Corinthianesque' capitals into this country the early designers used Doric forms, either the Rhenish 'cubical' cap for completing the various types of edge- and nook-shafting, or the curious Byzantine 'cushion' capitals for heavier work. It was the effect of the Corinthian type of capital upon the latter forms which produced the typically English 'coniferous' capital and later endowed it with the uncurling fronds of the Corinthian volutes.

There is something particularly charming about the miniature twelfth-century Corinthian cap. Though so different from its Classical prototype it seems nevertheless to have completely captured its spirit and converted it into a feature as gracious in its Nordic way as the opulent Mediterranean capital of antiquity. This is especially true of the smaller varieties employed on the shafts attending upon columns and imposts.

The full-scale capital of Classical origin does not pass into the thirteenth century, its place being taken by a system of mouldings such as was becoming the hall-mark of the early-medieval period. But the small capital or cap remains upon the shafting and continues to do so until the end of the Middle Ages. Always retaining the basic Corinthian form, its bell absorbs the volutes and formalizes their shapes. Then these shapes develop into magnificent carving based on English naturalistic forms, all this finally disappearing altogether in the general austerity of the later period and leaving the bell bare.

The weakest item of the Gothic ordinance is due to its failure to agree upon the proper form for a capital. The Corinthian, filtering down the centuries through the long distances from its homeland, reached this country retaining its three main elements, the abacus or impost moulding, the spreading bell, and the small astragal separating this from the shaft. The frond-like volutes continued for a while to endow the bell with its peculiar distinction, but if carvers were lacking to provide these items the bell might have to be left unadorned, leaving the capital forlornly incomplete, a poor substitute for the crowning features known to antiquity.

As a capping to a large pier or clustered pillar the three elements of the capital could be utilized, in typical Gothic fashion, to form a band of moulding, with the bell portion extended to provide a broad hollow. In first-class work of the fourteenth century this cove could be filled with carving (Plate 13), but in the parish church it might have to remain bare, looking particularly crude when exposed above a simple, as opposed to a compound, pillar.

During the fifteenth century all three parts of the capital were merged to form the typical profile of the period with its broad upper splay, the dullest, but at the same time the most confident form achieved by this troubled feature. From the fifteenth-century capital is derived the large cornice-type moulding which is the sign-manual of the end of the Gothic era. (Fig. 27d.)

In addition to the architectural ornament one finds in association with structural features such as capitals, there is a great variety of ornamental devices which are purely decorative. The pre-medieval churches were full of such. The zigzag or 'chevron' is a prolific motif (Plate 10), so is the 'billet' moulding of simple rolls sawn into pieces and with each alternate one removed. In antithesis to such barbarous ornament is the appearance of Classical floral scrolls winding along some wide roll. Again we revert to paganism with the beaked heads of Nordic mythology paying no tribute to any known style of architecture.

Another interesting form of pre-medieval ornament was the 'battlement'. This would certainly have nothing to do with the military feature as this did not come into use in this form until centuries later. The motif is probably allied to the Hellenistic fret and represents ornament copied from clothing, probably round the neck. An indication that ornamental features of clothing were copied in stone is seen in the diaper motif, clearly representing smocking, frequently encountered among these rich displays of ornament.

It is this array of repetitive ornament, displaying a great diversity of motifs, which has come to be called 'Norman'. It is however peculiarly English; that it continues to develop despite the Norman invasion is evidence of its vigour. Anyone who has come upon the tremendous turbulence of the chancel arch at Tickencote in Rutland, or the riches displayed by the whole church of Elkstone in Gloucestershire, must surely realize that art of this ebullience is native and never the product of imported carvers forced upon the local craftsmen. (Plate 29.)

A feature appearing everywhere throughout English architecture is the running motif of a system of small items of carving set along a hollow moulding. In pre-medieval days it was the little pyramids known as 'nail-heads'. Later these became cut into until

they were remodelled as a pile of four narrow leaves which antiquaries, seeing in them some resemblance to violets, have come to
call 'dog-tooth'. (See Plate 10.)

At the end of the thirteenth century the motif changes completely, being replaced by a curious little bud called a 'ball-flower'.
The broad hollows of the fifteenth century which replaced the
original deep channels required different treatment in the form of
square paterae formed of groups of oak-leaves.

The models for the semi-representational floral carving of the
medieval era cannot always be determined with accuracy. While
by the High Gothic period accurate representations of leaves and
flowers appear, as in such lovely achievements as we may find in
Exeter Cathedral or Southwell chapter house, the early-medieval
'stiff-leaf' with its crudely-carved leaves of clover-like form may
be nothing but a symbol of the Trinity. The 'crocket' which climbs
the sides of pinnacles and even spires is certainly derived from the
Corinthian 'volute', but does its English form represent any particular native plant? The Gothic finial or 'pommel' with its pair of
half-open cabbage-like leaves flanking a central one appears everywhere on buildings and bench-ends. Has it, too, some forgotten
legend to explain its origin?

Carving has always played an important part in the ornamentation of the medieval churches. While schools of carving must have
existed, the shaping of soft stone, such as clunch, with the aid of a
chisel, or even a knife, is a natural occupation and much of the
carved ornament of the Middle Ages must have been amateur,
enthusiastic if not actually inspired. Beautiful statuary may be met
with in churches, though of course by far the majority of such
achievements perished after 1539 or at the middle of the next century. But there are many smaller portraits to be found in corbels
and the like, especially heads of kings and queens, bishops and
abbots, which may well be true portraits. The accuracy of such
botanical studies as those of Exeter or Southwell suggest that the
sculptors of the Middle Ages were far from being all amateurs.

There appears to be a wide division between art of this degree
and the vigorous, irrepressible productions of the carvers of the
medieval grotesques. The pre-medieval corbel-tables formed the

29. The art of the Anglo-Saxons enshrined for ever at Kilpeck in Herefordshire

30. The dainty fan-vaulting of Cullompton church in Devon

first playgrounds of the amateur carver, for the corbel is always watching you as you pass—seeming always to be tempting you to glance up at it as it pokes its medieval fun at you. Nor did the stately architecture of the High Gothic venture to abandon the traditional grotesque from its art. Still the writhing dragons spew out the stormwater upon our heads while the funny little medieval peasants play their obscene japes to tease the ladies. As we look up into the vaulting of the porch we can never be sure whether its central boss will be some lovely wreath of foliage or a hideous mask putting out its tongue at us. Generally, however, the vaulting boss was a site for the more gracious forms of sculptured art.

Generally speaking, the masons and carvers of the early-medieval period strove to abolish the crudities of previous centuries and achieve an effect of refinement and delicacy. In the more important buildings this resulted first in the development of mouldings to lighten the structural features, then, with the coming of the High Gothic, in the use of fine carving to embellish them. Neither of these phases really penetrated deeply into the sphere of the parish church for lack of skilled masons and sculptors to carry them out.

The last phase, however, was the replacement of grace by a more disciplined approach to architectural embellishment represented by panelled designs. This was more in line with the capabilities of the parish church mason and during the fifteenth century, when his activities became more and more sought after, mason-made panelling, not sculptured ornament, became the keynote of the decorative system of his architecture. Under this influence pillars tended to become panelled piers as masons co-operated with the screen-making joiners who were increasing their architectural activities at this time.

While in antiquity the carver's art almost certainly developed from experiments upon soft stone, English carving is much more likely to have been first employed upon timberwork, as seen in the prows of ancient ships. After England had profited from its excellent supply of freestone to become a land of masons, the carvers followed their efforts in the new material. But the English 'wright', far from relinquishing his efforts to the mason, extended these until

by the fifteenth century he was producing magnificent achievements, both in the carpentry of his roofs (Plates 19 and 20) and
in the intricate joinery of his screenwork. (Plate 22.) Once again
the carvers followed the material, and many of the old masonry
forms—such as fan-vaulting—were translated into joinery, while
the masons were retaliating by copying the panelled motifs of the
joiners on their wall-faces. But the carpenters were winning, and
all the old masons' motifs, such as vaulting bosses, were appearing
as ornaments to mask the junctions of roof-timbers. (Plate 18.)

The Tudor era saw the use of badges as ornamental motifs,
perhaps the beginnings of political publicity in architecture. The
stylized five-petal wild rose of the Tudors took the place of the
earlier naturalistic achievements. During the sixteenth century
Spanish influence resulted in the open pomegranate with its cluster
of pips.

Heraldic emblems had been in use for a long time. The names
of our country inns—the Red Lion, the White Hart—remain to
remind us that during the Middle Ages such heraldic charges were
familiar to all. In an illiterate population the main features of local
heraldry—the sheaves of Hungerford, the bleak chevrons of the
great House of Clare—would be familiar to all the inhabitants of a
district living in the shadow of some noble landowner. Again our
inn-signs testify—the Beauchamp Arms, the Duke of Suffolk.
During the High Gothic phase, heraldry plays a large part in the
carved ornament of churches, often indicating some part of the
building built by the person thus commemorated. Roof-bosses, in
stone and wood, are the usual sites for heraldic displays. And the
shields are scattered thickly about the arcaded biers upon which
the knights and their ladies sleep down the centuries, where—

> 'for past transgressions they atone,
> by saying endless prayers . . . in stone!'

The early Renaissance ornament of the late sixteenth and early
seventeenth centuries exhibits two main characteristics. First come
the plain forms derived from the use of framed panelling with
moulded edges, the panels themselves being filled in with crude
geometrical forms such as flat pyramids. The other is the elaborate

carving which took many forms and was mainly derived from the Spanish 'Plateresque' or 'Silversmiths'' style of ornament which reached this country as a spate after the Reformation by way of its refugees. The architectural forms of this post-Reformation decorative style consist mainly of ill-digested Baroque shapes translated into a form of strapwork with the ends turned up.

The carving was in low relief, contrasting in this respect with the medieval work which knew nothing of such treatments. At the mid-sixteenth century roundels displaying imaginary portraits of Roman emperors were in vogue. The joiners who had been engaged upon church screenwork continued their efforts without a check. Existing parish churches continued to employ them to make not only screens but such items as pewing and the new pulpits. The first half of the seventeenth century saw a riot of sculpture spreading through parish churches, until it was all stopped with dramatic suddenness by the far more serious Reformation which removed the new Head of the English Church.

Important features to note during the Elizabethan/Jacobean era are those derived from Baroque architectural motifs converted, for lack of lathes, to a squared form. Of these the most important is the baluster, the bulbous colonette found everywhere in such situations as the king-posts of roofs. The most curious feature of all is the finial of the period, appearing as a kind of square onion, sometimes hollowed out like a pumpkin ghost. The same device appears as a drop, perhaps recalling in a somewhat shamefaced fashion the glorious pendants of the High Gothic twilight.

The Civil War which occupied most of the fifth decade of the seventeenth century was not the political revolution of a century earlier but a religious upheaval which put an end to all vestiges of the medieval Church. Architecturally its effect was to eliminate all ornament, not only omitting it from new churches but attempting to obliterate it in those already existing. In such Puritan districts as East Anglia the destruction was very considerable, windows in particular being deprived of their painted glass. It is fortunate that the chief architectural glories of the region, its angel-covered roofs, were too far off to be reached by the iconoclasts.

The Classical elements in Renaissance architecture, however, were at this time becoming acceptable provided they were austere and inclined towards the Doric.

After the zeal of the Puritans had faded and the more comfortable churches of the Georgians had replaced the preaching-houses, the Corinthian Order began once more to cast its spell upon the architecture of the churches. In this Order the cornices are most elaborate. Amongst its standard ornaments are the 'dentil course' cut into small square teeth and the rows of shaped brackets or 'modillions' which help to support the overhanging 'corona'.

As early as the twelfth century the walls of churches were being decorated with paint. The colours used were red and ochre and the designs were based on contemporary carved motifs such as the zigzag or billet. During the early-medieval period when so much attention was being paid to the excellence of masonry wall-faces, walls were sometimes whitened over and a system of jointing painted on the surface. Various representations of the 'stiff-leaf' motif may also be found.

The Byzantine churches were alive with mosaic portraits of the Deity and attendant saints. The greater English churches reproduced the same kinds of portraiture in paint. But it was not until late in the medieval period that representational art appeared in the parish church. As the decorator became artist the church wall became covered with life-size figures, certain parts of the building having their special assignment. Across the nave from the main door, usually that on the south side, we may often find a huge St. Christopher carrying Christ as a boy across a river. Over the chancel arch was a favourite situation for a 'Doom'. So much of this medieval art was removed during the whitewashing of Puritan days that it is difficult to appreciate today the extensive use of church walling as picture-books for the instruction of congregations.

Post-Reformation churches also had their wall-paintings, for the most part representing Baroque scrolls; lettered texts may be incorporated. Among the less attractive features of church ornament are the boards displaying the Mosaic Law and the Creed set beside the altar during the eighteenth century, an appeal to morality taking the place of the medieval threat of Hell Fire.

Ornament

The chief glories of the parish church will always have been its carved ornament. No other historical style—except possibly the Hellenistic in its latest manifestations—employed the carver to the same extent as the Gothic.

For the students of art there are the lovely forms of fourteenth-century capitals or the incredible richness of the screenwork of the following century.

And for everyman are the portraits. So many of them one feels assured are true to life, and one longs to know who they were. And as amusing as ever are the caricatures. Grinning and mowing, telling lies and plagued with toothache, our ancestors are still there, laughing at us down the centuries, caught for ever by the chisel of the medieval carver. The England that was, helping us to endure in our turn the England of today.

17

Furnishings

When one compares a cathedral such as Salisbury, gone through and swept out like a long-neglected attic by a late-eighteenth century 'restorer', with its neighbour Winchester, still packed with the accumulated history of eight centuries, one begins to appreciate the manner in which any old church, even the parish church of a small village, may contain within its walls a museum of historical objects quite independent of its architectural structure.

While down the centuries there have doubtless been occasions when some forward-looking individual has removed some despised feature and replaced it with something more fashionable, there are still plenty of items left over from all periods each of which adds to the history and interest of the village to which it has served for so long as a focus of parish life.

Some of these features are part of the structure, or semi-permanent partitions such as screenwork. But there are a number of movable items, decorative features or even furniture, moved about from time to time within the building as circumstance dictated. And notwithstanding their significance as memorials of the dead beneath, some of the objects which time has shuffled about the building are its tombs.

Beneath the paving of the village churches sleep the village forefathers, their bones turned over from time to time to make way for crowding successors.

Only in the great churches do we find early tomb-slabs with inscriptions. During the illiterate Middle Ages the indication as to who lay beneath had to be left to the skill of the engraver in brass.

From the thirteenth century onwards we find the memorial brasses, each with an inscription and usually a portrait of the deceased in helm and chain-mail, let into a matrix cut in the tomb-slab. By the Tudor period the brasses were no longer being set into the flooring where they were getting worn by the passage of feet, but were fixed to the sides of tombs or the architectural treatments above these. A large number of brasses have been worn away or removed so that only their matrices remain.

Not until the seventeenth century do we find many tomb-slabs bearing inscriptions. The lettering of these is usually crude, but during the next century it may become very fine, both capitals and script.

Figure sculpture has always been a popular method of indicating the nature of the occupant of a tomb. During the twelfth century the tomb of a bishop often had his portrait effigy set lying upon it, incised into the tomb-slab. By the early-medieval period the life-size effigy was finding its way into many parish churches where it is found lying in low-arched niches formed in aisle walls and transept ends to accommodate it. Mail clad-knights and their ladies, however, have far too often been shunted about their churches to make way for the re-planning schemes of the centuries since their deaths.

During the High Gothic era the so-called 'altar tomb' became the fashion. The feature represented a tall bier, arcaded about and often embellished with sculpture and heraldry, upon which lay the portrait effigy of the deceased. They are found everywhere in our old churches, some of them surprising examples of medieval furniture. Seeing them, one may be tempted to muse upon the lost loveliness shattered to ruin beneath the tumbling vaulting of the great monastic choirs.

The parish chancel had originally been reserved for the burial place of priests but during the Middle Ages important lay folk found sepulture there. By the end of the sixteenth century the Reformation had finally released these now somewhat discredited sanctuaries for them to serve as mausoleums for the new rich now denied tomb-room in the vanished minsters.

In life, the Elizabethan magnates advertised their riches in their raiment, in death they displayed it, in lieu of the plate-armour of their quarrelsome predecessors, on their impressive sepulchres. With the curious ill-taste of the age they abandoned the dignity of the medieval bier for the livelier setting of the four-poster bed. Many were the ponderous monuments they set up it this form, with themselves and their wives lying, fully clothed in ruffs and all the sartorial paraphernalia of the Elizabethan, upon these mighty couches, and arranging about them the kneeling figurines of their obedient offspring in attitudes of worship to God and their parents.

One cannot make mere mention of these and other Tudor tombs without drawing attention to the very fine artistry of many of the portrait effigies themselves. From the time of the Wars of the Roses onwards many of these effigies, especially those sculptured in alabaster, are breathtakingly beautiful. Little attention however is paid to them as their recumbent position allows them to be viewed only in a foreshortened aspect and it is usually impossible to see them properly without erecting some kind of scaffold. All the more glory to their sculptors who well knew that only Heaven would see in eternity the portraits they created.

So when one is feeling shocked by some monstrous Elizabethan sepulchre it is often pleasant to draw aside the curtain of the architecture and try to obtain a glimpse of perhaps some fine portrait statue lying serene amidst the meretricious nonsense about it.

Fortunately for the development of English sepulchral art the chancel of the parish church could not go on finding room indefinitely for such monstrosities. So lesser memorials came into fashion, fixed to the walls, depicting the Jacobean gentleman and his wife kneeling opposite each other in a pair of rounded-head niches ornamented in the curious sub-Renaissance of the period.

The change-over from floor to wall marked the trend of future sepulchral monuments in churches. The portrait statue remained, but now it was set in an upright position and surrounded by a Renaissance frame. Some of the noble dead of the Civil War were thus remembered. The standing figure remained until the end of

31. (a)
Masonry of the time
of the Conquest

31. (b)
Early Gothic
masonry

31. (c)
Late mediaeval
masonry

32. (a)
Pre-Gothic axed
stonework

32. (b)
Stonework showing
early use of the
bolster

32. (c)
Late mediaeval
diagonal tooling

the next century, but the tendency was for less expensive treatments with a bust of the deceased instead of the whole figure. Simple urns and sarcophagi appear in the eighteenth century. Some of the baroque monuments of the Georgian era are magnificent achievements, crowned by pediments and attended by cherubs, the whole in a setting of scrolls, swags, and here and there a skull.

In addition to these huge monuments we find a great array of simple wall memorials, slabs and cartouches, with a lettered inscription and a baroque surround to scale. At the end of the eighteenth century the Carrara slabs begin to appear, simple and austere with lettering which soon turns to ugly type. The sculpture remains, some of it bold but much of it in low relief. The loveliness of Flaxman's work sometimes shines in a village church.

Amongst the memorials of old parishioners are the 'hatchments' carried at the funerals of armigerous gentry and their wives or widows. These square canvases display the arms of the deceased, the divisions of the black and white backgrounds indicating his or her marital status and whether or not spouses were alive at the time. Accoutrements such as helmets and gauntlets, some made up specially for the purpose, may be found associated with late-medieval and Civil War monuments.

Once King Henry VIII had announced his title as head of the English Church in place of the Pope it became obligatory for the Royal Arms to be displayed in every church. Many of these still remain from the seventeenth and eighteenth centuries, far too often banished nowadays into some dark corner of the building.

Though usually far less prominent than the parish church's monuments, the font is often by far the oldest item of furniture in the building. Many a pre-medieval font, scene of the baptism of every villager for century after century, has survived the rebuilding of the church without having been replaced by a more fashionable successor.

This is surprising in view of the extreme crudity of many of these early fonts and indicates the veneration in which they must have been held in medieval days. The pre-medieval fonts were usually mere circular tubs of stone. The more primitive the shape of the font, the greater the likelihood of its being carved with lively sculpture of Anglo-Saxon type.

Twelfth-century fonts are often formed in the manner of coniferous capitals, mounted on a squat shaft and given a base similar to that of the contemporary pillar.

The tendency of the font was for it to grow in height so as to facilitate the act of immersion. The early-medieval design was to support the edge of the bowl with a ring of the slender shafts typical of the architecture of the period. The bowl was usually octagonal and often surrounded by simple arcading.

The High Gothic font was a sophisticated piece of furniture. Of what is known as 'chalice' form, it was octagonal and arranged so that bowl, stem and base were part of a complete design. It was often a fine piece of work with buttressed stem and sculptured figures and emblems. In its simpler form the sides of the bowl were ornamented with incised quatrefoils. The base is heavily moulded and often raised upon a step.

The post-Reformation font was far removed from the sturdy medieval form. Often formed in marble, it nearly always took the form of a baroque baluster of the more monumental type used not for balustrades but singly for a garden feature such as a sundial.

A font cover to keep dust out of the bowl was one of the features turned out by the splendid woodworkers of the High Gothic. It is usually fashioned as the aedicular representation of a very fine spire. Some late-medieval font covers are probably the finest creations of the Gothic Age. Post-Reformation font covers are plain boards supporting a fretwork finial formed out of crude baroque scrolls. During the eighteenth century they became small ogee domes.

While the sermon has always played a part in the parish Mass, no architectural provision for its delivery appears to have been made until late in the Middle Ages. The pulpit built into the wall and approached by steps formed in its thickness was generally to be found in the monastic refectories and there are a few examples to be seen in parish churches. One late-medieval example known to the writer is on the north side of an aisle-less nave immediately to the west of its lateral wing, a position which corresponds approximately with the monastic arrangement, though it is generally understood that in medieval days the sermon was delivered from the chancel arch.

Confirmation of this is suggested by the appearance, at the end of the fifteenth century, of the occasional tall slender pulpit, as at Holne in Devonshire, forming part of the elaborate timberwork associated with the rood-screen and elevating the preacher above the heads of the congregation in a church possibly still unprovided with fixed seating.

In view of the fact that after the Reformation the pulpit was the most important item of church furniture and that existing ones would presumably have been retained, one is forced to the conclusion that the pulpit was not a normal feature of medieval churches. Neither the great preaching naves of the friars' churches, nor the hall churches of the West, seem to have had them. But of course the medieval monastic pulpit built into the wall could hardly have been constructed in an aisled building, so that had pulpits been used in the average church it would have been necessary to build them up as a piece of detached furniture, presumably in wood.

The pulpit as an item of furniture comes in without warning during the sixteenth century and by the Stuart era it was to be seen in every church. The seventeenth-century pulpit is an interesting piece of furniture with its sides ornamented in Renaissance motifs and provided with a stair and balustrade. The usual rather crude fretwork scrolls carry it, and above is an acoustic device comprising a back-piece joining with an octagonal 'sounding-board' spreading out over the whole pulpit. Many of these huge pieces of seventeenth- and eighteenth-century joinery seem to have vanished today, their moorings to pillar or wall having become unsafe, threatening with extinction the preacher beneath.

During the eighteenth century the pulpit with its ever-expanding sounding-board remains the most prominent feature of the interior of the parish church. With the era of the 'horse-box' pews it had to be raised still higher above the congregation, becoming 'three-decker' and having incorporated into its lower stages a reading-desk for the lessons and a box for the 'clerk' who led the responses to the Protestant prayers.

Furnishings

As has been noted earlier, it was the emphasis upon the sermon, indicated by the introduction of the pulpit as a standard item of church furniture, which brought about the provision of a proper seating system within the parish church. Throughout the Middle Ages, congregations, when not kneeling in prayer, were forced to stand. In some churches, however, stone seats were provided around the walls of the building—giving rise to the saying 'let the weakest go to the wall'—and round the bases of pillars. Even as late as the last century some humble churches were still unprovided with enough pitch-pine pews, or even benches, and stone seating survived as the only form of furnishing. Worshippers forced to use these brought with them straw or bracken as insulation against the chill of the stone.

The introduction of fixed seating during the fifteenth century gave the joiners and wood-carvers of the period a full measure of experience. The seats themselves were ordinary benches formed of boards set at either end into heavy timbers called 'bench-ends'. As these lined the passages between the seated areas the bench-ends had to be embellished with some form of carving. The bench-ends of the fifteenth century were covered with carved ornament, often incorporating figures. Each bench-end was swept up into an ogee and crowned with a 'pommel' finial. By the sixteenth century the bench-end was still being richly carved but the Gothic pommel had gone and the top was square. Most of the finest examples are in the West Country. Elsewhere the interest in such costly furniture had been for some time on the decrease. In a Will of 1449 we find the testator providing for the re-furnishing of his parish church at Stamford in Lincolnshire; he particularly specifies *plain* desks, a *plain* rood-loft, and pewing 'not curiously, but plainly wrought'.

Throughout the history of parish church architecture in England, it will be noted that the South-West was always a century or so behind the times. Its parish churches date from a period at which the rest of England was already well equipped with buildings of all periods. The belated but vigorous burst in church-building was maintained right up to the Reformation and the arts of joinery and wood-carving continued unabated until the heavy hand of the Puritans came down upon them once and for all. During the Civil War the South-West was the staunchest in support of the Old Order, constrasting in this respect with the disloyalty of East Anglia and Yorkshire, older and more cynical regions.

The bench-end died out with the coming of the Renaissance when pews came to be framed up in sophisticated style and the ends were reduced to a panelled frame. Finials were sometimes introduced, either the 'square onions' of the Jacobeans or the rather charming acorns which succeeded them.

The next revolution in the seating of parish churches appears during the Georgian era and is concerned with the important consideration of bodily comfort. The monastic choirs had been warmed for the night offices by huge braziers set in their midst. The village churches presumably had no such amenities. Possibly the medieval congregation kept warm by stealthy movement; the introduction of fixed seating would however have put an end to this. The length of the Puritan sermon must have added to the discomfort of congregations sufficiently disciplined during the seventeenth century to sustain them but a century later becoming restless.

Among the many elaborately-carved items of furniture introduced into the parish churches of the first half of the seventeenth century were 'box-pews' seating two or three people, enclosed within waist-high screens and complete with doors, symptomatic of the middle-class attitude of the post-medieval era. This kind of display being of course anathema to the Puritan victors of the Great Rebellion, little of it can have survived this into the latter half of the century. But the idea had been established as a panacea to offset the hardships of winter sermons, so the intelligent Georgians completely re-seated their parish churches, providing a system of box-pews, almost man-high and provided with doors, to keep away draughts and perhaps allow worshippers in strategic positions to slumber undetected. The squire's pew sometimes had a fireplace set in an outside wall. Over all towered the panelled three-decker with its menacing sounding-board.

A great many of these 'horse-box' interiors were swept away during the restoration mania of the Victorian era. In their day the

Georgians probably destroyed a vast number of magnificent medieval bench-ends, only to have their own pews swept away to be replaced in their turn by feeble imitations of medieval pewing. Is it possibly due to the kindlier climate of the South-West that so many beautiful church interiors have been suffered to remain in their medieval form?

It was fortunate for Victorian congregations re-medievalizing their churches that they could now be warmed with piped hot water.

During the previous three centuries a considerable number of chancels appear to have become derelict or mutilated beyond hope of 'restoration', or simply to have disappeared altogether. A large number of new chancels were built during the Victorian era. In them, and in all the ancient ones as restored, lateral seating was provided, in imitation of cathedral stalls, to accommodate a surpliced choir brought thither from the demolished west gallery. With them came the pipe organ, to be re-sited in an 'organ chamber' extruded from the chancel wall and combining with a new 'vestry' to confuse still further the plan of many an ancient church.

The installation of some form of heating in an old parish church presents a problem which is however as nothing when compared with the provision of an appropriate form of lighting. One wonders what artificial lighting they had in medieval days when only the priest needed to read. Probably a simple boat-shaped oil lamp with a floating wick. Some of the isolated corbels found here and there in an old church may have been provided to carry such lamps.

Fortunate is the parish which has managed to keep its eighteenth-century 'spider' chandelier still scintillating above its chancel. In parenthesis it is pleasant to report that excellent reproductions of these charming features can at the present time be obtained; their lighting value may not be up to contemporary standards but their aesthetic properties more than make up for this deficiency.

On a summer Sunday the bells ring out over the English countryside. But how many of us think of the activity which fills the ringing-floors as the captain of each tower grunts his strange commands while the 'sallies' lift and plunge? How many people, admiring the pinnacled belfry stories of such glorious towers as that of Huish Episcopi in Somerset, think of the ancient machinery hidden behind the tracery of its windows, framing the lively bells which the whole magnificent structure was raised to carry?

Many of our bell frames are as old as their towers, their massive timbers solidly mortised together to hold firm against the tremendous whip of a ring of perhaps ten or more bells swinging in all directions in a great roar of sound. Each bell is strapped to a 'headstock' by a series of iron bands, the stock itself swinging in iron-bound 'gudgeons' strapped to the timbers of the frame. Attached to the headstock is a beautifully-framed wheel in the grooved rim of which the bell-rope is housed.

At rest, the bells hang down. In this position they may be 'chimed' by pulling on the rope and letting the bell rock to and fro. But before ringing a peal, the bells have to be 'pulled up' in a great clangour of sound until each is at rest mouth upward, held by a stay fixed to its headstock. A slight tug on the rope, and round goes the bell, sounding as it goes and coming to rest again at the other side of its swing. Then a tug on the fluffy 'sally' and round she goes again.

England is the only country with a tradition of 'ringing' church bells. In other lands bells are either chimed or sounded like a ship's bell by a rope secured to the clapper. In this country the tradition is of ringing bells in 'changes', each individual bell passing in turn through its companions until the original scale has been regained and the bells are once more 'in rounds'. This involves considerable skill, yet all over the country women as well as men continue to maintain one of the few genuinely traditional customs of medieval England.

Under the sound of the bells lies the parish churchyard. During the Middle Ages, and into the last century, the families of the squires were buried inside the building. The villagers went to the churchyard, and had no memorials other than the churchyard cross which most parishes seem to have raised on the south side of the church. These crosses vary considerably in the quality of their design, some being very humble and others fine monuments in the highest Gothic tradition, and are mounted upon a stepped base.

Furnishings

In the illiterate Middle Ages the poor had no epitaphs. No stones marked their graves. Not until the seventeenth century do we find churchyard memorials. But the great period of churchyard tombs was the Georgian, when the baroque 'table-tomb' came into fashion. Most of our village churchyards can show some of these impressive monuments with their panelled sides and balustered angles. The tiny church of Winson in the Cotswolds owns a fine series of these, the finest of all churchyard memorials.

Few churchyards seem to be without an ancient yew tree. As children we were solemnly told that these trees were grown in churchyards to provide timber for the manufacture of long bows. But a moment's thought will expose the improbability of such a theory. Farmers will tell you a different story. The churchyard yew is an insurance against defective churchyard fencing. For the foliage of the yew is fatal to cattle.

The parish churches played an important part during the Civil War. As public buildings of permanent construction they were used as armouries, magazines, and prisoner-of-war cages. Often they were actually garrisoned, usually in an emergency such as during a retreat, and many of them endured stern sieges. A surprisingly large number of them still show traces of battles fought around them: shot-holes in their towers, bullet-scars round their doorways. Perhaps the most dramatic incident was at Alton in Hampshire where Royalist cavalry under Colonel Bowles, trapped by a superior force, galloped to the churchyard and defended it behind a rampart of their slaughtered horses. Driven at last into the church, they died to a man, their colonel making a last stand in the pulpit. To recall this gallant episode in English history makes it difficult to enter Alton Church today without a sensation of awe.

The character of the parish church must have been strangely transformed to suit the cult of Puritanism which for a decade submerged them. And how glad they must have felt when they reached the year 1660 and they could once more display the royal heraldry upon their walls. To this day the 29th of May, birthday of King Charles II, is welcomed by the tall towers of Cornwall, each displaying above its battlements the branch of an oak tree in gratitude for the sanctuary it afforded him after a lost battle.

18

Notes on Dating

====

Visitors to an old parish church may view it through different eyes. To many there is the human interest presented by its memorials with their inscriptions and epitaphs. Aesthetically there are many aspects of old churches to delight the eye—the splendour of some fine late-medieval building has a different appeal from that of the humbler church in its setting of towering elms. Within, one may discover a narrow shrine of unknown antiquity or watch the play of light and shade in a pillared interior full of artistry in its sculptured memorials.

To the architect the interest lies in the variety of planning concepts and the ingenuity of structural devices of other days. But to the antiquary—who in order to study buildings should possess more than a smattering of architectural knowledge—the building presents a problem in historical detection. What are its origins, visible or conjectural, and what is its subsequent history of development?

It is hoped that among the foregoing chapters the student may discover observations which will help him with his research. But the writer thought it might be as well if he should recapitulate some of the items more particularly concerned with attempts at dating an old parish church.

Beginning with the building masses themselves, an interesting start can be made if the church should have a central tower. This may have started as a pre-medieval tower-nave. Crossing arches may be insertions of later date. Blocked-up arches in an old west tower may suggest that this began its existence as a tower-nave.

Signs of the lateral wings which indicate a pseudo-cruciform church of about the time of the Conquest may be looked for. These may be scars on the nave walls marking vanished roofs or walls. One may find signs of the actual arch which led into a wing. A difference in the form of the easternmost arch of a later arcade is often an indication of a vanished wing.

Timber towers rising at the west end of a nave, especially if they appear to have been built inside it, may be suspected of being the remains of an early timber church which has been absorbed within later walling. A half-bay at the west end of a nave arcade seems generally to indicate the site of the vanished eastern aisle of a timber church, absorbed by some westward modification of the nave built on to this.

Up to the end of the thirteenth century, aisles were narrow, eight feet or so in width. Many have been subsequently widened, but traces of the old spreading roof which once covered in one span both the nave and its aisles may often be found at the east end of the nave, on the tower, or on the west wall of a wing or transept. The new aisle may have been accompanied by the erection of a new arcade or, more rarely, a clearstory might have been raised above the old one.

Often in a Gothic church one may see traces of small round-headed arches above an aisle arcade. This is probably the remains of the high-set windows of a pre-medieval nave.

While one can find many old features in unexpected places within a church, one must not be misled into believing them to be in their original positions. A fine pre-medieval doorway in the wall of a wide aisle has certainly been carefully taken down and rebuilt. Such features were often more treasured than we might believe; it is no uncommon thing to find the early-medieval triplet of lancets which once formed the east window of the chancel re-sited in the east wall of a transept or even an aisle.

While one may thus find early features in a late wall, one is still more likely to find the reverse. Few early churches escaped being at least in part re-fenestrated during the High Gothic era. Inserted features can often be detected by the fact that the dressed stonework surrounding them is out of course with the walling about them. This is not however a certain clue as some of the early builders ordered ready-made windows from the quarry instead of having them made by a banker-mason on the job, as would have been the case with first-class work, the point being that both the walling and the dressings should have been raised course by course as the work proceeded.

The masons of medieval days were too concerned with their reputation to build with 'straight joints' when adding one wall to another. Thus one hardly ever finds straight joints to indicate a change of building period. On the other hand the new work would probably have its own course system so that the junction, however properly bonded, would be bound to show.

Changes in roof pitch are nearly always clearly indicated by the remains of water-tables on tower walls and above the chancel arch. Vanished additions can be detected by the vertical lines made by alternate quoin-stones left in the remaining wall. The actual internal angle of the vanished building can be seen as an absolutely vertical line of stone edges.

Dating stonework becomes more difficult when one cannot associate it with contemporary architectural features such as windows which by the pitch of their arches or the form of their mouldings give a fairly accurate date. There are, however, quite a number of clues to the date of walling visible in the arrangement of its stones.

Rubble stonework set 'herring-bone' is always an indication of pre-medieval date. The same is generally true of squared rubble set uncoursed or 'random'. After the twelfth century the mason would set his facing properly coursed.

When one comes to dressed stonework dating is helped by several factors. The first is the size of the stones. Until the early-medieval period these were squarish on the face but the medieval mason used stones about twice as long as their depth, typical of the neatness of the period. The High Gothic was raised with much larger stones, deeper in the course and up to considerable lengths. (Plate 31.)

The angles of a building can be most helpful in dating. Roman brick gives an early date. As the thirteenth century was coming in, quoins were often doubled, giving quite a smart-looking angle in conjunction with rubble walls. With the fifteenth century ashlar appears, stone which is laid in slabs set upright instead of flat. This appears in the angles of the building and is easily recognized. From then onwards, the properly-laid quoin disappears from all but the best-quality work. In rubble or brick walling the upright quoins becoming particularly noticeable, indicating all too clearly the deterioration of masonry.

During the seventeenth century the 'drafted margin' in which the face of the stone is heavily tooled along its edges, is often found. This is later developed until the face of the stone is left 'rock-faced' and not worked at all except along its margins. In Georgian days comes 'rustication' in which the joints are marked by square or V-shaped channels. At the end of this period one finds 'vermiculation', a raised pattern of flat strips wriggling across the stone. It is by looking for indications of this sort that one can date otherwise featureless additions such as buttresses.

Sometimes one may be surprised to find that the quoins of a building are not plumb but follow a wavy profile. This is an indication that the stone building was originally built against a timber one and that this has been destroyed.

Angle-buttresses give a useful clue to date. The 'French buttress' set diagonally does not make its appearance until the fourteenth century. During the thirteenth century appears a pair of buttresses set at right angles; prior to this we have the 'clasping pilaster' of pre-medieval days. (Fig. 21.)

If the west gable of the nave has a buttress-like pilaster passing up its centre it is likely to be of thirteenth-century date.

Any dressed stonework can be roughly dated if its tool-marks have not weathered away. Thus the pre-medieval stones, left off the axe, show its unmistakable uneven diagonal strokes. This rough-hacked finish is in complete contrast to the early-medieval bolster-work which is beautifully neat and is run dead vertically up each stone. The bolster continues in use throughout the medieval period (Plate 32) but after the thirteenth century its strokes are seen running in careless fashion diagonally across the stones.

The Renaissance masons seem to have exchanged the light bolster for a rather heavier tool which leaves coarser and much more untidy marks except where the margins are 'drafted', when more care is taken with the marks left along the edges of the stones.

One of the easiest ways of dating a portion of a building is to examine horizontal mouldings such as string-courses or drip-stones which follow a recognizable profile which remains more or less constant for each period. (See Fig. 27.)

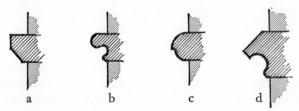

a   b   c   d

Fig. 27 *String-courses*
The standard profiles of string-courses and impost mouldings. The upper members of the caps of pillars; the top moulding in any horizontal system of ornament. Useful as an aid to approximate dating. (a) Pre-medieval. (b) The deeply-undercut early-medieval moulding equating to the water-holding base. (c) The fourteenth-century moulding equating to the triple-roll base. (d) The heavy 'cove' of the fifteenth century and onwards as long as masonry mouldings survive.

In the pre-medieval period the moulding was a square projection with its lower edge chamfered off. With the approach of the Gothic in the early-medieval period it changes completely to a rounded section, either a simple 'torus' or a slimmer roll deeply undercut and with a still smaller roll below. This is the moulding which accompanies the richly-moulded architecture of the thirteenth century and goes with the 'water-holding' base. During the mid-Gothic which follows the early medieval the hollows are filled up and disappear from both string-course and base. The basic moulding becomes a 'torus' with its upper radius greater than its lower and a small break where the two join. The last

Gothic period is marked by an unmistakable moulding which is a kind of coarse version of the early medieval in that it has a deep hollow with a small roll below it; the top however is a thin projection with a wide splay on its upper edge to throw off water. In all it forms a kind of Gothic cornice moulding but with a concave 'cove' instead of the projecting 'corona' of the Classical cornice. Incidentally, it is of interest to note that during the seventeenth century a large 'cove' is often found under the eaves of buildings. Usually run in plaster, it takes the place of the standard Classical cornice and appears to be a Gothic survival retained to mock at the rigid Classical ordinance of the Renaissance.

These basic mouldings are the most reliable aids to the dating of those portions where they appear. One finds the basic moulding in string-courses and round the drip-stones of windows and internal arches. They appear in the uppermost members of capitals, where they form the 'impost moulding'. At the responds of arcades and single arches the moulding is often compound, having below it a wide concave band representing a 'bell' as in the capital—often carved in the same way—and finished off below with the small 'astragal' roll.

The sizes of bricks can be a help in dating otherwise featureless walling. The Roman bricks, rather more than an inch thick, found in the rubble of walls and employed as quoins, suggest a very early date. From the thirteenth century—in the eastern counties only—to the sixteenth, one finds the 'two-inch' brick which from the end of the fifteenth century has a firm hold on the larger buildings of the day. During the sixteenth century 'Tudor' bricks are quite common. The seventeenth century uses rather wider bricks but still not quite running four courses to the foot as today. The standard two and five-eighths inches of the modern brick dates from the Georgian period.

Until the end of the sixteenth century bricks were laid as though they were rubble, without any pattern of coursing. There are more 'headers' than 'stretchers' showing in the walling. During the seventeenth century the 'bond' is 'English' having alternate courses of each; after this the 'Flemish bond', which alternates headers and stretchers in the same course, finally takes over. A feature of Georgian brickwork is the use of over-burnt headers called 'chuffs' to form patterns in the bonding.

Graffiti are often interesting and may help with dating. Geometrical 'doodles' made with a mason's compasses are medieval. If one of the primitive 'mass-dials' is found on the north side of a church the stone has been re-used. One may speculate on the significance of situations where one can see that men have gathered and gossiped while they sharpened a blade on some piece of ancient architecture known to serve as a good whetstone.

Initials and dates of the seventeenth and eighteenth centuries may be found. Earlier dates may be suspect, for Arabic numerals did not reach this country until the sixteenth century and were presumably unknown to the rustic vandal until the next.

While some of the additions and alterations to an old church will be connected with the improvement of its accommodation, others will be due to attempts to improve its stability, nearly always connected with trying to check distortion due to inadequate abutment.

The progressive widening of chancel arches led to spreading abutments and cracked gables. The eastern angles of new bell-towers damaged the western responds of the nave arcades and distorted the tower arch. New arches cut into transepts were cut without regard for abutment. Large windows were inserted without regard for the spread of their arches or the quality of the surrounding walling. Above all, an old 'close-couple' or cradle roof continued to spread and thrust against its walls while each generation watched the list increasing until at last it was decided to try to stop the trouble.

This kind of thing was going on all through the Middle Ages, as today. And it is of interest to see the measures taken to maintain the buildings of the parish churches against the stress of time. One can find old walling rebuilt in a new and more efficient fashion. And after the thirteenth century the real buttresses begin to appear, each generation adding its own, in its own fashion, as the old church calls for aid, to keep it standing still.

19

The Troubles of Old Parish Churches

Buildings grow out of the wants of men and are the embodiment of their wishes. In a parish church which leads a life prolonged through many centuries, its walls carry along with them memories not only of past worshippers but of those among them who strove to keep its stones alive and hand them down from generation to generation.

And as it was a thousand years ago, so it is today. Sturdy walls may defy the forces of disintegration while ancient roofs hold fast against the tempests of the seasons. But here and there the signal cracks begin to creep, on plastered walls faint stains are taking shape. Once more we are reminded that buildings, too, are mortal.

The student who takes pleasure in the store of history and art gathered by the centuries within the walls of an old parish church might once in a while give a thought not only to the men who built it but also to those who have undertaken the less impressive task of maintaining its condition. He might also remember that these same devoted guardians remain with us today, more often than not struggling with depleted congregations to scrape to-gether the funds necessary for the never-ending programme of restoration.

How often at holiday-time the visitor to the country comes upon a village fete? He may even pause to study the efforts being made by the villagers to gather in funds from amongst themselves, their neighbours, and with luck the passer-by. Perhaps after many hours of effort in arranging and carrying out the day's programme, the profits may be small. But it is by these means that the parish-ioners—not all of them worshippers—are able to keep their old church in being.

The visitor to an old parish church may see for himself what needs to be done. As he searches for breaks in the level of a plinth let him take note that he is being hindered in his search by an over-growth of vegetation which will cost money to eradicate. When he has noted with interest a settlement crack which indicates some change in the span of an arch the stability of which has as a result been threatened by centuries of cumulative strain . . . let him go on to wonder whether the rector has noticed it and whether such a small parish will be able to find the cost of restoring the situation.

The day is past when the study of old buildings was being considered only in the light of their aesthetic interest. It behoves the architectural historian of today to note the construction of a building and then go further to appreciate it as a living structure. He should teach himself to sympathize with the problems it encounters with the passing years. For someone has to, or there will be no more old buildings.

Very few of the guardians of our old parish churches are really amateurs of architecture. They simply have to try to keep their charges going. Their ignorance is an unfortunate handicap, and indeed traps them into situations which need never have been encountered.

They are actually helped in no small degree by the fact that the wilful jerry-builder was unknown in medieval days. Moreover his materials were natural and not synthetic, had been well tested by time, and could last for ever if given proper care. Their great enemy was the climate, especially the humidity due to too much rain and too little sunshine to dry things out quickly before deterioration begins.

There is an ancient saying concerning 'cob', that now-forgotten material of which so many houses have been built, to stand today after perhaps two centuries. It is said that all cob needs to stand for ever is a good hat and a good pair of shoes. This means that if you can keep the damp from rising through it and seeping down into it from above there need be no other reason for it to deteriorate.

Settlements due to foundation failure or structural thrusts excepted, the same saying could be applied to any wall of rubble, masonry, or timber.

Of the two deficiencies mentioned, the most serious would be absence of footgear. For while a wall might take some time to deteriorate downwards, let its base begin to disintegrate unchecked and its doom is sealed.

Some of the troubles of an old parish church are of a nature very easy to detect and remedy. Of these, the encroachment of vegetation around the base of the walls constitutes an assault which can hardly escape notice and which is easily remedied without expert assistance. A jungle of this sort keeps the base of the wall wet, prevents its drying out and leads dampness into the interior of the building.

Sometimes the encumbrance reaches a stage where the actual material of the walling is being attacked and its jointing being gouged out. Ivy is the great enemy in this respect as its sap will actually dissolve the mortar. Every scrap of ivy should be removed from walling and its roots treated with corrosive.

Another protection against damp walls is the ground gutter, often formed in brick, run at the base of the walling and drained by short lengths of pipe. Far too many of these gutters are allowed to deteriorate and become smothered with vegetation.

The graveyards surrounding many old parish churches have risen through the centuries until the lower part of the church walling, through which it needs to 'breathe', has become buried deep in the ground. Conservers of the last century often excavated a trench called a 'dry area' round the church to remedy this, but in many cases the purpose of this feature has been forgotten and it has been allowed to fill up.

So much for the 'shoes'. The 'hat' is more difficult. A most common source of trouble, however, is the rusting away of eaves, gutters and down-pipes for lack of paint, a defect which should be easily detectable and soon remedied. The inside of the gutter must not be overlooked.

In addition to the problems presented by the protection of the tops and bases of walling, one has to keep the wall-faces sealed against driving rain which in winter will freeze in the joints and burst the wall-faces asunder. A little attention with the pointing-trowel—neatly done so as not to offend the masons of old—will keep the wall-faces sound for ever.

In Chapter 12 the writer called attention to the disastrous aesthetic results of covering church walling with Portland cement rendering. Apart from its dead colour, it has no texture of its own, and will never weather, as other renderings do, by growing algae. Roman cement is nowadays difficult to procure, but an admixture of lime with the Portland cement will help to improve the colour to some small extent. The 'pebble-dash' used by the builders of cheap houses does help to give the rendering a texture but this is quite foreign to any existing in historical days. The stuff used during the eighteenth century was road grit washed by rain into the sides of the water-bound turnpike roads of the period. Today one can make do with crushed stone chippings, but these should not be larger than three-sixteenths of an inch in gauge.

The proper way to deal with damp walling is to remove internal plaster, apply a bituminous membrane, and re-plaster. But external rendering has a tradition behind it and is acceptable provided it be done with care for its appearance.

The most important part of the head-covering of church walling is of course the roof. While leaks in this may appear here and there above the building, the accumulation of stormwater is at the eaves, so that it is the walling, concealed from view, which bears the brunt of any seepage. Tiles of stone or burnt clay form a very good covering, but the iron nails which hold them to their battens, or the battens to the rafters, will not last for ever. The day comes when sagging lines appearing in the tiling indicate that the roof is due for re-covering if a tile-slide into the churchyard is to be prevented. But for the time being the annual replacement of missing and broken tiles costs little enough and keeps the 'hat' sound.

In this connection the writer would like to call attention to the insensitive way in which some church roofs are being patched. It is not so difficult to obtain second-hand old tiles. If however concrete tiles have to be used, they should be collected in at least two, preferably three, tones, approximately similar and mixed together before laying. A square patch of brown concrete tiles staring from the most prominent part of an old church does little to assist its aesthetic presentation.

Many post-medieval churches, and some ancient ones, have roofs covered with blue-grey Welsh slates. The traditional method for replacing slates is to hook the new one over its batten with a lead clip. The weight of the slate, however, opens out the soft lead clip and down it slides once more. Stout copper wire makes a much more reliable clip.

Churches with lead roofs have the best covering. But even lead will not last for ever. If the pitch is too steep the lead sheets will creep and slip. Over-large sheets will split themselves with the seasonal changes of temperature. The 'welts' joining the sides of sheets will crack. Spalls of stone will fall from the tower and hole them, and a lead sheet once broken can never be satisfactorily repaired, certainly not by solder which has a different coefficient of expansion. (Lead-burning was until recently believed to be the answer, but even this is now found to place too great a strain upon this somewhat pernickety material.) And lead eventually oxidises and loses its pliability, so that then there is nothing for it but removal and replacement.

Medieval lead was laid in much heavier sheets than are used today. It contained a certain amount of silver, and was more valuable than modern lead. It used to be possible to re-cover an old church for the salvage value of the old lead. Even today this asset must not be disregarded by those faced with the renewal of old lead roofs.

One occasionally sees preserved in some part of the church lead panels containing inscriptions recording a date and the names of two churchwardens. Such panels were cast into lead sheet at the time when a roof was being re-covered and were salvaged and preserved with the next re-covering.

The earliest dates are usually mid-eighteenth century and continue at intervals as successive parts of the church were dealt with. It would be interesting to know whether these dates represent replacements of the original lead of perhaps the fourteenth century, implying that this may have lasted for four centuries. Nineteenth-century lead is not lasting for half as long.

An important part of the leadwork of a roof is its gutters, for these collect the whole of its stormwater and quite a small fracture may discharge a large proportion of this into the building or its walling. Such gutters need to be constantly inspected, kept clean and examined for cracks. And cracked lengths should be replaced, and not patched with solder or asphalt.

The damage which can often be traced to a leaking gutter can be desperate indeed. The ends of main roofing beams or the feet of magnificent trusses can rot away unseen within their walls. The repair of such features is expensive, difficult, and frequently necessitates complete replacement. So watch the gutters!

A nice damp beam makes a desirable situation in which to found a colony of that scourge of old buildings, the death-watch beetle. This destructive creature has increased its depredations a hundred-fold since the fumes from oil-lighting were banished from the high crannies of the ancient roofs. Disinfestation is nowadays possible, but requires a desperate amount of scraping away of ruined timber before the beetle can be reached and destroyed.

The ironwork of doors, also—some of it maybe eight centuries old—is worth a dab of paint now and then. And the doors themselves, especially the unprotected west door, battered by the furies of English winters, will welcome a lick of varnish to bring back life to the grain of their boarding.

There are many qualities of stones. Some weather well, others decay all too soon. Sometimes a stone flakes or 'spalls' through settlement or through being burst by rusted ironwork. It is nowadays far from easy to discover a mason who will cut out and renew the defective stonework in a decent style worthy of an ancient building, but they may yet be found. Dabbing with cement looks squalid. The hard synthetic application soon pulls away, doing further damage to the old stone as it does so.

The key to the successful maintenance of an old building is found in regular examination—especially of the 'hat' and 'shoes'—followed by immediate repair of any defects discovered. Much can be done by a local builder provided he is willing to take pains not to contribute work of poor standard to that of his predecessors. Masonry work, repairs to glazing, and the renewal of lead roofing are of course the province of the specialist.

It is when structural failure occurs that expert advice has to be called in. The most common trouble is foundation failure. This is often of recent occurrence, as from the digging of graves too close to the building. But many settlements are of long standing and have been very slowly developing as some thrust increases, walling disintegrates, or foundations subside.

The bonding system with which all walling is constructed enables any length of wall to carry the walling above it in a line of about forty-five degrees outwards from any point. Thus any diagonal crack indicates that the part of the wall below the crack is sinking. Vertical cracks denote not sinking but a tearing sideways about the line of the crack, as in toppling, or the breaking of a joint between two walls. It is interesting to find that the earthquake damaged buildings round Peldon in Essex show plenty of such cracks.

To deal with major structural disasters such as the disintegration of walls or the threatened collapse of roofs through rot or the depredations of the beetle, it is necessary to call in an architect. Foundations may be underpinned, loose walling may be 'grouted'. But once a large timber beam has been deprived of its bearing on the wall it may be almost beyond human aid.

So, guardians of old parish churches . . . look to your lead!

Returning from roofs to walls, we shall find one of the most troublesome items in the equipment of the medieval church and probably the most expensive to deal with is its fenestration.

The window glazing of a church needs care and attention, for the lead 'calms' perish and the wiring oxidizes so that the whole window becomes loose and subject to damage from tempest. This needs the attention of the expert. But it is a small matter to keep the window ironwork from rusting away by painting it now and then.

Glass does not fulfil to perfection the task of waterproofing openings in external walling, and church glazing is formed of a number of small pieces held together by very slender strips of lead, each panel being sprung into narrow grooves cut into the stone-work and thereafter secured by wire ties to the vertical 'stanchions' and horizontal 'saddle-bars' which together form the window's 'ferramenti'.

A broken piece of glass—or 'quarry'—can easily be inserted by working it carefully into the lead 'calms', but once these become decayed or fractured, repair is impossible without removing the whole panel and laying it on a bench where it can be re-set with new leadwork by a skilled craftsman.

Lead is the most temperamental of metals and any disturbance is apt to cause it to become fatigued. Thus the flapping of a loose panel of glazing may start the disintegration of its glazing through the decay of its leading. The sound of a window giving to the wind is an indication that its security is threatened and that immediate attention must be given to its wire ties.

Ferramenti rust and need permanent protection by paint. If the rust reaches the ironwork embedded in the window surround it will split the stonework and thus become a source of extremely costly masonry repairs.

The most troublesome part of the fenestration of a church is its movable ventilators. One sees them rusted into immobility and letting in the winter tempests as well as the fresh airs of summer. They should always be kept rust-free and painted, their hinges and pulleys oiled, and their cordage intact and ready for instant use. Such maintenance as this is very undemanding and is a great help to the comfort of the congregation as well as eliminating those telltale stains which mar the decoration of the wall below the window-sill.

Stained glass, even though it should be of nineteenth-century origin, is an important part of the ornament of a church and is nearly always a memorial to some benefactor. While some of the designs may be regrettable, for the most part it represents the skill and devotion of some craftsman and should not be lightly torn out and replaced by plain domestic glazing introduced on the plea of improving the natural lighting of the building. It must be confessed, however, that heavily-pigmented Victorian glass in the clearstory windows of a tall church covered by a fine ceiling often conceals much of its carved detail, an aesthetic disadvantage which cannot but be deplored. The removal of such semi-opaque glazing can have dramatic results by abolishing the lowering shadows and providing the building with a glorious canopy soaring above its paving and emphasizing its true height.

The coloured glass filling the large traceried windows of the High Gothic was intended to provide a religious picture-book. The work was carefully detailed and produced a jewelled effect which can still be enjoyed at Fairford in Gloucestershire. But the religious bigotry of the seventeenth century swept away most of our medieval glass. What remains of eighteenth- and early-nineteenth-century glass shows it to have been of considerable aesthetic value, the pictures based on the masterly achievements of the contemporary painter and set out in large pieces of material so as to break up the scene as little as possible. Most of this Renaissance glass was removed at the Gothic Revival. The Victorian glaziers aimed at re-creating the medieval effect but traditional skill having been long forgotten there were no longer men capable of the work. The result was for the most part amateurish, in colouring either gaudy or drab, and quite unlike the gentle but brilliant glass of Gothic days. During the last fifty years an inevitable reaction has introduced pallid sub-aqueous treatments, less obstructive to light but lacking all the ancient warmth and liveliness.

Coloured glazing for a large Gothic window is nowadays a costly venture. But the writer has noticed how the charm of some small churches has been curiously enhanced by the introduction of plain coloured glass in a small window, especially if it should be near the altar where one's attention is naturally focused. Sunlight is not as golden as the poets would have us believe, but it can be lent a golden radiance from carefully-selected glass, so that the light may bring with it not the hard sheen of metallic gold nor the synthetic pigment of aureolin but something more resembling the natural glow of lichen on weathered stone.

A good deal of thought is being given today to the subject of how to brighten our churches by the development of more open planning (to say nothing of 'hotting up' services by introducing 'pop' accompaniment!). But so many of our village churches could be relieved of dreariness by giving a thought to their interior decoration. So many splendidly-proportioned buildings—austere perhaps for lack of architectural ornament—could come into their own for the cost of a couple of coats of distemper.

There is no need to invite glare by thrusting out the painted glass which, however indifferent its artistic value might appear to the cognoscenti, has been for so long a treasured feature in the life of a village church.

Light can enter in the train of the distemper brush.

20

Churches in Dissolution

———

Throughout the length and breadth of the land the parishes stoutly maintain the struggle to keep their old churches sound and watertight.

But what of the churches which have seen their parishes fade into history and no longer have priest or congregation to fill them and maintain their structures?

What happens to them?

As a small boy the writer was familiar with an ancient church in Buckinghamshire which had been abandoned by its parishioners for a new church and left in the fields to decay. Beyond its twelfth-century chancel arch it was still roofed, but over the nave only bare timbers remained; through them one could watch the clouds racing past a tall tower of the seventeenth century. The doors were open and the interior had become squalid with the debris of decay. A few years ago he visited it again to find it gone, smothered in a brake of brambles through which here and there an ancient stone remained to testify that here was once a parish church. Upon inquiry he found that some adventurous child had fallen to its death from the tower. So the Army had been called in to demolish the whole building as a military exercise.

There is something disreputable about this history. The church had undoubtedly become, in the modern phrase, redundant. So, like a regiment abandoning a temporary war-time cantonment, its parishioners had just walked out of it and left it, after perhaps a thousand years, to sink into squalor and in the end fall a victim to the breakers.

The writer has seen a number of derelict churches. Most counties can show them. Some of them have had their doors only recently closed for the last time while others have gaping roofs and pewing befouled. And some have become heaps of stones from which rotting beams protrude while they wait for bramble and briar-rose to give them decent interment.

Sometimes the situation results from a temporary breakdown in parochial organization due to the presence of an unsatisfactory incumbent or even a protracted period of sequestration during which the parish has lacked a priest. And without regular maintenance, especially of roofs, an ancient building can quickly reach a condition when repair becomes costly indeed.

Neglect the structure of an ancient building, and decay will creep in and flourish with increasing speed until a day comes when the situation suddenly bursts into crisis. It may be that insurers will no longer accept the building and closure becomes essential. With neglect broadened by this, the time is not far distant when the parish church becomes officially a 'dangerous structure', unapproachable and possibly even meriting demolition.

The devotion with which some sparsely-populated parishes will strive to preserve an ancient church the upkeep of which is quite beyond their means is well known. But the time may come when even such gallant communities have to give up the struggle and decay begins to get out of control.

Some of the most beautiful of the High Gothic parish churches are to be found in areas of the country that were once wealthy from the proceeds of a flourishing wool trade which financed their erection, areas now given over to mechanized agriculture and no longer able to support a large rural population. Such parishes are sometimes grouped together as many as four to one priest, who may in consequence have a number of magnificent buildings to try to maintain with the help of a population scattered over a few farms.

There are places in this country where the parish has not just moved its population to a new site but has vanished completely, so that the old parish church has literally no one at all to care for it. That such churches could ever be used again would seem inconceivable (though one such, at Chingford in Essex, was rescued from roofless ruin and restored to full use with the expansion of the town).

Some parish churches which have lost their villages through changes in rural circumstances have long been maintained by farming squires, against the day when their heirs, plundered through death-duties, will have to abandon the old buildings to inevitable ruin.

Was it proper that an architectural and historical monument such as an old parish church should have been allowed to sink into a state of squalor until in the end it became a dangerous structure and had to be, with its architectural treasures and its memorials of village history, summarily destroyed.

Many persons in this country have fought for years to preserve from dissolution some of the finer of our old parish churches. But the struggle may in some cases have become hopeless. In the end it has been necessary to make a cold-blooded survey of the whole situation and decide upon a workable policy for the country's architectural treasures. This policy will need to be more honestly administered than that which obtains at the moment for secular buildings, where attempts at preservation may be countered by delaying tactics while the structure concerned decays into a state where it is no longer capable of being restored.

There are possibly cases where an old parish church is passing through a bad period in its history and must wait for a new incumbent or a more enthusiastic congregation—who need not necessarily be regular worshippers to take a pride in their parish church. But amongst the thousands of old churches in this country there may well be scores which have indisputably reached the end of their history and if merely abandoned will simply slide into squalor, desecration and miserable decay.

The problem of redundant churches is at last being given authoritative consideration under the provisions of a new Pastoral Measure creating an Advisory Panel which will investigate the architectural merits of a church threatened with closure, and suggest what might be done to preserve the building, in whole or in part 'in the interests of the nation'. A Redundant Churches

Fund is to be created. An authoritative body such as this has long been needed and it is to be hoped that with its support the Diocesan Authorities will at last feel able to cope with the agonizing problem of the derelict churches of England.

Many of these buildings will contain features which are not only of considerable historic and aesthetic interest but may be of material use elsewhere. Furniture such as pews or screens might be acceptable to the congregations of other churches, especially those in the old Dominions or even the U.S.A. Better export than oblivion. Bells would certainly be welcome. Fonts also might take their history with them to other lands.

Many old churches suffer aesthetically from a lack of atmosphere owing to the absence of features of interest normally found in an old church. This is often due to a too drastic tidying-up during some 'restoration'. Valuable monuments such as medieval tombs or particularly fine Renaissance monuments, instead of being allowed to decay, might be moved to neighbouring parishes glad to add to the interest of their churches by preserving them. It is pleasant to record that the medieval effigies of Imber Church in Wiltshire, its parishioners driven from their homes by the Ministry of Defence, have been given a new home in neighbouring Edington.

While items of furniture such as these, however, may easily be transferred from one building to another, the greatest care is essential when performing the same operation with features belonging to the sphere of architecture. For the danger lies in creating the impression of a *museum* of architecture. Thus any item, such as an arch or doorway, transferred from its original site to a strange home, must be given an appropriate setting. This does not imply that a medieval setting must be created for it, but simply that it must be accorded the courtesy of an atmosphere suited to its age and dignity. Any sensitive architect should be able to achieve this by using materials appropriate, by virtue of their colour, texture or finish, for association with the transferred feature. It is the achievement of atmosphere, not the accuracy of detailing, which should in such circumstances be the consideration of the architect.

Thus if an old parish church were to be officially declared redundant and an order for its closure issued by authority, the first stage in its dissolution would be the rescue of its treasures.

We shall then have to consider the actual building. It is to be hoped that its windows contain no valuable old glass, but any which may exist would have to be extracted and found a new resting place. Not long ago, the Dean of York asked that any persons investigating the sites of Cistercian abbeys in Yorkshire should send him any fragments of old glass they might come across. From the pieces he received he fashioned a window in his Minster.

All roofing materials are valuable. The restorers of old buildings are always seeking tiles of clay or stone and will pay good prices for them. Lead, of course, is readily saleable for melting down and casting anew. Thus an old church in dissolution can itself provide some of the funds needed for a possible preservation as a monument.

In the middle of the last century a Wiltshire rector was waiting for a train on an East Anglian platform and became interested in some medieval timbers stacked there. Finding that they represented the roof timbers of the refectory of a local Friary which had just been pulled down, he decided to buy them, reconstruct the roof, and build under it a new church for his parish. At the Dissolution of the great monasteries a number of parish churches were able to employ salvaged roofs when enlarging their own accommodation. The roofs of dissolved parish churches might well be transferred to other buildings, endowing them with an architectural splendour no longer available by any other means.

Even the lesser timbers of belfries and porches might be salvaged and passed to persons only too glad to make use of them in houses undergoing restoration.

With all furnishings and perishable structure removed the old church will become a shell of masonry which is capable of being preserved as an ecclesiastical monument in the same fashion as a ruined abbey or medieval castle.

There are architects, especially those working for the Ministry of Works, who are nowadays quite expert in the treatment of such ruins. The parish-less church of Knowlton in Dorset has been preserved as an ecclesiastical monument by this Ministry.

It is of course essential to aim at the creation of a structure which will require the minimum of maintenance. Stone is a permanent building material but when it is set in mortar to form a wall the result is not immune from disintegration. Thus it is essential to point the wall-faces against the depredations of frost. Most important of all are the tops of the walls upon which rain falls and freezes. A layer of asphalt will provide a permanent waterproof cap.

Architectural detail cannot always be preserved in a ruin unless a certain amount of periodic maintenance can be envisaged. Thus the window tracery might have to be sacrificed; the dressed openings will stand firm enough without it. Parapets, especially if they should be elaborate, might have to be removed to enable the wall-tops to be waterproofed and save the scaffolding without which such high places remain inaccessible. Any delicate ornament, such as pinnacles, which might become loose and dangerous, might have to be sacrificed.

While the loss of such architectural features as parapets and window tracery might be regrettable, the transformation of a derelict parish church into a rural monument might be considered as an alternative to its removal as a dangerous structure or its segregation within a wire fence to rot away into squalor.

Let it rise from the land untroubled by fencing. Its yard can be kept from the plough by mere-stones. Suffer sheep to graze its sward in summer, folded within an electric fence which should give no great trouble to the farmer who will supply it.

Keep weeds away from its walls by sterilization, and touch up its pointing or rendering once in a while. Surely no parish would grudge their ancient church a small annual budget.

There is no building in all England that knows our country and its history so well as a village church. Its lines may have been marked out on the ground at the time when the Greatest Englishman was hammering the Danes at Ethandune eleven centuries ago. Generations of farming squires have knelt in it to bear witness to their Faith.

The Saxon farmer sadly handed it over to the Norman ruffian who as the generations passed became the stern Plantagenet and later, perhaps, crossed with the army to fight at Crecy or Poitiers. The happy breed of the wool-rich yeomen followed in that Merrie England which was later to turn to mourning for Englishmen clubbed to death by neighbours in the Great Rebellion. Then the peaceful era of the Georgian farmers, and the austerity, mellowed by sunny afternoons, of Victorian England.

Behind the squires, as they enter the south door of the parish church, file the whole of Englishry. Ploughmen, herdsmen, smith and miller, and the women who cooked and cleaned, and reared the children who played their games and put away their toys and grew up to make England.

What is so remarkable—moving even—is that they are all still there, every man and woman of them, gathered together within the compass of that small plot . . . for ever.

As you follow the path of the sun along the old processional way round the walls of a village church you may one day catch the mood and begin to realize that a thousand years of England is beside you as you pass.

Should not every old parish church be suffered to sleep out an honourable retirement in the midst of its great congregation, lapped by those friendly pastures which down the long centuries have been its neighbours?

Notes on Plates

Holder of Copyright indicated by italics
N.B.R. National Building Record

1. STOCK. A timber church of the twelfth or thirteenth century. Sheathing has probably been renewed many times but original framing remains inside. Structure has been retained to serve as bell-tower to later church, a practice met with elsewhere in stoneless Essex. Note the timber 'broach' or spire. *N.B.R.*

Page 16

2. WEST HANNINGFIELD. An interesting little timber church illustrating the cruciform 'West Byzantine' plan. Probably thirteenth-century framing; sheathing modern. Retained to serve as bell-tower to later church. Note broach. *C. J. Bassham.*

3. BARTON-UPON-HUMBER. Stone tower-nave, probably of the eleventh century. Ornamented with strips of stone arranged to imitate timbering. Note the Byzantine *bifora* windows in each storey, and the entrance doorway west of centre. A small 'west nave' remains. The tower has been retained to serve as a bell-tower to the later church. *N.B.R.*

Page 32

4. BREAMORE. A turriform nave probably of the twelfth century. The chancel has been rebuilt but the southernmost 'wing' can be seen, and the long 'west nave'. Note the fourteenth-century 'reticulated' east window. *N.B.R.*

5. WORTH. A fine 'pseudo-cruciform' church of the eleventh century, having the chancel arch and those leading into the 'wings' of unusually wide span but very crudely fashioned. *N.B.R.*

Page 84

6. WORTH. Typical 'pseudo-cruciform' church of the eleventh century but with unusually long aspidal chancel, possibly a successor to the original. A late Gothic window has been inserted in the south wing. Note the stone strip ornament representing timber posts and the Byzantine *bifora* lighting the nave. *N.B.R.*

7. HEATH. A twelfth-century church set out on the simple 'Celtic' plan of nave and chancel. Compare the rough rubble walling with the freestone 'dressings'. Note the 'clasping' pilasters at the angles and the provision for belfry openings in the apex of the west gable. *F. C. Morgan.* *Page 92*

8. IFFLEY. A twelfth-century church built on the so-called 'axial' plan in which the tower-nave has been retained as the nucleus of the design and the 'west nave' enlarged to medieval proportions. Beyond the tower is the small chancel. Note the slender angle-shafts beside the tower windows and rising up the angle of the clasping pilaster at the west end. The large buttresses are additions. *N.B.R.*

9. WHAPLODE. A twelfth-century interior illustrating the more massive 'Anglian' type of design. Note the heavy 'Doric' type of cap and its development into the 'coniferous' form. A typical twelfth-century 'impost moulding' crowns each cap. Note the early clearstory beyond. *Rev. Maurice Ridgway.* *Page 100*

10. STAPLEFORD. A twelfth-century arcade richly ornamented with zigzag and other repetitive elements. The pillars are of the circular 'Romanesque' type common to the Midland and Western regions. Their caps are based on the Corinthian and have bells tending towards the concave. Note the carved 'dripstone' band passing above the arches, embellished with an unusually early representation if the 'dog-tooth' ornament. *Bernard White.*

11. UFFINGTON. A cruciform church of the thirteenth century, possibly an attempt to emulate the form of a small monastic church. Note the chapel projecting from the east wall of the

transept. The octagonal tower was probably so transformed to facilitate the construction of a broach. Note the forms of the embryo 'buttresses', especially at the angles, and the fine 'reticulated' window inserted during the fourteenth century to improve the lighting at the chancel arch. *N.B.R.*

Page 108

12. AMESBURY. A fine 'crossing' beneath a thirteenth-century central tower. Note how the compound piers are assembled. *Bernard White.*

13. STOKE GOLDING. A fine medieval arcade of the period when the early-medieval style of the thirteenth century, with its deeply-undercut mouldings, was turning towards the more restrained profiles of the High Gothic. The 'botanical' caps, with their impost mouldings formed of broken rolls, are typical of the fourteenth century. The pillars are seen as a compromise between the shafted early-medieval type and the plainer 'cruciform' of the High Gothic. *N.B.R.*

Page 116

14. LOWICK. The fully-developed parish church of the High Gothic era with its large windows, in this example displaying 'rectilinear' tracery. Note the large 'wing' or transept provided to widen the nave immediately to the west of the chancel arch. Note the large north chapel flanking the chancel, and the octagonal corona at the summit of the west tower. *Rev. Maurice Ridgway.*

15. WALPOLE ST. PETER. A brilliantly-lit chancel of the High Gothic era displaying the maximum amount of glazing and the minimum of solid supports. Note the reduction in the rise of the arch spanning the east window, clear evidence of concern in the mind of the designer for the proportions of the opening. *N.B.R.*

Page 124

16. CHIVELSTONE. The West-Country 'hall-church' with its nave and aisles independently roofed and the clearstory omitted. Note the arrangement of the tower buttresses and the presentation of the tower-stair as an architectural feature of its southern aspect. *Noel Habgood.*

17. LAVENHAM. One of the finest achievements of the East Anglian parish church architect. Note the brilliance of the fenestration with the clearstory an almost continuous range of glazing. Note the elegance of the tower buttressing, the detail of the parapets, and the carefully-designed façade of the south porch. *Noel Habgood.*

Page 132

18. THAXTED. By the end of the High Gothic era the improvement in roofing systems permitted the provision of very wide aisles. The lead-covered roofs needed so slight a pitch that the undersides of their timbering could be embellished with carving and displayed as a ceiling. Note the carved 'bosses' masking the intersections of the timbers. *N.B.R.*

19. SOMERTON. The system of heavy roof trusses which forms the foundation of the High Gothic roof can be seen carrying the pair of longitudinal 'purlins' which in their turn support the rafters in mid-flight. The whole of the exposed timbering is framed together to display a panelled ceiling enriched with superb carving. *N.B.R.* *P. 140*

20. MARCH. Each of the principal trusses of this roof is constructed of an arched collar-beam carried at either end upon a pair of superimposed 'hammer-beams' the ends of which are masked by angels with their wings displayed. A pair of purlins pass along either slope of the roof. The brackets carrying the lowermost hammer-beams are taken down the walls to end in ranges of sculptured figures. *N.B.R.*

21. ST. ENDELLION. A wide-spread 'cradle-roof' of the West Country, formed of a series of primitive 'trussed rafters' strapped together with longitudinal timbers. The church is of the 'hall' type and has no clearstory. *N.B.R.*

Page 148

22. MANATON. One of the West Country's superb rood-screens with its loft over. The delicacy of the woodcarving contrasts effectively with the grim granite architecture. *Rev. Maurice Ridgway.*

23. WOLVERTON. A post-Reformation church, its body trying to recapture something of the liveliness of the medieval, but its tower frankly of the Renaissance. Note the typical windows of the belfry, the emphasis upon the quoins, and the elaborate Classical cornice with its plain parapet above. *N.B.R.*

Page 156

24. NORTH RUNCTON. A post-Reformation interior. Note the simple Classical columns with their rather ingenuous capitals, and the plaster ceiling which has replaced the primitive splendour of medieval joinery. *N.B.R.*

25. BURY. The typical English 'broach' which must have represented the almost universal method of roofing a tower-top prior to the introduction of flat roofs covered with lead sheets. The original sheathing of the broaches would have been of oak shingles. *Noel Habgood.*

Page 180

26. SLAWSTON. The timber broach reproduced in masonry. The dormer windows are interesting features seen in connection with stone spires of all types. *N.B.R.*

27. SOUTHEASE. A bell-tower of early date reproducing the Byzantine campanile. Built, for lack of freestone, in flint nodules, such towers are found in scores throughout stone-less East Anglia. Note the shingled roof. *Noel Habgood.*

Page 188

28. BOSTON. One of England's finest bell-towers, culminating masterpieces of the Gothic Age. Note the large belfry openings, the lofty windows of the ringing floor. In lieu of a stone spire, many of the later Gothic towers were finished with graceful octagonal coronas. *Noel Habgood.*

29. KILPECK. One can study this magnificent example of twelfth-century architecture without exhausting one's interest in the diversity of motifs available in the repertoire of the Anglo-Saxon sculptor. *Noel Habgood.*

Page 196

30. CULLOMPTON. The stone ceiling constructed as a series of cones sweeping fan-wise to meet each other across the span was the final achievement of the Gothic masons and carvers. *Rev. Sumner.*

31. The sizes of stones, and their proportions, are a help with dating. In the pre-medieval period stones were small and nearly square, probably for carrying in panniers attached to pack-saddles. In the early-medieval they were slightly larger and very neat and regular, generally about twice as long as they were high. In the High Gothic era stones were often much larger and very long on the bed, transported on sledges drawn by ponies. *Author.*

Page 204

32. The marks left on the faces of stones by the tools used by the masons are a help in dating. Pre-medieval stones have their faces roughly hacked with the heavy stone axe which left coarse diagonal scars cut irregularly into the face. The 'bolster' tooling of the early-medieval period was very carefully executed, the marks are neat and regular and always vertical. During the High Gothic period much less care was taken; the tooling was run diagonally across the face and no longer regarded as a decorative finish. *Miss P. Wynn Reeves.*

Glossary

abacus: uppermost member of a Classical capital

aedicule: a miniature reproduction of a structural feature used for ornamental purposes

apse: semicircular—or in some cases polygonal—end to a building

arcade: a row of arches

architrave: lowermost member of a Classical entablature (q.v.)

ashlar: freestone employed in thin slabs as a facing

aumbry: small cupboard in wall beside altar

baluster: miniature column of bulbous form supporting handrail of balustrade

banker: stone bench upon which a mason dresses stone

battlement: crenellated parapet alternating embrasures or 'crenels' with 'merlons' (q.v.)

bay: longitudinal division of a building

bell: spreading portion of capital (see also 'echinus')

'bifora': two-light Byzantine window

bolster: broad chisel used by masons

bond: method of arranging joints in walling so that no two appear immediately above each other

brace: a timber stiffener under tension

brattice: a boarded partition

broach: a spit, the medieval word for spire

buttress: masonry support against overturning pressure upon a wall

calm: lead strip holding window glass: pronounced 'came'

centering: temporary framework upon which an arch is turned *chamfer:* a bevelled edge

clearstory: a tier of small windows lighting the upper part of a building

collar: short timber tying a pair of rafters together near apex

coniferous capital: one having its bell fashioned to resemble a row of cones point-downwards

corbel: a stone bracket

corbel-table: a row of corbels carrying a tablement (q.v.)

core: the inner part of a masonry wall

cornice: the upper—projecting—part of a Classical entablature (q.v.) used in Renaissance architecture as a crowning feature

couple: a pair of rafters joined at the apex

course: layer of stones in masonry

cove: broad concave moulding

crocket: Gothic volute (q.v.) seen on sides of pinnacles, spires etc.

crossing: space under a central tower

cruciform: a church having a central tower flanked by transepts

cubiform capital: cushion (q.v.) having its angles cut away to reduce projection

cushion capital: Byzantine version of the Doric capital resembling half a domestic cushion

cusp: triangular tooth separating the 'foils' (q.v.) in Gothic tracery

dormer: window through a roof

dressings: dressed stone used in walling for lining openings and forming angles. Any worked stone as opposed to rubble

drip-stone: projecting stone band over window to prevent storm-water from wall overrunning down glazing

duplex bay: bay system having intermediate supports to main ones, often represented in English architecture by alternating character of supports in an arcade

eaves: the roof projecting over the wall-face

echinus: the projecting part, or 'bell', of the Classical capital

entablature: the principal feature of Classical architecture spanning the columns *fan vault:* late-Gothic vault elaborately designed as a series of stone fans

flushwork: an East Anglian form of walling appearing as a pattern of stone tracery filled with knapped flint

flying buttress: an arch carrying a thrust from a wall over to an isolated buttress

foliated: having a silhouette divided into a series of 'foils' by cusps (q.v.)

freestone: stone—properly speaking limestone—capable of being dressed by a mason

frieze: the middle or flat portion of a Classical entablature (q.v.)

gablet: a small gable

gargoyle: water-spout draining gutter, usually carved as a grotesque

groin: in early vaulting, line where two vaults meet

hammer-beam: end of a beam carried by a timber bracket from wall after middle of beam has been cut away

header: brick showing endways in a wall

hood-mould: similar to a drip-stone (q.v.)

impost: springing line of arch, usually indicated by a moulded band

jamb: side of a door opening

king-post: central feature of a roof-truss (see truss)

lantern: central tower carried above surrounding roofs and there provided with windows for lighting crossing below

lierne: short decorative rib in Gothic vaulting

lights: the divisions of a window

lintel: horizontal beam bridging an opening

lodge: a lean-to structure, especially that occupied by masons

masonry: dressed stonework laid in courses, or any other dressed stonework

Glossary

merlon: the projecting portion of a battlemented parapet separating the embrasures. In medieval times 'cop'

moulding: running ornament formed of continuous lines of rolls and channels

mullion: vertical stone member separating lights in a window

ogee: a double curve

order: a line of voussoirs (q.v.) in an arch carrying another over it

parclose: screen filling an arch and enclosing a chapel

pediment: a low-pitched triangular feature, the Renaissance version of the medieval gable

pier: an isolated mass of masonry carrying an arch

pilaster: a half-pier projecting from a wall, usually employed for decorative purposes

pillar: a slender support

piscina: stone basin set in walling on south side of altar for washing sacred vessels

pitch: angle of roof with horizontal

plaster: lime mortar used to cover a wall or ceiling

plate: horizontal timber carrying rafters on wall-top

pole: unit of measurement, originally sixteen feet

pseudo-cruciform: early type of church with wings or transept but no central tower

purlin: horizontal roof-timber passing between trusses (q.v.) to help support rafters

quarry: diamond-shaped piece of glass

queen-posts: pairs of posts forming features of trusses

quoin: angle-stone

rafter: sloping roof-timber carrying roof covering

relieving arch: arch set in walling above an opening to relieve pressure on its lintel

rere arch: arch carrying core of wall over an opening

respond: end of an arcade or jamb of single arch

reticulated: window tracery arranged like the meshes of a net *reveal:* an opening through a wall

ribs: slender members carrying a stone vault

ridge: apex of a roof

rood-beam: beam passing across church at chancel arch carrying crucifix or 'rood'

rood-loft: gallery above rood-screen

rood-screen: screen passing across church at chancel arch

rood-stair: stairs giving access to rood-loft

rubble: rough stone, undressed

saddle-bar: horizontal iron bar set in window as an anchorage for glazing

saltire: the diagonal cross formed by two timbers passing each other ✕

sanctuary: the part of the chancel containing the altar

scalloped capital: capital having its bell grooved in crude imitation of Corinthian capital

scoinson arch: arch carrying inner face of wall over opening

sedilla: stone seats set in walling on south side of chancel

shaft: diminutive of column

shingle: wooden tile for roofing

sill: horizontal timber of stone at base or feature

six-poster: timber church featuring six posts instead of the more usual four

sleeper: horizontal timber carrying posts

soffit: the underside of a feature, such as an arch

solar: an upper floor

spall: flake split from stone

spandrel: triangular space between arch and rectangular surround

squinch: an arch crossing an internal angle diagonally

stanchion: vertical iron bar in a window

steeple: the medieval word for a church tower; Renaissance spire

stoup: basin for holy water

stretcher: brick lying lengthways in a wall

string-course: horizontal moulding used for punctuation and for linking features together

strut: timber stiffener in compression

Glossary

tablement: medieval word for system of horizontal 'planks' of timber or stone. The tablement is the plinth

tail: rough end of stone buried in wall

teazle post: post set root-upwards so that thick butt end may be used to seat beams

template: a profile for a moulding

tie-beam: heavy horizontal beam first used for tying plates (q.v.) together, later the foundation member of a roof-truss

torus: projecting rounded moulding. Today 'bull-nose'

tracery: the system of bars in a Gothic window, also in wall decoration

transept: a lateral projection from a central tower, or a central area, usually one of a pair. Wider than a 'wing' (q.v.)

transom: horizontal member of window tracery

truss: system of timbering spanning church and carrying purlins (q.v.)

tympanum: space between lintel and relieving arch over

vault: stone ceiling

volute: angle projections of Corinthian capital; in Gothic becomes a 'crocket'

voussoirs: the wedge-shaped stones which make up an arch

wainscot: boarded ceiling

wind-bracing: system of timber arches beneath roof purlins (q.v.) to prevent roof from becoming distorted from wind-pressure upon ends

wing (ala): a small projection from the eastern end of the side wall of the nave

Index

A NECESSARY END

A NECESSARY END

J. M. Gregson

This first world edition published 2014
in Great Britain and 2015 in the USA by
SEVERN HOUSE PUBLISHERS LTD of
19 Cedar Road, Sutton, Surrey, England, SM2 5DA.
Trade paperback edition first published
in Great Britain and the USA 2015 by
SEVERN HOUSE PUBLISHERS LTD.

Gregson, J. M. author.
  A necessary end.–(A Percy Peach mystery)
  1. Peach, Percy (Fictitious character)–Fiction.
  2. Murder–Investigation–Fiction. 3. Police–England–
  Lancashire–Fiction. 4. Detective and mystery stories.
  I. Title II. Series
  823.9'14-dc23

ISBN-13: 978-07278-8441-1(cased)
ISBN-13: 978-1-84751-548-3 (trade paper)
ISBN-13: 978-1-78010-591-8 (e-book)

All Severn House titles are printed on acid-free paper.

Severn House Publishers support the Forest Stewardship Council™ [FSC™],
the leading international forest certification organisation. All our titles that
are printed on FSC certified paper carry the FSC logo.

Typeset by Palimpsest Book Production Ltd.,
Falkirk, Stirlingshire, Scotland.
Printed and bound in Great Britain by
TJ International, Padstow, Cornwall.

To Ellie, a young lady who reads much and will eventually go far.

It seems to me most strange that men should fear;
Seeing that death, a necessary end,
Will come when it will come.

Julius Caesar

ONE

E nid Frott needed to be in charge of something. She was
that sort of woman.

She hadn't admitted that to herself yet, though. She
was still constantly telling herself that you couldn't expect things
to be the same, once you'd retired. You needed to make adjust-
ments. You needed to slow down a little and create a different
way of life for yourself. You had plenty of interests, hadn't you?
You weren't stupid and you were well capable of making the
necessary adaptations to your lifestyle. Surely you'd thoroughly
enjoy the process, if you gave yourself a little time. You should
expect it to take time. Everyone said that, didn't they? You
couldn't expect to settle into the joys of retirement overnight.

It was three months now and time didn't seem to be helping
her much. Enid had always been contemptuous of clichés – lazy
thinking, in Miss Frott's view – but time was hanging heavily
on her hands. She couldn't think of a better way to put it, when
she looked the situation in the face. And she'd always made a
point of confronting things head-on. Anything else was a cop
out. Another damned cliché – or was it an Americanism? Perhaps
her mind was slowing up, as some people said minds did in
retirement. But no, she wasn't having that. Not at sixty-three.
Perhaps she should have insisted on staying on at work. But
she'd been too proud for that. She wasn't going to hang around
where she wasn't wanted.

Enid glanced at her watch. Time she was moving on. Twenty
minutes was quite long enough for a cup of coffee. When she'd
been working, she'd taken her coffee on the hoof, as often as
not. She'd liked to set an example to the girls in the office. You
could ask more of them when you didn't spare yourself. Flying
Frotty, they'd called her, when they'd thought she couldn't hear;
she'd heard them all right, but never reacted. Quite a flattering
nickname really, on balance. No one had ever accused her of
being lazy or incompetent.

It was quite pleasant up here after the chaos below. Good idea for the store to have its café on the top floor, away from the maelstrom of Christmas shoppers. She wouldn't have minded another few minutes at her table in the corner here, if she'd had something to read. Her own fault, that: she should have shoved a book into her bag. She enjoyed her own company, but she'd never been a great people-watcher.

There were a lot of people waiting at the lift, but she chose to walk past them and then down the stairs to the toy department. Good exercise. Excellent for the knees, her neighbour had said – not that she needed to be thinking about things like that. Not for ten or fifteen years yet. She tripped down the successive flights of stairs quite quickly and was scarcely out of breath at all when she pushed through the door on her chosen floor.

It was even more crowded now than when she had left the department and gone for coffee. She was trying to buy presents for her two great-nephews. Books would have been the thing, in her view. Educational as well as enjoyable, and a source of lasting joy if you chose the right ones. But she wasn't quite sure what was appropriate for boys of eight and six, and the girl on the counter had been totally useless. Better to go to a specialist bookshop if you wanted that sort of advice, the girl had said. She'd spoken as if Enid had been asking for some strange and esoteric novelty, when books should have been a standard purchase.

Her nephew's bitch of a wife had been no help to her, as usual. Computer games were more the thing now, she said patronisingly. She'd spoken as if she didn't expect Enid to understand, when a few months earlier the older woman had been instructing young girls in the mysteries and possibilities of IT in the office. Enid wished she'd had Althea under her control for a month or two there. She'd have had her skipping around and giving respect, not looking at her with that sneer she seemed to reserve for her husband's family.

Charles hadn't been able to offer her much in the way of present suggestions. He seemed content to leave all that sort of thing to his wife. Men were like that. But then it was probably fair enough to put it on Althea, since the bitch seemed determined to stay at home even now that the children were well established at school. Her nephew didn't even know what he wanted for himself. A sweater, Charles had suggested under pressure. But surely he'd need to select that for himself? She'd have to go to M&S. He could take it back himself if it didn't suit. Same for the bitch: whatever Enid bought for her was never acceptable.

She looked at a toy car with batteries for the six-year-old. But she wasn't sure he was the right age for it. And it was ridiculously expensive. She wasn't stingy, but you didn't want to throw money away, not when you were spending sums like this. And Enid wasn't sure what was the right amount to spend. You mustn't spoil children; everyone said that. She'd never had any children of her own and she didn't regret that. Not really. She'd told herself many times over the years that she didn't regret it. You couldn't have everything – well, you could now, but not when she'd started. Kids might have been welcome at one time, but she'd had a long and satisfying career. People should remember that.

Ms Frott took a long, despairing look at the crowds of people milling around the counters on the children's floor and decided to abandon ship. Another cliché, that, but she was fed up with this. She went outside and looked up through the gathering November gloom at the Manchester skyline, or at least at that section of it which she could see. She'd known Market Street and Piccadilly and the other shopping streets around it quite intimately at one time. She could have directed people to the best places to shop. Marshall and Snelgrove for good quality clothes at fair prices. Lewis's for good advice and keen prices on white and electrical goods. Had life really been simpler then, or did it just seem so from the distance of years?

She tried a couple of other shops, but they were even more crowded and people were even more frantic than in the big store she'd just left. A woman who was shouting for the attention of a salesgirl trod on her foot and scarcely bothered to apologise. Enid limped away with a thunderous face and went to queue for the bus to Altrincham. Leave it to Althea to get whatever presents she thought were appropriate, as she'd done last year. Or just give them money, which they seemed to like as much as anything. But that would just 'go towards' some major purchase they were saving for. It didn't give her as much satisfaction as buying a present might have done. As buying a book and seeing them read and enjoy it might have done. She'd do that next year, and bugger the bitch.

It seemed to take much longer to get out of the centre of the city now. It was the same in every conurbation, she supposed, with the traffic as dense as it was nowadays. She was lucky living in Brunton. The traffic was bad enough there, but the population was only a hundred thousand, and you were soon out of the town and into the Ribble Valley. She'd be quite glad to get back to her own comfortable and spacious flat.

They were running into Cheshire now, though you'd scarcely have known it, with the road just as busy and the houses almost as densely packed as ever. Althea always took care to tell people that she lived in Cheshire, not Manchester. Pathetic, really. If you were vulgar you were vulgar, wherever you lived. But jumped-up plebs never realized that.

She went and lay on the bed in her room when she reached her nephew's house. She was surprised how tired she was, and it saved her from making meaningless conversation with the bitch. She got up when she heard the boys come into the house from school. They liked her, in their noisy, boisterous way, and she was surprised how much she liked them and how easy she found it to talk to them. Young Thomas wanted to show her how much his reading had come on and Jason had been awarded a gold star in maths for his facility with fractions. Enid knew all about fractions and was delighted to show him that she wasn't the ignorant old biddy that he'd assumed she was.

She was glad when her nephew Charles got home from work. It was easier to talk to the bitch with him around. To talk to Althea, she told herself firmly: she must give the woman a chance and listen to what she had to say. There was a generation gap between them, that was all. Nothing between them but thirty-odd years, really.

'Aunty Enid had a bad time in town, darling. Didn't manage to get anything she wanted. I expect it was terribly hectic, a month before Christmas.'

She always speaks of me as though I'm not there, as if I

were a backward child, thought Enid. I'm being unfair again. 'I should have made a list of exactly what I wanted before I went. That would have made it much easier. Or shopped in Brunton, perhaps. I know my way around there, and some of the shopkeepers know me. I thought I'd get a better selection of things in Manchester, the way you used to do. But the choice was just the same, really.'

'We find it better to shop online, a lot of the time, don't we, darling? I could easily show you how to do that, Enid. It's much simpler than you'd think.'

'I've done it myself. Quite often, actually. But I like to see exactly what I'm getting, whenever it's possible.' Enid knew that she was tight-lipped, grudging, tense. She didn't want to be, but the bitch always got to her.

The children had left the table now. They'd eaten enough to earn their exit and they'd gone off to watch the telly in the other room. That's what seemed to happen nowadays. Not like when Enid and her brothers were young. You didn't speak until you were spoken to then and it was the adults who conducted the conversation, talking about things you didn't understand and didn't need to understand. It was all different now. The children were asked for their opinions about everything and you couldn't have a decent adult conversation about politics or music or books or anything like that. Probably just as well really: Althea wouldn't have been able to sustain an adult conversation for long.

Now who was being bitchy? Enid Frott hated herself for what she was thinking and tried to banish it, but she knew that she was never going to like this woman. Controlled neutrality would be the best she would ever manage. She said as brightly as she could, 'Would you like me to read the bedtime story to the boys? I could do it separately, if they have different ones now.'

'Oh, I'm not sure they'll have time for stories tonight, Enid. They've got homework to finish. And Jason's reading quite well himself now. He likes to have his own books.'

Enid smiled and nodded, biting back the thought that it was still good for kids to have stories in bed, that they liked being read to even when they could read for themselves. It wasn't her business, was it? And she must respect the views of the parents, who would know their children as she never could. She said carefully, 'I'll need to be off quite early in the morning. But I'll be able to wave goodbye to the boys as they go off to school.'

There was quite a long pause which no one seemed to know how to fill. Then Charles said with a false brightness, 'So how is retirement going, Aunty Enid?'

He'd asked her that before, scarcely twenty-four hours ago. But he meant well, so she mustn't snub him. 'Well enough, I suppose. I've been drawn into all the bridge I can take and I've joined the local branch of NADFAS.' She glanced at Althea's uncomprehending face and explained, 'National Association of Decorative and Fine Arts Societies. Quite a mouthful, really. Some of the men just call it the Fine Farts.' She grinned at Charles and enjoyed the look of shock on his wife's face. 'Takes a bit of time to adjust to life without work, but I'm getting there.'

Her nephew nodded thoughtfully. 'You need something to organize, knowing you, Aunty. You've always loved books and reading, haven't you? Why don't you start a book club and compare notes with other people who also read a lot? I'm sure you'd enjoy that.'

'It might be worth thinking about,' agreed his aunt.

And think about it Enid Frott did, in the days which followed.

TWO

Funerals were strange occasions, Enid Frott thought. When you weren't at the very centre of them, as widows and close relatives were, you could observe funerals and study them as the strange rituals they were. Touching, at times, but strange all the same.

She'd been Frank Burgess's PA for fifteen years, but he'd been eighteen years older than her, so that his death hadn't come as a great surprise. He'd been eighty-one and ailing for some time, and she hadn't seen him in the last few years. As she sat in the back row of the crowded crematorium, she regretted that. Grief was affecting her much more deeply than she would have expected.

Frank hadn't been a religious man, but he was being seen off with a clergyman and hymns. Curious how people lost the courage of their convictions, when it came to the end. She wondered if she would want hymns and prayers and a clergyman uttering pious, conventional thoughts when she went. Emphatically not, she thought: she'd always been a woman who knew her own mind. She'd feel she was losing face, if she didn't carry things through. Then she grinned at herself. What the hell would it matter to her, when she was gone? She wouldn't have any face to lose, would she? She tried not to think of how few people might attend her last rites. Enid dropped her head and studied her order of service sheet assiduously.

'The Lord is my shepherd' was over now; they were listening to the eulogy from one of Frank's sons. She was surprised how much she'd enjoyed singing the hymn. Memories of childhood and youth and that innocent and very different Enid Frott, she supposed. At least today they wouldn't be standing at a graveside in the freezing rain and throwing earth upon the lid of a coffin. She shuddered at the remembrance of her grandmother's and her father's funerals and the dark shadows of the hereafter they had brought to her as a young and impressionable girl.

She felt sorry for the clergyman here, as she had done at her last three funerals. He was a portly, balding man who could have modelled as a medieval monk. He would have fitted in better as a figure of fun than as the person in charge of this solemn procedure. He hadn't known Frank, but he had studied his brief from the family and was emphatically doing his best. The poor man was on a hiding to nothing, in Enid's view. If he spoke convincingly, people would say he had never known Frank and accuse him of hypocrisy. If he was less effusive about the man whose remains lay in the coffin behind him, he would be accused of shallowness and insensitivity to the grief around him.

Enid listened and tried to recognize in the vicar's description the man she had known. It was all a little too bland for her, but that was the way with funerals. You remembered the best in people, and that was probably how it should be. There was enough nastiness in the world, so let a man's life be remembered for half an hour here without bitterness. Good husband and father, good grandfather, ready now to be received into the Kingdom of Heaven, the vicar told them. Amen to that. But there were so few churchgoers among his audience that the vicar had to conclude his prayers with his own 'Amens'.

Ms Frott tried hard to be charitable. The vicar's pious account wasn't describing the man she had known, but this might be just another side of Frank. One man in his life plays many parts, as someone with greater insights than her had remarked. The vicar's version might well be the Frank Burgess that his family had seen and wanted to remember today. And this was their day, above all. Funerals were for those who were still here and living on, not for the man beneath the flowers in the box. The man who had gone before them and was being welcomed by God, as the vicar kept insisting.

They were into the Lord's Prayer now, and Enid voiced it with the vigour which would have been appropriate in a genuine believer. The joy of the familiar, she thought, as the words came ringing back to her from her youth, and with them came the vision of the high stone vaults of the church that she had found so awesome and forbidding as a child. It was curious how things you thought you had forgotten and laid aside many years ago came singing back to you at moments like this.

And then 'Jerusalem' and they were out into the relief of the open air. Frank Burgess would have liked that last hymn. Frank had known a thing or two about dark, Satanic mills and a thing or two about William Blake. And about the mills of God which ground exceeding small. Enid shook hands with the vicar and thanked him for his efforts, even as she decided that Frank Burgess would have given the clergyman short shrift. Which wouldn't have been deserved, because the poor man had been doing his best.

She went and conveyed her sympathy to the widow, who looked older, as was inevitable, but elegant and dignified in black. She'd been younger than Frank: fourteen years younger, if Enid remembered right, which she invariably did. That would make her sixty-seven, and wearing well. A small, illogical piece of Enid Frott's brain resented that.

Other people were giving the widow sympathetic hugs before they moved on to their own conversations and their own cars in the crowded park. Enid decided not to hug. She shook hands with Sharon Burgess and pressed her hand for a couple of seconds. They smiled guardedly at each other and the widow thanked her.

Neither was quite sure of the protocol for widow and former mistress at the conclusion of a funeral service.

Jamie Norris was not pleased with life. His girlfriend had stood him up last night, for the second time in a month.

He wasn't having that. When you were eighteen, you put up with anything, if you wanted a girl enough. It wasn't sensible, because it did you no good and you always came off worst in the end. But you hadn't the sense and the experience to see that, whatever other people told you. You were driven by your urges: you thought about what you had done in bed, and then everything else disappeared into some sort of sexual mist.

But when you were twenty-six and experienced, it was different. You could still be a bit stupid where women were concerned, but you were conscious of the danger. You put up with a certain amount if you really liked a girl, but you knew where to draw the line. And he was drawing the line after last night. Well, he was unless Annie came up with a really good explanation.

He'd been writing a poem for her, too. She'd never know
what she'd missed. He'd worked her name into a couple of the
lines, to make it personal. The sonnet wasn't complete, but he
thought it would really have been quite good if he'd been
allowed to finish it. And it wouldn't do for another girl later:
Annie was quite a difficult name to work into verse, and sonnets
weren't things you could mess about with. 'With which you
could mess about, Jamie,' his teacher would have said, years
ago. He could hear her voice in his head now, silly old bat.

They weren't especially busy in the supermarket today. Tuesday
was a quiet day, and it had been raining earlier. Bigarse would
have him, though, if he caught him slacking. Bigarse despised
poetry, and Jamie despised Bigarse. It didn't help that it was
Jamie who'd christened him that, and that Bigarse suspected it.
He was just looking for an excuse to sack him, and Jamie Norris
knew it. He knew also that he hadn't been here long enough to
give himself any protection against instant dismissal.

He stacked his trolley with tins of baked beans, sighed the
sigh of a much older man, and trundled towards the shelves.
Baked beans always sold steadily and they were on special offer
this week. Packs of four tins for £1.30: you couldn't go far
wrong at that price. Beans might mean Heinz, but they also
meant back-breaking work re-stacking the shelves, as far as
Jamie was concerned. Try making that into an advertising slogan,
you copywriters who sold your souls for money.

Jamie Norris thought sometimes that he should try selling
his soul for money. But he didn't seem to be presented with
many opportunities for merchandising his soul. And his soul
probably wouldn't be worth very much, as he hadn't given it
much attention lately. He decided that he definitely wouldn't
rework that sonnet entitled 'Annie Combing her Hair at the
Mirror' for anyone else, because that would be selling his soul,
even without money changing hands.

There was a sudden scream from the next aisle, out of his
view. Then a woman's voice shouted in anger, and provoked
the repeated screams of a child in tears. He was there in a
moment, taking in what was becoming a familiar scene to him,
even after only three weeks here. A child who was no more
than a toddler had taken a jar out of her mother's trolley and

waved it in her small chubby hand. It had slipped from those weak, unreliable fingers and crashed to pieces on the floor. Jamie shepherded mother and child away from the scene, gave them the routine 'These things happen' and went to fetch brush, mop and bucket.

He cleared the glass carefully, mindful of the health and safety briefing he had been given when he got the job, then slopped plenty of hot water and detergent around to make sure he cleaned the floor thoroughly. Too much water, as it turned out. His mop was too soaked to clear up all the water and he had to seal off the end of the aisle whilst he went for a dry one to complete the job.

He was almost back when there was a roared expletive and a bump which set cans shivering on the shelves around him. An impressive descent, in its own way. Jamie Norris found it even more so when he saw who sat splay-footed on the floor with his head in his hands and his back against the coffee jars on the bottom shelves.

Bigarse. And it was that eponymous section of his anatomy which had hit the floor with such a crash. Nothing was broken – well, there wouldn't be, with upholstery like that to cushion the blow. But a great loss of dignity, and a thunderous expression at the top end to balance the indignity at the bottom. Jamie waved his dry mop apologetically with a sense of impending doom. He strove heroically to control the grin which threatened to spread like warm syrup across his face.

'Oh dear! Are you hurt, sir?'

'Of course I'm bloody hurt, you fu— You young idiot!' Bigarse looked at the rapidly growing ranks of spectators at the end of the aisle and flung out a demanding arm towards his hapless employee. 'Help me up, you damned fool! And then try to explain yourself, if you can!'

There were irreverent titters from the children among his audience as he struggled painfully towards the vertical and clutched with a grimace the place which had borne the impact of the unyielding surface beneath him. The mirth was only ineffectively quelled by the adults who held small hands: modern parents do not share the strong disciplinary tastes of their forbears.

The customers' scarcely concealed amusement did not help Jamie. Bigarse sent him on his way with a torrent of abuse ringing in his ears and an injunction that he should never return. The manager then locked himself in his office to towel down his bruised rear and his bruised ego.

Jamie Norris went back to his bedsit and nursed a sense of grievance far into the evening. Perhaps it was this which prevented him from adding more than two paragraphs to the pages of the novel which had already defied him for almost a year.

At the very moment when the manager of the supermarket was damaging the most notable part of his anatomy, Enid Frott was taking a fateful decision. She had no idea that this had been going to happen. It took her as much by surprise as it did the other person involved.

The reception which followed the funeral service at the crematorium was held at the North Lancashire Golf Club. As was to be expected, the atmosphere was much lighter here than at the crematorium. Too light, Enid thought after a while. There was a buffet ready for the mourners, and most people helped themselves to the attractive selection of sandwiches, savouries and small cakes. They sat with friends, agreed that the earlier ceremony had been conducted with appropriate dignity, commented on the attractiveness of the golf course in the winter sunlight, and relaxed after the seriousness of the earlier part of the day.

People exchanged anecdotes about Frank's exploits on the golf course, where he had apparently been a competitor who gave little quarter but knew how to relax at the nineteenth hole after the game. To Ms Frott, who knew little of golf, the tales grew quickly boring. She smiled as politely as she could and downed rather more wine than she had intended to consume. She noted Frank Burgess's name a couple of times on the honours boards on the walls which recorded successes in various tournaments, but the other names there meant nothing to her.

She had meant to keep well away from Frank's family. That, she was sure, was the tactful policy for an ex-mistress at a funeral. But in an assembly where golf and golfing reminiscence seemed to dominate the conversation, she found herself chatting to two of Frank's grandchildren, the girl who had read a poem at the crematorium and a boy who was plainly more afflicted by his grandfather's death than most people in the room. They were both at university, and both felt that they owed much to Frank's encouragement and support in the last ten years.

'He was a good man, your granddad,' said Enid conventionally. She'd had to make herself use that word and she had to work on her face to deliver it properly. She'd never thought of Frank as a grandfather, not even after their affair was over and she knew she wasn't going to see him again. Unwelcome images of the younger man she had known and of the times they had enjoyed together intruded on her mind now, when she least required them to be there.

As soon as she could, she moved away from these pleasant, vital young people. She couldn't trust herself to deliver anything but the most anodyne sentiments to them, and that would bore them and irritate her. But, turning away from the increasingly noisy groups of golfing men, she found herself instead with the dead man's widow. Out of the frying pan into the fire: this unique day seemed to be a time when only second-hand thoughts and clichés were safe.

Sharon Burgess seemed happier than Enid was to be chatting like this. Could she really be as relaxed as she seemed to be, in these circumstances? For a moment, Enid Frott toyed with the idea that Sharon didn't know about her and Frank. But that was silly. They had both known all about each other when things had come to a head ten years ago. Could she be one of those women who knew that there were other women in her husband's life but chose not to acknowledge the fact? But then Enid noticed that her conversation was all about the trials and rewards of modern life and that Frank was never mentioned. This woman knew how close her marriage had come to being shattered by the woman with whom she was now making civilized conversation.

Sharon seemed genuinely anxious to know how Enid was coping with retirement and what her life was like now as a woman alone in the world. She drew parallels with her own situation as a widow, but Enid knew she was just being kind. Sharon might have lost a husband, but she still had children and grandchildren to occupy her, stretch her, and occasionally spoil her. Maybe Sharon was just being kind to her in suggesting that their lives had many things in common. That thought was surely more bizarre than anything else which had cropped up on this strangest of days.

They looked up the fairway towards distant figures, swinging stiffly as puppets in the early winter twilight. 'You've never taken up golf,' said Sharon.

Enid wasn't sure whether it was a question or a statement. 'No. I didn't feel I had the time when I was working. And to be honest, I've never seen the point.'

'Is there a point to any game, unless you're a professional? Aren't they just there to give us fun and pass the time?'

'Frank was a decent player,' said Enid. She'd ventured at last on to dangerous ground with the mention of that name. She gestured towards the honours boards in mitigation. 'Are you a good player yourself? Do you enjoy golf?'

Sharon smiled. 'I don't play. I had a go at it for a month or two many years ago, but I suppose like you I never really saw the point of it.' She paused to watch one of the figures on the course make elaborate preparations and then dump a short shot into the bunker beside the eighteenth green. 'Frank said something to me once about you and golf. He said that if you couldn't do anything well, you wouldn't be interested in doing it at all.'

'I don't know about that. I've never really thought about it.' Enid gave a short laugh, anxious now to be away from the subject and from the mention of Frank. 'Have you any plans for the future yourself?'

She'd almost said 'as a widow' and that was obviously what she'd meant. Crass of her: she'd never been crass, in her working days.

But Sharon Burgess seemed quite willing to talk about her plans. Perhaps like Enid she wanted to get away from the dangerous subject of Frank. She talked about her bridge and her work with University of the Third Age and how she was helping to run the local library on a voluntary basis to save it from closure during the latest cuts.

'Do you read much yourself?' asked Enid.

'Yes. But like most people, not as much as I intend to do.

I've always enjoyed reading and books. But I need to be more organized, really. I don't read half the books I mean to read.'

'I think we're all like that,' said Enid sympathetically.

And then she said something she could not explain to herself when she reviewed it later, as she did many times. 'I'm thinking of starting a book club. You know the kind of thing. We all read the same book and then talk about it together. Perhaps once a month. Would you be interested in joining?'

THREE

Dick Fosdyke didn't have many friends in Brunton. His marriage had broken up three years ago, and a lot of the people around here seemed to blame him for that. It didn't greatly worry him. He'd always been a bit of a loner, he supposed. He didn't need many friends, and he would choose them for himself. Most of the people he was close to nowadays were people he had worked with. One or two of them were in London, but most of them were in Manchester. Modern technology meant that he didn't have to be in the newsroom every day, as he had in the past. In any case, he was freelance now and much more dependent on his own efforts than the team ethic. It wasn't altogether a bad thing that he didn't see his colleagues as much as he once had. Journalists tended to drink a lot, and when you are with them you drink too much yourself.

Dick was a cartoonist, and a surprisingly good one. It had surprised him, anyway. He had drawn ever since he was a boy, but he'd never been to art college and never thought that he would make a living from it. He'd been freelance for seven years now, after a dispute with one of the national dailies, and it had worked quite well. He knew who had got him sacked, but so far he hadn't been able to do much in the way of revenge. But he was a patient man. Freelancing made his financial situation more precarious, but it gave him independence. And money hadn't been a problem, so far. Dick was versatile. He did sporting and even occasionally music drawings now, but his main work had always been political cartoons. He had a sharp eye for not only the characteristics in a face which could be exaggerated to make it immediately recognizable, but for the contradictory statements from public figures which provided openings for the satirist.

He also selected items from the daily news which offered him opportunities for the lighter humour he underlined with sharp one-liners. His efforts featured increasingly on television when people reviewed the papers and he now had a national reputation for pithy comment on political events. In an era when the reputation of politicians was at an all-time low, people were eager to welcome even the most cynical comments on their leaders, and Fosdyke's capacity to add humour to acid made his efforts even more welcome. Twice in the last month his work had been cited in the hourly review of the morning papers on Radio Four's *Today* programme, when one would have thought that radio was not the natural medium to discuss the work of cartoonists.

Dick had moved to a small flat near the centre of Brunton after the break-up of his marriage, abandoning his large detached house to his wife and the new partner she had acquired with suspicious speed. He felt a considerable bitterness about this, but he kept it to himself: he'd heard too many other men boring people in Manchester pubs with tales of how wives and their lawyers had exploited divorce settlements. He'd listened to reactions and found they tended to be on the lines of, 'Well, the poor sod's suffering now, but he probably behaved like a bastard when he was married, or she wouldn't have been able to do that.' Better to shut up and get on with life. He wasn't short of women, when he wanted them, but he was wary of getting himself into another long-term relationship.

He had taken to working much of his day in the library. He used the reference facilities there to check on any historical or biographical facts he needed – he was still old-fashioned enough to find Google less illuminating than his own researches. And he preferred to check all the morning papers there when he was looking for openings for cartoon humour, and decide which of the nationals were most likely to accept his barbed drawings and comments. Modern technology meant that he could dispatch his finished efforts swiftly from his PC at home to whatever organ he thought most likely to welcome them and reward him most handsomely.

He was generally protective of his efforts, even secretive about them. He didn't welcome company whilst he was working, and the last thing he wanted was someone looking over his shoulder as he drew. He needed no distraction as his swiftly fashioned lines shaped themselves into telling pictures. His best work was in itself an ironic comment on the events of the day, or the questionable conduct of a senior government minister. Humour was a serious business: it was only those who never produced it who thought otherwise.

That is why the tentative friendship which he had lately developed with one of the part-time workers in the library had surprised him. Almost as much, he suspected, as it had surprised her. She was much older than him: mid-sixties to his forty, he guessed. She was a voluntary worker and he always respected those. Some people would have been surprised by that. They thought of Fosdyke as a hard-headed journalist, who should have despised people who worked for nothing as hopeless idealists. But Dick liked to surprise people and he genuinely cared about libraries. They'd never had books in his working-class household; without the public library and the taste it had given him for reading and enquiry he'd never have achieved what he had in life.

Their alliance came out of nothing, really. It certainly wasn't sexual, but perhaps that was a relief for both of them. He first spoke to her on a cold mid-December morning, when they were both wringing their hands together for warmth after escaping from the chill wind outside. 'You seem to be here more than you used to be.'

She looked at him cautiously. 'You're very observant.'

'I'm here almost every day. You get to notice the comings and goings.'

'The library's run almost entirely on voluntary staff, since the council cuts. They seem to need me more than they used to do.'

He grinned. 'Make sure they don't exploit you. The willing horse always gets more and more weight to carry.'

She smiled back. 'I'm not sure I like your choice of metaphor, but I appreciate your concern. Actually, I quite enjoy the work here and I'm glad to find worthwhile things to occupy me, at the moment.'

'Have you taken early retirement, then?'

This time it was she who grinned, and the mischief lit up her face and banished the wrinkles. 'Flattery will get you anywhere, kind sir. But I'm past retiring age and I wasn't working anyway. It's just that I recently lost my husband. He died a month ago.'

'I'm sorry to hear that. I lost my wife three years ago. But she didn't die. She found a new man and kicked me out. After an expensive divorce.'

He thought she'd say that she was sorry about that and then they'd go their individual ways to their separate tasks of the day. Instead, she looked past him and said dreamily, 'I almost got divorced myself once. It seems a long time ago and in another place, now.'

'Do you get a break?'

'Eleven o'clock or thereabouts. We give each other half an hour if we want it. Privilege of the unpaid. Allows you to get a bit of shopping, if you need to.'

'I can take half an hour as well. Privilege of the self-employed. Do you fancy a coffee in the place next door?'

And so, almost by accident, a friendship began between Dick Fosdyke and Sharon Burgess.

Jamie Norris wasn't looking forward to Christmas. The episode with Bigarse and his subsequent sacking had seen to that.

He went to sign on for his unemployment benefit and was given a hard time about losing the job at the supermarket. The woman behind the desk looked at him with some distaste. They had to be careful what they said nowadays, but he knew what she was thinking from the way she looked at him. 'You're a man now, not a youth. And you shouldn't be unemployed. Not with good health and an education. You've got six GCSEs. You should be holding down a regular job. You shouldn't need us to help you.'

It was pep-talk time this morning, then. Usually he just sat and accepted things dully and was apologetic. But this woman was so sure of herself that she annoyed him. 'You don't help me. You send me to interviews with people who've no intention of employing me. Whatever work I've had I've obtained for myself.'

She looked at him dispassionately for a few seconds. 'Are you on drugs?'

'No.' You couldn't count a bit of pot as drugs, not nowadays. Even the police didn't count a bit of pot as drugs, nowadays. 'Do I look like a junkie?'

'No, not to me. But I'm not quite sure how a junkie does look. I'm asking because you've got some education but you don't seem to be able to hold down a job.'

He didn't want to get involved in a discussion with this woman, who obviously didn't like him. But he had to give some account of himself. He needed to defend what he was doing, as much to himself as to her. 'I'm trying to be a writer.'

'Any luck?'

She wasn't sneering, as he had expected her to be. That made it worse: he wasn't used to people like this taking him seriously. 'Not much. I've had a poem published in the *Brunton Times*.'

'So you wouldn't call yourself a successful writer?'

He listened for the contempt in her voice, but she sounded quite neutral.

'Not financially, no. It takes time. Even the good writers struggle, at first.'

'And you're not one of them, are you?'

It should have been nasty, but she sounded quite sympathetic. 'Probably I'm not. But you'll never know what you can do, if you don't try.'

She glanced down at his file. 'You're twenty-six, Mr Norris. How long are you going to go on trying to be a writer?'

'I'm going to give it one more year.' Jamie surprised himself by being so specific; it was a decision he'd taken only as he spoke.

'And meantime you have to support yourself. You need work.'

'Yes. I'd rather work. I don't like taking benefits.' He'd really no idea whether that was true. He hoped it was.

'You need to get yourself a job, Mr Norris. You need to carve out some sort of career for yourself. You can go on writing in your spare time. If you're successful, really successful, you can then consider becoming a full-time writer.'

It was what other people had said. It was what he'd told himself, often enough. But he resented it, coming from her. 'Expert on the subject of writing, are you?'

'No. But I know quite a lot about work and the way it's

central to most people's lives. And I'm supposed to give advice to the people who come and sit where you're sitting now. That's part of my job: perhaps it's the most important part.'

She smiled at him and he found himself smiling back, even though he hadn't meant to do that. 'So give me some work to support my writing.'

'I can't give you work. You know that. I can send you where you might get work, if you show the right attitude.'

He sighed. 'So send me.'

She flicked through a few cards in front of her. But both of them knew what she was going to say next. 'I can't offer you anything very grand, because of your previous record. You haven't worked anywhere for very long. Three months is your longest period of continuous work, and it's mostly been measured in weeks. You need to hold down a job and give good value to an employer. Show him or her that you're reliable as well as honest. Then you should move up the ladder – you're not stupid and people will recognize that, if your attitude's right.'

The pep talk again. Jamie resented the fact that it made sense. 'So send me somewhere.'

She looked at him hard. 'There's only temporary work. You'd expect that, with Christmas coming up. But if you show promise, you'll probably be offered something more permanent.'

He looked at her, studying her face for the first time. She was perhaps forty-five, with neat, short hair and grey eyes which looked at him steadily. He'd had an aunt like her, before he'd moved here and left all that behind. She looked as if she really wanted him to take notice of her. That was something, he supposed, after all the impersonal stuff he'd had here, with people barely looking at him. He said without a smile, 'Isn't this the point where you say that it's really all down to me?'

It was she who gave the smile. 'I can't say that. You might give complete satisfaction and still be laid off in a week or two. That's the nature of temporary work. But your best chance of making it permanent is to keep your head down and work steadily. That's not specialist knowledge; it's common sense.'

He sighed inwardly, but spoke quite evenly. 'Where do I go?'

'Tesco's. They need people to cope with the Christmas rush. After that, it's up to you. They'll need cover for the regular staff who're entitled to time off after the holiday rush. And they're open Boxing Day and New Year's Day. That's to your advantage, if you really want work.'

'I can't give them references. And I've just been sacked from a supermarket.'

'You probably won't need references, for temporary work. Convince them that you're honest and that you really want to work. It's up to you. No one can do it for you.'

'I'll give it a go.' He picked up the card and slid back his chair.

'Sell yourself to the employer, Mr Norris.' She looked up at him as he stood up and gave him a smile of genuine encouragement. 'Regular work really is the only way to support your writing. And please accept that this is meant in the best possible way: I hope I never see you again, Mr Norris.'

Three hundred yards away from the employment centre, a very different exchange was taking place in the café beside the public library.

'It's a while since I invited a woman out for a drink,' said Dick Fosdyke.

'It's only coffee. Perhaps I should insist on buying my own. I don't want you to get the wrong idea.' She'd been wondering how many years had passed since she'd last drunk even coffee alone with a man, other than Frank.

'You're safe enough with me. Especially in the middle of town at eleven o'clock on a cold December morning.'

'I feel very safe indeed. Not least because I've got a son as old as you.'

'I can hardly believe that. You must have been a child bride.' But both of them knew that he wasn't serious, that he was guying the philanderer's approach rather than making any serious play for her.

It was much easier now than when you were younger and had to decide whether every man was trying to get his hand up your skirt, Sharon thought. Easier, but not as exciting. There wasn't too much to be said for age and maturity. 'I've seen you a few times in the library. I suspect that like me you like being surrounded by books, Mr Fosdyke.'

She knew his name. That must be from the library records and the books he'd taken out, he supposed. Or perhaps she'd checked him out during the morning, after he'd arranged to come here. It was strange how he felt uneasy and at a disadvantage with someone who knew more about him than he did about her; he'd never thought about that before. 'It's Dick, please, not Mr Fosdyke. What did your husband do?'

'He ran his own firm. Burgess Electronics.'

One of the biggest units on the industrial estate to the east of the town. No wonder she didn't need to work. 'I'm sorry. I'd forgotten he'd died so recently. Perhaps you don't want to talk about him.'

'No, that's fine. It's something of a relief, actually. People tiptoe around you as if they're on broken glass; they take great pains to avoid any mention of Frank. It's quite a relief to be able to talk about him. His death wasn't a shock. He was fourteen years older than me, so I suppose I'd been preparing for his death for years. But it still shocks you, when it comes.'

'I'm sure it is. But it should be, don't you think? When death ceases to move us, we're diminished as human beings.'

She nodded, studying her coffee whilst she stirred it thoughtfully. 'I'm Sharon, by the way. What do you do for a living, Dick?' She used his name as if she were trying it out.

'I'm a cartoonist. Political, mostly. I try to be the "abstract and brief chronicle of our time". But in fact I also do anything I'm asked: I'm a whore with a pencil, really. You have to be, when you're freelance.'

'Are you very cruel?'

'Very cruel and very unfair, sometimes. It's part of the cartoonist's brief. You can make a point very quickly in a drawing. I tell myself that I'm satirising silly or outrageous conduct rather than the individuals themselves. You can't afford the luxury of a delicate conscience, when you've got a single picture and perhaps a few words to make a telling comment.'

He was an interesting man, Sharon thought. He'd quoted from *Hamlet* a moment ago. Not many men did that at a first meeting. And he talked about serious things immediately. She liked that in a man. It was many months since she'd talked about anything serious with anyone. Except for Frank's illness.

She said, 'It must be a very special skill. I've never really thought about it before.'

He said, 'The skill comes in making a point quickly. Ideally, without using any words at all.' He turned over the menu card on the table and drew swiftly and boldly upon the back of it. It took him no more than ninety seconds in all, but his concentration was intense and he spoke not a word whilst he drew. When he passed the card to her, she saw two very different images of Queen Elizabeth II. One was a benign old lady, totally harmless and smiling as softly as a saint. The other was of a witch-like creature who would bring only evil to anything she chose to touch. Both were immediately recognizable.

'That's very clever.' She was quite sincere and very impressed. There were only a few bold lines in each sketch, but they presented two very different images.

He grinned at her. 'It's not completely off the cuff. It's a bit of a party trick. I used to do it when I was much younger, to sell myself to newspaper editors.'

He wouldn't have revealed that to a younger woman, he thought. But it helped you to relax when you felt you could really be honest. There was a pause whilst she studied his handiwork. She must have been a very pretty woman, when she was in her prime. He said, 'I used to know someone who worked for Burgess Electronics. It's a long time ago now. You wouldn't know her, of course. Except that she had the kind of odd name you tend to remember. Enid Frott.'

'I spoke to Enid only a couple of weeks ago. She became Frank's PA eventually. He relied on her a lot.'

Dick Fosdyke noticed how studiously neutral they had both become with the mention of Ms Frott.

The manager at Tesco looked at Jamie Norris coolly across his desk. He wasn't many years older than the man who wanted to stack his shelves, which Jamie found an unnerving thought.

'So why do you want to work here, Mr Norris?'

'I need to work. It's that or the social.' Jamie pulled himself up there, trying hard to think of something the man might want to hear. 'And Tesco's is a good firm to work for. I know that I'd be starting at the bottom, and I can't expect to do anything else. I've frittered away a lot of time, but I want to think about a career now.'

'You've frittered away opportunities, as well as time.' The manager glanced down at the brief summary in front of him. 'This is the record of a man who doesn't seem to be able to hold down a job.'

'I know. There are reasons for that. But I'm not on drugs and I never have been.'

The man didn't ask about reasons. Jamie didn't know it, but the manager had allocated himself only five minutes for this meeting, and he didn't intend to take more. 'Your last job was in a supermarket. Why did you leave there?'

'I didn't leave of my own accord. I was sacked.' Might as well be honest – that question meant that he wasn't going to get the job here now. Visions of Bigarse flashed across his vision. 'I had a clash of personalities with the manager.'

'Shelf-stackers can't afford personalities. They get on with their work and keep their heads down.'

'That's what I was doing. I'd just mopped up a mess after a kid had dropped a jar of baby food. The manager slipped on it before I could post the warning notice. He fell on his fat arse and slung me out.'

He hadn't meant to use those words, but they'd come upon him without warning, as words did very occasionally as he struggled with his poetry. The man behind the desk said, 'And who was this man with the sensitive posterior?'

'Mr Garner.'

The manager's face was twitching. Jamie thought at first that he was annoyed, then realized that it was mirth which he was struggling to suppress. 'Start tomorrow morning. Seven o'clock. Don't be late.'

FOUR

Christmas came and went. Jamie Norris went back to Leeds and tried to feel at home in the midst of his fractured and rather distant family He pretended to his mother and the rest that he was doing well in Brunton and that his writing career was looking promising. No one believed him.

Dick Fosdyke found this a lonely time, though he affected to be unworried by that. There were no newspapers on Christmas Day, Parliament was in recess, and the world's more public idiocies had shut down for a time. There was precious little for a cartoonist to comment upon. A woman he had slept with in November offered to take him to her parents' home for a family Christmas. Dick was tempted for all of two minutes, but he declined. Better not to get involved. Better to meet her again on his terms, not hers. He made a drawing of his wife beside a roaring fire in their old home, with an acid comment beneath it, but he didn't send it to her. Instead, he put it on the mantelpiece above the gas fire in his flat, alongside the other three cards he had received.

Sharon Burgess spent Christmas cocooned in the warmth of her family. They were kind and welcoming and she felt glad to be with them. She beamed with the others as the grandchildren grew boisterous over their presents; food, wine and bonhomie flowed freely round the very warm room. But she was conscious throughout the day of people keeping an eye on her, knowing that this was her first Christmas without Frank. They didn't know everything about that relationship and they never would, she reflected. No marriage was completely public and Sharon was pleased about that. It seemed to give her the shaft of independence she needed amidst all this tenderness.

Enid Frott turned down an invitation to spend the day with Charles and Althea and the boys in Cheshire. She hoped the children would be a little disappointed by that, but she knew the parents wouldn't be. It was good of Charles to ring her at eleven o'clock on Christmas morning, but she could detect the relief in his voice. She spoke briefly with her nephews, but Althea was busy cooking the lunch and didn't pick up the phone. But Althea sent thanks through Charles for the beautiful M&S sweater. No doubt the bitch would change it in the next few days.

Enid walked a brisk mile with a present to the home of one of her bridge partners, who was also alone, having been divorced three years ago. They downed mince pies and a considerable quantity of mulled wine and felt quite cheerful together. Her friend asked if she wanted to watch the Queen's Christmas message and Enid's reaction was unprintable, causing both women to descend into giggles quite unsuitable for sexagenarians. They both agreed that Christmas without a man was a great improvement. A solitary bed was much better than the complications which men brought with them. Or women either, no doubt – more giggles, followed by the ceremonial opening of the cognac Enid had brought.

It was towards the end of Boxing Day that Ms Frott received the unexpected phone call. 'Enid? It's Sharon here. Sharon Burgess. Belated compliments of the season and best wishes for the coming year and all that jazz. This is about something you said at Frank's funeral.'

Enid couldn't think for a moment what that might be. 'I hope I didn't cause any offence. They're emotional occasions, aren't they, funerals? For you most of all, I'm sure.'

A slight, half-muffled giggle. Had Frank's widow been indulging herself with the Boxing Day booze, in the bosom of her considerable family? Enid sought desperately for the names of the grandchildren she had chatted with at the funeral reception at the golf club, so that she could speak glowingly of them and win herself some neutral-ground brownie points. Those pleasant adolescents would surely have been safe ground, but the names wouldn't come to her. Then Sharon said, 'They are emotional occasions, yes, and I'm sure we all behave out of character – well, those who were closest to the deceased, anyway. But this is nothing to do with Frank.'

Enid divined suddenly what was coming, but she couldn't work out on the spot what her reaction should be. Dismissive,

or welcoming? Did she really want any further contact with
this woman, in view of the history they carried? She switched
the television off and said formally, as if she was back at work,
'How can I help you, Sharon?'

'It's your suggestion of a book club. I think we both thought
it was a good idea.'

'Yes. I haven't gone any further with it.' Enid was still playing
for time.

'Perhaps we could meet, then, to discuss whom we might
invite to join us. It might be important to get that right. I fancy
that once you invite someone, you're stuck with them. We'd need
to give it some thought. You could come round here, if you like.'

Enid Frott had to summon all her resources to make herself
polite, yet friendly. She needed time to think about this. 'Yes.
Excellent idea, Sharon. We could meet early in the New Year.'

The snow fell softly and silently, but steadily. It was picturesque,
almost hypnotic. The large white flakes descended inexorably,
softening the uglier lines and shapes in the Tesco car park. It
was the seventh of January. The snow had come too late for a
white Christmas, as usual.

Jamie Norris was still working here, even with all the regular
staff back after the holiday. He wasn't permanent yet, but the
manager had said he might be, soon. The manager had even
said he was pleased with his work. Jamie tried to despise himself
for being so absurdly joyful over that crumb of praise.

It was seven o'clock in the evening now. He had used his
tea break to come to the door with his beaker and gaze out at
the snow. There was no wind, which was what allowed the
flakes to fall like this, obscuring the night sky behind them,
slowly enveloping the landscape in their descending curtain of
white. There must be material here for a poet. But only the
conventional words and the conventional phrases would come
to Jamie, as he stood and allowed himself to be mesmerised by
the monotonous beauty of the vision.

'Have you mark'd but the fall of the snow / Before the soil
hath smuch'd it?'

The voice was quiet and even, but it made Jamie start
nonetheless.

He turned and saw a figure in the shadows, wearing a trilby hat so that the brim gave further shade to the thin face beneath it. Jamie said as if he resented it, 'That's verse. But I don't know whose verse.'

'Ben Jonson. He isn't much read now. It's a love poem really: "Have you seen but a bright lily grow / Before rude hands have touch'd it?"'

The figure stepped forward and took off its hat. It was a man. A man with a sallow, experienced face, heavily lined but not old. A man in his forties, Jamie reckoned. He said, 'I don't know any Ben Jonson. I try to write poetry myself, sometimes.'

The man seemed to have expected that. He didn't seem shocked or alarmed or amused, the way most people did. 'That poem's a celebration of maidenhood and chastity and innocence. Those aren't popular qualities, in our secular age. You wouldn't expect them to be celebrated nowadays. But fresh snow always reminds me of innocence and chastity.'

Jamie Norris didn't know how to reply to that. He'd had quite a lot of trouble with chastity in his short time upon this earth. He'd never thought of celebrating it in his attempts at poetry. He turned to look again at the steadily falling curtain of snow. 'There's not much wind, so it shouldn't drift. But it will be quite thick by morning, if it keeps on like this.' He paused for a moment, willing the man to speak, but he heard nothing from behind him. 'I was trying to think of some lines about the snow. I wanted to catch its beauty and its power in words, but phrases from other poets keep coming into my head. Better phrases and better lines than I can think up.'

'It's inhibiting, knowing what others have written. You need to read poetry, because it excites you and it tells you what good verse is about. But it gets in the way when you try to write yourself.'

'That's just how it is, yes. I love reading Philip Larkin, but when I go into an old church myself, his verse always seems so much better than anything I can manage. I end up discarding even what I think were promising images, because his always seem so much better.'

'You should keep working at it, though, even if you often have to throw your efforts away. It's only by hammering away

at it that you get better. Mediocrity is something you have to
go through to produce the good stuff.'

It was encouraging, Jamie supposed, even if the man made
writing seem even harder than he'd supposed it would be when
he'd set out to be a poet. And he was sure that what he said
was true: it echoed what he had been discovering for himself
by the hard process of trial end error. It would be nice to have
a few more successes and a lot fewer errors.

He said, 'You sound to me as if you write poetry yourself.'

The wan features melted into the first smile Jamie had seen
there. 'I've written a little, yes. Most of it isn't allowed to see
the light of day. I end up burning or shredding most of it. But
it sharpens your appreciation for the efforts of others. For Philip
Larkin and Ted Hughes and Seamus Heaney. I don't know any
of them personally, of course, but they seem like old friends
by now.'

After not moving at all since he had first spoken, the man
stepped forward into the light, removed his trilby, and held out
his hand. 'Alfred Norbury.'

'Jamie Norris.' He took the hand and shook it, noting how
cold and sinewy it felt.

'I don't like the Alfred and I hate Alf. But I'm stuck with it.
"They fuck you up, your mum and dad." Didn't mince his
words, Larkin.'

'Alfred was good enough for Tennyson.'

'True. And he wrote some good stuff, did Alfred. Even after
they made him Poet Laureate, unlike most.'

'I'd like to write just one poem as good as his.'

'*The Lotus Eaters*, that's what you should use as your model.
Or *Morte D'Arthur*, if you like. Not the charge of the bloody
light brigade – though if you want to know about the rhythms
of verse, you could learn a bit there.'

'I'll look at them. I don't know enough poetry.' Jamie was
afraid of being exposed as a sham by this strange man he had
never seen before.

'Read as much as you like, but don't stop writing. Don't let
the masters inhibit you. Find your own voice. Larkin did.'
Norbury stood back a pace and looked at the uncertain young
man in front of him. Not as young as he'd thought at first: late

twenties, probably. But young for his age; young and probably vulnerable. 'What time do you finish here tonight?'

'Eight o'clock. Sometimes there's a couple of hours of over-time, but there won't be tonight. People won't be coming out in this.' He looked back at the steadily falling flakes which had stubbornly failed to inspire him.

'You could come round to my place if you like. Discuss this further. I've got quite a lot of books of poetry there.'

Jamie Norris was suddenly back in his childhood, with his mother telling him that he must on no account go anywhere with strange men. But he hadn't even been allowed to speak with them, and he'd certainly done that. And that was then and this was now. He was a grown man and he could look after himself, couldn't he? It would be a poor thing if he couldn't do that when he was twenty-six and knew all about these things.

'I haven't got a car. I can drive, but at the moment I—'

'It isn't far from here.' The man scribbled a note on the slip of paper he drew from the pocket of his coat. 'They're flats. You'll see the name Norbury among the others. Ring the bell beside the name.'

Jamie glanced down at the address. Wellington Street. An old street of high, posh Victorian houses. Near the centre of the town and not far from here, as Alfred Norbury had said. Four hundred yards, perhaps. He had his wellies in the staff cloak-room and he could easily walk that, even through the snow. Wellies for Wellington Street. He liked that thought, but he didn't think it would amuse Alfred. Perhaps he might get an idea or two for a poem, on the way.

Jamie Norris said with a sense of impending doom, 'All right. I'll be there.'

They often went to the pub after the evening class. That was the advantage of adult education. Mature students were only there because they wanted to be. They really enjoyed learning and they often wanted to continue discussions informally, after the official class was over.

The night of the seventh of January was different, however. The attendance was thin, for a start. Snow had been forecast and it was falling steadily by the time the class began. Many regular and enthusiastic attendees decided that discretion was the better part of valour and reluctantly conceded this night's class to the weather. They had only eight instead of their more normal eighteen. They packed up early as the snow deepened outside the church hall where they met; they agreed that this was no night for the pub.

Jane Preston had prepared well for an evening on William Thackeray, but she'd scarcely begun her spiel on Becky Sharp and *Vanity Fair* when the session was aborted. She told herself that it was just as well: she'd have a bigger audience for her pearls of wisdom next week and the discussion which followed would be much livelier with a full complement. She really enjoyed teaching this group and she felt that Thackeray, who was nothing like as well-known or well-loved as Dickens, would give them all food for thought and provoke productive arguments.

She put on her coat and the fake-fur hat which the oldest member of the group had said made her look a little like Julie Christie in the film of *Dr Zhivago*. Pity the two younger men weren't here tonight, but you couldn't have everything. There was nothing to prevent her wearing the hat again next week.

Meanwhile, it would be good to get home. She turned the collar of her coat up and prepared to dash to the car. She'd need to watch for wheel-spin in the side street, but the main roads should still be all right. Good thing they'd packed up early, though.

'No chance of a drink tonight, I suppose?'

Jane was startled by the voice behind her, which seemed unnaturally close in the silence. She turned and smiled, searching desperately for a name as she recognized the speaker. It was the pleasant older woman who had asked her earlier how important she thought George Eliot was as a successor to Thackeray. 'Not tonight, I'm afraid. I think we all need to get home as quickly as we can, don't you?'

'Yes, of course. It's a pity, though, because I had something to ask you, Ms Preston.'

She forced a smile. 'It's Jane to my friends, of which you are emphatically one, Sharon.' The name had come to her just

in time: much better than 'Mrs Burgess'. She embellished it
with one of her wider smiles.

This young woman looked very pretty in her fake fur hat and
crimson coat, thought Sharon. More Red Riding Hood than
Lara in *Dr Zhivago*, perhaps, but no doubt that depended on
your point of view. 'It's a simple enough thing. I could ask you
here, really. I don't need a couple of gins to give me the courage
for this.'

It was still snowing steadily, as Jane could see through the
gap beyond the door she had begun to open. She shut it again
reluctantly and forced a smile. 'Is it connected with our course
her on the nineteenth-century novel?'

'No, not at all. Well, only very indirectly.' Sharon was abruptly
embarrassed when it came to the moment, when earlier this had
seemed to her a simple and reasonable request. She blurted it
out all at once, like an embarrassed child who was anticipating
refusal. 'I'm starting a book club. Well, two of us are, really.
We'll all read a book and then discuss it. Perhaps once a month,
we thought. Would you be interested in joining?'

Jane Preston didn't really want to get involved. Probably a
lot of old biddies discussing books she'd never have dreamed
of reading for herself. But that was unfair and ageist. This was
an intelligent woman who'd made good contributions to their
discussions here and supported her loyally. The trouble was,
she didn't really want more commitments with an unknown
group. But then she thought of the man she wanted to contact.
He was part of the Brunton literary set, wasn't he? He might
even be a member of this group. Or she might in due course
be able to suggest him as a member, if she joined.

Jane Preston heard herself saying, 'Yes, I'll probably give it
a go. It sounds fun. Can I ring you in a day or two to give you
a definite decision?'

Jamie Norris had a shock in Wellington Street.

He found the house easily enough. Number twenty-three. A
high, gabled Victorian house, looking even taller as it towered
blackly above him amidst the falling snow. Before he could
mount the steps to locate the right bell and ring it, the door
opened. But it was not a man but a large dog which stood at

the top of the steps. It looked to Norris like the Hound of the
Baskervilles, its dark outline massive and forbidding against
the orange light of the hall behind it. The beast gave a single
deep bark and hurtled down the path towards him.

Jamie didn't like dogs. He hadn't thought about it much
before, but in that single moment it was clear to him that he
abhorred them. He shut his eyes and waited, not wishing the
see the eager fangs as they prepared to attack his defenceless
body. He wanted to cry out, but he knew there was no point.
He thought he had probably emitted a strange, strangled croaking
noise, but he wasn't even sure of that.

And then there was a warm head against his hand, a snuffling
insistence that he gave attention, a soft, damp tongue nuzzling
against his palm. A voice from the doorway of the house said,
'A traveller, by the faithful hound / Half-buried in the snow
was found.'

Alfred Norbury stood benignly above him as the dog frisked
around him, excited by the snow to a display of impromptu
gymnastics. Friendly, thank God, despite its size. Norbury said
as Jamie cautiously moved nearer, 'Drinkwater. No one reads
him nowadays. Probably they should do, but they don't.' He
stood aside to let man and dog past him, wiping the animal's
large paws with a towel as Jamie stamped his wellies on the
top step to get rid of the accumulated snow.

Jamie said, 'I'd better take these off.' He removed the wellies
and banged them vigorously together beside the top step before
he followed Alfred and the dog down the hall and into the
door of a ground-floor flat. There was a gas fire which was
so good that he thought at first that the flames were real.
Ten-foot-long curtains, maroon with gold tracery, concealed
what he was sure was an impressive window. The television
in the corner had doors on its front, an appendage he hadn't
seen since he was a boy visiting his grandmother's house. He
wondered if his strange new friend had had them specially
made to mask the ubiquitous presence of the most insistent
of modern media.

But the most impressive item in the room was the floor-to-
ceiling bookcase on his left, of which every shelf was crammed
with books. Norbury saw him looking at them and said, 'There

are lots of poets there and a whole variety of novels. You must borrow whatever you want, Jamie.'

It was the first time Alfred had used his first name, the first time he had called him anything. Jamie felt that the relationship was running too fast, moving out of his control. He sat down in the armchair his host indicated, looked down at the canine head which appeared immediately upon his thigh, and said, 'I don't know much about dogs. I was quite frightened of him at first.' He tried to laugh at himself, but didn't get beyond a sickly smile.

'Oscar's a golden retriever. They're very rarely fierce. This one's a real softy. Daft, but totally harmless. I'm looking after him for a week for a friend. He seems to have taken a shine to you.'

The dog gazed up at him with wide, guileless brown eyes, as if anxious to reinforce this view. Jamie stroked its soft head cautiously and felt very stupid as he said, 'Good boy, Oscar.'

'You need a whisky after trekking through the snow. I've got a good single malt. Is that all right for you?'

Jamie Norris signified that it was. He didn't think he'd ever tasted malt whisky in his life, single or double. He wanted to say that, so that he wouldn't be a sham, but Alfred Norbury seemed to know and to tolerate everything anyway, without being told. Jamie managed to hold his own when they talked about poetry, or at least to think he did. He was glad when they got on to Seamus Heaney, because he'd bought the selected poems of Heaney when he died. He remembered some of the poems and quite a lot of the introduction, which gave him intelligent things to say about Heaney.

They seemed to agree about Heaney and about his Irishness and about the need for a united Ireland, wherever the political lines which were drawn. Perhaps Alfred was indulging him, feeding him questions to which he found the answers easy. He'd been worrying about his wellies, which would be leaking their remaining wetness on to the mat by the door, but after a couple more whiskies the world seemed pleasantly warm and unthreatening, and his wellies less important.

He wasn't sure how much time elapsed before Norbury went across and parted the maroon curtains to peer out into the night.

He closed the gap carefully again before he said, 'It's still snowing out there. Perhaps not quite as heavily, but still steadily. We're much better off in here.'

As the older man smiled down at his guest, Jamie Norris raised his glass a little unsteadily, clinked it against Norbury's and said, 'I'll drink to that!'

FIVE

Three days later, there were still four inches of snow in Brunton. But a rapid thaw was forecast in the next twenty-four hours.

Alfred Norbury drove out to climb Pendle Hill whilst it was still in its winter white. The main roads were clear of snow, but he had to be careful over the last few miles as he drove round the hill to Barley. He usually climbed it from the Brunton flank and walked along the long top to the summit, but the ascent from Barley was easy: a long, steady pull which was perfectly graduated for these difficult conditions. He put on the boots he had worn for many years now: quality was always the best investment, if you gave it long enough.

He climbed steadily, drawing in long breaths of the winter air, panting a little with the sheer pleasure of the crisp, cold air. Pendle wasn't a high hill, not much more than 1800 feet – he didn't favour the modern fashion of reducing numbers to metres; that seemed to him to diminish his favourite climbs. But Pendle amply repaid the trouble of scaling its modest heights. It gave splendid views of the Yorkshire Dales to the east, of the Pennines to the north, of Longridge Fell and the long descent to the Fylde coast to the west. You could see all of these today. Snow gave extra definition, as well as extra drama. He made the summit, as he had planned, almost exactly at noon.

There were few people abroad in these conditions: he passed one couple descending as he neared the summit, and that was all. Even the hardy Pendle sheep were sticking to the valleys and the lower slopes today. It was bitterly cold up here, but Alfred hardly felt it, filled as he was with the vigour of his activity and the exhilaration of his achievement. He stood, breathing hard, savouring the immaculate cleanness of the frozen snow around him, enjoying the cold that cut like a knife at his cheeks, the one section of his flesh which he had cared to expose.

Norbury glanced at the clear blueness above him. One felt
nearer to the sky up here. Nearer to God, for those who believed
in such things. Hills and mountains put things in perspective,
especially when you climbed alone. You felt cleaner in mind
up here. You felt as if you could leave behind the squalor which
seeped into your life in the world below. He looked down
towards Sabden and the homes of the Pendle witches. And he
wondered as he had done many times before how much was
fact and how much was superstitious fiction in the tales of
those wretched women who had been hanged at Lancaster in
1612. Modern man had left such things a long way behind
him, hadn't he?

Part of him wanted to stay up here longer and preserve this
feeling of cleanliness, this clearing of moral ambiguity. A kind
of serenity had been afforded him by the climb and the solitude
and the long views over the frozen landscape. But he knew
that it was impossible to stay here for long. Already the cold
was attacking the tips of his fingers beneath his gloves: you
did not have to stand still for more than a few seconds up
here to be reminded of the temperature. He took a last, long
look at the panoramas in each direction, then dropped his head
and turned to his descent.

He moved towards the pub when he was down in the valley,
then thought better of it. He wanted nothing but his own
company for as long as possible. Only in solitude could he
preserve the cleansing which occurred when he had been
alone amidst snow and ice on the long hill which now towered
above him. He didn't even put the radio on in the car as he
drove slowly back to the streets of Brunton and the life which
awaited him there.

There was a message waiting for him on his phone, left for
him at 10.41, exactly four hours earlier. He pressed the '1'
button on his phone reluctantly, knowing that in doing so he
was rejoining the familiar world from which he had escaped
for the earlier part of the day.

'Alfred? It's a voice from the past. This is Enid Frott.' Then
there was a pause, which was long enough for him to feel that
this might be all there was. Then, hesitantly, 'Could we meet?
I've something to ask of you. Nothing very important, but it

would be good to talk. Ring me back, please. The number hasn't changed.'

He met her in the small café beside the market hall. She'd suggested her flat or his, but Alfred had said he would prefer to come here. Neutral ground was best. She hadn't argued. She'd thought he might refuse to meet her anywhere.

Alfred Norbury was already sitting alone at a table when she walked into the busy little place. Enid Frott had known he would be. He'd always been meticulously punctual, almost obsessively so.

He hadn't ordered. He went now to the counter and turned to look at her whilst he waited to be served. He came back with two white coffees and two flapjacks. She looked at them, gave him a taut smile, and said, 'You remembered.'

'The flapjacks? I remembered, yes. If you don't want yours, I can always eat two of them.' He stirred his coffee and looked into her face from no more than two feet. She had lines round her clear brown eyes now, just a wisp or two of grey in the light brown, short-cut hair. He said very deliberately, 'You're wearing well.'

It was a statement, not a compliment, as if he was listing a simple fact of life.

She responded with facts of her own. 'I've never had children. That helps, I suppose. You're looking older. Are you eating properly? You were always careless about that.' She bit into her flapjack, her white, regular teeth suddenly bright in the subdued light.

'You're retired now.'

Another statement of fact, not a query. She wondered how he knew that. She didn't think she'd put that in the message she'd left on his phone or stated it during their brief exchange when he'd phoned back to arrange this meeting. She'd been too nervous for anything save the basics. But then Alfred had always known things you didn't expect him to know. She said, 'I didn't ask to meet you to talk about old times.'

It sounded rude, or at least abrupt, She hadn't intended that, but she was nervous. He looked hard at her and then said, 'Pity. We'd have quite a lot to talk about.'

His tone sounded menacing, but she saw a smile on his face, so it was presumably all right. Perhaps she was reading too much into things: she knew she was anxious. She was wondering why she'd done this, asking herself now, when it was too late, where it might lead in the long run. Enid wasn't used to being nervous and she was finding this difficult. 'Have you got a partner at the moment?'

It was a straightforward enough question, but he took a little time and an unhurried sip of his coffee before he answered. 'No. I find it more difficult to commit myself to others, as I get older. You're still in the same flat. Does that mean that you haven't a significant other in place?'

He delivered that phrase with a slight curl of his saturnine lips. She had the impression again that he already knew the answer to his question. 'No. Commitment's easy when you're young, even when it's entirely unsuitable. I find it becomes more difficult as I get older. You get fonder of your own comforts and your own idiosyncrasies and you're not prepared to give them up. I'm like you in that, Alfred.'

She used his first name as boldly as she could, acknowledging that it was an attempt to move towards an intimacy they had once enjoyed. Norbury did not respond to it. 'I live my own life. I do not care to open it up to others, except on my terms.'

'It was always on your terms, Alfred. You were generous enough to others, so long as it was you who called the shots.'

He watched her finish her flapjack and her coffee, as if challenging her to say more. When she did not, he gave her the smallest of smiles. 'You said in your phone message that you had something to ask of me. What would that be?'

'It's a small thing, really. I've made it bigger by arranging a meeting, when I could have done this on the phone. But I wanted to see you again. And I suppose I thought you'd be more likely to say yes if we met face to face.'

His eyes seemed to be set even more deeply in his sallow face than she remembered. He said, 'I should be intrigued by this. I'm certainly curious. What is it you want?'

'I'm starting a book club. Well, two of us are, really.' She looked up into the dark, intelligent eyes, searching for a reaction; she found none. 'We plan to meet once a month and talk about a book we've all read. I thought you might be interested. I'd certainly like to have you there: I'm sure you'd be an asset in a group like that.'

He looked hard into the oval, intelligent face, as if he hoped to read more there than she was prepared to tell him. 'You know me. I'm a loner, not a team player. I wouldn't fit into a group. I'd probably be too trenchant with my opinions. I'd give offence to your friends.'

'They won't be my friends – well, not most of them. And if you don't like it, you don't have to stay. That applies to everyone. It's tentative and entirely voluntary.'

'You said there were two of you involved. Do I know the other person?'

She'd hoped he wouldn't ask her that. She'd been planning that he'd only find out at the first meeting. She looked down at the empty coffee cups, trying hard to be nonchalant and knowing that she wasn't succeeding. 'You're not going to believe this. I'm still not sure how it came about.' She looked up at him, hoping for the encouraging smile which he didn't volunteer. 'Its Frank's widow. Sharon Burgess.'

Now at last Alfred Norbury did smile. Not a very pleasant smile, Enid thought. 'All right, I'm in. I wouldn't miss this for the world!'

The internet was a fine thing for discovering all kinds of information. Everyone said that. Jane Preston's experience was that it could also be a great time-waster.

She was having second thoughts about this book club business. She'd half agreed to take part in it because with the snow falling steadily outside she had been anxious to get away from Sharon Burgess. She'd taken the line of least resistance in a bid to get home safe and dry last Tuesday night. It was surely too much to hope that the man she wanted to get near would be there.

Now she wasn't at all sure that she wished to be a member of the enterprise. Was she to be a trophy for the older woman to brandish in the group – an expert on the nineteenth-century novel and on books in general whom she could wave in the faces of her fellow members and produce as her own expert?

Or was she being paranoid, her brother's favourite word to taunt her? Sharon Burgess seemed a nice enough woman, an enthusiast for the classic nineteenth-century writers and a great asset in Jane's class on the subject. Even if this group never involved her target man, it might be amusing. And given time, she'd bring him in. Jane knew she was a persuasive woman, once she put her mind to something.

She googled Burgess Electronics on her PC and found that it was a small but prosperous private firm which had carved out a niche for itself in the electronics field and grown steadily over the years. Its founder was Frank Burgess: she knew that Sharon was a widow, so presumably the founder of the firm was her husband, who had recently died. Sharon must be a rich widow. Rich and likeable, Jane told herself firmly: there was nothing pretentious in the woman. Indeed, she had been very supportive in the early stages of the evening class, when no one knew each other and the adult students had been sizing up their teacher.

Don't close your mind to new experiences, Jane Preston. You don't do that at twenty-seven, because of one unhappy love affair. If the book club doesn't work out after a couple of sessions, you can always say it's not for you. And there is always the possibility that it will get you nearer to the man you're looking for.

She rang before she had time to dither any further. A female voice spoke to her – a young voice, she thought. Jane asked for Sharon Burgess and the voice asked for her name and then said, 'I'll see if Mrs Burgess will speak to you,' as though administering a rebuke. A maid, perhaps? How very Agatha Christie! Jane didn't think she'd known anyone with a maid before.

But Mrs Burgess, when she spoke, was as friendly and informal as usual. Jane said, 'I said I'd let you know about your book club. Yes, I'd like to give it a go. You could give me further details when the class meets again on Tuesday.'

Jane Preston wondered as she put the phone down why a simple decision like that should feel so significant.

Enid Frott didn't choose neutral ground for her meeting with Sharon Burgess, as Alfred Norbury had done.

There was ample room in the driveway of Pendle View, the impressive Burgess house, but Enid chose to park on the road outside it. The house was familiar to her, but it was years since she'd been here. She had stood here years ago, after Frank had told her he was ending it with her, studying the big house and wondering exactly where he was inside it. She'd wondered also what he was doing inside those walls, when she'd chosen to torture herself in those months of pain. Time healed, they said, and she supposed that it was true. The wounds were still there but they had thick scabs upon them now. The pain was all but gone.

The big detached house had been impressive, but new and raw in those days, its fresh bricks rising stark and harsh against the sky behind it. The house on the summit of the hill had been an affront to nature, in her anguished thoughts. It had matured now, as she had. The flowering cherries and the rhododendrons had partly obscured and certainly softened the outline of the house, sculpting a more varied and rounded silhouette for the whole against the winter sky.

And Frank was dead. She had seen him off with others at the crematorium. She had conversed with Sharon at the funeral reception and they had spoken like civilized women, not harpies scrapping over a corpse. Death brought a close, with lovers as certainly as with parents. It was difficult to retain a passionate hatred for a dead man.

It was quiet here. The few other houses in this exclusive road were as big as Pendle View and widely spaced. There was no one else in the road and no presence visible in the Burgess home. She studied the house for a little longer, making sure she was composed before she walked slowly up the drive. There was a white frost upon the grass today, but the lawns were straight and sharp and the borders were filled with sturdy polyanthus and wallflowers, ready to burst into colour with the advent of spring. They would employ a gardener, of course, one who knew his stuff. Sharon would have a gardener, she should say. She must get used to saying that. It would be a good job for a gardener, working for Sharon.

She rang the bell and was surprised when Sharon opened the door herself. She was in a dark blue dress with heels which lifted

her a little but were not absurdly high. Becoming but not ostenta-
tious. That seemed to be the keynote of Mrs Burgess, who now
smiled at her and said, 'You're commendably prompt.' She gave
Enid a smile which could have meant anything or nothing. 'But
of course, you knew where the house was, didn't you?'

She led her into a huge lounge with a view down the long
back garden to a border of roses which were no more than
sticks, having obviously been pruned in the autumn. A low
winter sun had burned away the frost here: the grass looked
surprisingly green for January. A coffee pot steamed gently
beside two china cups and saucers on the table. Sharon offered
her home-made biscuits but did not take one herself. She
watched her guest nibble one and said, 'You were always slim,
Enid. You can afford to indulge yourself.'

A second reference to the past. Enid didn't like that. But she
hoped Frank's widow might feel some of the embarrassment
she was enduring herself at this moment. You tended to search
for common ground when you were fumbling for things to say.
She determined to remain in the present. 'So, the book club.
Do you still think it's a good idea? I was speaking rather off
the cuff when I suggested it to you. I shan't be at all offended
if you tell me to go away and forget it.'

She's not talking about the idea of a book club itself, thought
Sharon coolly. She means do I think it's a good idea for us to
run one together. And she's right: it's a bizarre notion for two
people with our history even to think of any sort of social
exchange. But she's put me through the mangle in the past and
if she's uncomfortable now I find that quite satisfactory. 'Oh
no! Rather the reverse. The more I've thought about it, the more
I think it an excellent idea. We're both retired and we both like
books. It's quite a logical development really for us to try to
give that a more formal framework.'

No, not for us, thought Enid. Not for two women who've
slept with the same man and competed for him and agonized
over him. What would Frank think of this if he could see the
two of us now? Would he be appalled or would he be amused?
Bemused, more likely. I'm pretty bemused myself, and it was
I who suggested the preposterous idea. But I'm not going to
give best to this woman. 'I'm glad you still think it's a good

idea. I've got a couple of people I thought we might ask to join us. Would you like me to run them by you?'

This wasn't a woman to underestimate, Sharon thought. But she'd known that for many years, hadn't she? She'd found out the hard way. She took a deep breath and said breezily, 'That would be splendid. I've got a name or two as well. I thought we should start by establishing one or two principles for the group. Perhaps we should do that before we even discuss names.'

'All right. You've obviously given this matter much more thought than I have.'

Sharon doubted whether that was true. Enid Frott had done very little without giving it careful forethought, in the past. But the past was a different country. They did things differently there, someone had said. L.P. Hartley, she thought. This was the here and now and she must banish the past. Otherwise, why get involved with the woman at all?

They were two intelligent women in their sixties pursuing a common interest, or they wouldn't be here talking abut forming a book club. No one had forced either of them into this. She poured more coffee, noting with approval the steadiness of her hand. Enid watched her without a word. Then she picked up her cup as carefully as if she were responding to a move she'd anticipated in a game of chess. Sharon Burgess was dictating the terms of this strange game. She was sitting in her own house and controlling the evolution of their joint enterprise.

Yet the woman seemed suddenly diffident, when she had previously been assertive. Sharon said unconvincingly, 'I haven't given it a great deal of thought. And this was your idea in the first place, so you don't have to accept any of this unless you agree with it.' She paused for interruption or dissent, but her visitor studied her refilled coffee cup and gave her nothing save the slightest of nods. Her hostess plunged in. 'I didn't want our group to be all female. Most of the clubs I've heard about seem to be either exclusively or predominantly female. I'd like ours to be different.'

'I agree. I envisaged us as a mixed group. We don't want to insist upon an exact balance; that would be silly. But I think we should certainly have men there. If we can recruit suitable ones, of course.'

'Of course. That goes without saying. And that would apply to females as well as males. I'm sure neither of us intends to bring people along just because they're friends. They must be interested in books and interested in discussing what they read.'

They were pussyfooting around each other, Sharon thought. Stating principles and watching for reactions. But that was surely natural enough. Even women who were bosom pals would have been treading carefully as they moved into a new enterprise. And she was certainly not a bosom pal of Enid Frott's. Rather the opposite, whatever that might be. 'Good. We're agreed upon that, then. The other thing I thought was that we should go for a mixture of ages in the group. It might be much easier if we simply invited a group of women of around our own age to join us, but in my view it would be much better for us to have both sexes and a variety of ages.'

'You have been thinking about this, haven't you?' Enid's smile was almost mischievous. 'I'd say we need to remember that we're doing this for pleasure. We need to suit ourselves and have some enjoyable evenings, not bog ourselves down with ethics and principles.'

'Unless they're principles we both agree with, of course. I just think we'll have better discussions and more thought-provoking evenings if we have young and old together.'

'With us as the oldies, I suppose.'

'With us as the experienced and wiser older heads who can give a sense of perspective to the exchanges.'

Enid smiled. 'I like that. And I don't object to a couple of youngsters. Let's show them that they can't shock us, whatever they produce. And I think we should have one or two in-betweenies, to complete the set.'

Sharon tried not to sound surprised as she said, 'We seem to be more or less agreed on the composition of the group. It will be easier once we have a nucleus. Once we are functioning, we can put any new suggestions to the group. Any new members then would have to be sanctioned by the existing club.'

'And no doubt you now have one or two suggestions to be founder members.'

Sharon said tartly, 'I'm hoping we both have. It's the only way to get things going. And it should be simple to agree, shouldn't it? There are only two of us and we each have the power of veto.'

Enid wondered suddenly what part the efficient Mrs Burgess was taking in the running of Frank's old company. Frank had been retired for years before he died and all that was behind her, but she had worked on at the company and been in charge of the office for years after Frank had gone. Enid was suddenly jealous of this woman's power at Burgess Electronics, a world which she had left abruptly and unwillingly only six months ago.

It wasn't an easy combination for her to secure, but Enid tried to sound bright and neutral at the same time. She put her empty coffee cup back on the tray and said, 'Let's have your suggestions. I can't really think I'm going to black-ball any of them.'

'I've only got two. One is a youngster, in our terms. I suppose the second one is what you just called an in-betweeny.'

'This is quite exciting, Sharon. It's like interviewing people for a job, without having their tiresome presence to inhibit us and make us polite.'

Her hostess smiled conspiratorially. 'I'm glad they can't hear us. I'll do the younger one first. She's a young woman called Jane Preston. I'm attending a WEA course on the nineteenth-century novel and she's my tutor. She's very knowledgeable but very approachable.'

'You don't think she would inhibit us? I'm feeling reticent already at the thought of an expert. I suppose people who know me might think that was a good thing.'

'Jane's very unassuming and I'm sure she wouldn't hog the discussion. She certainly knows a lot about the nineteenth-century greats, but she probably knows no more than the rest of us about contemporary writers. It could be quite a coup for us to get her.'

And thus give you the edge over me, thought Enid. I didn't think this was going to be a contest over who could produce the most impressive recruits. But we've got a history: perhaps I should have expected it. Or perhaps I'm a lonely, bored, retired woman who's in danger of seeing sinister motives where no offence is intended. 'I'm sure your Jane Preston will be a valuable member of our group. Who else are you proposing?'

She remembered Jane's name, where I would instantly have forgotten it, thought Sharon. But then Enid had been Frank's PA, so you'd expect that – amongst other things. 'My other candidate is quite different. I haven't even asked him yet – I thought I should have your approval first.'

Which implies you've already invited La Preston, I suppose. But let's not be too sensitive about your appropriation of what was once my idea. 'This is a male, then. Hence your remarks about including the young and the male: you're providing us with one of each.'

'Only if you approve, Enid.' She'd forced herself to use the name for a second time, but it felt very unnatural. 'And it's a shot in the dark, really. But I think you'll find him an interesting man. You may already know the name: Dick Fosdyke. He's a cartoonist who appears regularly in the morning papers. He works as a freelance and spends a lot of time in the library.'

'I do know of him. I've seen some of his work. Have you known him for a long time?'

Enid was suddenly quite tense, Sharon thought. 'Not long, no. I met him in the library on one of my voluntary stints there. He comes in most days and does a lot of his work there. I don't know a lot about art, but I'd say he's very talented. He has a sharp wit and a sharp mind. If he'll join us, I fancy he might be an asset in the group.'

'I agree. Let's have him.' Enid didn't trust herself to say more. Several seconds passed before she said, 'My one suggestion is also male.'

He would be, thought Sharon bitchily. 'Do I know him?'

'Yes. I think you do. And you can veto him, if you choose to.'

'And why should I wish to do that?'

'Probably you won't. I might, but you'd be far too fair-minded to do that.' Enid contrived to make that sound like an insult. 'I think he'd get discussions going for us. But you might choose to reject him in view of what's happened in the past. That would be fair enough and I would instantly accept it. His name is Alfred Norbury. I think we both know that he's an intelligent man and a stimulating man. But he's also a dangerous man, in some respects. He's possibly bisexual or possibly gay, but he isn't dangerous to women like us. I don't think he'd be a predator within the group, and as a contributor to our debates, he'd be an asset. He'd certainly hold his own with your Jane Preston. He knows a hell of a lot about poetry: he's written some himself and he lectures about it when called upon to do so. Alfred is better read than anyone else I've met. And I know he's prepared to join us. He's the only one I've already approached.'

'What does he do for a living nowadays?' Sharon didn't much care about that: she wanted time to think.

'That's not as straightforward a question as you'd imagine it to be. He has private funds, which means he doesn't take on anything except what appeals to him. He lectures for the Open University, but I'm not sure how much work he does for them.'

'I'm sure we're lucky to get him.' Sharon Burgess spoke so evenly that it was impossible to be certain how much acid she intended. 'Is it in order to ask how long you've now known Mr Norbury?'

'Of course it is. I've known him for over thirty years.'

Sharon waited for a while, but Ms Frott offered no more details. 'I didn't know him until about a dozen years ago.'

Both of them knew the heavy implications of that simple statement, but neither of them wished to investigate it at this moment. Sharon took a deep breath and said, 'We should arrange a date and an agenda for our first meeting. Do you want it to be here?'

'No. We can manage in my flat. There'll only be five or six of us. I can handle that easily enough. We don't need any formal agenda: we need to introduce ourselves to each other and agree on the first book we're going to tackle together. I think it will be easier to do that in a more intimate setting. It might even help if we're crowded together a little.'

She's asserting her right to be in charge of this, thought Sharon. Well, fair enough: Enid was the moving spirit behind the whole idea in the first place, and she's accepted my suggestions about age and gender and membership. Why then am I still so wary about her? Why are we treating each other with such suspicion?

We have history and we can't get away from that, however

much we try to live in the present. Things might become easier as time passes. She said brightly, 'We've made good progress, I think. Don't be afraid to give me a ring if anything crops up. We seem to be in agreement about most things.'

'So when shall we have our first meeting? I suggest next Monday night at seven thirty.' Enid was back in her PA mode, efficient and impersonal. Sharon accepted the suggestion immediately.

Enid Frott was glad of the walk back down the drive in the cool winter air. When she was outside the gates, she looked back at the big house, with the sun now a little higher and the sky bluer than ever. She was glad to have her book club enterprise up and running. Too many bright ideas seemed to remain just that, when you were retired. It had helped that she'd had Sharon Burgess to push her forward and come up with ideas of her own. They seemed to have similar ideas, even if previous events meant that they could never be kindred spirits.

As she climbed into her car and started the engine, she still couldn't believe that she and Frank's widow were working together on this.

SIX

D ick Fosdyke decided that he was pleased with his morning's work. It was vicious but fair, he decided.

The British troops were being withdrawn from
Afghanistan at last and he wanted to point out how futile he
thought the whole exercise had been. Thousands dead, women
constantly abused and downtrodden, drugs rampant, victims
being stoned. And now we were moving out and leaving all
that behind. You couldn't put all that into a drawing: he needed
words as well, but as few as possible. And he knew that he
drew a good image of David Cameron by now. He set him
moon-faced in the middle of his drawing, looking absurdly
pleased with himself beneath a 'Mission Accomplished' sign.

He was so engrossed in the smooth rounding of the Prime
Minister's cheeks that he wasn't conscious of the woman in
front of him until she said, 'Got time for a coffee?'

He looked up and saw a smiling Sharon Burgess. 'I haven't,
really. I want to get a final version of this finished and off to
an editor before midday. It's a competitive market and I'd like
to get there first.' He glanced up at her. 'You can look at it if
you like. Offer any comment you like, as long as it's grossly
flattering.'

She moved round behind him, knowing that it was a great
privilege he was offering in even showing her his work, let
alone inviting her to comment. She gasped at what she saw,
then wondered if he had heard her. 'It's pretty brutal.'

He nodded contentedly. 'Vicious, isn't it? That's what I
intended. The cartoonist has to be extreme. It's the nature of
his calling. And in this case I think it's justified. There's been
carnage on both sides out there, and what has it all achieved?'

Sharon gazed at the drawing and said woodenly, 'I voted for
David Cameron in the last election.'

'I admire your conviction.' She supposed he was being ironic,
but she couldn't be certain of it. 'I didn't vote for anyone,

myself. You tend to become cynical, when you're making almost daily comments on the political scene.'

'This particular comment's justified, I suppose. You've made your point pretty effectively.'

'He's just the fall guy. I fancy it could have been whoever was the prime minister at the time. It's my view that they'd all have followed the Americans in there.'

'I'd say that you've made your point more trenchantly than most people would have done with a lot of words.'

'Thank you. That's what we try to do. You have to keep your lines simple and your comments very direct. A cartoon gets thirty seconds at most to make its point. Much less, with some people. The quickest ones are usually the most telling.'

'I'll leave you to get on with it. I'm glad I'm not a politician.'

He said as she moved away, 'I could do lunch. I'll be finished by then.'

They'd never had more than coffee together. It was surely quite a compliment to be invited to eat with this man, who preserved his privacy so carefully. 'All right. I don't finish my stint on the counter until one, though.'

He was waiting for her when she finished. He took her to a small pub in a back street, where the people behind the bar clearly knew him. She'd never been in here before. The staff were obviously trying to work out her relationship with Dick. Mother, perhaps? Or aunt? That's what their ages would have suggested to casual observers. But Dick treated her cheerfully as an equal, a person who might have views on what was happening in society which would interest him, whether he agreed with them or not.

The food was unpretentious but good. She said in a tone which made it clear she was sending herself up, 'Do you come here often?'

'Oftener than I used to, since I was divorced. It's a bit down-market, for someone like you. But the woman who does all the cooking buys her vegetables from the market and her meat from the local butcher. And the regulars have given up trying to engage me in casual conversations. I can read my newspaper or my book and enjoy my food without interruptions, like the miserable bugger I am.'

'I wanted to have a word with you about books, actually.'

'I gave a lot of my old ones to the library last year. You mean to re-read the best ones, but you never do.'

She smiled. 'It's not that. A couple of us are starting a book club. I'd like you to be one of the founder members.'

He looked at her in surprise, then shook his head firmly. 'Not my scene, I'm afraid. I enjoy books, but I like to choose my own. And I'm too opinionated to talk to other people about them. I'd get excited and give offence.'

'I'm glad to hear it. We need people to get excited. The last thing I'd want is bland agreement on the merits and de-merits of a book. I'll encourage you to state your views as trenchantly as you like, so long as you give others their turn and don't shout them down.'

He shook his head again, but less vehemently, perhaps even a little reluctantly. 'I'd be too argumentative.'

'You need the odd argument in a book club. You certainly need vigorous discussion. How much of that have you had, in the three years since you were divorced?'

'Not much. Are you offering me this as therapy?'

She grinned at the thought. 'Emphatically not. I'll want your opinions on whatever we've read, and I'll want you to listen to the opinions expressed by me and the other members of the group.'

This time he pursed his lips as he shook his head. 'How many?'

'Five or six to start with, if you come in with us. We might recruit one or two more, if we're successful. That would be up to the group.'

'Women don't like arguments. They prefer it when people agree with each other.'

'Not all women. And there'll be men there as well as women. Two or three, I hope. That would be including you.'

'I've lived in Brunton for a long time now. Would I know many of the people there? It might be embarrassing on both sides if I did.'

She got the impression that he was ticking off his objections one by one. 'I don't know all of them myself yet. There are a couple of people who teach literature professionally. One of them's a man who's a little older than you. The other's a young woman who teaches me about the nineteenth-century novel, and you'll like her. She's blonde and curvy and quite a dish. Fit, they call it now, don't they?'

'They might. I don't. And I'm more likely to be frightened of your bluestocking than attracted to her.'

'Jane's no bluestocking. And the other woman is almost as old as me. She used to be my husband's PA, a long time ago. Before Frank retired, of course: remember he was fourteen years older than me. Her name's Enid Frott.'

She thought that he knew that name, that he was going to comment on it. His lips tightened for a moment, then relaxed into a smile. 'I'll give it a go. On condition that I don't have to stay if I decide it's not for me. When do we start?'

Jamie Norris was trying to combine iambic pentameters with stocking shelves at Tesco. He wondered if he was the first person to attempt this. Possibly not: poets were a strange crew and they popped up everywhere.

Not successful poets, of course. Byron had made a fortune from poetry. 'Mad, bad and dangerous to know', Byron had been. Jamie had always rather fancied those epithets for himself, but he knew now that he wasn't going to make it. Tennyson had made himself into a lord and been revered by the Victorians. But no poet made big money nowadays. And no modern poet was adulated like Tennyson, not even Betjeman. Good old Philip Larkin had needed a librarian's wage to support his muse. At the moment, Tesco was supporting Jamie's muse, such as it was.

Tesco and Alfred Norbury: another unlikely combination. It was Alfred who'd set him going on the iambic pentameters. Jamie knew what they were all about, of course. Shakespeare had used them, after all. But Alfred Norbury had pointed out that even Shakespeare had needed to learn his craft, that the early plays creaked in a way you could scarcely credit when you saw the mastery of the famous later passages.

So Jamie had been set to work on iambic pentameters. Back to basics, Alfred said. It would be easy enough, but it would give him the foundation for lots of other verse. Jamie wasn't finding it easy enough. He conjured up lines of ten syllables easily enough, but getting the stresses to drop naturally on alternate syllables was rather more tricky. And you needed to do that to secure the poetic effects you wanted.

Jamie had always thought of himself as a free verse man, but Alfred said that was lazy thinking. You could only kick over the rules effectively when you knew exactly what the rules were and when you could write effectively within them. Otherwise, breaking rules was a kind of cheating.

Jamie Norris had understood all of this and accepted it. But he wasn't finding it easy to implement. Yet he knew that what Norbury said was true: he'd be a better poet when he'd studied and mastered different forms of verse. He'd managed sixteen lines in iambic pentameters, on the theme of the supermarket in snow and the effects snow had upon the people who used it.

He wanted four more lines to finish off what he thought might be a neat and balanced little poem, with one or two quite vivid images within it. He mustn't be self-indulgent, though, and he must be ruthless in pruning his verse. That was another thing upon which Alfred insisted: you must cut out anything which was even faintly second-hand or second-rate.

Norbury was right and Jamie could see that the little he did produce was of better quality. But standards didn't make things easy, and when your thoughts were constantly interrupted by calls for more tinned peaches or more lasagne, it didn't help your muse. John Keats had never had to contend with a frantic yelling for bags of frozen peas. But then Jamie Norris wouldn't have to contend with consumption, so it seemed a fair exchange. And physical labour was a kind of release, when you couldn't for the life of you form a bloody iambic pentameter.

It was towards the end of his shift that Jamie Norris was called into the manager's office. Mr Jordan looked worried: even if he'd reached his exalted position whilst only three years older than Jamie, management wasn't all milk and honey, the younger man realized. Jordan's face cleared and he smiled when he saw Norris. Everyone enjoys the luxury of having good news to deliver.

He said, 'You've been here for a little over three weeks now.

Your work has been generally satisfactory and you've happily accepted whatever shifts we have asked you to undertake.'

'Yes. I've been glad of the work, sir. And especially glad of the overtime.'

'Are you happy with the way you've been treated?'

Jamie knew the proper answers to the standard questions; you couldn't reach the age of twenty-six without learning some at least of the standard ways of survival. 'Very happy, sir. I get on well with my colleagues and I have been well treated by my superiors.'

'I'm glad to hear it. The work is repetitive at times, I know. That's inevitable, I'm afraid. But it's what you choose to make of it, in the main.'

Jamie wondered what that meant – wondered whether even the man who had stated it had any real idea what it meant. What the hell were you expected to make of it? But he said dutifully, 'I appreciate that, sir.'

'That's good. That's good for us as well as for you, Mr Norris. Because I like to think that we're a team here. And I have some good news for you.'

He paused and Jamie accepted his cue. 'Good news, sir?'

'I am happy to tell you that we are now able to offer you permanent employment.'

'Thank you, sir. I shall try to give satisfaction.'

'And we like to think that there are no dead-end jobs here, Mr Norris. You don't need to be a mere shelf-stacker for ever. If you continue to give satisfaction, you will be afforded more responsibility. We shall expect you to spot where shortages are likely to appear and take anticipatory action. That will take you into the realm of planning. In due course, if all goes well, you may be put in charge of other workers. You may even eventually take charge of a particular shift. I'm speaking long-term now, of course.'

'Of course, sir.'

Jamie Norris went back to the shelves and the tins of fruit in a golden glow of satisfaction. After twenty minutes or so he felt quite guilty. It was absurd to be so pleased about securing permanent employment at Tesco. He was almost more pleased than he was with his iambic pentameters.

*   *   *

Half a mile away from Tesco, in the large modern red-brick police station, Detective Chief Inspector Percy Peach was having a trying day.

At three o'clock on this January afternoon, the lights had already been on for an hour in the station. Percy glanced out at the dying grey of the day and thought it replicated the amount of light he had been able to cast upon this particular incident. It was a serious affray and he wanted to charge someone, but he knew now that he wasn't going to be able to do that.

That realization didn't improve his temper. This had been ruined for the rest of the day by a pep talk from Chief Superintendent Tucker. Even though it was only the middle of January, Tucker was already Percy's candidate for Prat of the Year. A hotly contested award in the police service, but one for which T.B. Tucker was invariably a short-priced favourite in Percy's book.

Peach glared at the young Asian man who sat four feet away from him in the interview room. 'You were bent on aggression, the whole gang of you. And you were the ring-leader, Mr Maqsood.'

'That is not true. We were not a gang. We were innocent people going about our business when we were attacked without provocation.'

'You came to Lord Street last night intending aggression. You spread yourselves across the thoroughfare to prevent any escape for the youths you had already planned to ambush there.'

'No. Your English trash carried out a planned attack upon us. We did no more than defend ourselves.'

'You were carrying knives. You came to the scene prepared for violence. Possibly murderous violence. You are lucky that you are not today being charged with murder.'

The brief who had not spoken until now cleared his throat theatrically. 'There is no case here for any sort of serious charge, DCI Peach.' He made an elaborate show of consulting his watch. 'You will have to release my clients in a few hours, and all of us know that. I suggest that you save valuable time for all of us and conclude this farce now by setting these men free. Whether they choose to sue you and your colleagues for wrongful arrest will of course be up to them.'

It was a prepared speech he'd been waiting to deliver, thought Peach sourly. It didn't help his temper that the local white lawyer with the white youths incarcerated elsewhere in the building was more hesitant and less articulate than this smooth operator. He ignored the brief and said to Maqsood, 'The only reason you didn't use the knives was that you were prevented from doing so. Both of them were removed from you by your intended victims as soon as you produced them. They were more prepared for your assault than you had expected.'

'You can prove this, can you, DCI Peach? It sounds like yet another instance of institutional police racism, to me.'

They'd have been charged and in court by now, if he could have proved it. The Asians knew that as clearly as Percy did, and they had grown more confident as the day had dragged past without charges. No need for the racism card really, their brief thought; that was a tactical error. Reserve the racism suggestions for when you were driven into a corner. There was no corner here, unless it was the one which DCI Peach and his colleagues had built for themselves. He contented himself with a bland smile when Peach glanced at him.

Percy said, 'Your colleagues are being interviewed elsewhere. They will contradict you, and your whole case will collapse about your ears like a house of cards.'

But he knew in his heart that it wasn't so. The others would be mouthing the same safe, rehearsed phrases that Maqsood was producing here. This was an experienced group, bent upon serious mischief. They'd been through all of this before. They were used to police questioning and to the restraints which were imposed upon it. They knew precisely what the CID could do and, much more importantly, what they couldn't do.

Sooner rather than later, there would be serious bloodshed on one side or the other between these rival gangs. Perhaps deaths, and perhaps on both sides. And then the press and the television would weigh in with pieces about the police failure to maintain order. And police officers wouldn't be able to cite all the hours they'd given to this today, because they'd been unsuccessful and they'd look stupid.

He said to the detective constable who stood behind his adversaries, 'Take Mr Maqsood back to his cell. We'll see what nonsense his companions come up with, and what the eye witnesses have to say about their actions.'

But he knew that he'd no eye witnesses to the key happenings, that Maqsood's fellow-fighters were too well-versed to contradict themselves, that he'd end this by releasing both sides with no more than a police caution. For a man who thrived on success, it was a depressing prospect.

There hadn't been a decent crime for months now. Not one you could get your teeth into and get some satisfaction from. They'd had a couple of manslaughters, but they'd both been domestics and solved within an hour. A proper murder would make life more interesting in these darkest months of the year.

Fat chance of that.

SEVEN

Enid Frott's flat was an interesting combination of the old and the new. A substantial Georgian house ('mansion' in estate agent's terms) had been converted just over twenty years ago into four spacious flats.

The amenities were modern – the kitchen, for instance, was spacious and had modern built-in appliances, most of which Enid had recently renewed. The bathroom had power-shower, bidet and mirrors which could be distressingly revealing to those sensitive about the effects of the passing years on human flesh. The central heating was both economical and efficient.

But the long Georgian windows had been carefully preserved and the rooms were spacious and surprisingly light. The four residences here were impressive from within and without. Enid had secured perhaps the best of them, the south-facing ground-floor flat which was adjacent to the communal front door of the converted mansion. She had no intention of leaving here until age or infirmity compelled it. For a spinster without children, extreme old age can be a desperately lonely business, but Ms Frott was a vigorous sixty-three year-old with much life to live before confronting such possibilities.

Like most people of her age, she consoled herself with the thought that dangerous frailty might never happen. She might be carried off by a heart attack in the throes of some illicit and highly vigorous passion, she told those whom she wished to shock. Who knows, she might even marry, she said: all possibilities were still open nowadays to the emancipated female. Her more private thoughts on such adventures she kept strictly to herself.

She had agreed in a phone call with Sharon Burgess that her hospitality on this occasion would be modest. Although everything was subject to discussion at this first meeting, the plan was that the book club would meet in the home of each of its members in turn. In view of this, you didn't wish to set standards which other people might find it difficult to maintain, and still less to introduce the sort of competition which dictates that each participant feels he or she has to outdo whatever has been provided before. The books must be the things, the two women agreed, and everything else must be merely incidental.

Enid Frott nevertheless thought it sensible to have a bottle of wine at the ready for her visitors, with a couple of others hidden in the fridge against emergencies. You had to be prepared to grease the wheels if you wished them to run smoothly in a vehicle like this, in which everyone was travelling for the first time. She wondered as she set out three dishes of nibbles how far this particular vehicle would run and how closely she would be able to control the route it followed. She had accepted now that control was important to her. She had been able to exercise a considerable degree of it in her working life and she had relished that. With no husband of her own and no children, she had needed to make few of the compromises which others had accepted as part of working life.

Now she acknowledged to herself that she might need to make a few revisions in the way she lived. She told herself firmly that retirement needed different attitudes from those she had exercised as office manager in her final period at Burgess Electronics. Being flexible in your approach would prove to yourself as well as to others that retired women could still be lively and adaptable.

She didn't need the wine, as it turned out. Sharon arrived first, as she'd expected. Then another woman and three men arrived in quick succession and her sitting room rang with a welter of introductions and nervous small talk. Four other bottles had arrived with these guests, who were obviously as anxious as she was that the occasion should not founder on the social rocks. Her only problem was persuading people to sit down in the rough circle of chairs she had prepared for them. No one seemed to be prepared to be the first one to descend into a chair; it was as if sitting would be a confession of some form of social weakness.

There was unease at first, which was not unexpected. Part of this was the natural uncertainty of people meeting each other for the first time. They were sizing up human beings with whom they planned to spend a considerable amount of time over an indefinite period, whilst simultaneously trying to give the impression that they were not doing that. It is a strange contradiction and one which besets the British more than most, and the English most of all. You wish to be relaxed and to encourage others to be relaxed, yet you wish at the same time to gain as much knowledge as you can about the personalities of these people. You might be meeting them for years, if this club works as it is supposed to do. You stand, or eventually sit, with a glass of wine in your hand and make small talk, hoping desperately that it will tell you far more than small talk usually does.

There was one person here whose presence no one had anticipated, apart from Alfred Norbury, the man who had insisted on bringing him here. The lean, dark-haired figure led the rather gauche young man in behind him and said, 'This is Jamie Norris. He is a young man with an interest in words, a writer who plans to shape words to his own purposes. Jamie is a poet and a wordsmith who shows considerable promise: I am sure he will be of great benefit to our group dynamic. He reads books like the rest of us, but writes as well, and he will bring a different perspective to our discussions.'

'We're all different, I'm sure,' said Enid Frott. 'I'm delighted to see Jamie here and to welcome him on your recommendation, Alfred.' She gave Jamie Norris a wide, automatic smile, as if to assure him that no personal insult was intended in what she was about to say. 'But the idea that our views will not be diverse without him is surely wrong.'

The lank-haired, saturnine Norbury took this as his cue to take centre stage. He moved a careful pace nearer to the centre of the room. 'We shall be able to test that in due course, no doubt. My own view is that Jamie will bring something quite different from anyone else to the group. I think we may expect what I would venture to call an informed naivety – I do not believe that is a contradiction in terms. He is well-read and anxious to test his own skill in words. But he will bring an unsullied mind to our deliberations because he has not been tainted by much previous formal instruction in the great works of our literature. In other words, he has not been told what to think, as many of us have.'

Jamie Norris thought it high time that he spoke up for himself. 'I don't remember learning much about books when I was at school. That might have been because I didn't pay much attention or because I wasn't there most of the time – I don't think the teaching was much good, but I wagged off quite a bit.'

Jane Preston thought that she should give some sort of support to the person in the room who was nearest in age to her. 'You'll probably have much more original views than I have. I've been stuffed to the gills with the orthodox critical views on all the great poets and all the great novelists. I was a dutiful schoolgirl in a private school, and I sometimes think I haven't got a really individual idea in my head. I'd love to write short stories or poems, but every time I try I find that what I've been taught over the years bounces into my brain and stifles creativity.'

Jamie glanced at her gratefully. 'Alfred says you should cast aside all preconceptions and start from scratch. Pen a few iambic pentameters of your own and just try to be original. Then you move on from there.'

Norbury moved between them. 'That isn't a general precept, Jamie. What's right for you might not be right for Ms Preston. I try to tailor my advice to the requirements of the individuals concerned. And that of course means that I have to get to know the people themselves quite well, before I feel equipped to offer any thoughts on what they might essay in the way of writing. I look forward to getting to know Jane much better in the months ahead of us.'

He turned the full focus of his dark, deep-set eyes upon the lady in question. Beneath his wide black eyebrows, his face looked in that moment quite Mephistophelean.

'If things go well, we shall all get to know each other much better in the months to come,' said Sharon Burgess brightly. Her words sounded almost like a rebuke, but Norbury looked quite unrepentant as he held out his glass for a refill. He looked at Jane Preston as if he wished to make her his ally in defying the older woman and her conventional sentiments, but she turned away from him to talk to Jamie Norris.

Enid Frott watched the exchanges with interest from the edge of the gathering. Then she stepped forward, holding her glass against the light and affecting to assess the colour of her red wine. 'Alfred is good at controversy. It's a way of life with him. That's one reason why I suggested we include him. With Alfred Norbury around, we won't be short of stimulating ideas about whatever books we select for our joint delectation. I'm sure that if any of us are reluctant to voice an opinion, we'll be stimulated by something outrageous from Alfred.'

Norbury gave her a little bow, like a matador making his preliminary pass at the bull. It was the sight of this which prompted a contribution from Dick Fosdyke. The cartoonist had been watching Norbury closely but making no comment on what he said. He now smiled and said, 'I suppose I should welcome controversy. It's the lifeblood of cartoonists. We thrive on the controversial and the outlandish. But it's one thing making a sardonic comment with a few lines and quite another responding in words. I feel inadequate already. Perhaps I'm here under false pretences.'

Norbury looked at him steadily. 'Even Dickens needed his Phiz until he'd established himself. The sketcher has his place in literature.'

'Just as the writer has his contribution to art. Even Hogarth needed some trenchant words beneath his work to provide the full and vicious irony in his depiction of the Rake's Progress.' Fosdyke looked hard for a moment at Norbury, then visibly relaxed as he addressed the rest of the company. 'I read all sorts of things – a real ragbag of books. A lot of the time I'm looking for ideas for cartoons. It's pretty demanding, thinking of a theme for every day. I can draw things and make my point quite swiftly, once I've decided on the point I want to make.'

Norbury was watching the cartoonist closely, as if he thought he would give something away about himself as he spoke. 'Fascinating. I'm sure writers find the same thing. Even my own modest efforts would support that. Once I know where I'm going, I can proceed quite quickly. It's deciding on my theme that gives me trouble – selecting my target, as I'm sure a man like you with a political message would put it.'

Sharon Burgess had a lot of experience of anticipating and suppressing spats. She waved the bottle enticingly around her five companions and said, 'That's an interesting idea. We're throwing up stimulating thoughts already, when strictly speaking we haven't started yet as a book club. Perhaps it's time for us to sit down and think a little about books.'

Enid Frott spoke with a surprising edge. 'Just when it was getting interesting, Sharon? You were always good at pouring oil on troubled waters.' She glanced round at the surprised faces, wondering which of them knew the facts of her history with Mrs Burgess. 'We're all civilized people here, aren't we? This isn't a back-street pub. We can have our little differences and enjoy them, without coming to blows.'

It was the third woman in the room who now spoke up when people were least expecting it. Jane Preston said, 'I find any discussion of the creative process fascinating. I've already said how difficult I find it to produce anything original, how inhibiting I find what I have learned about the writings of others is to my own creative efforts. I'd love to hear whether other people in this group have my problems and if so how they go about solving them.'

'It's a very private process. I'm not sure I want to start analysing it publicly.' Jamie Norris surprised himself by asserting this. He was emboldened by Jane's presence, he thought. He was enormously grateful not only for her being here but for what she was saying; it was surely helping him to speak and make his contribution, where he would otherwise have stood awkward and silent.

Perhaps Alfred Norbury was startled by this initiative in his protégé. He took a step towards Norris, looking for a moment as if he was about to put a hand upon his shoulder. Then he thought better of it and said, 'This is captivating, but as I understand it we did not gather here to discuss our own muses and our own creative processes, riveting as that might be at a later date, when we all know each other much better.' His smile flashed around his five companions. Jane wondered if she was being vain as she wondered whether or not it dwelt for a little longer upon her than the others. Whether she was right or not, she found this saturnine attention disturbing.

Sharon Burgess said immediately, 'Agreed,' though she knew that nothing had been agreed. 'Perhaps we should all sit down and address ourselves to the matter of books.' She glanced at Jamie Norris's too-revealing face. 'Other people's books.'

She was acting as host in Enid Frott's flat. The real host glanced at her, then forced a smile. 'I'm sure that's right. That's the object of the exercise, after all. Let's settle a couple of things and then get back to drinking and friendly argument, if that's what we wish to do.' She set the example by sitting down herself and waving a wide arm towards her sofa and the armchairs she had set alongside it. She watched her visitors acquiesce with varying degrees of reluctance and then said with a smile, 'I'm sure Sharon has given our first choice of book some thought, as she has so many other matters connected with this initial meeting.'

If Mrs Burgess detected a barb beneath the honeyed words, she gave no sign of it. She looked a little nervously round the expectant faces and said, 'I'm in your hands. I thought we might start with something in a genre which we all read.'

Alfred Norbury smiled his dangerous smile at the company, then said, 'Start on familiar ground, find our feet, and then perhaps move out into deeper waters. That sounds an excellent strategy, although I hope whatever writers we choose will avoid the string of clichés I've just used.'

Jane Preston looked deliberately away from him and into the apprehensive face of Jamie Norris sitting beside him. 'Crime fiction, perhaps? Everyone reads that, or has done at some time, according to what I read in a review the other day.' She waited for a response, but did not receive any. 'There are all sorts of crime novels, so we really would have quite a wide choice, if we chose to go that way.'

Most of them looked at Alfred Norbury for a reaction. He did not dismiss the suggestion out of hand, as Jane had thought he might, but said instead, 'The police procedural seems to be the most popular nowadays. You get the impression from the television versions that everything's under control, whereas in my experience anarchy grows ever nearer to most of us. I carry a loaded pistol in my car as a protection against the attentions of the citizens of modern Britain in our splendid multi-cultural society.' He looked round to assess the effects of his bombshell, but no one rose to the bait. Perhaps the ones here who had not met him before did not know whether to believe him or not.

Norbury appeared satisfied with the mixture of surprise and shock his statement had created. He sat back on the couch and said, 'You will all be pleased to hear that I propose to shut up now and leave the floor to others.'

There was a pause before Jamie Norris said unexpectedly, 'Historical fiction is very popular at the moment. And I believe that the quality of it is very good. I haven't read much of it myself. Perhaps it would further my education if I did.'

Enid Frott said, 'I think that is an interesting suggestion. We can learn a lot from what happened in the past.' Her eyes fixed automatically upon Sharon Burgess, then switched hastily away as her old adversary met her gaze.

Dick Fosdyke was looking at Norbury. He said, 'Should we go the whole hog and opt for history itself? We could read some of Pepys' diary. I've always meant to do that and never got round to it. Or perhaps we should consider a biography of Pepys – there's an excellent one by Claire Tomalin.'

There was a lively discussion, more wine, and the last of the season's mince pies, which Jane Preston had brought along and produced almost apologetically. They were on to the coffee by the time they agreed that their first book would be Jim Crace's *Harvest*, shortlisted for the Man Booker prize and the subject of recent rave reviews.

'I've never really understood what the Enclosure Acts did to the rural poor,' said Enid Frott. 'It's high time I remedied my deficiencies.'

'I'm sure you already know more than most of us,' said Sharon Burgess loyally. 'It will be interesting to have a literary treatment of history as well as a few facts.'

'And Alfred says it isn't overlong,' said Jane Preston modestly. 'I've always been much too slow a reader for someone with a busy life. It seems that almost every best-seller these days has to be a blockbuster; they take me far too long to read and don't usually repay the effort.'

This self-effacing contribution from the person in the room most highly qualified in literature cheered those who feared being eclipsed in this challenging company. The group broke up shortly afterwards, having agreed to meet next at the home of Sharon Burgess on the seventeenth of February. They left congratulating each other on the success of this first meeting and assuring themselves that it would surely be the first of many such convivial evenings.

None of them realized at the time that they would not meet again.

EIGHT

'Low-key', they said this operation had to be. The mysterious 'they' who made all the unpopular decisions. The intangible 'they', who couldn't be identified and thus couldn't be the recipients of your complaints.

The only thing that was certain was that they were obscure bastards: so obscure that you weren't even sure whether they were from the higher echelons of the police hierarchy or from somewhere beyond that and even more difficult to identify. MI5, perhaps. Or even the politicians who controlled – or miscontrolled – all policing and made the ultimate decisions on security.

Low-key. Presumably that was why they put a mere detective sergeant in charge of this. An inspector or a superintendent might have drawn too much attention to it. But it was more likely that the higher ranks didn't want any involvement in a cock-up. They'd prefer to be able to stand aside and say 'I told you so' when things went pear-shaped.

Detective Sergeant Clyde Northcott didn't consider a further possibility: that higher ranks might have opted out of this because of the physical danger involved. When you went into houses where the occupants possessed firearms, death or serious injury was always a possibility, and more so when those occupants were young and likely to panic. Northcott wasn't stupid and he knew that. He was a big target; he didn't carry a surplus ounce of fat, but he was six feet three and weighed 215 pounds. There was a lot of him for a bullet to hit. He was also very black: some people were even more likely to shoot first and ask questions afterwards when you were black.

Northcott chose not to entertain the possibility of physical injury because he considered such risks natural for him. He had been a murder suspect himself before being recruited unexpectedly into the police service. He had never had a criminal conviction, but he had dealt in drugs and lived on the other side of the law for

several years before he had seen the light and been offered unexpected redemption. This had come in the unlikely form of
Detective Inspector 'Percy' Peach, who had cleared him from
suspicion of murder, then enlisted him first into the police service
and then two years later into his own CID team.

Peach had recognized in the massive Northcott the 'hard
bastard' he said he needed for his team. He had noted in the
big black man the experience of that darker criminal world
which would be useful. He had seen also a shrewd detective
brain, which Peach chose in the main not to acknowledge but
which he drew upon whenever it suited him. Northcott was the
man who had replaced DS Lucy Blake as Percy's chosen assistant when marriage and police protocol had determined that the
curvaceous Lucy could no longer work closely with her husband.
Neither Peach nor Clyde acknowledged the fact, but both of
them knew that Northcott's swift promotion and transfer to this
role were huge compliments to his skills and standing.

As he sat in the unmarked car outside the unremarkable
terraced house, Northcott knew that he hadn't been sent here
by DCI Peach. Percy would have been by his side: he never
shirked physical danger himself, though he was decently prudent
in the precautions he took. Very likely Percy had protested about
his bagman's presence here today, and been overruled by that
mysterious higher authority. The thought that Percy might have
opposed his involvement in this made Clyde even less anxious
to explore what might lie behind the innocent-looking front
door of number thirty-four.

The street lights were still on. It was just after half past seven;
not much past dawn on this cold, grey January morning. If you
caught your victims still in bed, you had the advantage over
them; if they were naked and with a partner, so much the better.
It wasn't just dignity they lost; not many men found it easy to
be aggressive when they were bollock naked. Early morning
snatches were police favourites for all sorts of reasons. There
was one major reason on this day. An early-morning snatch
probably offered the best chance of safety to the men who were
making it.

The guidance in the station said they should have a woman
officer with them, if at all possible, in case there were women to

be searched in the house. Clyde had decided against that when he had selected his three. The rules said all sorts of things about gender equality, but young men still tended to protect a woman, to try to ensure her safety even at the expense of their own. Chivalry overrode police regulations, even in those who had scarcely heard the word. He'd grabbed the only Asian officer available to him: there still weren't anything like enough of these in multi-racial Brunton.

He glanced at the three plain-clothes constables in the car with him. This was probably their first security exercise. They weren't so many years younger than him, but he felt immensely older and more experienced than them, and thus very much responsible for their welfare. He wanted them alert and prepared for any sort of surprise beyond that door. Yet he wanted them to think that this was a routine, everyday exercise for him, which it emphatically was not.

He looked up and down the street, which at this hour was still full of cars. 'You lads would be better employed checking tax disks.' Relax them; let them think this was all likely to be an anti-climax. Yet you needed them to be poised and ready for action, as soon as they crossed this step. The responsibilities of rank did not come easily to Northcott. He risked his own skin without a moment's hesitation, but looking out for the safety of others gave him all sorts of problems.

He rapped at the scratched blue front door, rang the bell beside it, heard not a sound from within. Bloody daft procedure: you warned the buggers inside, lost all the advantages of surprise. He motioned to the burly man with the heavy metal door-crasher, who stepped forward and swung the heavy implement viciously at the wood beside the lock. Two crashes saw the wood splinter and the lock shatter. They were into the house immediately, ignoring the four curious faces in the street behind them, bursting noisily into the narrow, empty hallway with Northcott at their head.

There was no one in any of the sparsely furnished downstairs rooms. But in the rear bedroom they found three men. Between twenty and thirty, Clyde estimated: he always found beards made it more difficult for him to be certain about ages. Asian – he wouldn't speculate beyond that vague epithet. And hostile:

their fierce eyes and the hatred in their narrow faces told him that he was the infidel.

He waved the search warrant at them and uttered the formal, official words which he was not sure they understood about what was now going to happen. The phrases were gabbled out so breathlessly that he scarcely followed them himself; he realized in that moment how nervous he was. Then he directed his companions towards the systematic search which was their mission here. It was swifter than he would have anticipated because the furnishings were so minimal. He wondered how long these men had been here and whether the house was merely a temporary base for them. He didn't know the full picture, but he was not resentful about that. He was much happier supporting Percy Peach than in this complicated, specialist policing. These men were terrorist suspects, and the unit which dealt with terrorism had its own staff and its own methods.

The problem was a mammoth one. There were hundreds of suspects in Brunton alone. But the terrorism unit moved only when an actual plot was suspected and innocent life was considered to be in danger. If they moved too early, they arrested a series of fanatical young men who were prepared to die for the cause, their idealism warped and intensified by their minority, militant branch of the Muslim religion. Unless you had clear proof of their murderous intent, your efforts ended in frustration with their eventual release through lack of evidence. Meanwhile, the major criminals who were orchestrating the violence would move on scot-free to their next intrigue. If you delayed arrests a fraction too late, disasters on the scale of the London bombings of 2007 and perhaps much worse would certainly ensue.

DS Northcott was glad he was only on the periphery of anti-terrorist action. The suspicion here was that arms were hidden in the house, stored there in preparation for use in some major but so far embryonic attack. He rapped out a series of warnings and explanations to the three men who sat resentfully together where he had directed them to sit, on the edge of one of the three single beds in the room. He read understanding in the face of the one he judged to be the eldest, but the man gave him no verbal response.

His men found nothing in the kitchen, nor in the two other

rooms on the ground floor. The bathroom and the large bedroom at the front of the house yielded nothing, even when rugs were stripped away and the floors investigated. It was only when he moved the hostile trio from the bed where they sat to one on the other side of the room that he detected a reluctance and a glance from one of them towards the area of the room which he thought might be significant.

Clyde set one of his men to keep careful watch on the men, who had already been searched for guns and knives. They sat reluctantly as he indicated on the third bed and watched him with brown, malevolent eyes. He shifted the bed where they had sat until now and rolled up the tattered strip of matting which was the only floor-covering in this room. He kept one eye on his seated adversaries as he eyed the floor, feeling that they might fly at him like feral animals if he really had located something here.

The floorboards in this room had been here for 120 years. But one at least of them had been raised recently. The tongues and grooves which had anchored it had been broken: the board was loose and noisy beneath his foot as he tested it. He looked at the youngest of the men and read fear in the narrow, mean face.

The floorboard and the ones adjacent to it lifted easily with a screwdriver. The man he had looked at tried to rise, but was pushed roughly back on to the bed by the constable who stood over him. Northcott and his other two companions carefully removed nine dangerous weapons from the shallow space beneath the floorboards.

Armalite rifles, oiled and ready for use. And beyond them, ample supplies of ammunition. Many thousands of pounds worth of armoury. More importantly, the means to kill hundreds of British citizens. He stood looking into the defiant faces of the men on the other side of the room and felt hostility rolling like a cloud of poisoned gas between hunted and hunters.

DS Northcott pronounced the words of arrest and went through the rigmarole about them not having to say anything but needing to be aware that anything they did say might be used in future court proceedings. As he had anticipated, the men said not a word, but stood sullenly defiant whilst they were handcuffed and taken to the police van now waiting outside. Higher minds than theirs had issued them with their orders in the eventuality of arrest.

They were taken to the station and formally charged with the illegal possession of dangerous firearms. They would undergo detailed interrogation in due course. No doubt they would have been warned about that also, and would have the assistance of an expert brief, who would encourage and assist them to be as obdurate and uncooperative as possible.

DS Northcott was relieved to see them taken from his sight and locked into a cell. He was glad that it wouldn't be he who had to question these three.

A mile away from the dramatic events which were being enacted in that shabby terraced house, Jamie Norris was struggling with quite different problems in the brightly lit aisles at Tesco.

He was on early shift and he'd started at six. The big vans had made their deliveries during the night and he had spent the first two hours of his shift transferring fresh vegetables and fruit to the shelves and replenishing the freezers with hundreds of ready meals. A boon to working mothers, these were; he'd kept his ears open and heard that view expressed repeatedly by the customers.

A knowledge of how customers felt and of the geography of the store were the two things which carried you through public exchanges in the supermarket. People mostly wanted information as to where they could find various products. Those who chose to offer him more than questions and opted to pass the time of day with him wanted their own prejudices reinforced, not challenged. It was far better to agree with them about how convenient and sensible these pre-packed meals were than to reminisce nostalgically about how their mums and grandmas had laboured lovingly to produce balanced meals for them. Customers wanted to feel sensible, not guilty.

These words were provoked by a short exchange he had just had with Mr Jordan during his breakfast break. He now called the manager by his name, rather than 'sir', except when there were customers around and he needed to boost the man's prestige. Mr Jordan had said that he seemed to be developing a good relationship with the customers. They were a curious lot, the manager had implied, and far more difficult to please than most of the public ever knew. Jamie thought it was pretty easy to get on with them, so long as you talked about the weather and took care to reinforce purchasing prejudices which they sometimes didn't know they possessed. If you looked at what they already had in their trolleys, you were on pretty safe ground.

These easy and rather random thoughts diverted Norris from more serious problems. The first of these was his latest attempt at verse. The iambic pentameter stuff had helped him: he was prepared to admit that, though he had found it humiliating at the time, for he had thought he had moved beyond that stage. But you were never too old to learn, as many people said and few of them practised. Back to basics had reminded him of the advantages of rhythm and of the need for discipline in your writing.

He had produced a sonnet which was quite tight and well-finished, with some trenchant phrases and no padding. It had taken him a while; he had refined it and sharpened it over several days and enjoyed the processes of doing that. It was a love sonnet. It wasn't addressed to a particular girl, but rather to an amalgam of womanhood, to the best and most desirable in the various girlfriends who had passed through his hands over the last few years. Well, not always through his hands. He'd found it difficult to get his hands on the more delectable parts of the ones he fancied most. But that was life, wasn't it? Life constantly enticed you and constantly disappointed you. This wasn't a perfect world: another of those statements which people enunciated philosophically but still resented.

Jamie thought he would keep the sonnet in his secret drawer and produce it when he had his next serious girlfriend. He would call it 'To Becky' or whatever the girl's name might be. It would be easy with a few minor amendments to make it seem quite personal. Girls like poetry much more than men do; with a bit of luck, this still anonymous girlfriend would be pleased and flattered by his sonnet. Perhaps even pleased enough to pass through his eager hands.

He wouldn't show it to Alfred Norbury, much as he would have welcomed his mentor's grudging praise. That was the second of his serious problems. Alfred had taken him over, and Jamie wasn't comfortable with that. The older man had been generous to him, and he undoubtedly knew a lot about literature. He seemed genuinely concerned to make Jamie a better writer and his advice had been practical and effective. Jamie understood more about the way good poetry worked now, and his own verse had improved as a result of that. The practical exercises Alfred had urged upon him were taxing, but they were productive.

He would like to keep the tuition and advice, but dispense with other Norbury intimacies. But he was becoming aware that he couldn't do that. You couldn't pick and choose what you took from Alfred. It wouldn't be fair. The older man would make him acutely aware that it wasn't fair. This wasn't a problem Jamie Norris had needed to deal with before and it made him very uneasy.

But sooner or later, he would need to do something to dispense with the attentions of Alfred Norbury.

Detective Chief Inspector Percy Peach was having a trying day. He was used to trying days in the Brunton CID section, but this one was a belter.

He'd spent most of the morning with a youth who'd crashed his fist into the face of an old lady when she had surprised him during a burglary at her council flat. He'd finally got the seventeen-year-old to admit to his crime. But for almost an hour, the young brute had maintained that the lady had fallen over a chair and hit her face on a corner of the table, whilst his mother had sat beside him and interjected at every opportunity the view that Jason was 'a good boy who wouldn't hurt a fly'. Peach pitied the woman in her delusion, but was at the same time intensely irritated by her interruptions.

Her son had been duly charged and would plead guilty. His age and lack of previous criminal convictions meant that he might well escape a custodial sentence. Probably he'd be remanded for psychiatric reports and given a hundred hours of community service, Percy reflected darkly. The Crown Prosecution Service would eventually inform him wearily that it had all been a waste of police time. But an eighty-year-old woman who had kept the law throughout her blameless life would be permanently marked, fearful for the rest of her days, and would probably never come out of care and back to the independent home she had loved. Peach should have been insulated by experience against such things, but they still brought him much pain and depression.

His choice of toad in the hole in the police canteen at lunch time had afforded him another bad experience, less enduring perhaps, but still a source of internal turmoil. He'd forgotten that the regular chef had left and he had suffered for his omission.

And now he was closeted with Chief Superintendent Tommy Bloody Tucker for a pep talk. The end of a perfect January day in CID. 'I thought we should have a few words together at the beginning of a new year!' said T.B. Tucker bracingly.

They were now twenty-two days into the new year, but that was par for the course for Tucker. An appropriate metaphor: Tucker was one of the worst golfers as well as undoubtedly the worst chief superintendent Percy had ever encountered. He tried to sound a cheerful note. 'Another year nearer to pension, sir.'

Tucker bristled. On other days, this would have given Peach some pleasure, especially if he was sure he had provoked it, but on this bleak January afternoon it afforded him no comfort. The bristle became a glower. 'Are you implying that my pension dominates my thinking, Peach?'

'No, sir. I'm sure that it is no greater a consideration for you than it has been over the last three years, sir.'

'I invited you up here for an informal chat, Peach. When I directed you to sit down, it was certainly not an invitation to you to insult me.'

Percy looked round the familiar penthouse office. It had wide views over Tucker's domain, looking out over the Brunton which constituted the bulk of their criminal patch to the vales and hills of the Ribble Valley beyond the town. He said dully, 'Sir, it has been your practice to remind me over the last three years at least of the proximity of your pension and of the need to take no action which might possibly endanger your securing of that holy grail.'

'I remember no such occasions, Peach.'

'Your capacity for amnesia is one of your more remarkable attributes, sir. I'm sure it has been instrumental in your progress to the rank of Detective Chief Superintendent, sir. Along with your multitudinous other qualities, of course, sir. That goes without saying.'

Tucker endeavoured to pin Peach to his chair with the beam of his basilisk chief superintendentorial eye, but he found his junior's gaze fixed resolutely upon some high point in the corner of the room. 'We need to go carefully this year. The need for economy has been urged upon us by the Chief Constable.'

'Economy is always urged by chief constables, sir. It's part of their job: it's a nervous reflex to stress the need for economy. Probably built in as part of their training: when you have no useful thoughts to offer, stress the need for economy.'

'This is more than cynicism, Peach. This is something nearer anarchy. I must warn you that I will not tolerate it in one of my senior officers.'

'Our overtime claims have been extremely economical, sir. We have hardly disturbed the budget at all over the last three months.'

'I was planning to congratulate you on that, Percy, had you given me the chance before embarking upon this scurrilous attack on our much-respected Chief Constable.'

The man was using his first name. That was always a danger signal. 'No personal attack upon our respected leader was intended, sir. I was merely sounding off about the habits of bureaucracy.'

'You're claiming that our CC is a bureaucrat?' Tucker looked as if he had accused the man of fraud or smuggling.

'All really senior policemen have to be bureaucrats, sir. The more so as they move up the hierarchy. That is why I have never been interested in promotion beyond my present rank. Men like you and me wish to remain near the crime-face, do we not, sir?'

He waited for a reaction from this man who avoided the crime-face at all costs. Tommy Bloody Tucker looked as puzzled as he always looked when he suspected an insult but could not pin it down. He eventually said, 'That should be "you and I" you know, Percy.'

'I think you'll find it's "you and me", sir. Following a prep-osition, you see. And I can't guarantee that the overtime claims won't rise steeply over the winter months, sir. The last three months of the year were unusually quiet on our patch. Almost dull, in fact, for a man as interested in nailing villains as you are.'

'Now look, Peach, we have to be realistic about this. We want to keep our spending within bounds and our clear-up rates high. That is a recipe for success and for congratulations from the CC.'

'You're suggesting we should keep our noses clean and not excite too much attention, sir.'

'If you like, yes. There are virtues in quiet efficiency, Peach. You tend to underestimate the advantages to us of keeping our noses clean. It is much better not to chance your arm, if you wish to get on in the police service, Peach.'

Back to surnames again; Percy felt much safer. 'Yes, sir, I can see the advantages of that. Especially for any senior officer who is approaching the end of his service and taking care that nothing should jeopardize his pension.'

'You are impertinent, Peach.' Another bristle was in the offing.

'Sorry, sir. I thought I was enunciating your CID policy for the coming year.'

'You will show respect to your seniors, Peach. And you will exercise a proper control over your juniors.'

'Not easy, sir, when the DS on whom I place great reliance is summarily removed from my control and sent out on anti-terrorist operations.' He watched Tucker's plump features sag towards bewilderment. 'DS Northcott, sir. A vital man for me. Deployed against my wishes and without consultation in anti-terrorist arrests at thirty-four Boston Street this morning.'

'Ah! Yes. I was asked for local expertise in this matter by the anti-terrorist unit. I decided that DS Northcott was the appropriate officer for the task. That is my right, Peach. That is part of my job.' He waited for the inevitable rejoinder, but Peach offered him nothing to bite on. Tucker decided diver-sionary tactics were the best option. 'I've never been quite sure about DS Northcott, you know, in view of his record before he was recruited into the police service.'

'Poacher turned gamekeeper, sir.' Tommy Bloody Tucker looked as if he'd never heard the expression, but Percy wasn't going to help him out. They'd had this conversation several times before.

'He was suspected of murder, you know.'

'I do know, sir. It was I who decided that Clyde Northcott was not involved. It was I who made the eventual arrest of the guilty party in that case.'

'Technically, yes. And it was I who subsequently had you promoted to Detective Chief Inspector. You should remember that, Peach.'

'I remember it, sir,' said Percy grimly. In order to secure his own promotion to chief superintendent and the fat pension which was now his sole concern, T.B. Tucker had been forced to recommend the elevation of the man who made the arrests and kept the clear-up rates for serious crimes among the best in the north of England. Percy sighed extravagantly. 'DS Northcott found an illegal cache of arms beneath the floorboards this morning and made the appropriate arrests. Will you be conducting the interrogations yourself, sir?'

Percy enjoyed the look of horror which now suffused the revealing features of his chief – predictable, but satisfying nonetheless. Tucker said sternly, 'We must leave that to the anti-terrorist officers, Peach. Our job is done in this matter. And now I think you have occupied my day for quite long enough. It is time you were about your business, Peach.'

Percy descended the stairs dolefully, pausing at the window to gaze out over the grimy old town he loved. What he needed to animate him and to dissipate his resentment of Tommy Bloody Tucker was an interesting major crime, of which there had been a serious dearth over the last four months.

DC Brendan Murphy, the large, fresh-faced officer who was a local, despite his name, was waiting for him in the CID section. 'I'm glad you're back. Something's just come in.'

'You're brighter than you look, Brendan. It's the only virtue I can see in you, sometimes. Your bearing tells me that this is something interesting. So spit it out.'

'Man shot in his car, sir.'

Peach raised the impressive black eyebrows beneath his bald

head. Brunton wasn't Los Angeles: gun crime was still the exception rather than the rule here. 'Suicide?'

'Too early to say, sir. Seemingly not a burglary, though. Victim's wallet intact and well-filled. Name of Alfred Norbury.'

NINE

Wellington Street was a quiet residential road near the centre of Brunton. It had been the finest street in the town in its Victorian heyday, when cotton had been king, a hundred chimneys had belched smoke from the town's mills and foundries, and a few fortunate men had made huge fortunes.

It was still one of the best and most convenient roads in the town, but smaller family units and the cost of domestic help meant that only two of the houses had survived as individual residences. The others had been converted into flats. But unlike many units in more rundown urban areas, these were mostly owner-occupied and changed hands infrequently. The major aesthetic decline from Victorian days was in horticulture. Where geraniums and lobelia and alyssum and snapdragons had flourished in long front gardens behind low front walls, the motor car now dominated.

That ubiquitous and many-hued modern marvel had replaced horticultural design and beauty with a random and constantly changing parade of metal. The front walls and the railings which had topped them had disappeared a long time ago. Huge slabs of grey concrete had spread where many years ago there had been lawns and flowers. Tyres came and went where once gardeners had worked with loving care to set off the high brick houses behind them. Progress is sometimes the enemy of beauty.

It was only four o'clock on this Wednesday afternoon and many of the vehicles which parked here overnight were still at the owners' places of work. But the early January nightfall was already beginning to envelop the scene of crime. That is what the area outside 12 Wellington Street had been designated, even though no one had yet officially established what crime had been committed. The ribbons defining it as such were already in place, enclosing a rectangle of twenty metres by eighteen metres in front of the high building, which looked more sinister in the developing darkness.

Because of the quietness of the area and the chill of the January evening, there were fewer curious spectators than usual standing around to observe the police activity. But the word would get around quickly enough and the rubbernecks would gather. This was the best area of the town. There was always an additional frisson of excitement when crime and scandal struck among your supposed elders and betters.

As was usual on such occasions, there was very little for bystanders to see, beyond the official comings and goings. The chilled and gloomy spectators watched the scene of crime team, who were mostly civilians, and the plain-clothes officers. These were the people who were going to decide what crime, if any, had taken place here and what police resources this death warranted. The vehicle which was at the heart of this was surrounded by a high temporary fence of canvas, so that the onlookers could see nothing of the most vital activity.

Within the wider areas of the crime scene outside this hidden nucleus, a young man and a young woman stooped low over wet concrete to gather whatever peripheral evidence they could acquire. They were constables gaining experience, the only police service members of the SOCA team. Every officer needed to know how a meticulous scene of crime chief worked, and this also gave two raw young newcomers their first fringe contact with a suspicious death. They used tweezers to pick up cigarette ends, chocolate papers, even the plastic wrapper from a loaf of bread, then transferred them with scrupulous care into small plastic bags.

Peach and Northcott took in the scene for a moment, then slipped plastic covers over their feet and moved down the designated track to the small gap at the rear of the inner enclosure which was not visible to the public. Jack Chadwick, former police colleague of Peach's but nowadays a civilian, was watching the fingerprint expert removing powder from the rear door handle of the car which was now revealed to them. He looked up into the formidable black features of Clyde Northcott. 'No offence, son, but I preferred Percy's last bagman – baglady would give entirely the wrong impression.'

'We all preferred Sergeant Lucy when she was Blake. Only

one of us got any further than that. I reckon Percy pulled rank to make her Mrs Peach.'

'Animal magnetism,' said Percy calmly. 'If you can't spot that from a mile away, you're no detective. What news, Jack?'

'Very little, so far. Suspicious death is as far as we can go.'

Northcott bent to look at the slumped figure in the driving seat of the car. It had very black hair, which just failed to conceal a surprisingly neat bullet hole in the right temple. There was less blood visible than he would have expected. The hand at the side of the corpse, invisible until you stood beside the vehicle, held a medium-sized pistol. 'Suicide?'

'Possibly. The pathologist has been and gone and wouldn't commit himself. Says he'll give you more when he's had him on the slab and cut what's left to pieces: you know the form.'

Percy looked at the gleaming dark blue metal. 'Nice car.'

Chadwick nodded. 'Valuable, too. Triumph Stag Mark One, in sapphire blue and with not a spot of rust visible.' He glanced down at the registration number. '1972. And only ninety-one thousand on the clock. I'd need convincing of that, but she's a lovely motor.'

Peach ran his eyes along the sleek flank of the vehicle. 'You should sell 'em, Jack.' He gestured towards the figure he'd hardly looked at as yet. 'Didn't do chummy much good, did it? How long do you reckon he's been dead?'

Chadwick shrugged his highly experienced shoulders. 'Pathologist will give you his opinion tomorrow. He agreed to make it urgent. He's only got a road death to occupy him, other than this.'

'And your opinion?'

Jack grinned for a second at his old colleague. 'He's as cold as an Arctic nun. My guess would be that he died last night.'

Northcott looked back at the street, then the other way, towards the entrance to the house at the top of three stone steps, where a series of bells rose neatly beside the names of the people who had flats here. 'And has lain here ever since? Surely someone would have seen a body and reported it earlier?'

'You'd think so, but you and I know that people don't want to get involved nowadays. They ignore things they should report and get on with their own lives. Remember that Catholic

priest who lay dead for three days in a supermarket car park
before anyone reported that he was there? Ignorance is a safe
way of life for a lot of people. You can't see the pistol, unless
you come and peer through the window. And this is a quiet
place. It isn't the sort of house where old ladies peer out from
behind lace curtains.'

Peach nodded and looked resentfully at the long and impressive Victorian bay windows in their stone surrounds. He'd
collected a lot of useful information over the years from
inquisitive old women of both sexes, with or without lace
curtains. 'I suppose people who were parked on the concrete
here could have come out in a hurry and at the last minute to
get to work. I don't observe much myself when I'm running
late.' He looked up at the heavy grey sky. This was one of
those dreary winter days which are scarcely more than intervals
between long nights. People racing off to work in the grim
half-light of the morning might well have failed to register
the figure in the Stag. And Chadwick was right: a depressing
proportion of the modern British public would have left it for
someone else to report, even if they'd suspected something
might be amiss.

Jack said, 'There are garages round the back. According to
the woman who also lives on the ground floor, each of the flats
has one. Assuming chummy was a resident here, he'd probably
have one of the garages.' He glanced back appreciatively at the
Stag. 'This car certainly looks as if it's spent most of its life
in a garage.'

It was something to be borne in mind, one of a whole series
of routine questions which would need to be asked of the people
who lived here, over the next twenty-four hours. Where, when
and how were the three major questions with a suspicious death.
It looked pretty certain that this man had died here. Chadwick
had given them an informed guess about when. Now they were
starting on how. It was pretty obvious that this man had died
by a bullet from the gun in his right hand. But exactly how?
Who had pressed the trigger?

As if he followed Percy's thoughts, Jack Chadwick grinned
mischievously and volunteered a thought. 'My team's almost
finished here. You'll have to wait and see what the pathologist

says. It's my view that you've got a murder on your hands, Percy Peach.'

The setting for Clyde Northcott the next morning couldn't have been more different from Wellington Street. That place had been emphatically urban, albeit upper-class urban.

This house was in gently undulating Cheshire countryside and barely within sight of its nearest neighbours, which were over half a mile away. It was a low stone farmhouse, in contrast to the high brick Victorian town house outside which the body of Alfred Norbury had been discovered. But this was no longer a working farm. The land it had once controlled had been taken over by a larger neighbouring farm, invisible behind a copse of trees at the top of the slope behind it. This building had now been converted into a luxurious private residence.

The two CID officers parked on the large cobbles which must once have been a farmyard. The adjacent labourers' cottages had been demolished and replaced by a huge conservatory, where the buds of camellias were already showing colour in gentle heat. A woman in there noted their arrival and appeared a moment later at the front entrance of the farm to meet them. Clyde said, 'I rang earlier. I'm Detective Sergeant Northcott and this is Detective Constable Murphy.'

The building must be more than two hundred years old, he reckoned. He wondered as the woman led them indoors how many black men had crossed its threshold in all those years. The ceilings were low and he had to bend his head to pass through the doorway into the lounge – a large, comfortable room which was almost square, with a Turkish carpet and long sofas which looked as if they had been designed for the room. The only evidence of the building's original more humble station were the small windows, which had been carefully preserved. They seemed to emphasize the thickness of the cream-painted walls around them.

The woman wore black leather low-heeled shoes beneath black jeans and a blue top which looked to Northcott's inexpert eye very expensive. He said, 'I think you should sit down, Mrs Tilsley.' She gestured towards the sofa and the two big men sat down as carefully as if it had been much more fragile. She watched them with a small smile. Only when they were seated did she sit in an armchair opposite them and cross her elegant legs.

Northcott said. 'I must first of all check that we have our facts right. Are you the former wife of Alfred James Norbury?'

'I am indeed. You hinted when we spoke on the phone that you had bad news. He's dead, isn't he?'

'I fear he is, yes. I'm sorry to be the one who has to tell you this.'

'You've no need to treat me with kid gloves. I stopped having tender feelings for Alfred a long time ago. We've been divorced for twelve years. I haven't seen him since the details of the divorce were finalised. There were no children, so it was a clean break. That suited me. I haven't spoken to Alfred for ten years and I had no intention of ever speaking to him again.'

'Thank you for being so plain. May I ask how you knew that Alfred was dead? There has been no official announcement.'

'I heard on the radio that there had been a suspicious death in the centre of Brunton. Ten minutes later, you rang me, said you were CID, and established that I had once been married to Alfred Norbury. I made an assumption.'

'A correct one. You've indicated that you are not overwhelmed with grief. I hope it is not impertinent of me to say that you also do not seem to be very surprised that your former husband should have died violently at the age of forty-six.'

'I've had a couple of hours since you rang me to get accustomed to the idea. I was more shaken at first than I feel now. But no, it's not impertinent, and yes, I suppose it's true that his death is not as much of a shock as I would have expected it to be.' She gazed past them and through the window to a patch of sun moving swiftly across the swathe of green outside, weighing her opinion as coolly as if she had been asked her view on new curtains.

Brendan Murphy spoke for the first time. 'Neither of us has ever met Alfred. As far as we are aware, he has had no dealings with the police. There is no official verdict yet, but it appears that he might be the victim of a violent crime. We know nothing about him and he can no longer speak for himself. We have to try to build up a picture of him through those closest to him.'

'I can see that and I'd like to help you. But I've already told you that I've had no recent dealings with him and had no intention of renewing our acquaintance. I believe that suited both of us. I have been happily married for the last eight years to a very different man and I have two young children, who are at present at school. I suppose I should be sorry that Alfred's dead, if only for old times' sake. Every man's death diminishes me, and all that stuff. But I'm afraid I feel nothing. To be strictly accurate, I suppose I feel a certain relief that an unfortunate chapter of my life is finally and irretrievably closed.' She clasped her hands in front of her and looked at them thoughtfully. 'I'm sorry to be so frank, but I hate hypocrisy.'

Northcott had moved not a muscle of his dark, solemn face through all this. 'We much prefer frankness, Mrs Tilsley. It saves both us and you a lot of time. But as my colleague said, we have to build up a picture of a man about whom we know nothing. Even after ten years, you know much more about him than we do. And I'm sure that if he has been the victim of violence you would like to see the person or persons involved brought to justice, despite your differences.'

She didn't give him the conventional assent he expected. Instead, she stared steadily out of the window for a few seconds, then gave the curtest of nods, almost as if she was reluctant to recognize a weakness in herself. 'He was a difficult man from the start. We should never have married. I was six years younger than him, only twenty at the time. It was a huge mistake.'

'Was he violent?'

She glanced at him sharply. 'Are you sure this is relevant?'

'Probably not. We shan't know until the end of the case exactly what was relevant. But people who are violent often provoke violence in others. That might be a factor in whatever relationships Alfred has established since his time with you.'

'He wasn't violent to me. Not physically violent. His cruelty took other forms. He sometimes enjoyed inflicting suffering on others. He could do that without inflicting physical blows.' She looked from one to the other of the two very different young, attentive faces. 'But you are thinking, "How much reliance can we put upon what this woman says? How much is her own bitterness colouring the picture of the man she is painting for us?" I cannot answer that for you. I hated Alfred by the time we parted. My hatred is not as sharp as it was, because of the life I have now. But if he was around, I know I would hate him still. I cannot think he changed much in the years which have passed.'

She had appeared so controlled when they had come into her home that the passion with which she was now speaking was a surprise. Brendan Murphy said softly, 'You indicated earlier that his death had not come as a great surprise to you. Could you offer us any thoughts about who might have wished him dead?'

'No.' A mirthless smile. 'I have no idea of his recent acquaintances. I took care to cut myself off completely from Alfred and all his associates. I have no idea who might have been close to him recently. Or whom he chose to favour with his attentions.' The bitterness she had stored for at least a decade hissed out in her last sentence. Then she looked at them as if seeing them for the first time. 'You've come quite a distance. I should have offered you some refreshment. Would you like coffee or tea? Or perhaps something stronger?'

Northcott smiled, happy to lighten the tension he felt in her. 'No thanks. We need to be on our way, once we are convinced you have nothing more to tell us. But thank you for the thought.'

'Once you are convinced that I have nothing more to tell you. It's difficult for me to appreciate that you really know nothing about him. Alfred isn't a man you would forget, if you'd known him at all. I'm not going to resurrect all the details of our battles and our separation. That would upset me and it wouldn't help you.'

She looked as if she was about to reveal something, but there was such a long pause that Clyde feared she might be having second thoughts. He took advantage of her silence to ask, 'Where were you last night and this morning, Mrs Tilsley?'

She looked at him, allowing her lips to lift at the corners in what might have been amusement or might have been contempt. 'You really think I might have killed him?'

Clyde shrugged his formidable shoulders. 'It's a question we shall no doubt be asking a lot of people over the next few days. Unless we get a confession from someone, of course. Or unless this proves to be a suicide.'

She shook her head immediately. 'It won't be suicide. Alfred's not the type to do the decent thing. Or to do anything to help others out. And I didn't kill him. I was here from four o'clock yesterday until you arrived this morning with my husband and two children. But if you really do know nothing about him, there are facts you should take away from here. He enjoyed causing me pain and he enjoyed taunting me. Sexually, whenever he could. He played for both sides, as he put it. He made great play of being bisexual, of saying how little I knew and how little I'd lived, and how inadequate I was as a partner for a man like him. In my view, he should never have got married: it was just another of his sexual experiments. I was the one who had to suffer to further his research.'

'You're suggesting that his death might be sexually motivated?'

'I've no idea how he died. I suppose it's possible that sex might have had nothing to do with it. But you should bear in mind as you try to discover what sort of man he was that he was essentially homosexual.'

TEN

Whilst DS Northcott and DC Murphy were learning whatever they could from the dead man's wife in Cheshire, two other people who had known him much more recently were discussing Alfred Norbury in the Brunton public library.

Dick Fosdyke looked up from the single note he had made on the sheet in front of him. 'You're not normally here on a Thursday.'

'And a good morning to you too. Nice to see you,' said Sharon Burgess resentfully.

'Sorry. My mind was elsewhere and I wasn't expecting to see you here. It's a bit late after you've prompted me, but good to see you, Sharon.' He forced a smile as he had forced her forename. He still wasn't quite easy with that, though he couldn't think why. Mrs Burgess was a generation older than him, but that had no bearing on such things nowadays.

'You've heard?'

'Heard what?' He thought he knew what she was going to say, but some sort of superstition made him reluctant to voice it himself.

'Alfred Norbury's dead. I went round to Wellington Street before I came in here. They've cordoned off the area in front of his house. His car's there, I think, but you can't see it. It's all screened off with canvas.'

'He won't be in it.' It was out before he could stop the words. He'd no idea why he'd said it.

She looked at him curiously. 'You didn't know him, did you?'

'No. Well, not before Monday night.' He looked down at the blank sheet in front of him. 'I think I'd heard of him. He was quite a local character, I gather.'

Sharon Burgess glanced round the library, which was busy. 'I said I'd give them an hour, but I'm not on the official rota for today. We could go for coffee now, if you like. It would be a bit more private than here.'

She thought he would say that he needed the time for his drawing, since he didn't seem to have made even a start on his cartoon for the day. But he said immediately, 'Yes, let's do that. We might need to compare notes about Alfred Norbury.'

Enid Frott had determined to be calm and get this over with quickly, but she was surprisingly nervous when she opened the door to the CID man.

'I'm sorry I'm late.'

'You're hardly late: five minutes. Visitors rarely come at the time I suggest. Some of them even think it more polite to be a little late.'

'But this isn't a social call, Ms Frott. It's more efficient to be on time, in professional matters. I expect you found that in your working life. I'm Detective Chief Inspector Peach.'

He was smaller than she would have expected, but vital, with a fringe of dark hair around a bald pate. Late thirties, she thought, although baldness usually made people look older. Not at all the sort of build and appearance she'd anticipated in a senior detective, but he seemed to exude energy and alertness as he followed her into the sitting room of her flat. He accepted her offer of coffee.

He seemed the sort of man who would genuinely take pride in being punctual. She wondered if he'd accepted coffee simply so that he could have a good look round the room where she spent so much of her life, without her present. Even if she was right, there was nothing she could do about that.

He looked at her steadily as she brought him the coffee; refused biscuits; watched her as she sat down opposite him as if her every move might be telling him something. She'd been determined to leave it to him to make the moves, but because he'd already made her nervous she heard herself saying, 'I thought you usually operated in twos.'

'Very often, yes. My normal sidekick is out in Cheshire, talking to the murder victim's wife.'

'Alfred Norbury is a murder victim?'

'Purely my opinion, at the moment. Be confirmed officially by the end of the day. Either that or I'll look a fool.' He didn't seem to feel threatened by that prospect. He stretched his legs out and inspected the highly polished toecaps of his black Oxford shoes. 'I'm on my own because I don't feel the need for anyone to record what you're going to say or to provide a witness in the case of any disagreements about what we've said. I can come back with someone else if you don't feel easy with that. This is an informal chat with a citizen doing her duty and providing the senior officer investigating a crime with whatever information she can.' He beamed at her, his dark eyes as alight with mischief as those of an impish boy.

Enid made herself smile. 'I'm quite happy to see you on your own. But why do I feel so threatened? Why do I feel as though I need to watch everything I say to you?'

He beamed as if she had accorded him great pleasure. 'I can't explain that, Ms Frott. It almost sounds as if you feel you have something to hide, doesn't it? Which of course it would be my duty to investigate, as a conscientious CID officer.'

'I've nothing to hide.' She sat primly on the edge of her seat, wondering how she could feel so defensive in her own home.

'That's good to hear. Although I suppose I should point out that professionally nothing would give me greater satisfaction than a swift confession and a swift solution to the problems of this case. My chief superintendent, the man in charge of Brunton CID, is much preoccupied with our clear-up rates for senior crimes and very anxious that we should not fritter away public money on police overtime.'

'Would that be Chief Superintendent Tucker?' She was glad to throw in the name. Perhaps the fact that she had met his superior would keep this bouncy little man in check.

'You know the man?'

'I have a slight acquaintance with him. I have met him and his wife socially.'

He looked at her sympathetically, like a man about to offer his condolences after a tragic revelation. But he said nothing. After a pause he offered briskly, 'I need you to tell me everything you know about Alfred Norbury. The man, his character, his habits, his friends, his enemies. Particularly his enemies, perhaps. But assume I know nothing. Treat me as the ignorant but eager policeman I am.' He beamed at her and folded his arms, as if preparing for a long session.

'It's difficult for me to know where to start in response to that. I didn't know Alfred Norbury as well as you seem to think I did.'

Again that infuriating grin, as if he knew the subtleties behind her simple words and understood everything she was trying to conceal. 'You could start by telling me when you last saw the man who is now the subject of a post-mortem.'

He made her denials sound sinister; he was surely using everything he could to disturb her. Enid tried not to picture the body she had known, which was now on the slab – tried to thrust aside the vision of the dismemberment which might be going on at this very moment. 'Monday night. I last saw Alfred on Monday night.'

'As recently as that?' The black eyebrows arched high beneath the bald head, as if her reply was evidence that she had been on far more intimate terms with a murder victim than she had so far admitted. 'The exact time of death is still to be established, but that may be less than twenty-four hours before he was brutally killed.' Peach inched forward on to the edge of his seat. 'You may very well be the last person to have seen the victim alive, Ms Frott. Such people are always of great interest to us when there are suspicious deaths – but I expect you already know that.'

She tried hard to answer his irritating smile with one of her own, to show how little he was worrying her. But she found she could not do that. 'I wasn't alone when I saw him on Monday night.'

He looked disappointed, then nodded a couple of times. 'Perhaps you'd better tell me all about it.'

Enid wanted to say that she'd always intended to tell him, that he wasn't wringing the information from her unwilling lips, as his attitude seemed to imply. 'Alfred came here along with four other people. We drank wine, exchanged views. It was a relaxed and civilized social occasion.'

'I see. I see also certain implications. If this was a relaxed and civilized social occasion, you must all have known each other before Monday night. Was this some sort of party? Had the six of you met before on other occasions? Remember that I need to discover all that I can about a murder victim who died very shortly after you had exchanged these views and enjoyed this social exchange.'

He had her on the back foot again. It would appear that what she now had to tell him had been dragged from her unwilling lips when she would otherwise have concealed it. 'We didn't all know each other. Sharon Burgess and I already knew Alfred. And obviously the young man he brought here with him already knew him. As far as I know, the other two people who were present had not met Alfred before.'

'As far as you know. I see.' He nodded, as if committing to his memory some key revelation she had made. 'And did your party go well?'

'It wasn't exactly a party. It wasn't purely a social occasion, I suppose.' Again she was annoyed with herself, because it came out like an admission.

'I see. So please tell me exactly why Mr Norbury was in this room on Monday evening.'

'We were thinking of forming a book club.'

'A book club?'

He was like Lady Bracknell with that famous handbag. He made it sound an outrageous and highly reprehensible idea. 'Yes. The idea is that you all read the same book and then discuss it. It's supposed to add to the pleasures of reading.'

'I know what a book club is, Ms Frott. My wife has even made tentative moves towards starting one and suggested to me that I should participate. I don't think I shall do that.'

He contrived to make it seem as if she had insulted him as an idiot and yet at the same time made book clubs seem irregular and outlandish associations – something like those gatherings where people exchanged child porn materials, she thought. 'Well that's what it was. The first meeting of a book club. The preliminary meeting, if you like.'

'If you like, Ms Frott. I am entirely in your hands on this. But I would appreciate it if you gave me as full an account as possible of what took place at this preliminary meeting. With special reference to Mr Norbury, for obvious reasons. We're lucky it was so recent, aren't we? It means that a woman with your background will have excellent recall of it.'

She wondered exactly how much of her background he knew.

She wanted to ask him about that and about how he had gathered the information, but no doubt he would treat it as an evasion. She took a deep breath. 'It was the first time we had all met together. We didn't all know one another. A fair amount of wine was consumed. Wine helps to grease the social wheels on occasions like that.'

'It does, doesn't it? And one can always get a taxi home if one's over the limit. Not too difficult, on a Monday evening.'

'As it happened, most people lived within walking distance of here. That's one of the advantages of living near the centre of a small town. I think only Mrs Burgess came by car, and I'm sure she was careful about her alcohol consumption.'

'Are you, indeed? But of course you'd be in a fortunate position yourself, as host. You'd be able to drink as much as you liked and simply collapse into bed when they'd all gone.' He stared at the wall behind her, as if speculating about the secrets of the bedroom beyond it. Then he said suddenly, as though trying to catch her out, 'Who invited Mr Norbury to join the group?'

She should have anticipated this, she thought. But then she might have anticipated lots of things, if she'd only known that she was going to be confronted by this extraordinary man, who contrived to suggest that she was trying to deceive him at every turn, whilst remaining on the surface scrupulously polite. 'I did.' It came out like an admission, of course, instead of merely an innocent fact. 'The book club was my idea in the first place, so I felt entitled to invite Alfred.'

'Of course. So did you invite all of the people who were here on Monday night?'

'No. The club was originally my idea, as I said, but I'd put it to Sharon Burgess and she was enthusiastic about it. So we had a preliminary meeting at her house and discussed a few names – people we thought might be suitable. It was all very tentative – neither of us had been involved in anything like this before.'

For some extraordinary reason, it came out as defensive. It was as if she was having to defend her involvement in something secret and dubious, rather than an innocent literary experiment. Peach had steepled his hands and put his fingertips together now, and was nodding slowly, as if he considered a book club highly suspicious. 'I take it you and Mrs Burgess must be old friends.'

'Not really.' She sighed. 'I used to work for her husband's company, Burgess Electronics. I was his PA for several years. Then, when he retired, I was in charge of all the office services at the firm.'

He nodded, frowning a little, as if this competence and responsibility in her was something he had to digest and commit to memory. Then he shook his head briefly; it seemed there was something here which was still puzzling him. 'You say you and Mrs Burgess were not friends. But you must surely have known each other for many years?'

'Yes. I was simply saying that we weren't close friends. We didn't meet regularly. As a matter of fact, I hadn't seen her for quite some time before I attended her husband's funeral. Frank was much older than both of us.'

Had the man raised those expressive eyebrows again when she used the name Frank, or was she merely imagining all sorts of sinister things now? 'We got on well at the reception after the funeral. That's when I mentioned my idea of a book club. Sharon was enthusiastic about it. As a matter of fact, it might never have got off the ground, if she hadn't rung me to remind me of my suggestion a couple of weeks after the funeral.'

'So you met at her house to discuss how to begin.'

'Yes. Neither of us had been members of book clubs before, so we wanted to compare our thoughts on how to proceed. It was pretty straightforward really, as far as that went. We decided that we would meet about once a month and that, once we were established, any suggestions for additional members should be approved by everyone. But obviously to get the thing going, Sharon and I had to decide who our first members were going to be. We were quite relaxed about it.'

She remembered that strange, spiky meeting at the Burgess house, where the two women had watched each other closely and sized each other up for the future. What would Sharon say about it, if he questioned her like this? Peach looked as if he was filing away everything she said within that remarkable head; she had no doubt that he possessed a formidable memory. 'So you agreed on the six people who attended the first meeting on Monday night.'

'Not quite. It wasn't as formal as that. We agreed the date for the first meeting and one or two names. But we kept in touch by phone, so that we both knew whom we were expecting on Monday. Apart from one of the six.'

'And who was that?'

'A young man called Jamie Norris.' She found that she was relieved to be able to talk about this. It would surely take the man's intense scrutiny away from her. 'Alfred brought him along to the meeting. The rest of us didn't know him. But none of us objected. He seemed a pleasant young man who was interested in books and writing, and we were happy to take Alfred's recommendation. Sharon and I had already agreed that we wanted a balance of the sexes, if we could achieve that – there are far more women than men who are interested in book clubs. And Jamie was young: we'd agreed also that we wanted a healthy mixture of young and old, because we thought we'd get livelier discussions that way.'

She was talking too much. Perhaps that came from the simple relief of diverting attention away from herself. She expected Peach to pursue the matter of this rather strange young man who had turned up without warning alongside the man who was now dead. When he didn't offer any questions, she blurted out, 'I think Norris was a protégé of Alfred's. Mr Norbury liked to foster creativity.'

Peach nodded. She expected him to enquire about how Norbury sponsored and attempted to develop young talent. Instead, he said, 'You said earlier that it was you who invited Alfred Norbury to be part of the group. Why did you want him there?'

'Because I thought he would be an interesting and stimulating member of our group.'

'I see. What kind of man was he?'

She forced a smile, trying to simulate a calm which she had long since ceased to feel. 'I used the word "stimulating" and I think everyone who knew Alfred would accept that. He could also be abrasive – well, downright rude at times, I suppose. But I was prepared to take that and I convinced Sharon Burgess that we should have him.'

'She knew him?'

'Yes. We all go back quite a long way. Neither of us had ever been a bosom pal of Alfred's but we both knew he was well-read and would provide us with some interesting ideas. Some outrageous ones too, no doubt, but that would be part of the fun. In my view, you need people like Alfred in a group to get things going.'

He leant forward in what was almost a tiny bow towards her. 'I might like to be in a group set up by you, Ms Frott. I don't think it would ever be uninteresting.'

She managed a rather melancholy smile of acknowledgement. 'Thank you. I don't think the one we initiated on Monday night will be going anywhere now.'

'I expect I shall meet all of the surviving members in the next day or two. Unless we have a quick solution, that is. Which of them do you think might have killed Mr Norbury?'

He seemed to have this talent for asking shocking questions as though they were perfectly normal. And Enid had to admit that she had been wondering before he had come here whether he would raise exactly that question. It did not make it any less shocking to hear it asked so baldly, as if he were speculating about the price of milk. She felt very prim as she said, 'Surely you aren't presuming that it was necessarily one of our book group? There is a whole range of other possibilities. I'm sure that Alfred Norbury had lots of enemies.'

'Are you indeed? That's very interesting.'

Those black eyebrows were moving again. The simple statement sounded pregnant with sinister implications as he set his empty cup back on her tray. She said, 'I told you he was abrasive.'

'You did indeed. But lots of people are abrasive, Ms Frott. It's interesting that you think Mr Norbury was abrasive enough to excite the hatred which leads to murder. But I'm sure you know best.' He stopped for a moment with his head a little on one side, inviting her to enlarge on her account of Norbury, but she remained resolutely silent. 'Perhaps you should have been a detective. I'm constantly having to remind the officers who will make up my team on this case that they must consider all possibilities, not just the obvious ones. They're eager and willing lads and lasses, but they haven't all got the experience of life which you and I can boast.'

If he was in his late thirties, as she thought, he had a quarter of a century's less experience of life than she had. But he made her at this moment feel like an infant as far as experience of anything like this went. She said stiffly, 'I haven't even thought about who might have done this.'

'Really? Well, that's remarkable. I should have thought it was only human nature to speculate about that, once you heard that this stimulating and abrasive man was dead. Well, I'd like you to start thinking about it right now, Ms Frott. You knew both Mr Norbury and the people in your group far better than I do at the moment. You are an intelligent, experienced woman and I would welcome your input on this.'

He stood up and Enid felt immensely relieved that he was going. She said, 'I'll give it some thought. I suppose I'm still in shock. I've never been involved in anything like this before.'

He managed to look as if he found that surprising. Then he said, 'Where were you last night, Ms Frott?'

She told herself that she wouldn't give him the satisfaction of seeing her outraged. It was a question he had to ask, wasn't it? Part of his job, no doubt. 'I was here. From about four o'clock yesterday afternoon until this moment.'

'Is there anyone who could confirm that for us?'

'No. I had a telephone call from my great-nephew in Cheshire, thanking me for my Christmas gifts. That was at twelve minutes past nine. I remember checking the time because I thought he should probably be in bed and asleep. He's only eight.'

'Thank you. That might be helpful, though I have a feeling Mr Norbury was killed well before then. I must take my leave, Ms Frott. Please go on thinking about the people involved in this. I'm sure your views will be valuable. I've no doubt that I shall need to see you again in the near future.'

He gave her the last of his range of smiles, but his final words nevertheless felt much more like a threat than an assurance.

Sharon Burgess was not feeling the sort of pressure which DCI Peach was exerting on her co-founder of the book club as she drank coffee at the same time with Dick Fosdyke. She was surprised nevertheless by the tension she felt.

Dick initiated it when he said, 'We're all going to be suspects, if this is murder.'

'Do you think it might be?' He was only voicing what she had thought herself, but it seemed shocking nevertheless to have it spoken aloud.

'The radio bulletin said that a man had been shot. And it spoke of a suspicious death. That usually means the police think it's murder.'

She was abruptly very fearful, though she had known in her heart that it must be so. 'And you think they'll have us down as suspects?'

'I reckon he was dead within twenty-four hours of our meeting on Monday night.' He looked into her eyes as they widened apprehensively and added hastily, 'Or not much more than that, anyway.'

How could he know that? How could he sound so confident about when Alfred had been killed? For some reason she could not look him in the eye. She stared down at the steam rising slowly from her latte. 'I hadn't thought of it like that. I've never been a suspect in any crime.'

'We'll need to watch our steps. Be careful what we say. The police will be eager for a quick arrest.'

'You sound like an expert in these things.' She meant it to be a joke, but it didn't emerge as one.

He didn't react to it, but pursued his own train of thought. 'A lot depends upon what Alfred did yesterday. If he was out and about and saw lots of people, that would increase the range of suspects. The police will be investigating his movements now, I expect. They'll have a big team on this. They always do, when there's a murder.'

She wished he wouldn't keep using that word. She could hear the horror creeping into her voice as she said, 'And you think it might be one of us?'

He produced a smile at last. 'I didn't say that. I said that the police might think that it was one of us. They're paid to think the worst of people, and they're usually rather good at it.'

Sharon said dully, 'I suppose it just could be one of that group who drank and chatted together so happily on Monday night. It just seems incredible to me, but I expect we have to consider the possibility.'

'The police will. They'll be on to us quickly, once their initial enquiries throw up the fact that we met on Monday night. We'll need to be careful what we say to them.'

She wasn't sure whether Dick meant just the two of them or the other three as well. She wished on an impulse that they could all be together again, comparing notes and preparing themselves for interrogation by the police. She didn't like the idea of someone else implicating her, whether deliberately or unwittingly. She said quietly, 'Do you think Alfred was shot with his own pistol?'

He stared at her dully. 'What do you mean, his own pistol?'

'Alfred told us on Monday night that he carried his own pistol in the car because he feared being attacked. I thought it was over the top at the time, a typical bit of Norbury boasting. He liked to shock and he liked to be the centre of attention.'

'Yes, I remember it now. I'd forgotten all about it. I suppose I thought it was just a typical bit of Norbury braggadocio and didn't take it seriously.' He finished his coffee and gave her a taut smile. 'I must get back to the library and concentrate on other things. I've got work to do.'

Sharon Burgess went back there with him, but they didn't exchange many more words. She spent a busy hour on the counter, and Dick had left the building by the time she was free again. She went out to her car and drove home very thoughtfully.

What he said about treating the police with due care made sense. But one thing worried Sharon. Dick Fosdyke had been so alert about everything else that she couldn't really believe that he'd forgotten all about Alfred Norbury's revelation that he carried a pistol in his car. So why had he pretended to do that?

ELEVEN

J amie Norris waited anxiously all day for the visit he felt
must surely come. He'd heard the early-morning announcement on Radio Lancashire and he'd observed the scene of
crime tapes around the area in front of Alfred's house in
Wellington Street. Then he'd gone to Tesco and tried to work
through the long hours as if nothing had happened.

It wasn't that he wanted the police to come whilst he was at
work. Rather the reverse, in fact. It wouldn't do him any good
here if the police turned up and wanted to question him about
an event like this. No smoke without fire, people always said.
They were mean and ungenerous, those people. But you couldn't
just ignore them. It was a fact of life that once you were linked
with something you were never quite clear of it.

His apprehension affected his work. He wasn't his normal
reliable self and he wasn't anticipating the need to replenish
the shelves as quickly and accurately as usual. His lack of
concentration brought him a rebuke from his immediate super-
visor and he thought he also saw Mr Jordan looking at him
curiously from the other end of the bread and cakes aisle. He'd
had nothing but praise and approval from the manager so far:
he didn't want something like this to affect his retail career
whilst it was still in embryo.

He was glad that the phone call from the police came during
his lunch break. It was put through to him in the staff rest room
and no one who mattered even knew about it. The police offered
to see him after work and he seized upon that eagerly. Half
past seven would be fine, he told the female voice at Brunton
station. She noted his address carefully and said that Detective
Inspector Peach and Detective Sergeant Northcott would be
round to see him at that time. He tried not to be as awed as
the police officer obviously was by these names.

He heard the bell ring, but he had to descend the stairs and
Mrs Jackson was at the door before him. He experienced the

first of his shocks before he had even spoken. The presence filling the front doorway of the old house was massive and very black. You saw lots of Asian faces in this area, but very few black ones. Black men were the perpetrators of violent crime, rather than the solvers of it, in Jamie's mind. He realized immediately how that mind had been conditioned and rebuked himself silently for allowing that to happen.

Then he said rather uncertainly, 'You'd better come upstairs to my apartment. That's all right, Mrs Jackson, isn't it?' His landlady looked highly disapproving of both her tenant and his visitors, but she signified with a nod that it was permitted.

The black man didn't look any smaller when Jamie had shut the door carefully on the world outside and invited him to sit. There was scarcely room for Northcott and his chief on the tiny sofa which was the only seating in the room apart from Jamie's own small armchair, which he now turned away from the television to face them. Peach must have realized Norris was intimidated by his bagman's size and appearance; he hastened to accentuate that apprehension rather than dissipate it.

'Big bugger, isn't he, DS Northcott? I like to call him the hard bastard. He's very useful when things turn ugly – or when members of the public are anything other than cooperative.' He beamed his approval of this, first at the inscrutable Northcott and then at the fearful Norris. He didn't say anything further, but looked hard first at Jamie and then at the room around him, as if it was important to him to commit to memory every detail of the place where this man lived.

After what seemed to Norris a very long time, he said, 'Nice place you have here.'

No one had ever said that before, but it didn't sound like sarcasm. Jamie said apologetically, 'It's only a bed-sit. I'm hoping to get something better, once I get established at work.'

The bed-sit was in fact very tidy and very clean. They saw many scruffy and some outright filthy rooms in the circles where they moved. Peach said, 'That's at Tesco, I believe.'

'Yes. I've only been there for about a month, but I seem to be doing all right.'

'That's good, isn't it? Especially after a series of jobs which don't seem to have lasted for very long.'

They'd done their homework before they came here. That was disconcerting. He wondered exactly how much they knew about his previous life. 'I was trying to become a writer. A professional writer, I mean. It's not easy. Very few people manage to live on their earnings from writing.'

'So I believe. Have you given up the idea now?'

'No. I'm planning to go on developing as a writer, but to do that in my spare time. I want to hold down a job – perhaps even develop a career. That can even help your writing, you know. Working full-time keeps you in touch with people and with life. It gives you all kinds of ideas and material which you can use in your writing.'

'Oh, I'm sure you're right about that. Is that what Alfred Norbury told you?'

It was a brutal introduction to the reason why they were here, the more so because it hit the nail very firmly on the head. Jamie had been repeating almost word for word what Alfred had said to him a fortnight earlier. 'I think that was his opinion, yes. We discussed things like that a little. But I was already working at Tesco when . . . when I first met him.' He'd almost said 'when he picked me up'. That would have given them exactly the impression he was trying to avoid. It just showed how careful you had to be.

'Recently, was this?'

'Boxing Day, I think. It was snowing at the time. I was standing in the car park and trying to compose a poem about the snow, but I wasn't having much success. I couldn't think of anything original.'

'Took you in hand, did he, Mr Norbury?'

A crude double entendre leapt into Jamie's mind when he least wanted it: the human brain is a strange and often unpredictable organ. 'He offered me a bit of advice, yes. As far as I can remember, that is. It was really more that he took me seriously, that he understood what I was trying to do. I was grateful for that. A lot of people just make fun of you, when you're trying to compose poetry.'

'Do they really?' Peach tutted noisily. 'The world can be a very cruel place, can't it? We see a lot of its cruelty, don't we, DS Northcott?'

'We do indeed, sir. We see people dying of heroin, whilst the ruthless sod who has supplied them grows fat on the Costa Brava. We see people beaten to death because some loan shark has lent them far more than they can possibly pay back and they default on the instalments. We see children being groomed for sex because they haven't a soul in the world who cares about them. And then we even hear about people being unsympathetic to poets. It's a cruel world.' Northcott's face was like ebony as he stared at the ceiling in the narrow room.

'I wasn't equating people who think that poetry is nonsense with those sorts of things! I was just trying to explain that poetry is difficult anyway and that it's even more difficult when people think it's rubbish and make fun of you.'

Peach smiled happily. 'You must forgive DS Northcott, Mr Norris. He's had a hard life. He hasn't got the kind of sensitive soul which you and I possess, but we must make allowances. He hasn't had our advantages.'

'I didn't have many advantages.'

'Really? That's interesting. Good schooling in Leeds and quite a string of GCSEs, I heard. University material, if you hadn't got into bad company, my informant said. DS Northcott didn't learn anything except fighting at his school. But he made himself pretty good at that. With or without knives.'

Jamie glanced at Northcott, who had remained impassive throughout this strange eulogy. It was the black man he had feared, but he was beginning to learn that it was his bald-headed chief who was the really dangerous one here. He had been determined before they came to keep his previous life well hidden, but this bouncy, cheerful little man had somehow induced him to bring it up himself. He said helplessly, 'I came to Brunton to get away from Leeds. I wanted to begin a new life here.'

'I don't wonder at that. Lucky to stay out of stir, my informant said. Attacking someone with a knife is still regarded very seriously by the law courts, even in these violent times.'

'It wasn't my knife.'

'Makes a difference when you're stabbed, does it, that?'

'I'm only saying that I didn't take a knife out with me. I was attacked. I managed to take the knife from the lad who was planning to use it. It was self-defence.'

It was the defence Norris had offered at the time and it was probably true, Clyde Northcott reckoned. He said, 'I wouldn't be surprised if someone claims that he killed Mr Norbury in self-defence. Why did you come to Brunton, Mr Norris?'

Jamie wished they wouldn't keep using that title. It made him feel as if he was already in court, or at least about to be charged. 'I had a pal here. But he didn't stay around for long. The main reason I came was to get away from Leeds and what was happening there. I just knew I was going to get into trouble if I stayed there.'

'And you wanted to be a writer.' Clyde made it sound as exotic as an astronaut.

'That would have happened wherever I was. It's not as outlandish as you make it sound. Lots of people have a go at it. Mostly they don't succeed, so you don't hear much about it. None of us wants to broadcast his failures, does he?'

Peach grinned at him. 'That's true, Mr Norris. You don't hear DS Northcott talking about his skill at darts or snooker. Very understandable, that is.' He'd beaten his junior in both of these recently and he saw no point in modesty. 'Would you describe yourself as a protégé of Alfred Norbury?'

Jamie was suddenly on the spot here, when he had been marshalling all his resources to defend his conduct in Leeds. 'I suppose some people would see it like that.'

'I'm sure they would. But I asked how you saw it.'

'I don't think I'd known him long enough to develop that sort of relationship.'

'But it was he who took you along to the first meeting of the book club on Sunday night, wasn't it? I'm not aware that anyone else had suggested your name to the others.'

'That's right. I'm pretty sure that none of them even knew I existed until I turned up with Alfred. I didn't want to go: I felt that I'd be out of my depth amongst highly educated middle-class people. But Alfred said it would be good for the bourgeoisie to be shaken up by a working-class intellectual. It was he who called me that, not me. I have to say they made me feel very welcome.'

'Was that because of Norbury, do you think, or your own obvious charisma?'

Jamie glanced up furiously at Peach, but the man was studying the ceiling. 'I don't think it was because of Alfred. I got the impression that some of them didn't much like Alfred.'

'And why was that, do you think?'

'I think they found that he was what my mother used to call "too big for his boots". Intellectually, I mean. He could be rather overbearing, you know.'

'No, I don't, Mr Norris. I never met Mr Norbury, and here I am in a situation where I need to know all about him. Which means that your explanation of what you mean by "overbearing" will be most welcome.' He gave Jamie a wide beam which the young man found more disturbing than the fiercest of frowns.

'Well, Alfred could be quite patronising when the mood took him. Without actually insulting anyone on Monday night, he behaved as if he knew all about literature and the other people there knew very little.'

'I know the type. Very annoying.'

'In fairness, I should say that Alfred did know a hell of a lot. And he was generous with his knowledge and his time, so long as . . . so long as . . .'

'So long as he felt in control and it was quite clear that you were his intellectual inferior?'

'I suppose so. On Monday night, he seemed to be trying to take over a group which other people had set up, and I think they resented that.'

'Not unnaturally. Thank you for being so frank. I'm beginning to get the picture.'

'I feel bad talking about him like this, especially now that he's dead.'

'Yes. But I asked you to be frank, and presumably you've done your best to be that. His death must be particularly sad for you, as his protégé.'

'I'm not sure I ever accepted that description. I think I said I hadn't known him long enough to feel that I was that.'

'So tell us about your relationship with Alfred Norbury. We need all the detail you can supply.'

Peach looked as eager as a schoolboy, and Jamie was conscious of the other man's black hands beside him, manipulating a notebook which seemed far too small. He gulped. The best way to lie was to incorporate as much of the truth as you could, so long as it was harmless to you. A young lawyer had told him that when he was seventeen and he'd always remembered it. 'He was interested in my ambition to become a professional writer. He gave me tips and he examined most of the things I did and made suggestions.'

'And did you find this helpful?'

'Yes. I think Alfred regarded it as a teaching process and me as a writing apprentice rather than the finished article. But I didn't mind that. I was prepared to learn and I felt I was doing that, under Alfred's regime.'

'And what did this regime involve?'

'Well, he took me back to the beginning as far as my poetry was concerned. He got me to use iambic pentameters, which sound complicated but are actually quite a simple form. Shakespeare used them, so you couldn't have a better model, could you? What I was doing was undertaking exercises in writing, rather than aiming for the finished product, but that was part of the learning process.'

'And you didn't mind it? Didn't mind going back to school, so to speak?'

'No. Don't forget I left school before I'd completed a term in the sixth form. What I'd learned about verse before I met Alfred, apart from one book on writing I bought for myself, had come almost completely by trial and error. Alfred said that if I was prepared to go back to the beginning, he'd teach me the mechanics of writing. What I made of them then would be up to me. He said he could teach me the craft, but the art would be up to me.'

'And you were quite happy to go along with that?'

'I'd have been a fool not to. He knew a hell of a lot and he'd done quite a bit of teaching, at different times. And he'd written himself: articles about novelists and poets. It would have cost me many hundreds of pounds to get what Alfred was offering me free of charge.'

'Did he point that out to you?'

Jamie wondered if he was blushing. He looked down at the low, scratched table between them, wondering how long it would be before they picked up the school exercise book which lay there and examined his efforts within it. 'I suppose he did, a couple of times. As I said, he liked to be in control. But that was fair enough: he was very generous with his time and his criticisms made sense. He'd made me much more self-critical, which is one of the things you need to be to become an effective writer. And he had a terrific library, to provide examples of what he meant. He let me borrow anything I wanted to read and he made his own suggestions. He was very generous.'

'I see. I must say you sound very like a protégé.'

Jamie smiled. 'I suppose I might have become one, given time. Alfred said he'd introduce me to useful people, when he felt the time was right. I suppose Monday night was perhaps the first instance of that.' He felt more relaxed now. Talking about writing had brought out his enthusiasm; he'd even forgotten for a moment or two that these two were police.

The next questions brought him swiftly back to earth. Peach said abruptly, 'Was there a sexual relationship between the two of you?'

'No. I'm not gay. Alfred offered me advice about writing and access to his library. That's as far as it went.' His mouth set in a thin, determined line.

Peach looked at him for seconds in silence, then said, 'So who do you think killed your mentor, Jamie?'

It was the first time the DCI had used his forename. He hadn't time to dwell on the significance of that; his mind was reeling before the challenge of the query. 'I don't know. Someone from outside, I expect, not someone I know. I'm sure he had a lot of enemies.'

'Are you? Why is that?'

'He could be very caustic. Even painful. He didn't trouble to disguise his feelings. That upset a lot of people.'

'You seem very definite about that.'

Jamie smiled wryly. 'It's what he said himself. I'm almost quoting him.'

Clyde Northcott's pen twitched over his page. 'We need the names of his enemies, for obvious reasons.'

'I can't give you any, I'm afraid. I know very little about his past life, apart from odd things he let drop. No names.'

Northcott stared at him steadily for a moment. His deep-set

brown eyes seemed laser-like to Jamie; he wouldn't want to make an enemy of this man. 'Where were you on Tuesday night, Mr Norris? We need an account of your movements from late afternoon onwards.'

For a moment, Jamie was tempted to say he had been at work until late in the evening. But that would be madness. They would check at Tesco, and then he'd be in trouble with Mr Jordan and, much more seriously, with this formidable pair. 'I was on early shift on Tuesday, six to two. I did two hours' overtime and then came back here. I was pretty knackered, as you can imagine.' He glanced automatically at the curtain which concealed his tiny kitchen area, where he microwaved the meals for one he bought cheaply at work.

'You didn't see Mr Norbury on that night?'

'No. I came back here and ate. I worked for a while on a poem I was writing. I watched a little television. Then I went to bed.'

The phrases poured out rapidly, with scarcely a pause. It sounded like a prepared statement. But it would be understandable if he'd anticipated having to account for his movements. He'd undergone police questioning before: they weren't sure how many times. Clyde made a show of recording what he said exactly, then asked, 'Is there anyone who can confirm this for us? Should we speak to your landlady?'

'No. Mrs Jackson wouldn't know when I came in. We all have our own keys.'

'When was the last time you saw Alfred Norbury?'

'On Monday night. At Enid Frott's flat, at the first meeting of the book club.'

'Did Mr Norbury keep a pistol in his car?'

'Yes, apparently he did. I didn't know until he told us on Monday. Even then I wasn't quite sure how serious he was about it. I thought it might be just a bit of bravado.'

They left him then. Jamie Norris was surprised how exhausted he felt. He'd been on edge throughout and they'd been two senior men, so that was understandable, he supposed. But it had gone reasonably well, he thought. He thought he'd handled the bit about the pistol rather well. And he hadn't told them more than he'd intended to.

*   *   *

It was an hour after the CID men had left that Jamie's mobile phone shrilled on the table beside him. It made him jump. He'd been immersed in an episode of *Silent Witness*, guiltily fascinated by the gory details of the dismemberment of a body found in a burnt-out building.

The voice which spoke to him was female and nervous. 'Hello! Is that James Norris?'

'This is Jamie, yes. Who is that, please?'

'Hello, Jamie. Sorry to ring so late. It's Jane Preston here. Is it all right to speak?'

For a moment, he couldn't remember who Jane Preston was. Then it came to him and he was pleased. 'Jane Preston from the book club? Yes, it's perfectly all right to speak.' He pressed the mute button on his remote control; the blackened stomach looked even more ghoulish when it was lifted from the corpse and brandished without sound. 'What can I do for you, Jane?'

He'd hardly spoken to her on Monday night. Not because he didn't want to, mind; she was blonde and very attractive and the only person there in his age range. He'd been rather over-awed by her beauty and even more so by her learning. He hadn't wanted to risk any sort of public brush-off in front of those older people, but he'd been determined to get to know Jane better at future meetings.

She said, 'You've heard about your friend Alfred Norbury?'

'Yes.' For some reason, he wanted to say that he wasn't really a friend, or at least to define and modify the term, but that seemed unfair to Alfred. And it might make him seem petty to Jane if he denied being friendly with the man who had introduced him to the book club. 'The police have already been to see me about it, actually. It's not long since they left.'

'Really? I expect they'll want to see all of us, won't they?'

He sensed that she wanted him to deny that and reassure her, but he rather enjoyed the image of her apprehensive and looking to him for support. 'I expect they will, yes. But I can't think that you'll have anything to fear from them. It will just be routine, you know.'

'Do you think they regard us as suspects?'

Now that she had put him on the spot, he realized how little they had revealed about the crime and what they thought about it. 'They don't give much away, the police. They played it very close to their chests.' Two clichés already, when he wanted to impress this bright and willowy woman. 'They seem pretty sure Alfred was murdered.'

'Yes. We'd hardly be suspects otherwise, would we?' A little tinkle of nervous laughter in his ear. 'Sorry. You were trying to tell me what you could about the police.'

'There isn't much I can tell you, really. They seemed to be top brass, the people who came here. The detective chief inspector in charge of the case and a detective sergeant who was his sidekick. You might get someone further down the line, someone who is just part of the team.'

'Yes. I expect it would have to be someone very important like you to get the man in charge of the case. I'll probably get some probationary girl who's just out of school.'

She was teasing him. He could see that small, ironic smile on her face which had so intrigued him on Monday night. He tried not to sound too serious as he said, 'I just meant that they couldn't possibly think that you had any connection with Alfred's death. That's why they'd just allot a more junior member of the team to you. It wouldn't be anyone wet behind the ears, though. It will almost certainly be CID, and to be CID you have to have served for years in uniform first.'

'I didn't know you were such an expert on the police.'

'Oh, I'm not an expert!' said Jamie hastily. 'I've picked up the odd bit of knowledge, I suppose. I'm not sure where from, though. Books I've read, or crime series on the box, I expect.'

There was a silence. He wondered what she was assessing. Was it him, or something else entirely? Then she said, 'I'm a bit nervous about the police, actually. I've never been involved in anything like this before.'

'Like all of us,' said Jamie hastily.

'Yes, like all of us. Like you and me, anyway. We don't know what these older people have been up to in their earlier lives, do we?' She giggled again and this time Jamie, knowing that it was nothing to do with him, found her amusement quite delightful.

'You're right. There's no knowing what Mrs Burgess and Miss Frott have been up to, is there? Probably a pair of serial killers!' This time they laughed together, and he thought he could hear her relaxing.

Then she said, 'Do you think we could meet? Fairly quickly, if possible – before the fuzz come round and put the bracelets on me. You could give me some idea of how I should behave with them.'

Jamie was about to deny his expertise when he realized how asinine that would be. He'd be risking turning down a meeting with this creature he'd thought exotic and unattainable until a few minutes ago. 'I don't start until twelve tomorrow. We're always busy on Friday evening and the manager likes to have me around then. He says I'm good with the public.'

He regretted that crass little boast immediately. But she said, 'I'm sure you are, Jamie. Just as you'll be good with me. Could we meet in Booth's café for coffee? Say ten fifteen? I'm sure I'll feel much more fitted to face the fuzz after a session with you.'

TWELVE

Everything in Alfred Norbury's flat was impeccably tidy. In the kitchen and dining area, there was no sign of his last meal, no *Marie Celeste* remnants of a life so abruptly terminated.

The sitting room was quite dark on this gloomy January morning, despite the long window at the end of it. The fact that one wall was completely lined with books seemed to accentuate the dimness. The shelves of volumes had a further, rather strange effect. Books are such personal things that something of the occupant seemed to be still here. It felt to the CID men investigating his death as if Norbury was observing their movements and preparing to pass his sardonic commentary on their conduct.

This was an alien environment for Clyde Northcott. He had never in his life been in a room quite like this. A scholar's room, he supposed, whatever other virtues and vices the occupant had exhibited. He was quite relieved when Percy Peach said to him, 'You take the desk and I'll make a start on the books.' Clyde wondered what he meant by a start. It could take you days to thumb through that lot, he reckoned, and he wasn't even sure what you'd be looking for. DCI Peach would be the right man for that task: he knew a lot more about books than he ever admitted at the station. Funny bugger, Percy: you never knew what depths he had and he didn't encourage you to plumb them.

Peach was already finding interesting things on those packed shelves, though he wasn't sure if they were going to have any connection with the case. There was a neatly printed inscription above one of the higher shelves which was obviously a fragment of verse:

> Change in a trice
> The lilies and languors of virtue
> For the raptures and roses of vice.

That was Swinburne. He wouldn't have known that, but the poet's name was helpfully appended at the end of the quotation. He wondered if that had been Norbury's motto for life. An exciting but dangerous approach – but from the material about him which they were beginning to assemble, that might have been the sort of existence he craved and counselled to others.

There was a complete collection of Swinburne on the shelf below the quotation. One of the great Victorians now much neglected, thought Percy. But lately a source of much interest for intellectual gays, if he remembered it rightly – which he probably didn't.

He moved along to the shelf housing the novels of E.M. Forster, where the newest one, *Maurice*, seemed to protrude a fraction, as if it had recently been returned to its place there. There were slips of paper at two points in the book. He wondered if Norbury had been using it to demonstrate something about the craft of writing to Jamie Norris. Protégé, or something more than that?

His conjecture was overtaken by something more concrete from his bagman. Two of the drawers of the desk were locked, but the key was in the top one; evidence perhaps that at the time of his death Norbury had felt in no danger and not threatened by any intrusion here. Clyde Northcott was investigating the drawers methodically, moving carefully through a world which was totally new to him.

It was when he turned the key and opened the bottom drawer on the right-hand side of the desk that he found something more familiar in his world. It was a packet scarcely bigger than a large matchbox, but with contents which were much more sinister. Bullets: short, low-calibre and neatly packaged, looking as innocent as small electric batteries. But suggesting, as these two experienced men looked down at them, violence and death.

'Spare ammunition for the pistol that killed him, the one he kept in the car,' said Peach thoughtfully. 'Shows he thought he might have occasion to use it, I presume. We should check whether he was a member of a gun club, I suppose. See whether he kept himself in practice.' He didn't think a man who was already emerging as secretive would have cared for anything so public.

Twenty minutes later, DS Northcott was examining the deep double drawer which was the bottom one on the left-hand side of the desk. It was there that he found something much more interesting than bullets. This drawer was a built-in filing system and he found within these a slim file which particularly interested him. It was one devoted to Enid Frott, and it went back twelve years.

Ms Frott had claimed when they interviewed her that she had little previous association with Alfred Norbury.

Jamie Norris had passed Booth's café often enough before, but he had never before set foot inside it.

It was much plusher than anything he was used to. There were carpeted floors and a waitress who showed him to the table for two he asked for and took his order for coffee. She didn't curl her lip in contempt at this awkward young man, or even show surprise that he was here. He supposed they were trained to do that. He told himself firmly that his money was as good as anyone else's and that he had as much right to be here as anyone else; he didn't manage to convince himself of those things.

He was glad that he'd put on his best shirt and sweater and the newer of his two pairs of trousers. For a horrible moment as he sat at the table and stared around him, he thought that he had forgotten to comb his hair. He raised his right hand surreptitiously to his head and ran it awkwardly over his pate. All was well: the parting was certainly there, and the style of his short fair hair, such as it was, was in place.

The other customers on this cold Friday morning were all middle-aged and elderly women. He felt them looking at him, resenting his inappropriate presence here. But that didn't last long. None of them was alone and they quickly resumed their conversations. Probably these now included observations on this alien youthful intrusion, but that was no doubt inevitable. He'd grown used to being an object of interest and even sometimes of bawdy female speculation in the supermarket. You lived with these things, when you worked with the public and were a man of the world. He hoped that Jane Preston would arrive before too long.

She was worth the wait. She was wearing jeans, he was happy to see, though they were very new and of a quality he had never possessed. Her green top was in no way tarty, but it accentuated her charms. Jamie found it difficult to detach his eyes from the breasts beneath it and his speculation about what support, if any, they were receiving. Jane said, 'Oh, you've already ordered!' and he realized that he had perpetrated his first social faux pas.

She handled the waitress far better than he had, receiving her attention with a smile of welcome and a briskly delivered order for a cappuccino. Jamie had just ordered ordinary coffee and was surprised when it now was delivered in a pot. He poured a small amount of milk in carefully from the jug provided and stirred his coffee thoughtfully, trying to look as if he did this all the time. Then he gave Jane a bright smile and said, 'And how can I be of service to you, fair damsel?'

She gave him a wide smile. 'I don't feel very fair this morning. And I'm not quite sure what a damsel is supposed to look like in the twenty-first century. But thank you for being my knight in shining armour.' She looked very fair indeed, to Jamie, in her bright green top and new jeans. Smart casual, they called it. He wished he felt as smart and as casual as Jane looked. He wasn't up to being a knight in shining armour, but he was grateful for the thought. He said stoutly, 'I can't think that you've anything to fear at all from the police.'

'Can't you? After all the tales we hear? I didn't think you were as naïve as that.'

He wanted to prove to her that he wasn't naïve, without admitting exactly how much he did know about the police. He'd given that some thought this morning, but it wasn't going to be easy. 'The police want convictions, there's no doubt about that. But this is a serious crime and it will get a lot of publicity. They won't try to rig the evidence or frame anybody, with so much at stake. They could end up with egg on their faces if they tried to frame someone who was innocent.'

'You see! You do know all sorts of things that I don't. What you just said might seem obvious to you, but it's all new to me. When I was a student, I heard such awful things about the police and what they do.'

Jamie smiled, feeling more confident now. 'You shouldn't believe everything students say. They like to dramatise things, to make out that the police are all vicious pigs and that they themselves are whiter than white. Whatever the police would like to do, they have to be careful, nowadays. You don't even have to say anything, if you don't choose to. They can't even grill you with a brief beside you unless you've been charged with an offence. And even then, you can give them the old "no comment" if you think that's the best line.'

'There you are! You know all sorts of things that I don't. If I have any trouble, I shall insist on having you at my side as they give me the third degree.'

He grinned, aware by now that she wasn't entirely serious. 'I don't think that would be a very good idea. If they do come to see you, just remember that you are a private citizen with nothing to hide, who is merely fulfilling her public duty by giving whatever help she can to the police in their enquiries.'

She sipped her coffee without comment. He imagined those full, efficient lips pressed against his, exploratory perhaps at first, then moving forward into passion. Surprised, perhaps, by his adeptness and his urgency, giving herself to him, journeying onwards and upwards into other and as yet unspecified amorous adventures. Bloody hell, Jamie!

'So you want to be a writer.'

The words seemed to come from a long way away, banishing the images which were racing like an express train across his fevered brain. 'What? Oh sorry, yes.' Supposed to be a writer and not even articulate. 'Yes. I write a little. Well, quite a lot, really, but I throw most of it away. That's part of the process. You have to be self-critical to improve. Chucking things out may be the most important part of the creative recipe, you see.'

'Yes, I do see. It makes good sense. Did Alfred Norbury tell you that?'

That was puncturing his posturings, wasn't it? Particularly as he'd been quoting Alfred almost word for word. 'I suppose he did. I think I was working it out for myself, but he put it into words for me. Shortened the process. I'm grateful to him for that. He made me more optimistic, in a way. I used to simply despair of myself when I thought what I'd composed wasn't very good, but now I see it as a necessary part of the process. The secret is to spot the worthwhile phrases and the worthwhile ideas amidst the dross. Then you keep those and polish them and add to them, if you can.'

'You really believe in this, don't you? And it all makes sense. I've tried bits of poetry, like most people, but I've always been so disappointed with the results that I've just chucked them away in disgust.'

'You shouldn't do that. Spot the good bits, even if it's only a word or two, keep them, and use them to stimulate more.'

'Perhaps we could have a go together. Show each other what we've written, I mean. That's if I can bring myself to show my sorry efforts to anyone else.'

'You should do that. Humility is one of the foundation stones of creativity.' That was him, not Alfred and he wanted to let her know that. But was it as profound as it had sounded, or merely pretentious nonsense? 'It would be good if we could try bits of writing and then show them to each other. It's a very lonely business, writing. You have to develop self-critical faculties, as I said, but there are times when a second opinion would be very welcome.'

Jane gave him that smile again and her blue eyes brimmed with a friendly humour. Jamie forgot about words and thought about flesh again. She said firmly, 'I'm making no promises – I'm not sure that I can bring myself to show my puny efforts to anyone else, even someone as obviously sympathetic as you. I expect you're missing Alfred.'

He didn't like the switch back to his mentor, but if he rejected it he would feel disloyal. He said slowly, 'I think we'd gone as far as we could go.'

'I see.' She was looking hard at him, patently trying to assess how genuine his statement was.

'Alfred was very generous. Both with his time and with his resources. He told me to take any books I wanted from his library, and even made suggestions. Helpful ones, in the main. And he was a good teacher, I think, one to one. He knew a lot about literature and a lot about the processes of writing. And he was a good communicator.'

'Yes, I see.' She took a large gulp of her coffee, drummed

her fingers on the immaculate white tablecloth, paused for so long that he wondered if she was waiting for him to speak. Then she said, 'Was there a sexual relationship between you?'

He wasn't shocked. He hadn't been expecting it, but when she asked the question he felt that it had been coming all along. 'The police asked me that.'

'And what did you tell them?'

He waited until she looked up, then gazed hard into those very blue eyes. 'I'm strictly heterosexual, Jane. I think you might have realized that.'

His hand stole daringly across the table and covered hers.

The Burgess house was certainly impressive. There was white frost on the lawn, but that only made the front garden seem even longer as they drove up and parked on the gravel before the double front door. The modern red brick of the front elevation rose above them, seeming impossibly high against the crisp blue of the winter sky beyond it. 'You probably won't need to display your hard bastard skills this morning,' said DCI Peach to DS Northcott.

The maid who opened the door viewed the tall black man with interest rather than suspicion when Peach announced their identity. 'Mrs Burgess is expecting you. You're to come into the morning room,' she said. They followed her through a huge hall with impeccable parquet flooring to a room on the left which looked over their car and down the front drive to the leafless flowering crabs and cherries by the gates. They had less than a minute to conduct their habitual CID assessment of the room before Sharon Burgess arrived and offered them her hand.

Peach was looking at the contents of a glass-fronted bookcase when she arrived. She said aggressively, 'Casing the joint, are we? And what are your findings?'

Peach smiled benignly. 'A nicely proportioned and pleasantly furnished room. Well kept, which in this context argues excellent domestic staff rather than the direct attentions of the owner. Very little used. I was wondering when a book was last removed from that bookcase.'

'Entirely correct, Sherlock. Coffee will be along in a moment, but I can't remember when it was last served in here. We're only here now because my cleaner is busy in the sitting room. And I suppose because my maid thought it a suitable place to accommodate curious policemen.'

'Nice for you to have a choice of rooms.'

Mrs Burgess said, 'I rattle around here. I keep thinking of moving to somewhere smaller and I shall probably do so eventually. But the children and the grandchildren like it when they come to stay and I can afford it. My husband left me comfortably off and Burgess Electronics continues to prosper.'

She was sizing them up during this initial fencing, when Peach felt that it was he who should be assessing her. Wealth gives certain advantages in the one-upmanship stakes, and this woman was clearly used to exercising those advantages. He said briskly, 'We're heading the enquiry into the death of Alfred Norbury, at the hand of person or persons unknown. How long had you known Mr Norbury?'

'I didn't know him well. I suppose about a dozen years. I'd probably heard of him earlier than that. Alfred was quite a well-known local figure, as I'm sure you're aware.' She looked at Clyde Northcott rather speculatively on that thought, but the coffee arrived as she had promised. The DS helped himself to one of the flapjacks she offered and then held his china cup and saucer with immense care, like a child on its best behaviour. She tried not to be distracted by this strange presence in her morning room. 'I didn't know Mr Norbury particularly well.'

'And yet you saw fit to invite him to be one of the founder members of your book club.'

Peach was looking at her with his bald head a little on one side and his dark eyes bright with interest, like a blackbird about to sample a particularly succulent worm. Sharon decided that she had much better give her full attention to the senior man. 'It wasn't me who invited Alfred. And it wasn't my book club.'

'Collective adjective, Mrs Burgess, that "your". And if you didn't invite Mr Norbury, you certainly sanctioned his presence at that meeting on Monday night. Or am I quite wrong? Did you oppose his membership? Were you overruled?'

The questions were coming at her like machine-gun fire. She hastened to answer before the fusillade could continue. 'It was

Enid Frott who invited him. And yes, I was consulted: I sanctioned Alfred as a member, I suppose. It was all very informal
and tentative.' She sighed. 'The book club was Enid's idea, but
I welcomed it and encouraged her to set it up. The first problem
was obviously to get a number of suitable people interested. We
decided that we would start with six and then add to that as we
went along, unless the whole thing collapsed around our ears.'

'Which it did in spectacular fashion, with the murder of one
of the founder members. One of the best-read and therefore
most promising of the founder members, if what I have heard
already is correct.'

It was a reminder to Sharon that they had been in touch with
the other people who had been there on Monday night and with
other people who had known Norbury. She needed to control
everything she said here. She felt deflated as she said, 'I expect
the book club will disintegrate now. Well, it never got off the
ground really, did it?'

'Murder isn't the best of starts for any sort of club, is it?'
Peach gave her an irritating grin, as if he found the thought
amusing. 'Do you think Mr Norbury would have been a useful
member of the book club?'

This was a question she hadn't expected. It was only later
that she realized it was an invitation to tell them everything she
knew about Norbury. She said carefully, 'He had all the attributes to be a good member, if he was willing to participate. I'm
sure he was quite the best-read person there on Monday night,
despite the presence of Jane Preston, who is well qualified and
works in the field. He is – was – articulate and stimulating.
Enid and I wanted him because we knew that he would initiate
lively discussions on whatever we had read.'

'I see. That confirms what other people have told us. I think
you said, "If he was willing to participate." Did you have doubts
about that?'

It showed how careful she needed to be: this man would pick
up any unguarded phrase and use it against her if it suited him.
'I had certain reservations about Alfred, yes. He could be too
bright for his own good, sometimes. He liked to show off his
knowledge and I felt that might inhibit others who weren't as
confident as he was.'

'I see. Well, that makes sense. It also shows quite a knowledge of the man, in someone who didn't know him well.'

He was throwing her own phrase back at her again, suggesting that she was concealing things she knew about Alfred. She said firmly, 'I discussed these things with Enid Frott, who knew him better than I did. We agreed that on balance Alfred had things to offer which would outweigh his disadvantages. I watched him on Monday and I think that would be a fair summary of his conduct. He was lively and stimulating. Controversial, probably, at times. But people listened and responded. That's what we wanted of him, I suppose. No one was going to be neutral, with Alfred around.'

'Someone certainly wasn't neutral. Someone killed him the next day.'

'But not necessarily someone who'd been at the book club meeting on Monday night. Someone else entirely, in my opinion.'

'And why do you say that?'

'Because I saw nothing at our meeting which would suggest a murder. I've been reviewing it in my mind ever since I heard Alfred was dead, and I can't think of anything said there or any action taken there which would suggest that anyone present on Monday night had murder in mind.'

She was the oldest of their suspects at sixty-seven, but the calmest and seemingly the most secure they had spoken to so far. Wealth and power brought a certain assurance, Peach supposed. This woman was used to being in control, especially here, in this huge house where she reigned supreme. 'We are tracing Mr Norbury's movements and contacts prior to his death on the day which followed your meeting. So far we haven't found anyone who admits to being in contact with him on Tuesday. Was anything said on Monday which suggested that violence might follow?'

'No. I thought I'd already answered that. I told you, I've been over it in my mind and haven't come up with anything.'

'Did Mr Norbury himself say anything which might suggest violence?'

There was a tiny pause whilst she considered her reply. 'No. Alfred had rather tense exchanges on literature and the writer's craft with Jane Preston and with Dick Fosdyke. But that was the sort of thing for which we'd included him and it wasn't unpleasant. Alfred gave us a few thoughts about crime fiction and then said he proposed to shut up whilst we chose our first book to read and discuss.'

'And he didn't say anything more shocking than that?'

'No. He shut up then.'

Peach eased himself back in his chair a little and stared at her steadily. 'I wonder why people have such selective recall about important details. You are the second person who has chosen to omit the most significant thing Mr Norbury said.'

'I can't think what you mean, Chief Inspector.'

But the denial came too promptly on the heels of his remark; she had begun it almost before he had completed his assertion. He said coldly, 'I think you know exactly what I'm referring to, Mrs Burgess. Alfred Norbury told the company at large that he kept a pistol in his car at all times. Your recall of other things he said seems commendably precise. I cannot think that you have forgotten such a dramatic statement from the murder victim. I therefore now have to ask myself why you chose to withhold that information.'

His adversary – she had no doubt by now that she was that – looked at him resentfully for a few seconds, but did not lose her nerve. Sharon knew she had made a mistake, but surely not a vital one. Her greater secret was safe still. 'All right. I probably shouldn't have left that out, but perhaps you can understand why I did. I'd already told you that I knew Alfred from way back. I'd agreed that we should invite him to join us. I thought that if I told you that he had that weapon in his car I'd have immediately become your number-one suspect. It may have been foolish to withhold the information, but you can surely understand why I did it.'

Peach had watched her with raised eyebrows during her explanation. He glanced at Northcott, gave the slightest shrug of his shoulders, and said, 'Mr Norbury brought a younger man with him and requested that he should be made a member of your embryonic book club.'

'Yes. Jamie Norris. It was a little unfair, because we could hardly have rejected him without embarrassment to ourselves and to Mr Norris. In the event, it brought us a welcome addition. Mr Norris seemed a pleasant young man, with a real interest in books and in the processes of writing. I think he would have been a valuable addition to our group. Enid Frott and I had already agreed that we wanted some young members to balance our aged selves. Jane Preston, whom I had introduced, and Mr Norris were going to be just that.'

'What do you think was Mr Norbury's relationship with Mr Norris?'

'Shouldn't you ask Jamie that?' It was the first time she had used his forename.

'We already have. I'm now asking you.'

'Jamie was definitely Alfred's protégé. How far it went beyond that, I couldn't say, but he did drive him to Enid's place in that Triumph Stag which he was so proud of.' She glanced from one to the other of her questioners. 'I gather Alfred has a history of liaisons with men. From his attitude on Monday, I suspect he had plans for a sexual relationship with Jamie Norris. I may of course be quite wrong, but you asked me to speculate.'

'I did indeed. And your thoughts on this, as on other things we have discussed, will remain confidential. Who do you think killed Alfred Norbury?'

It was so abrupt, so transparently challenging, that she almost laughed. 'I have no opinion on that. I have given the matter some thought, but come up with no useful possibilities. I am as baffled as you seem to be.'

Clyde Northcott looked up from his notes and said in his deep, sombre voice, 'Where were you on Tuesday afternoon and evening, Mrs Burgess?'

She felt as if her stomach was dropping away inside her. 'I suppose you have to ask that. You might record that I didn't kill Alfred. I was in this house during the whole of that time. As a matter of fact, I began during the evening to read *Harvest*, the book which was to be our first book club choice.'

'Can anyone confirm that you were here during those hours?'

'I fear not. Mrs Waterson, the lady who let you in, has Tuesdays off. She lives in this house, but at the other end of it from me. I have no idea whether or not she was in her quarters during those hours. I made one rather lengthy phone call to our product manager at Burgess Electronics, but that was early in the afternoon. As far as I can remember, I took no calls after that other than nuisance calls – recorded advertising messages which I always ignore.' She watched Northcott scribbling a note on his pad. 'Was Alfred shot with the pistol he claimed to carry in his car?'

Peach nodded. 'Almost certainly. I expect it to be confirmed within the next few hours.'

'Is it possible that he shot himself?'

'It is possible but extremely unlikely, in the opinion of the very experienced scene of crime officer who examined both the body and the weapon at the scene. I agree with his thoughts on the matter.'

He thought she would ask him about the technicalities of that view, but she merely nodded and said, 'He wasn't the suicidal type, Alfred. Whatever that type is.'

He gave her his card with the injunction that she should ring the station immediately if she had any more thoughts on the crime. She showed them to the door herself, then watched them turn the car and move down the drive and through the gates, as if she wished to confirm with her own eyes that they were clear of her home.

Clyde Northcott knew better than to initiate any discussion: that had to come from the chief. They had driven about a mile when Peach said, 'She'll repay further research, Mrs Burgess. She knows more than she's told us this morning.'

His DS negotiated a pensioner who stepped suddenly into the road twenty yards from a zebra crossing. 'I felt more had happened in the past with Alfred Norbury than she was admitting to.'

'I'm sure you're right. She knew not only that he had a classic car but the make and the model. Unusual in a woman, that. Especially in a woman of her years. But that's probably ageist and sexist.'

'You've got to play to your strengths, sir. You're good at being ageist and sexist.'

'And you're a cheeky young sod. A black cheeky young sod. There you are: racist as well. That's the hat-trick. I never had one of those when I played cricket. But I think you're right, Clyde. Tommy Bloody Tucker won't like it, because he hates annoying the local gentry. But we can't be afford too much respect for the recently widowed Mrs Burgess. We need to investigate exactly what she was doing in the past with the late Mr Norbury.'

THIRTEEN

The post-mortem report and the forensic findings from the scene of crime gave them little which was new or unexpected.

A bullet lodged in the top of the passenger door of the Triumph Stag confirmed that the instrument of Alfred Norbury's death had been the Beretta semi-automatic 92 FS pistol which had been found beneath his right hand in the vehicle. There were no prints other than his on the pistol, but in the views of both the pathologist and the police forensics personnel, death had not been self-administered. Norbury had been shot through the left temple, which would have been awkward and highly unusual for a right-handed suicide. Norbury was right-handed. The angle of the attack also, with the bullet passing slightly from rear to front in the skull, would have been almost unique in anyone who had elected to shoot himself. Finally, the powder burns and 'stippling' around the entry wound indicated that Norbury had been shot at close quarters, but not with the muzzle pressed against the head, as would normally be the case with a suicide.

There was no record of Norbury having a licence for the firearm, and no paperwork had been found during the police examination of his home. But the Beretta was not a difficult weapon to obtain. It had been the primary side-arm of the US Army, US Marine Corps and US Air Force for well over thirty years. The initial contract had been for 500,000 pistols, but there were probably over a million of these weapons in existence by now. They were fairly common and easy to purchase in the undercover markets which existed now in most European countries. The state of the pistol and of the ammunition found in the car and in his desk indicated that Alfred Norbury had probably possessed both of them for several years.

The interior of the car had been tidy, but it had not been valeted in the recent past. This left a situation beloved of the forensic staff. The Triumph Stag had now been examined in detail. A variety of clothing fibre, human hair, and dirt from footwear had been bagged and labelled and subjected to laboratory examination. They were available as and when required for matching purposes at a later date. That was not as promising as it sounded. Proving that someone had been in Norbury's car would not provide significant evidence for a court of law, unless it could be proved that the person concerned had been there at the time of the murder.

Percy Peach made a private note that for all save Jamie Norris, evidence that they had been in the Stag would argue much closer links with the murder victim than had been so far admitted. There might be possibilities for a little bluff in the days to come; he licked his lips at the prospect.

One of the tangible things the post-mortem examination provided was a more accurate indication of the time of death. Analysis of the stomach contents indicated that Norbury had eaten a substantial meal involving fish, mashed potatoes and vegetables about an hour before his death. This tallied with the 'meal for one' plastic container the police team had found in his disposal bin in the kitchen of his flat.

The team had also discovered through diligent routine enquiries that Norbury attended an art group which met in the adult education centre on most Tuesday evenings. Their sessions began at seven o'clock and Alfred Norbury was invariably punctual. Along with the analysis of the stomach contents, this gave a strong indication that the victim had probably died at around twenty to seven on the evening of Tuesday the twenty-first of January. No one had yet come forward to say that he or she had been in Wellington Street at that time, or had witnessed anything in any way suspicious.

'So anyone familiar with Norbury's habits would know that he would be coming out to his car at some time shortly after half past six on Tuesday evening,' said Peach thoughtfully. 'And I think that some of the people we've already spoken to knew his habits much more thoroughly than they've so far admitted.'

'Twenty to seven on a bitterly cold January night in a quiet street which is not a thoroughfare,' said Clyde Northcott. 'It's not surprising that we have no witnesses to the crime.'

Peach nodded grimly. 'And not surprising that the body should have sat undetected, getting colder and colder through the long, dark night. I don't think anyone would be aware that there was anything amiss before daylight on Wednesday. Apart from our killer, of course.'

Dick Fosdyke, like Alfred Norbury had, lived alone in a flat. But the two residences were very different.

Whereas Norbury's spacious, book-lined sitting room had suggested much about the tastes and the habits of the dead man, Fosdyke's living quarters were much more anonymous. He lived in a modern flat which was scarcely three years old and a mile from the centre of Brunton. You would have thought from the look of the place that the cartoonist was anxious to conceal rather than reveal himself. The first impression was of a place where a man slept and which he used as a base of operations, rather than making it the centre of his life.

Peach gazed around unhurriedly and without embarrassment when he was invited to sit on the sofa in the warm, comfortable but characterless living room. Fosdyke watched him for a moment, then glanced at Clyde Northcott. He received no support from that unyielding source. He eventually spoke first, as Peach knew he would do, when the social pressure upon him increased with the silence. 'You won't discover much about me from looking round here.' He spoke almost apologetically.

Peach turned to him with an affable smile, as if he had not realized until then that the owner was present. 'More than you realize, perhaps, Mr Fosdyke. I would think that this place is not particularly significant for you, in that you could move somewhere else tomorrow without any great regrets. Modern flats do not generally inspire nostalgia, unless the occupant brings something to them which makes them individual and quite different from other flats around them. I judge that you have made no particular effort to do that. This flat looks as if you have no great interest in putting your stamp upon this or perhaps any other home.'

Fosdyke looked hard at him, but chose not to respond directly to his remarks. 'I haven't been here long enough to put down roots. Almost three years, I suppose, though it seems like much

less than that. My marriage broke up and I had to find somewhere as a base. You aren't particularly interested in where or
even how you live, when you've been through the emotional
trauma of a divorce. This is what I could afford and it suits me
pretty well, I suppose.'

Peach nodded. 'I've been through the same process, but it
was many years ago and I was glad to be rid of my marriage.
The partnership was a mistake and it didn't last long. There
were no children. But like you I didn't pay any attention to
where I was living next. It was somewhere I slept and whence
I ventured forth to work. I've moved on now and got a new
wife. She tells me how much I've neglected the place and points
out how much needs doing. I'm sure she'd say it's sexist, but
it's my view that men aren't natural nest-makers.'

Dick Fosdyke grinned. This sort of discussion was the last
thing he had expected. He'd been preparing himself to stonewall
resolutely through the routine police questioning, but this strange
DCI who had bounced into his flat in an unexpectedly smart
grey suit was a surprise. A pleasant one, he told himself hope-
fully. 'As you say, work dominates your thoughts and your
lifestyle. Necessarily, in my case. I have to work to live, and
also to give the support the court decreed appropriate to my
wife and two children. Hobbies seem like an indulgence.'

'And yet you chose to join a book club.'

'Yes. I felt it was time for me to dip my toe again into the
dangerous waters of society. I surprised myself when I accepted
the invitation. I suppose when you've set yourself up as a loner,
it's flattering to be asked to join anything.'

'Who did the asking, Mr Fosdyke?'

The questions were coming now. And he wasn't stonewalling
as effectively as he'd intended to do. Perhaps this strange little
man with the large and threatening black sidekick was more
cunning that he'd thought. 'It was Sharon Burgess. I met her a
few months ago in the library, where she works as a volunteer.
We got into the habit of having coffee together. It's an unlikely
alliance, I suppose – she's from a very different and much more
affluent background than mine, and she's twenty-seven years
older. Perhaps it was the fact that there was nothing sexual in
the friendship that helped it to develop. Sharon was recently

widowed and I was still shell-shocked from divorce, so we probably both wanted something unthreatening.'

Peach looked at him with a sparkle in his very dark pupils. 'Sex is not unknown between people who are a generation apart.'

Dick felt quite at ease. He wasn't going to take offence at such a comment, especially as he thought the man might welcome that. 'I can assure you that there is no sexual liaison here. So you can abandon the image of a steamy partnership plotting together to secure the death of Alfred Norbury.'

'You both had reason to wish him dead then, did you?' Peach's eyebrows arched high beneath the shining whiteness of his bald head.

For the first time, Dick was ruffled. They had somehow moved much nearer to his feelings about Norbury than he had intended. 'I didn't say that. You've no right to assume it from anything I said.'

'True though, isn't it? You didn't much like the man. I'm sorry, but we have to be pretty direct, when we're investigating murder. Bluntness is allowed, you see – even encouraged. We wouldn't get anywhere quickly without a certain directness, Mr Fosdyke. And speed is of the essence. You may know that the chances of a successful conclusion to a murder investigation decrease sharply with each passing week.'

'I think I have heard that, yes. In which case, you should probably be using your time more usefully somewhere else at this very moment. Because I know nothing about this death.'

Peach looked at him and nodded slowly. It was impossible to be sure whether he was digesting the information or the reaction it showed in his subject. 'Was Mr Norbury a friend of yours, sir?'

'Not a friend, no. We didn't know each other well enough to be friends or enemies.'

'I see. You didn't know him before you met him at the inaugural meeting of your book club, then?'

That was exactly the impression Dick had intended to give them. But now this suddenly aggressive little man was asking the question directly and he needed to be careful. 'I knew of him. He's quite a well-known local character and I've lived in

Brunton for years. It would be strange if I hadn't known a little about him.'

'Indeed it would, sir. How well did you know him?'

Fosdyke looked down at the low table with the art magazine on top of it. 'Not well at all. I suppose I've probably met him before, but I feel as though my first real meeting with him was on Monday night. That's an odd feeling, because the next thing that I heard about him was that he was dead.'

'And what impression had you formed of him on Monday night?'

Dick took his time. This was the crux of these exchanges and he must get it right. 'I was trying to reserve judgement. Or at least to remember his good points.'

'Which were?'

He frowned. 'Is what I felt about Norbury really relevant? Shouldn't you be asking about times and places? Or better still, questioning people who might have had some reason to kill the man?'

Peach gave him the blandest of his smiles. 'We're still building up a picture of a man neither DS Northcott or I ever met. We're finding out all sorts of interesting things about Alfred Norbury and the people who knew him. The views and reactions of an intelligent person like you are sure to add colour and definition to the portrait. As an artist, I'm sure you can appreciate that.'

'A sometime artist, I suppose. I make my living by using a few swiftly drawn lines to make political or sporting comment.'

'And I'm sure you consider yourself an artist, Mr Fosdyke. Your views on Mr Cameron's treatment of his coalition partners in the cartoon published yesterday would be much less trenchant without the sharpness and selectiveness of the drawing.'

It was flattering but also disturbing. He had thought this man knew nothing about him. Now he found that he knew not only what he did but something of the way he thought. You revealed a lot about yourself in your drawings and your comments. How much more research had Peach done before he came here? How much more did he know about the past and what had happened between him and Alfred Norbury? Dick said carefully, 'I suppose we're artists in our own minds. The public scarcely consider us that. With the great names – the Italian old masters, for instance – mere preliminary sketches for paintings can now be worth many thousands of pounds. Original newspaper cartoons rarely sell for more than a few hundred, even when they are by acknowledged masters of the craft.'

He was riding a hobby horse, but a safe one. Whilst he was indulging himself here, he was safe from further probing on Norbury. Peach flicked a glance at Northcott, who said calmly and menacingly, 'Where were you on Tuesday evening, Mr Fosdyke?'

He had the story ready, of course. He'd rehearsed it long before they came here. He tried nevertheless to make it sound spontaneous. 'Tuesday evening. That's when he was killed, isn't it? You're asking me to account for my movements at the time, treating me as a murder suspect. Just routine, I suppose.'

Northcott ignored his nervous smile. 'So where were you, Mr Fosdyke?'

'Tuesday, let's see.' Dick put his hands together, steepled his fingers, allowed them to play against each other for a moment. 'I went down to the library as usual in the morning. I read the newspapers, surveyed the market for cartoons, thought up a couple of possible themes for drawings which would make political comments. I checked a few facts in the reference section – very much a routine day, really. I didn't see my friend Sharon Burgess, who obviously wasn't on the library duty rota for that day. Bit of a disappointment, really: I'd been looking forward to comparing notes with her about our book club meeting on the previous night.'

'And what would have been your comments on that, if she'd been there?'

This was Peach, his head a little on one side, looking like a cat inviting a bird to make a wrong move. Dick wished he'd shut up and let him concentrate on the important matter of his whereabouts at the time when Norbury had been killed. 'I suppose I was rather confused really. I'd never been to a book club and I didn't know quite what to think about our first meeting. That's why it would have been interesting to have a chat over coffee with Mrs Burgess.'

'I see. What did you think of Mr Norbury's contribution to the evening?'

'I suppose I was rather irritated by it, if I'm honest.'

'Do be honest, Mr Fosdyke. It's much the best policy.'

Dick told himself not to show his annoyance: that would no doubt delight the man. 'He seemed to be trying to take the meeting over. He seemed to regard it as his natural right to be the leader of the discussion and to dictate the direction of our thoughts. I found him rather patronising. But I suppose he'd been brought along to speak up and offer his views when we were all feeling our way with each other. Perhaps I should have been grateful to him for offering his opinions so freely. That's the sort of thing I'd have liked to discuss with Sharon Burgess, if she'd been around the next morning.'

'And what about the other people there? Did they find Norbury as galling as you did?'

He wondered for a moment whether to object to that adjective. But this was an opportunity to divert attention away from himself, to assert to them that others as well as he had found Norbury irksome. 'Well, that boy he'd brought along was under his wing, as you'd expect. And the two older women seemed amused rather than upset by Alfred, if I'm honest. But the young woman, Jane Preston, seemed to take against him rather. I think she resented the way he came on strong with her.'

'Our information is that our murder victim was homosexual.'

'Bisexual, perhaps. But let's not argue about that: I didn't know the man well enough to give an opinion. He certainly seemed to leer a little at the fair young Ms Preston. But I wasn't thinking just in sexual terms when I said he came on strong with her. He seemed to be challenging her expertise. She's well qualified in English literature and pursuing a career in teaching it. Alfred seemed to want to argue with her, to encourage her to state her opinions just so that he could disagree with them. It was all in a jokey manner, but I think she found his whole attitude disagreeable. Perhaps I'm being unduly sensitive on her behalf – you'd need to ask her about it.'

'Which we shall do, Mr Fosdyke. Where were you between six-thirty and seven on Tuesday evening?'

Dick smiled, trying not to look too pleased with himself. 'I was out for a meal with an old friend. In the restaurant at the White Hart. I can recommend it, Chief Inspector, though I'm no gourmet. Simple but excellent cuisine and well-kept local beer. We ate early because Ernie lives in Bolton and had to get home afterwards.'

'We'll need the name of your companion.'

'Of course you will. Ernest Ainsworth. Seventeen Goldstone Avenue, Bolton. Former colleague from the days when I worked full-time for our national press. Ernie still does: he's based with the *Daily Express* in Manchester.'

He looked at the card Peach had given him thoughtfully when they had gone. Then he picked up the phone to speak to Ernie Ainsworth. It was good to be able to call in a favour from an old friend.

Percy Peach got home to find his mother-in-law in the house.

That stark fact would have led to deep depression in many of his police colleagues, reared as they had been on northern comedians and robust jokes about the species. But Percy and his wife's elderly parent had got on like happy children from the moment they had met, which was shortly after her nubile daughter had been assigned to Percy as a detective sergeant. Percy and Lucy had worked together happily and productively until their marriage, whereupon police protocol determined that they could no longer work closely with each other. Clyde Northcott, rescued from a life of crime and trained up for CID by Percy Peach, had been the best man at their wedding and had subsequently replaced Lucy as Percy's bagman.

Agnes Blake had been prevailed upon to share the evening meal in the Peach household. With Lucy in the kitchen, she and Percy discussed England's dismal performance in the Ashes tests in Australia with feeling and considerable expertise. One of the things which had bound them inextricably from the first was a love of the arcane mysteries of cricket. Percy had been a prominent batsman for East Lancs, the Brunton side in the Lancashire League, and Agnes had followed his exploits long before she had met him. He was now thirty-nine and had retired from serious cricket three years earlier – much too prematurely, in Agnes's view.

She was a widow of seventy-one, vigorous and acute, but intensely aware of the passing years and the absence of grandchildren in her life. She had produced her only child at forty-one, and it was in her view high time that Lucy was providing her with the brood she had always envisaged. Her daughter had sternly forbidden her even to introduce the subject with her spouse. Lucy was all too aware of the unholy alliance into which these two dropped naturally whenever her interests were threatened.

Agnes scrupulously avoided the subject of the murder which was dominating local headlines as they demolished their lasagne. Lucy had long since convinced her that Percy couldn't talk domestically about his current cases and she accepted that. Mrs Blake confined herself to a couple of barbed references to foreign food and how basic English cooking was suffering with so many women doing full-time work outside the home. She was secretly delighted that Lucy as a detective sergeant was enjoying the sort of career which had never been open to a mill-girl like her, but she pretended to disapprove. Over dessert, Lucy responded to a query about her latest work with the news that she had recently been working with the rape unit. Agnes informed her that this was not a suitable topic for discussion over rhubarb crumble.

She eyed her daughter's stomach with undisguised curiosity, searching for the expansion she dearly wished to see there. Percy cleared the table and prepared to load the dishwasher his wife had recently had installed. He winked at Agnes from behind Lucy as he passed. He listened to the conversation as he conscientiously stacked the dishes, reflecting that he needed a little amusement after a trying day.

It didn't take long for Agnes to arrive at her favourite conversational topic. 'Any news yet on the – the family front?' Percy smiled, imagining his mother-in-law's grey head jerking sharply towards her daughter's stomach.

'No, not yet. We're in no hurry. I'm enjoying my career, Mum.' The sentiments she had voiced so many times before.

Percy hastened back into the sitting room to make mischief. 'She may be in no hurry, Mrs B, but she shouldn't speak for me or for you, should she? She may be a young slip of a girl, but we have to consider our years, don't we? Ever at our backs we hear time's winged chariot hurrying near.'

'Oh, go on with you, Percy! You're off with your poetry again, and I can't be doing with it!' Agnes cackled delightedly nonetheless, then turned seriously back to her daughter. 'But he's right, our Lucy, isn't he? Percy doesn't want to be a doddery old dad and I don't want to be a gran who can't run along hand in hand with my grandson, do I?'

Agnes sighed. 'I'm no slip of a girl. I'm thirty now, Mum. I've got a biological clock ticking, the same as anyone else of my age. And for your information, I'm not on the pill. We're trying for a baby. I can't help it if nothing has happened as yet!' She glared darkly at Percy, who had ignored his usual armchair and sat down happily beside Agnes on the sofa.

He donned an expression of outraged innocence and addressed his remarks to the older woman beside him. 'They've no shame nowadays, these modern young women, have they? They bring the bedroom into the living room and strip life down to its barest essentials. She'll be telling you about her new blue pants with the lace edges next. It's just not seemly and it shocks me, Mrs B! I've no idea what it must do to someone of your delicate sensibilities.' He clasped his hands across his stomach and closed his eyes sententiously, then rocked back on the sofa and shook his head in deep dismay.

Agnes was as usual delighted with his efforts. She swayed backwards and forwards with laughter and said, 'Oh, you're a caution, Percy Peach, you really are!' Then she straightened her face and addressed herself solemnly to her daughter. 'But he's right, isn't he, our Lucy? He and I aren't getting any younger and your biological whatsit is careering along, as you admitted. So it's high time you got on with it.'

'And it's high time you shut up and found something else to talk about, Mum!' said her outraged daughter.

'You see what I'm up against, Mrs B!' Percy shook his head dejectedly. 'I'm doing my best to make me a father and you a grandmother, but I'm ploughing a lonely furrow here!' His dark eyes caught the very blue ones of his wife on what he was sure was a double entendre, then sparkled at the images it conjured up for him.

'This is not a suitable subject for a post-dinner discussion,' said Lucy as firmly as she could. She tried hard to be sanctimonious, but it did not come naturally to her and she destroyed the effect with an involuntary giggle.

Percy seized upon it. 'You see what I have to contend with, Mrs B? The wanton hussy of conversation becomes the cold nun of rejection at the very prospect of conception. Life is much harder with your daughter than most people could ever imagine.' He sighed extravagantly with the pain of it all and the pressure of the marital secrets he had to conceal.

Agnes Blake hugged herself with laughter. 'I'm going to go now and leave you two lovebirds to it! I know my daughter's in safe hands with you, Percy.'

'None safer, Mrs B. And none more active, when they're given free rein.' He cast his eyes unsmilingly to the heavens, as if he were describing some religious ritual.

He took Mrs Blake out to her car and watched her drive away into the night, then returned to the house to pursue her interests. An hour later, he did his very best to secure the grandchild she so dearly desired. As duties came, it was a highly pleasurable one. So much so that he made a second attempt an hour later.

No one would be able to say that Percy Peach had shirked his responsibilities.

FOURTEEN

They were coming to see her at last. Jane Preston had been waiting since the announcement of the murder on Wednesday for this. By Saturday morning, her tension had increased considerably.

They had interviewed all the others involved in that fatal book club meeting now; when they made the arrangements to see her, she had gathered that she was the last of the five to be questioned. What had the others said about her? What information should she relay to the police this morning? How much could she safely conceal? They held all the key cards. They had done this many times before and she had never been involved in anything remotely similar.

She made sure that the sitting room in her small modern house was tidier than usual, then went into the kitchen and set beakers, sugar, milk and biscuits on a tray. She found that she was doing simple things with elaborate care and taking twice as long over them as usual. She was trying to fill the time before they arrived with actions rather than thoughts, because she had already been over what she needed to say to them so often. Further thought could only make her more nervous.

They were not what she had expected, even though she had had no clear anticipation of what they would be. A very tall black man told her that he was Detective Sergeant Northcott and that the smaller, watchful man beside him was Detective Chief Inspector Peach, who was in charge of this case. Strange name for a detective, Peach. And hadn't Jamie Norris told her that the man's full name was Percy Peach – an even more ridiculous and unthreatening combination?

The man didn't look unthreatening. Despite the formidable presence of Northcott upon her sofa, it was Peach who alarmed her. He accepted her offer of coffee enthusiastically, then prowled around her living room as she prepared it. She had left the kitchen door open to keep an eye upon them, but he made no attempt to disguise either his movements or his curiosity. He was looking at the photographs of her family on the side table when she carried in the coffee. There was one of her mother and father standing behind their two children, taken twenty years ago and still one of her parents' favourites. Her father's hand was resting fondly on her head and her mother's hand was on her brother's shoulder. She must have been only eight then and Adam was at least a foot taller than her, almost as tall as Mum.

Peach hadn't picked up the photograph but he was studying it closely, though what he could hope to gain from such an innocent family group Jane couldn't imagine. She was surprised how much she resented his interest; it felt as though without speaking a word he was intruding upon her privacy. He accepted the coffee politely enough and thanked her for her efforts. Then he said abruptly, 'Did you know Alfred Norbury well?'

'No. Not well at all. His death was nevertheless a great shock to me.'

'Yes, I suppose it must have been.' He sounded unconvinced. 'But not a source of any great grief.'

'Why do you say that?'

Peach shrugged his surprisingly broad shoulders. 'You hardly knew the man, you say. One would presume therefore that his death, whilst shocking, caused you no real anguish.'

The black arcs of his eyebrows rose interrogatively towards the shining bald pate above them. They were too prominent, those eyebrows. They dominated the questioning which followed, perpetually mobile, perpetually questioning the veracity of what she was delivering in the way of answers. Jane said coldly, 'I didn't know Mr Norbury well. But it would be highly insensitive to feel no sorrow that he is dead.'

'And you have a sensitive soul, I'm sure, Ms Preston. Did you like what you saw of him on Monday night?'

Another query which was brutal in its brusqueness. Jane made herself take her time. This was a question she had expected, after all, though she hadn't expected it to be so confrontational. She forced a smile. 'Alfred was stimulating, if you approved of him. If you didn't, he was disagreeable.'

'And which camp did you find yourself in?'

'I found him both intriguing and irritating. Not necessarily at the same time.'

Peach beamed and agitated those too prominent eyebrows. 'Could you enlarge upon that, please?'

'Well, he seemed to want to dominate the conversation: that was rather irritating. But we were all rather diffident about voicing any opinion at this first meeting. Therefore his contributions were no doubt stimulating. When I look back, he was instrumental in getting the conversation going and encouraging the rest of us to voice our opinions. We would have been grateful to him for that, if the book club idea had gone ahead. Now it looks as if it will be an abortive venture. I certainly don't feel like carrying on after a beginning like this.'

'Do you think Mr Norbury was deliberately irritating people – I'm assuming you were not alone in your reaction to him?'

'It's difficult to be certain about things like that when you're meeting someone for the first time. Other people seemed to be more used to him than I was. I got the impression that he liked to dominate whatever company he was in. That he was prepared to take the centre of the stage by any means available to him.'

'I see. So this means that you weren't the only one irritated. Other people had reason to dislike him, as well as you.'

'I don't think I spoke of anything as strong as dislike. Still less of anything as strong as the hatred which would lead anyone to kill a man the next day.'

It was meant as a rebuke, but this man was not at all quelled. 'Good point that. So it was something outside that meeting which prompted his murder. Some more long-standing grievance against Mr Norbury. Yes, that's a very useful observation. That's the kind of thing that it's useful for us to know.'

'It's only my opinion.'

'Of course it is. But it's the kind of thing that's helpful to us, fishing around as we are in the early stages of a murder investigation. And you will probably be pleased to learn that your views on this coincide with what other people we've questioned have said.'

'I wasn't suggesting that anyone who was at the book club meeting killed Mr Norbury. It seems to me most unlikely.'

'Does it really? Well, that's most interesting. Make a note of that, DS Northcott, will you? Ms Preston found our murder victim both stimulating and irritating, but didn't think he did anything at Monday night's meeting that would have provoked murder. She thinks that derived from some deeper-seated and longer-standing grievance.'

'I said it might have been someone who wasn't present at our meeting on Monday night.'

'Indeed you did, and it's a suggestion we are bearing in mind. We haven't so far come up with any other possibilities, but we continue to search diligently. Do you think Alfred Norbury was seeking deliberately to irritate his audience on Monday?'

He was back to that fatal meeting and her part in it, like a terrier refusing to give up its bone. 'He might have been. He might have been mischievous. He might have been prepared to go on being contentious until he provoked some sort of reaction in his audience. It can be quite an effective teaching technique, when you have a group of people who are reluctant to offer anything in the way of opinions.'

'Ah! You're a teacher yourself, so you would be aware of these things.'

She smiled, a little more at ease now. 'It's a ploy I've used myself, when I've had a class who were unwilling to offer thoughts of their own on a particular author or a particular book.'

'I see. At the University of Central Lancashire, that would be, I suppose.'

'Yes.' She should have known that this man would have explored her background before he came here, but it felt like another intrusion into her privacy. 'I've been teaching there for the last year.'

'In Preston. Quite a coincidence, that. With your name being Preston, I mean.'

Jane smiled. 'Coincidences occur. They aren't always sinister.'

'No indeed. I wasn't suggesting there was anything sinister in this one. Interesting, though. You moved there from a similar post in Birmingham. Promotion was it?'

She wanted desperately to say that it was. But they'd check. They'd check everything, when they were following up a murder. She tried to speak as casually as she could. 'No, it wasn't a promotion. It was more interesting work. I specialise in the literature of the nineteenth century, and the post at the University of Central Lancashire offered me that. I'm a single woman without family. Finance wasn't my first consideration.'

She was tight-lipped and dismissive. Peach studied her for a few seconds, registering just that. 'I believe that you were born and bred in Penrith.' He glanced round the room. 'I'm surprised you haven't got pictures of the fells in here. Great county, Cumbria.'

'I grew up there, yes. But when you're a lonely child, you don't seem to make the circle of friends who take you back there. I've scarcely been back since I completed my university studies. Like lots of other graduates, I go where the work is and where the work seems interesting. I can't think that is of any relevance to your case.'

'Can't you, Ms Preston? Well, you may be right. But we have to have magpie minds. We have to pick up all sorts of things. We have to consider lots of details about the people involved. Most of them have not the remotest connection. But we turn up the occasional gem and that justifies the effort and all the other irrelevances we have to discard. We do study people's backgrounds and what they do in their normal working lives outside the case. You'd be surprised how often that throws up things which prove significant in our investigation.'

'I see. Well, in that case your magpie minds will also wish to collect the information that I teach an evening class in Brunton on the nineteenth-century novel.'

It was meant as a rather petty assertion of her independence, as a claim that she did other things of which he would not know, but Peach merely nodded, lowered his eyebrows and said, 'And this is where you met Mrs Burgess, one of the moving spirits behind the formation of the book club.'

Jane tried not to be disconcerted by how much he already knew of her. 'It was Sharon Burgess who in fact invited me to be a member of the book club.'

'Yes. How did she react to Mr Norbury's posturings?'

She wondered for a moment whether she should object to his use of that word, then decided that it might be justified from her description. 'I can't remember that she seemed anything other than mildly amused. I got the impression that she and Enid Frott knew Alfred from way back and knew what to expect. I think it was probably Enid who had invited him to join the group.'

'You think correctly.'

It was another reminder to her that they had spoken to others before her and that she needed to be careful with what she told them now. 'The two older women seemed to expect Norbury to behave in the way he did. I think they were amused by it, but I could be wrong. It's just an impression: they didn't say much.'

'And Dick Fosdyke? What impression did you form of his relationship with the man who is now deceased?'

Jane didn't like the way he'd picked up her word 'impression' and put just the slightest ironic emphasis upon it as he delivered it. Or was she being unduly sensitive? She mustn't go looking for trouble, not with experienced people like these two. 'I hadn't met Mr Fosdyke before. He seems an interesting man. Very bright, I'd say, though he didn't say much. I thought he was studying the other people in the group and making up his mind whether to proceed with it, but that might be quite wrong. He didn't say a lot, but he might have been taciturn for other reasons.'

Jane waited for a moment, watching Northcott making a note in his notebook, hoping that Peach would ask the question she wanted to give her the cue for what she now proposed to add. But he said nothing, watching her as though he was waiting for her to make a wrong move. She was forced to go on without prompting. 'For what it's worth, I got the impression that he didn't much like Alfred Norbury. He seemed irritated by the way Alfred threw out his opinions and tried to hog the attention, when we talked a little about books and what we proposed to do. I might be quite wrong and quite unfair, because I didn't know either of them well, but I thought there might be some previous history between the two of them.'

'Oh, I'm sure you're not wrong, Ms Preston. I'm sure you are very shrewd in matters like this. And thank you for your speculation. It is something we can only encourage, during a murder enquiry. It will remain confidential, unless it proves material to the case.'

'Thank you. I don't think there is much else I can add to this.'

The eyebrows shot upwards with alarming speed. 'Ah, but there is, Ms Preston! We need to know your own reaction to these events. We gather from what others tell us that you were the central figure in all this. That Mr Norbury turned the spotlight of his attention upon you, as if he regarded you as some sort of challenge.'

Jane fought down a feeling of panic. How fully had he questioned the other four and what had they offered to him about her and Norbury? She tried very hard to speak calmly. 'I suppose it might have been like that. When you're at the centre of things, you don't always see it as clearly as the people on the sidelines. Yes, I suppose it's possible that Mr Norbury turned his attention principally towards me, when he was showing off his knowledge and his opinions on literature and on books. I was perhaps the person in the room with the best formal qualifications, as well as the only one making a living from the teaching of literature. I suppose I was the natural target for his more controversial remarks. I don't think there was anything more sinister in it than that.'

'You were also the most attractive woman in the room. That might also have been a challenge to a mischievous man like Mr Norbury. Wouldn't you say so, DS Northcott?'

'I would indeed, sir. I would of course be speaking in a wholly objective, non-sexist way. But I think a red-blooded male of Mr Norbury's age would be very likely to see a woman like Ms Preston as a sort of challenge, sir.'

His smile was quite different from that of DCI Peach, she thought; less threatening, more genuine, and even broader. His teeth looked large and very white. She said as coldly as she could, 'I understand that his tastes were not for blonde young ladies.'

Peach nodded sagely. 'We have received that suggestion from a person well placed to know. But we have also had the suggestion from one of your fellow book club members that Alfred Norbury "leered" at you in the course of these exchanges. We have to follow these things up.'

He spoke apologetically whilst he was thoroughly enjoying

himself, she thought. 'I was not aware of anything sexual in his approach. If there was, there was certainly no response on my part.' She felt like an ageing spinster. She had a maiden great-aunt of eighty who would have spoken in just her tone.

'You will be aware that it is not entirely unknown for people to exhibit bisexual tendencies and tastes. It has always seemed to me inordinately greedy and selfish, but it's a fact of life. Thank you for clarifying the matter for us. What do you think was the nature of Mr Norbury's relationship with Jamie Norris?'

Another startling switch, as if it was the most natural progression in the world. As she supposed it was, after what they just been saying. She was forced to admit that to herself. She said stiffly, 'You would need to ask Mr Norris about it yourselves.'

'As we have done, Ms Preston. We are now asking you for your thoughts on the matter. As a confidante of Mr Norris, if you prefer to see it that way.'

They knew that she'd met Jamie; they knew that the two of them had compared notes. They seemed to know everything, these two. But there was a huge team on a murder case, and no doubt they made it their business to know everything which was going on between suspects. Suspects! She was admitting now that she was a suspect. They'd won that battle. 'My impression – and please accept that it is no more than an impression – is that Mr Norbury was interested in taking things further, in conducting a sexual relationship with Jamie, but that Jamie was not. Alfred had been very generous to Jamie in giving him advice and furthering his progress in his own writing. Jamie says his advice has been really useful and practical. He didn't mind being a protégé of Alfred's as far as his work went. But he was anxious that it shouldn't go further than friendship. He didn't want a sexual relationship with Norbury.'

'Or he says he didn't.'

'He says he didn't and that there wasn't. And I believe him on both counts.'

She let her annoyance out in saying it. But there surely couldn't be any harm in that. He was being intrusive and she was defending a friend. And anything that took their attention away from her and what she had thought of Alfred Norbury must be a good thing. Jane wondered if he would press her about how she knew that and whether Norris had pursued an association with her, but he seemed prepared to accept what she said. He told her again that all of this was useful in building up a picture of a murder victim and 'those closest to him at the time of his death', of which she was plainly one. Then he asked her to go on thinking about this murder and to communicate any other information she discovered about the other people involved – a plain invitation to investigate Jamie Norris and report on him, she thought.

She cleared away the coffee cups and the biscuits when they had gone. That black detective sergeant had been quite a dish, she thought with a smile. He carried an air of power and danger behind that calm exterior which gave so little away. In other circumstances . . .

But she mustn't think like that. When this was all over, everything might be different. In the meantime, things had gone reasonably well this morning, despite the intense and demanding attention she had received from that man Peach. It hadn't been pleasant, but they hadn't discovered much more than she'd intended to tell them. So far so good.

The murder victim's computer software proved more difficult to enter than the police had anticipated.

Harry Mercer was the police expert who had never been beaten by a laptop. It took him two days and much ingenuity to solve the problems left behind for him by the intricate mind of Alfred Norbury. But Harry cracked the password problems eventually and what he then revealed was quite startling.

Norbury had detailed computer files on his finances and share-holdings, which showed that he was a rich man, who could well afford to behave as independently and even eccentric-ally as he had done sometimes. He had also compiled files on other matters, which were much more interesting to the team assembled to investigate his murder. There were many files with individual names; these contained information which could be best described as 'very private'.

Certainly the individuals concerned would be aghast if much of the information they contained was ever made public. A quick scan of what they contained set the pulses of CID officers racing. There was information here about several noteworthy Brunton figures. Some of the information and thinking here needed to be followed up, which would lead to embarrassment and perhaps even some prosecutions.

It was now late Saturday morning and most of the team had been stood down for the weekend. DCI Peach called DS Northcott and DC Murphy into his office to discuss the implications of Mercer's treasure trove. 'Do you think Norbury was blackmailing people?' was DS Northcott's first question after he had been apprised of the findings.

Peach shook his head sadly. 'You always seem to want to think the worst of people, Clyde,' he said sententiously.

'I never used to be like that. It must be a result of working continually with you,' said Northcott with an impeccably straight face.

Murphy grinned. 'This looks like a hoard of material built up by a blackmailer to me too. Sins great and small, strengths and weaknesses – particularly weaknesses.'

Percy grinned. 'Pity there aren't files on you two in there. There'd be infinite possibilities for a resourceful chap like me. But there's no evidence that Norbury was blackmailing anyone. Some of his personal files show that he had ample private means and plenty of good investments. He didn't need the money he might have made from blackmail. And everything we're learning about him shows that, whilst he was no angel, he wasn't the kind of underhand character who goes in for blackmail.'

'Why all these files on individuals, then?' said Northcott.

'Because he was the kind of man who liked to be well-informed about his acquaintances. Or to put it in less flattering terms, the kind of man who liked to build up a store of information which would give him a hold over people, if he ever wanted to exercise it. From what we've heard so far, he liked power, and power over people in particular. The fact that he knew these things would give him control, even if he used his knowledge only judiciously and infrequently.'

Murphy nodded. 'I haven't seen this stuff yet. Is there anything on the people we've been questioning this week?'

Percy smiled approvingly on the big fresh-faced Lancastrian

with the Irish name. 'Indeed there is. There are files on three of the people who attended what seems to have been Norbury's last meeting with other people on Monday night. These are people who were to be members of the book club. Those three are Sharon Burgess and Enid Frott, the two people who set up the whole thing, and Dick Fosdyke, the man who claimed to us that he hardly knew our murder victim.'

Northcott licked his lips. 'We already possess Norbury's old-fashioned manual file on Enid Frott. That presumably dates from his pre-computer days. It was Enid Frott who invited Norbury to join the group. It sounds as if we now have the material for further interviews.'

'Exactly so. An unexpected gift from the gods for deserving and persevering coppers. There is also a fourth file, but I haven't included that, because it's on Jamie Norris and there's nothing in it, except for the details of where he works and when he started there. That was obviously just the beginning, as far as Norbury was concerned. It shows that he had serious intentions of some sort about Norris. I doubt whether he saw him as merely a literary protégé.'

Brendan Murphy checked on his notes. It was he who had been feeding the mass of accumulating information on the Norbury case into the police computer. 'But there were five people who were at that Monday night inaugural meeting for the proposed book club. You've seen all of them this week.'

'Yes. The fifth one was Jane Preston, whom Clyde and I saw earlier this morning. There's no file on her.'

The night of Saturday the 25th of January was clear and starlit. There would be a hard frost by morning. The Rovers had managed to win their home match and Brunton wrapped itself up and prepared for the winter night. The young folk were out, but not many others. The restaurants had been busy as usual, but people had eaten early and left early. Even the pubs in the town centre were much less crowded than they usually were on Saturday nights The Scots in the town were saving themselves for the delights of Burns night on the morrow.

Sharon Burgess had not expected a visitor at this hour, though any sort of company was welcome enough. There had been much sympathy for her after Frank died, but widows are not invited out very much. She was finding her social life much diminished since Frank's death. She hadn't realized until now how much she would resent that.

Dick Fosdyke had said he would bring a bottle of wine when he rang to invite himself, but she had vetoed that. Wine implied a prolonged stay and she wanted to feel free to terminate this meeting whenever it suited her. In fact, he put himself out to be pleasant and she found after an awkward beginning that she was enjoying the evening.

They drank a couple of glasses of Merlot: her wine on her terms, she told herself. She must have got the temperature just right; the rich red wine tasted more smooth and mellow than she could ever remember it before. And Dick seemed to appreciate the nuts and the crisps she had set out for him. Men who lived alone usually ate meals from containers and drank alone in front of the telly, she thought. A little pampering brought more appreciation from men like Fosdyke than from men who lived with wives in comfortable middle-class homes.

It was over half an hour before he felt able to broach the real reason for his visit. 'I expect the police have spoken to you about Alfred.'

'Yes. Just routine, they said. But they gave me more of a grilling than I'd expected. They came here: the detective chief inspector in charge of the case and a big black chap who didn't say much but watched me all the way through as if I might be trying to steal his watch. I suppose it's their job and they weren't doing much more than going through the motions. But I felt wrung out and stretched out to dry by the time they left.' She smiled, trying to lighten her effect. 'I must be getting old and sensitive.'

Dick grinned and prepared to flatter her shamelessly. 'Old and perceptive, I'd say. A woman running a business as big as yours is more than a match for a couple of plods.'

'Oh, I'm not running Burgess Electronics. Even Frank wasn't doing as much as he used to do, by the time he died. He was fourteen years older than me, you know.' She was annoyed with herself for asserting that yet again: she seemed to be saying it wherever she went. Was it mere vanity, or was it a reminder to others that she was still vigorous enough to be a force in the firm and in life in general? She frowned after another sip of her wine. 'I don't think you should underestimate those plods. Not if you got the two I had.'

'Oh, I agree. I think that chap Peach knows exactly what he's about and the other one pretends to be thicker than he is. I felt as you did, that I'd had quite a grilling by the time they left me.'

'I suppose it's to be expected. As far as I can gather, the members of our book club are the last people who saw Alfred alive.'

He glanced up at her sharply and found her watching him steadily, studying his reaction to that thought. He realized in that moment that they were assessing each other. They were each trying to decide whether, in this large and comfortable sitting room, with its wine and its nibbles and its courtesies, they were in the presence of a killer. It might be bizarre, but the whole business of murder was bizarre. And to them, but not to the police, quite novel.

At one time, he would have lit a cigarette at this point. You didn't do that now, not in other people's houses. And he'd given up, hadn't he? And he didn't miss it, did he? Dick folded his arms and said as casually as he could, 'Did you get the idea that the police felt they were getting near to an arrest?'

'I felt that they weren't. I felt that they were still gathering information and feeling their way. But they didn't give much away yesterday. Even if they'd been on their way to your place to arrest you, I don't suppose they'd have given me a clue about that.'

He gave a brittle little laugh. 'They weren't. Actually, I had a good alibi for the time of Alfred's death. I was eating a meal with an old journalist friend of mine from Bolton. I think they were duly impressed by that. I expect they'll check it out – they have to do that, when they're investigating a serious crime. But they'll find it's absolutely true.'

'Of course they will. Whereas the woman who helped to set up the book club which now figures so largely in their thoughts has no such witness to account for her movements at the time of Alfred's death.'

'I'm sure they can't entertain you as a serious suspect.' He wondered if he should express more sorrow about Norbury's death. But Sharon didn't seem to regret it any more than he did. Both of them were more concerned with what was happening after the event than with any concern for the victim.

'I'm not really sure what they think about me. Alfred and I had our differences, in the past. I didn't tell them anything about that. Not their business, I thought.' She grinned mischievously at him, and he glimpsed the very attractive young woman she must have been forty years earlier.

It emboldened him to say, 'I can't think that they would suspect you. Except of course that it was you who ensured that Alfred was at that meeting on Monday.'

'No. It wasn't me.' She was abrupt and very serious. 'That was Enid Frott's idea. I agreed to it, but it was her suggestion.' She topped up his glass. 'You and Alfred had previous, didn't you? Did you tell them about that?'

It was strange to hear that odd underworld phrase dropping from these gentrified female lips. He said, 'That sounds quite sinister, "had previous". We went back a few years, yes, but there's nothing significant in that is there? But I didn't talk to the police about it, no. I'm not quite sure why. I suppose I thought there was no point in muddying their investigations.'

'I see. Well it's all rather unpleasant, isn't it? We are talking about murder, whatever we both thought about Alfred Norbury. Let's hope they make an arrest soon and leave us to get on with our lives.'

They clinked glasses on that, embodying as it did the comforting thought that neither of them had anything to fear in the matter. She insisted that he drank strong coffee before he left, then stood in the doorway of her house to watch him walk the length of the long drive to his car at the gates. The sky was very clear and the night still and cold now. Myriad stars shone white and steady against a dark blue canopy.

Fosdyke's last words stayed with Sharon as she went back into the big house. 'Best that we don't say anything to those nosy policemen about past times, I think. No point in wasting their time and stirring up trouble for ourselves.'

FIFTEEN

Enid Frott knew what she was going to say when she opened the door to the CID men. Keep it as light as you can, she'd decided. But let them know that you had friends in high places, that you weren't merely a woman alone. 'Well, I must say I'm impressed. I didn't expect to find you working on Sunday morning! I shall commend your actions to Chief Superintendent Tucker, when I get the chance to do so.'

Peach ignored the mention of higher rank and the connotation that he should tread carefully here. 'All in the line of duty, Ms Frott. Murder overrides more petty policeman's considerations like connubial bliss. Or overnight liaisons, in DS Northcott's case. He wasn't present when we last met. He's a formidable presence, don't you think? As Wellington said about his army, I don't know what he does to the enemy, but by God he frightens me. He's my hard man for when things turn nasty. But I'm sure they won't do that this morning.'

He gave her his bright Sunday-morning smile. But his words sounded in her ears as if he were responding to her warning about Tucker with one of his own. She asked if they wanted coffee, but he waved the offer aside and said it was still too early for that. 'Won't take long, this, Ms Frott. Well, it won't if you are more cooperative and less obstructive than when I spoke to you last time. Perhaps I should have had DS Northcott beside me on that occasion, after all.' He looked up interrogatively into the carved-ebony face of his companion, but received no affirmative expression from it.

Enid tried to be firm. 'I'm sure I was perfectly frank with you, Chief Inspector Peach. If I concealed anything you now think I should have revealed, it must have been purely accidental on my part.'

'We now have access to Mr Norbury's computer files, Ms Frott. He had also kept a more conventional manual file on you, dating back twelve years. Would you care to revise your attitude, in view of this?'

Enid swallowed hard, telling herself that she had always expected this. 'So I knew him in the past. What of it?'

'You will need to tell us that, Ms Frott. At present we are interested in why you chose to conceal your history with Mr Norbury at our meeting on Thursday.'

'I'm entitled to keep some things private, surely.'

'In a murder investigation, very little can be kept private. We are allotted a large team to make sure that all the information surrounding the worst crime of all is available to us. Much of it, of course, will prove to be irrelevant and will be treated as confidential. When we unearth material which people have chosen to conceal from us, it will inevitably be examined in detail.'

'You said on Thursday that you were here for an informal chat.'

'Did I, indeed? Well, we always try to put people at their ease.' He issued this blatant lie with the straightest of faces. 'I seem to recall that I also said I needed you to tell me everything you knew about Alfred Norbury. This you patently omitted to do.'

'I don't recall this. I'm sure you must—'

'"Assume I know nothing," I said. I made it plain that I needed enlightenment, Ms Frott. You were eminently capable of delivering that to me and you conspicuously failed to do so. In such circumstances, we regard ourselves as justified in presuming some ulterior motive in our interviewees, do we not, DS Northcott?'

'Indeed we do, sir.' Clyde Northcott did not move, but he looked at the diminutive Enid Frott as if he might at any moment pick her up and hurl her against the wall of her property. 'In such circumstances, we are entitled to interpret silence as a hostile response.'

Enid wondered if he was quoting from some manual of police procedures. She said sullenly, 'I didn't mean to be obstructive. I merely kept quiet about certain things. I didn't tell you any lies.'

Peach was inexorable. 'I suggested at one stage that you and

Mrs Burgess and the deceased must be old friends. You denied that. You denied any previous close association with either Mrs Burgess or Mr Norbury.'

'I think I said at one stage that we went back quite a long way. I told you that it was I who invited Alfred to join our book club group. I believe I said that I did that because we could rely on him to be both irritating and stimulating, and to get discussion going when others were more reticent. That surely implied previous knowledge of him.'

'I accept that. But you also wanted me to think that such knowledge was relatively recent. It is such deceptions which make us wonder why you really wanted him in your group. Was it to give yourself the opportunity to wreak revenge, we are forced to ask? Did Mr Norbury prompt you towards thoughts of violent retribution, when he mentioned that he always carried a pistol in his car?'

'That's ridiculous! Why on earth should I be seeking revenge?'

'That is something we must now investigate, Ms Frott. Why did you conceal the fact that Mr Norbury had mentioned this pistol on Monday night when we spoke on Thursday?'

'I didn't, did I? Well, it must have slipped my mind. I know I meant to mention it, before I saw you.'

'Not very convincing, that, is it? That statement about the firearm was surely quite melodramatic. From what we have now learned of Alfred Norbury, I can only assume that it was meant to be so. It seems to me very strange that you should have chosen to omit it from your account of the meeting on Monday night.'

'I didn't choose to omit it. It slipped my mind, that's all.' But that sounded ridiculously unlikely, even to her as she spoke it. She sighed. 'All right. I didn't tell you about the pistol precisely because it was melodramatic. It was the sort of thing Alfred produced to make him the centre of attention.'

'So you didn't believe him? You didn't think it was important?'

'I believed him. It was the kind of precaution he would take – he always said he believed in self-help.'

The contempt came out as she spoke. Peach said quietly, 'You didn't like Alfred Norbury, did you, Ms Frott?'

She spoke very slowly now. 'No, I didn't like him. Everything I said about him being intelligent and lively and stimulating and useful within the group is genuine. But I didn't like him. I realized how much I didn't like him when I saw him in action on Monday. I saw the way he was planning to humiliate the youngest woman in the group and I detested it. He saw Jane Preston as a challenge and he was going to take her on and try to make her look silly.'

'Jane Preston struck us as a woman well capable of looking after herself.'

'Maybe. But Alfred was ruthless, once he was determined to get the better of you.'

'As you know to your cost.'

Peach spoke very quietly, but she knew with that simple phrase that he had won. It was a statement, not a question, and it told her that he knew what she had wished to conceal. She said with a world-weary resignation, 'As I knew to my cost, yes. You say that you have access to his files.'

'We'd rather have the full story from you. What Norbury recorded are facts and opinions which are entirely his own. I'm sure we'll have a more balanced version if we now hear your account of events.'

He sounded sympathetic, almost therapeutic. This was a radical change from the aggression he had shown in their meeting on Thursday, when she had told him almost nothing and thought she had fended off the CID attention. Enid wondered now how she could have been so naïve as to think that. She said dully, 'You know about Frank?'

Peach glanced at Northcott and the big man shut his notebook and put away his ball-point pen. Percy said softly, 'I presume you mean Frank Burgess, your late employer. Yes, we know that you had a relationship with him.'

'A long-term relationship.' She smiled bitterly. 'It was the classic businessman's affair, if you take the bare facts. High-powered, self-made tycoon falls for his PA and seduces her. He sees a younger woman who's available: she is bowled over by the trappings of wealth and power and is only too willing to leap into bed with him. Except that it wasn't quite like that, or it didn't seem so to us: I expect everyone says that, though. We resisted for a long time – by which I mean that we both knew we were attracted to each other but didn't acknowledge it for months and didn't go to bed together for several more months.'

'You're saying that this was a serious and prolonged relationship.'

Peach was pushing her on and she recognized it. 'It was. Frank said he was going to leave Sharon and set up house with me. I had no ties and was free to do as I pleased. Embarrassment was the only thing I had to contend with: it would surprise you if you knew how strong a factor that was for me. I'd been Frank Burgess's PA and in unofficial charge of the office for ten years. I'd been a pillar of respectability. I was now going to break up the boss's marriage and carry him away as a rich trophy to set up house with me. I wasn't looking forward to the reactions among my colleagues.'

'I can appreciate the upheaval and gossip that would cause in a small but prosperous private firm.'

'Can you? Well, I suppose you might be able to. Except that I didn't really have the power to carry it through, when it came to it. They say the wife always wins in the end, if she wants to, don't they? And Sharon Burgess wanted to. I don't blame her. Frank Burgess was a very lovable man. Worth fighting for.'

It seemed for a moment as if this neat, controlled, sixty-three-year-old woman might burst into tears. The thought of what might have been is one of the most powerful of all human emotions; that thought for a moment excluded all other considerations from her mind. It was left to Peach to drag her back to the matter of murder. He said gently, 'We need to know how Alfred Norbury relates to all of this.'

Her sigh was so deep that it shook the whole of her slim body, so radical that they wondered for a moment if it was the prelude to a confession. 'It's simple, really. Alfred Norbury found out about our relationship. We thought we were being very discreet, but lovers are always absurdly over-confident about that, aren't they? And always wrong. People always get to know. But not the wife. She's usually the last to know, isn't she? You may not believe this, but Frank and I were both very concerned about Sharon. She'd been a good wife and mother and she'd done nothing wrong. We wished to hurt her as little as possible.' Enid gave a brittle, unexpected laugh. 'Doesn't that sound trite?'

Peach gave her another prompt. 'What did Norbury do, Ms Frott?'

'He taunted me for a few weeks. I think he wanted to see what he could get out of me, what he could gain from the situation. But I had nothing to give him, and Frank wasn't prepared to be held to ransom. I think Frank thought he could call Norbury's bluff, because he never understood men like Alfred. He was a bigger man than that and he couldn't believe that Norbury would be so petty as to tell Sharon about us merely to gratify his own pique and display his own sort of power.'

'But he did just that.'

'Yes. Alfred did it in his own warped way, of course. He planted a rumour with one of the town gossips whom he knew wouldn't be able to control her tongue. Within a couple of weeks, Sharon heard about us, as he knew she would. She confronted Frank and brought matters to a head. He didn't deny it. And as I said, wives always win in the end, if they wish to. Sharon wished to.'

'And yet you two are friends now. You set up the book club together.'

There was a long pause before Enid said, 'Friends of a sort. She invited me to Frank's funeral. He was much older than both of us, of course, so it seemed inevitable that we should both be around when he died. She rang me to say that she wanted me there at his funeral. I said that it wasn't appropriate, but she said that she'd given a lot of consideration to the matter and she thought that it was. We were the only two women who'd been really important in Frank's life and she wanted us both at his funeral. I appreciated that and I attended. It was a little while after the funeral that she revived the idea of the book club; it was my idea in the first place, but it became from that time onwards a joint venture.'

'But it was you who suggested that Alfred Norbury should be a member of the group.'

'Yes. I suppose I thought that my resentment of him had cooled over the years, but I found that it hadn't.'

She allowed herself her first smile in many minutes. It was

a bitter one. She followed it by staring challengingly at Peach across her living room. The DCI responded with a mirthless smile of his own. 'The obvious question now. Why did you invite a man who had done so much damage to both of you to participate in this new venture?'

Another sigh, not as radical or as body-rending as the previous one. 'Obviously you have to ask that and obviously I was expecting the question and prepared for it. I could say passions cooled over a decade, and with Frank dead that is true to an extent. It would also to be true to say that I, and I suppose to a lesser extent Sharon also, wanted to see whether Alfred would have the bare-faced cheek to accept an invitation to join something as innocent as a book club. I hadn't seen him for years, and I don't think Sharon had either. Everything I said earlier about him making a stimulating and active member of the group is absolutely true. I think both Sharon and I wanted to see him again after a number of years of recovery from his earlier efforts to destroy one or other of us. Call it female curiosity, if you like. Call it what the hell you please!'

Her fury against the dead man sprang out in the last sentence. Peach let her anger and frustration hang for a moment in the quiet, warm, elegant room. Then he asked solemnly, 'Did you invite him to join your new book club venture so that you might give yourself the opportunity for revenge, Ms Frott?'

'No, I didn't. I consider that a logical question to ask and I don't resent it, but the answer is no.'

She was gazing at the carpet, so it was a surprise when the next question came to her in DS Northcott's deep, emollient voice. 'You said that Mrs Burgess took the initiative in pushing forward the idea of the book club, although it had been your suggestion in the first place. Do you think she sanctioned Mr Norbury's membership because she had intended harm towards him and thought the club would provide her with opportunities?'

'I don't believe that, no. But you would need to ask Sharon Burgess herself. We are not bosom friends and I had not seen her for years until Frank's funeral.'

She looked up to see that the black officer had resumed his

note-taking. It was Peach who said evenly, 'Did you kill Alfred Norbury, Enid?'

It was the first time he had used her forename and it represented an invitation for confession. Enid's tone was steady as she said, 'No. To be honest, I don't know what I'd have done to him, given time and opportunity.'

'You had the opportunity. He offered it to you on a plate, when he told you about the pistol in his car.'

'He offered that opportunity to everyone. He went out of his way to be flamboyant. That was his way and he paid for it, in the end. I can't say I'm sorry, after what he did to me. But I didn't shoot him.'

'Did you know that he attended the art group on Tuesday evenings?'

A long pause whilst she considered the implications of her answer, or perhaps whether she could get away with a denial. 'Yes. I knew someone else who painted with him on Tuesdays. But I wasn't the only one who knew about it in the group. Alfred had been attending those sessions for years.'

Northcott looked up from his notes, sounding at that moment as if he was calmly and affably signing a death warrant. 'So you knew exactly when he would be leaving his house on Tuesday evening.'

'I did. I could envisage him going out to that old car of which he was so proud. I could envisage exactly where he kept the pistol he'd boasted about. But I wasn't there and I didn't fire it. I was here, as I told you on Thursday.'

Peach gave her a tight smile. 'So who do you think did pull that trigger, Enid?'

She answered his smile with one equally minimal. 'I've no idea. That's your business, isn't it, Chief Inspector? I look forward to hearing of your findings.'

The CID pair let themselves out of the spacious modern flat in the Georgian house. They left her sitting in her armchair, a small, upright, defiant figure.

DS Clyde Northcott was enjoying the feeling of being in charge. He'd been delighted to fill the role of Percy Peach's bagman when Lucy Blake became Lucy Peach, but it didn't allow you to display a lot of initiative. Percy took his advice from time to time and made no secret of his high regard for his assistant, but that is what he was: an assistant. Percy Peach controlled his cases and everyone involved in his team; one ignored that fact at one's peril.

So it was a pleasant change for him to be in control of this little expedition with DC Brendan Murphy. Sunday evening wasn't the ideal time to be out and about on police business, but if it gave him a chance to show a little of his own initiative, fair enough. And this was better than capturing caches of Armalite rifles at 34 Boston Street in Brunton, which was the last time he'd been in command of an operation. This was less dangerous, for a start: you weren't in any danger of getting your head blown off by militant Muslims on this one.

That was the sentiment he conveyed to Murphy as his fresh-faced companion drove them through Darwen and then over the moors on the A666 to Bolton. 'The devil's number,' said Brendan. 'I'm surprised they haven't renumbered this road before now.'

Clyde didn't react to that. His thoughts were elsewhere. They were about to pass the lay-by where he had examined the body of a murder victim in the course of an investigation a couple of years earlier. He still felt obliged to show a certain deference when he passed the scene of a serious crime. That death had been particularly bleak and isolated; he shivered a little as they raced past the scene.

'We may need to lean on him a little,' he said to Murphy as they drove into Bolton. He smiled at the prospect, making no secret of the pleasure it afforded him. Northcott in fact rarely laid a finger upon even the most violent of villains. His formidable physical presence was usually enough to secure their respect.

They were surprised how humble the house was. This man was a journalist with an established post on one of the great national dailies. They had expected him to live in something grander than an end-of-terrace in one of the rows which had originally run down to the now long-defunct cotton mill at the end of the street.

Ernie Ainsworth must have noticed their unspoken surprise.

He said ruefully, 'Welcome to my humble abode. When you've had three marriages and three divorces you're lucky to have any sort of roof over your head, I suppose. My exes all live in greater comfort than me, at my expense.' He spoke without apparent rancour: he had obviously grown used to the situation and the ritual protests he uttered about it.

The house was in fact well decorated and comfortably furnished, much brighter and more welcoming inside than its grimy exterior had suggested. The two big policemen sat close together on the neat little sofa in front of the surprisingly convincing dancing flames of a new electric fire. 'One or two things need to be cleared up, Mr Ainsworth,' DS Northcott opened ominously.

'Always happy to help the law,' said Ainsworth with a cheerfulness he didn't feel. He didn't know what Dick Fosdyke was up to, but he hadn't liked this business from the start.

'That's good. Cooperation will be much the best option, for all concerned. It will minimise the effects and the consequences of any infringement of the law which has occurred. I'm sure there will be no call for violence here.' Clyde studied the black kid gloves he had donned before he entered the house and nodded his satisfaction at Murphy, who was jammed so tightly beside him that he too was studying his companion's formidable fists as they turned and twisted beneath the fine leather.

Murphy struggled to withdraw a single sheet from the rear pocket of his jeans. 'Our visit is in connection with your account of your activities on last Tuesday night, Mr Ainsworth. I have here a copy of the statement you made about your presence in Brunton between the hours of six-thirty and eight-thirty.'

'Yes, so I understood when you rang me. The times are a little approximate, because I wasn't expecting that they would be important at the time, as you can appreciate. But I'm sure there's nothing which can't be easily sorted out.'

He received no reassurance from the unsmiling black countenance of Clyde Northcott. 'Are you, sir? Well, that's good, I suppose. You'll forgive me if I'm not as optimistic about these things as you are. That comes from experience. Tricky thing, the law, and we need to treat it with respect.' He flexed his powerful fingers thoughtfully beneath the leather, then took the

paper from Murphy. 'You say here that you entered the restaurant at the rear of the White Hart at shortly after six-thirty p.m.
alongside Mr Fosdyke.'

'That is correct, yes. It was the first time I'd seen Dick in
almost a year and we were laughing and joking. I wanted to
eat quite early because I had to be at the *Daily Express* offices
in Manchester by eight o'clock on Wednesday morning. Early
to bed, early to rise, for us journalists nowadays!'

'Really, sir. I wouldn't know about that. It's the activities of
Mr Fosdyke on that evening which concern us, as you no doubt
appreciate. Any attempt to deceive us about those would be
regarded most seriously.'

'Yes, I can see that.' Ernie licked his lips, which seemed
suddenly much drier than they normally were. 'I suppose that this
is connected with the murder case in Brunton I've seen reported.'

'Indeed it is, sir. And if the journalistic grapevine is imbued
with its normal accuracy, I'm sure you know that Mr Fosdyke
is involved in our investigation of that crime.'

'Is he? Well, knowing Dick as well as I do, I'm sure he has
nothing to fear from even the most searching of investigations.'

'Are you, Mr Ainsworth? Well, no doubt he will be glad to
have a man like you speaking up so forcefully on his behalf.
What time did he join you on Tuesday evening?'

Ernie was conscious of the pen poised over the paper in one
pair of hands, of the other pair which continued to twist against
each other beneath black leather, of the white face and the black
face both tilted slightly to one side as they examined him. 'It
would be about twenty-five to seven, I think. We went in to the
restaurant section together, were shown to a table, and studied
the menus we were given. It didn't take us long to make our
selections and—'

'You're sure Mr Fosdyke was with you at this time, are you?
That's what is recorded in your statement, of which DC Murphy
has a copy for you to check if you wish to.'

'Yes, Dick was with me. I'm sure of it. Is that not what he
says?'

'Yes, that is emphatically what he says, Mr Ainsworth. We
wanted to check that you were still of the opinion that this is
what took place.'

Ernie tried hard to ignore the unfamiliar presence of two large plain-clothes policemen upon his sofa. 'It seems perfectly straightforward to me, Officer. Dick Fosdyke and I met to eat together and to chat about old times. We had a pleasant meal and a bottle of wine which went down swiftly. This took place between six thirty-five and eighty thirty. Having taken care not to exceed the legal limit for alcohol, I drove carefully back here, had a large beaker of coffee, watched a little television, and then went to bed relatively early. It seems straightforward and unexceptional to me.'

'And to us, sir. We have no doubt that these events did take place on Tuesday evening last. The problem is that other accounts of them do not tally with yours.'

'Other accounts?'

'In a murder enquiry, sir, what people tell us is checked scrupulously against other testimony, as I'm sure you would expect.'

'Well, if Dick says something different, I'm sure he's correct. As I say, I wasn't—'

'Oh, Mr Fosdyke's account tallies exactly with yours, sir. Almost suspiciously so, you might say. There's no discrepancy there.'

'Well, where's the problem then?' Ainsworth forced a smile he did not feel.

'The problem is with the owner of the restaurant at the White Hart, sir. And with the young lady who fulfilled your order and was grateful for the tip you gave her at the end of the meal. They both remember things a little differently from you.'

'In what respect?' Three feet away from him, the hands had ceased to twist beneath the black leather. They looked bigger than ever to Ernie.

'As they remember things, Mr Fosdyke arrived considerably later than the time given in your statement. As they recall events, he came into the restaurant and joined you at seven o'clock, or even a minute or two after the hour. They agree with you about the other events of the evening.'

'All right. I got it wrong. What they say is probably correct.'

'Probably, Mr Ainsworth?'

He was sweating now. Why the hell had Dick Fosdyke

dragged him into this? Calling in a favour was one thing; pitching him into a murder enquiry was something quite different. It was time to cut his losses. 'Well, definitely then. Look, Dick asked me to say that, and I owed him a favour. I shouldn't have done it.'

'Do you now wish to revise your statement?'

'Yes. Yes, I do. I'm sorry for any trouble I've caused you.'

'I can't guarantee that you won't face charges, sir. I hope they won't include being an accessory to murder.'

SIXTEEN

A light dusting of snow covered the streets of Brunton on Monday morning. No more than quarter of an inch, but enough to make commuters curse as they cleaned the windscreens of their cars and persuaded reluctant batteries to turn cold engines.

The car park at Tesco was scarcely a third full when Peach drove into it with Northcott at nine-thirty. A few mums and three house-fathers had come here dutifully after dropping their progeny off at school; the rest of the populace had delayed shopping until later in the day, when there might be a rise in temperature.

Jamie Norris was enthusiastically restacking his shelves after the weekend when Mr Jordan brought the two senior detectives to see him. 'It's in connection with this murder in Wellington Street. You'd better use my office. Ignore the phone if it rings. I'll take any calls in the staff rest room: it's quiet enough there at this time of day.' The manager looked at Norris curiously as he left, as if he sought clues in that unlined countenance about the dark event which was dominating the local press and radio.

Clyde Northcott thought that Jamie Norris looked less stressed than their other suspects. He had youth on his side of course, but his fair hair was neatly combed and there was colour in his cheeks and a spring in his gait as he led them into the room suggested for this meeting. When they refused coffee or tea, he said with a light little laugh, 'Pity, I could use a drink. I've been here since six. But don't worry about me, I had breakfast an hour or so ago.'

Jamie was trying to behave as naturally as if this was no more than a routine meeting, where he might be asked about his views on tinned soups or the rising popularity of the new meals-for-one range. He'd determined this would be his strategy before they came. He'd always known somehow that they would come back to see him again. You should always use their names if you knew them: the personal touch. That was good retail practice. He spread his arms a little, as he'd seen Mr Jordan do when people came in to see him from their suppliers, and said, 'What can I do for you, Detective Chief Inspector Peach?'

'You can answer more honestly than you did on Thursday, for a start.'

Peach and Northcott sat down on upright chairs, scarcely five feet from Norris, who was on the other side of his manager's desk. The room was a closed, windowless cube, not dissimilar from an interview room at the station. That suited Percy admirably. Jamie swallowed hard and said with a curious formality, 'I told you no lies.'

Peach flashed him a smile which signalled only danger. 'You were economical with the truth, Mr Norris. DS Northcott has a record of those economies. I would strongly advise you to be more forthcoming this morning.'

'I can't recall that I was anything other than cooperative.'

Peach looked at him steadily for five seconds, then said without taking his eyes from the young face, 'Remind Mr Norris of his omissions, DS Northcott, will you?'

Clyde flicked open his notebook and ran his finger down the page. He appeared to be making a selection from many damning statements from the nervous young man in front of him. 'Mr Norris told us when asked about our murder victim that, "I know very little about his past life apart from what he told me." We know now that this is not true. In fact in the week before Mr Norbury's death, Mr Norris made extensive enquiries about his previous activities. He contacted people who attended the same art club meeting as Mr Norbury on Tuesday evenings; he spoke to people who had been taught by him when he worked part-time for the Open University; he even questioned a young man who had attended a creative writing group Norbury had run as long as eight years ago.'

Jamie felt himself turning paler as each of these groups was mentioned. It was almost like hearing charge sheets read out in court. He said weakly, 'It was natural that I should try to get to know as much as I could about Alfred. He'd mentioned these activities – he seemed to be almost inviting me to follow them up. And I wanted to know everything I could about him. He was threatening to take over my life and I wasn't happy about that.'

'That is exactly the kind of information you could have given us on Thursday. I explained to you then that we knew very little about our murder victim and needed to find out as much as we could as quickly as we could. You chose to be obstructive when you could have been helpful. We now have to ask ourselves why.' Peach nodded several times and reserved his smile not for Norris but for Northcott beside him on the upright chairs.

'There's nothing very complicated about what I was doing. I told you on Thursday that Alfred was treating me as a kind of writing apprentice. He was rather patronising – that was his way with everyone – but I didn't much resent that, because he was generous in so many ways. He allowed me full access to his extensive library. More importantly he allowed me full access to his extensive mind.'

Norris stopped on that, as if he wished to savour his last phrase and memorise it for future use. Peach said dryly, 'He was using you, Jamie. He wanted to display you as his latest protégé. You were to be the young man who had come through a difficult adolescence and missed out on the formal education system, a promising young writer now rescued and developed by sensitive intellectual Alfred Norbury.'

Jamie knew this was meant to challenge him, but it encapsulated so much of what he had been thinking himself that he felt immediately uncomfortable. It was as if this man whom he had never seen until three days before had been looking over his shoulder as his relationship with Alfred had developed. Developed and soured: he didn't want these people to know about the souring, but he wondered now how he was going to conceal it from those all-seeing dark eyes beneath the shining bald pate. He said stubbornly, 'Alfred was very good to me. He was honest about my poetry and he didn't pull any punches when he thought it was trite or overwritten. But he was constructive. The exercises he gave me were useful and he really was giving me pointers to improving my writing.'

'Why then did you wish to cool your relationship with this most helpful and sensitive of mentors?' It was spoken quietly and it was a shot in the dark. Peach didn't know that there'd been a crisis between the two immediately before Norbury's death, but something indefinable, some slight uncertainty in Norris's words to them this morning, had suggested it to him.

The shot hit home. Norris assumed, as people often did with Percy Peach, that the DCI knew far more than he did, that what he ventured was not speculation but fact. 'I suppose I didn't like being paraded as a protégé. I felt when Alfred took me along to the first meeting of the book club that I was being exhibited as a pet animal who was learning a series of clever tricks from Alfred. He was being very good and very helpful to me, so perhaps I should have been more grateful, but that was the way it felt. The fault might have been in me rather than Alfred, but I was finding him overbearing. I felt I was becoming his creature and I didn't like it.'

It was more or less what he'd decided to say before they came, if he was pressed on this. He was quite pleased with the way he'd delivered it. When things were very close to the truth, it was much easier to deliver them convincingly, he thought. He remembered again that old advice from the lawyer years ago: the way to lie convincingly was to use as much of the truth as you safely could. He was nevertheless unnerved by the way Peach studied him unblinkingly, as if he saw through his words and into his very soul. Then seeming to confirm that resistance was futile, Peach spoke as though putting forward the next item for revision. 'You told us on Thursday that you did not have a sexual relationship with Mr Norbury. Would you now care to modify or develop that statement?'

'No, I wouldn't. What I said was correct.' Jamie wanted to shout this at them. He wanted to assure them that his fantasies last night were all of the female curves of Jane Preston; to tell them that any thought of a bed shared with Alfred would have revolted him. For a moment, he wished to show them the sonnet he was still polishing about Jane Preston, which he thought was really quite promising.

He did none of these things, of course. He reaffirmed his denial of a homosexual relationship with Alfred and sat tight. Most people were secretive about sexual things, and he was going to be no exception. At this moment, with these two contrasting coppers watching his every move, he wanted to be as conventional as he could about this and other things.

Peach wasn't willing to let it go. 'But Alfred hadn't accepted that the two of you were going to be platonic, had he, Jamie? Alfred wanted to take things further, and he wasn't a man who was easily resisted.'

There was a long pause before Norris said, 'That is true. Alfred didn't take no for an answer very easily. He took a lot of convincing.'

'I'm sure he did, Jamie. Was that why you were driven to fire a pistol into his head?'

The questioning had been leading to this over the last few minutes, Jamie told himself. Yet when it was baldly stated like that, it was nevertheless shocking. More shocking than anything else he had heard in his young and eventful life. He wanted to sound outraged at the very idea that he might have done this, but his voice sounded to him quite dull as he said, 'I didn't kill Alfred. I don't know who did. I hope you find out who it was.'

Clyde Northcott spoke for the first time, his deep voice sounding even more solemn than Peach's. 'I need to be clear about what you wish me to record, Mr Norris. Did Mr Norbury make any sort of sexual advance to you?'

'Yes. In the week before he died, he became more and more insistent.'

'And you rejected these advances?'

'Yes. I told him that I was sorry but the idea revolted me. I told him that I was heterosexual and could never be interested in having sex with him.'

Jamie was staring straight ahead, willing them to believe him. Northcott made a note and said, 'You realize that this provides you with a motive for murder?'

'I realize that it gives me a motive, yes. But motives don't always lead to action. I didn't kill Alfred. I rejected his sexual advances, but I was grateful for what he had done for me – for what he was still doing for my writing at the time of his death.'

Peach had never taken his eyes off his quarry. 'How did Norbury react when you told him sex wasn't on the cards?'

'He wasn't pleased. But he assumed he would carry on giving me guidance with my writing. I think he thought I'd eventually be so grateful that he would overcome my resistance. He wouldn't have done.'

'I see. You said on Thursday that the last time you saw Alfred Norbury was at the book club meeting on Monday night.'

'Yes. That is correct.' Norris spoke almost before Peach had completed his sentence.

'It wasn't, though, was it?'

Jamie had driven himself into a corner. Now he held on to his story even when he knew it was about to be disproved, like an obstinate child who can see no other course. 'Yes it was. I didn't see Alfred after I left him on Monday night.'

'That's not what an independent witness is telling us, Jamie. I advise you to reconsider this.'

The use of his first name again, as though the man was a friend and not a pig trying to pin this on him. Beware, Jamie. But what could he do? He took a deep breath, then exhaled slowly, trying to keep control of his speech. 'All right. I was working six to two on Tuesday, same as today. I went round to Alfred's place in the afternoon, after I'd finished work.'

'Time, please.' DS Northcott spoke as calmly as if he was checking a bus timetable.

'I had something to eat first. It would be some time between three and half past.'

Peach gave him a sudden, unexpected beam of approval, which lasted for all of three seconds. 'This is better. This tallies with the time given to us by our independent bystander. They're always useful, independent bystanders. Judges tend to believe them. Why did you choose to lie to us, Jamie?'

'I – I knew by then that Alfred had been killed. I thought you'd fit me up for it, if you knew I'd been there.'

'We don't fit people up, Jamie. It's not in our benevolent natures, is it, DS Northcott?'

'No, sir. We much prefer genuine arrests, wherever possible.'

Peach nodded happily. 'Purpose of visit, Jamie? We'd better have purpose of visit, if you can think of one.'

Jamie felt in his bones that this was going to sound feeble. 'I wanted to apologize. Alfred had tried to get me into bed the night before and I'd told him to fuck off. I wanted to remain friends. I wanted him to go on helping me to improve my writing and making suggestions about it. I wanted to clarify our relationship. Master and apprentice, I was aiming at, with no sexual contact.'

'Did you know about Alfred Norbury's art classes?'

It was a bewildering switch of questioning, but Jamie saw the reason for it immediately. 'Yes. I knew he joined the group on each Tuesday evening.'

'I see. So you knew exactly what time he would be leaving the house.'

'Yes. The sessions began at seven, so he always left at around twenty to seven or just afterwards.'

'Think about your answer to this, Jamie. It will be much better for all of us if you are honest. Were you waiting for Alfred in or around his car at twenty to seven on Tuesday evening?'

'No. I was at home in my bed-sit, as I told you on Thursday.'

'You told us a lot of things on Thursday, Jamie, many of which you have now admitted were wrong. Can you offer us anything further to confirm to us that this one is right?'

'No. I know it looks bad, but—'

'It looks very bad indeed at the moment, Jamie.' Peach stood up and Northcott followed his lead. 'You've just admitted to us that you are the last person known to have seen Alfred Norbury alive. Not a pleasant position for anyone to be in, that. Perhaps you need to review your account of events.'

Peach nodded affably to Mr Jordan, the curious manager who had just appeared at the office door. Then he thanked him for the use of his office and departed.

Peach's mood was not improved when he arrived at the station to find that there was a direction waiting for him to see the Head of CID immediately. Tommy Bloody Tucker was the last thing he needed on a bitter Monday morning in January.

Chief Superintendent Tucker didn't ask him to sit, but nodded curtly towards the upright chair in front of his huge desk. 'I'm not happy, Peach.'

It was to be a bollocking, then. He could cope with that. Tiresome, as always, but better than those creepy sessions where Tucker addressed him by his first name. 'Is this a domestic issue, sir? Are you not basking in the connubial bliss which has always been your marital lot?'

'This has nothing to do with Barbara, Peach. And I'll thank you to keep your opinions on my relationship with my wife to yourself.'

Peach was not in the least inhibited by the warning. He cast his eyes to the ceiling and assumed the strangest of smiles as he thought about the bedroom joys afforded by the woman he always thought of as Brunnhilde Barbara, whose Wagnerian build and volume had always filled him with awe. 'Happy the man who is content at home, sir. Happy the man who can sally forth daily into our sordid world from a wife who ministers to his every spiritual and carnal need.' His smile grew, filling the whole of his face as he contemplated the joys of physical fulfil-ment with Barbara.

Tucker took a deep breath and tried to thunder. He wasn't good at thundering, but this man warranted it. 'I'm not happy, Peach. This is not a domestic issue; I'm not happy because of what is happening here. Or rather what is *not* happening here.'

'I'm sorry about that, sir. Weight of work, is it?' Percy contemplated the empty acres of his chief's desk.

'I'll tell you what it is, Peach. It's this Norbury case. A murder in the middle of our town and my Chief Inspector doing bugger all about it!'

'Where were you on Saturday and Sunday, sir?'

'That's my business, Peach. Don't try to divert me.'

'We could have done with you at the weekend, sir. Your experience and your incisive questioning of suspects would no doubt have been of great value, had it been available. DS Northcott and I and the key members of the team worked through the weekend, sir. I hear the golf course is in excellent condition for the end of January, sir. I haven't been able to sample its delights myself.'

Tucker considered denying he had been on the golf course, but decided against it. Peach knew all kinds of things: he had mysterious sources of information which he never revealed. 'You know that it is my policy never to interfere with the teams assigned to major crimes, Peach. I maintain an overview and contribute as I see fit. In return for this, I expect diligent and efficient work from my officers. In short, I expect results. And I find results so far lacking in the Norbury case.'

He hadn't managed genuine thunder, but he now produced a thunderous brow. He was much better at thunderous expressions than thunderous volume. He could be positively Churchillian in the severity of his countenance, having studied wartime photographs of the great man at the hours of his most notable pronouncements.

Peach watched Tommy Bloody Tucker's countenance with interest but no sign of fear. 'We are making progress, sir.'

'Don't give me that guff, Peach. Save that for the public. "Making progress" means that you have nothing to report. Any copper knows that!'

'Nevertheless, it is sometimes a fair summary of events, sir. We know when, where and how Mr Norbury was killed and we have the murder weapon. We have whittled the suspects down from the very large number possible when a victim is killed in the open rather than in his house to no more than five. We have not entirely eliminated some other and more random agency, but I am personally confident that our eventual arrest will be made among these five.'

'Don't try to blind me with science, Peach! I'm too old a hand for that. I go back a long way, you know. I would remind you that I served as a young copper with Jack Slipper, head of the Flying Squad. A man who had played a leading part in the investigation of the Great Train Robbery of 1963.'

'Really, sir? I'd no idea you were as old as that. You're wearing very well.'

'This was in the eighties, of course, as you know very well, Peach. I wasn't around at the time of that crime itself. I was a small child then.'

Peach laughed heartily at the rather alarming vision of his tormentor as a cherub. 'Of course, sir. I saw a BBC documentary on the Great Train Robbery of 1963 a few months ago. Detective Chief Superintendent Butler was the man who really cracked the case.'

'Yes. Great man, Butler. My kind of copper.' Tucker was anxious to claim even the most tenuous association with the team involved in the so-called 'crime of the century'.

'Really, sir? He seemed to be my kind of copper as well. I actually made a note of something he said about his career.' He reached into the inside pocket of his jacket as Tucker beamed his approval and produced a small piece of card from which he read his quotation. 'DCS Butler said at the end of his career: "No matter how far you go or how high you climb, there's always a wanker boss in charge." Clearly a man of great wisdom and experience, as well as a good copper, sir.'

Percy Peach descended the steps which led him back to the real world with a quiet satisfaction. The wanker boss was repulsed for the moment.

'How's the writing going?' Jane Preston had locked the door of her tutorial room before she picked up the phone. She now launched the conversation shamelessly with the line she'd chosen, even though she feared Jamie might recognize it as a deliberate ploy.

'Oh, not too bad. Alfred's death was a distraction, of course, but I've made myself carry on working.'

It was all right: Jamie Norris suspected nothing. Writers were notoriously egocentric, almost as much as actors. They had to be so, she supposed: they had to concentrate on the words they were producing at the expense of almost everything else. She didn't really know much about that. Although she had learned a lot about literature, Jane's was a critical rather than a creative intelligence. She said, 'Yes, I'm carrying on too, even in the face of this awful thing. It's easier when you've got students. They expect you to be there and to produce, whatever's going on in your private life. You're very much concerned with yourself and your own problems, when you're nineteen or twenty. Thank heavens we're past that age!'

She was treating him as a mature man, when he felt anything but that. It gave Jamie an enormous lift, quite out of proportion to the small compliment involved. He wanted to tell her that he had a poem to show her, a poem that he had written about her. But he held back. Something told him that it would be better to produce it casually, as if it were merely a modest afterthought to something raised in their conversation. Perhaps he really was maturing, as she'd said he was. He said earnestly,

'It's been a help to me working at the supermarket, these last few days. It's undemanding intellectually, but it keeps you busy physically. It gives you a certain rhythm in your life. I think my writing's actually improving, now that I have to treat it as a part-time occupation.'

'Really? Well that's very interesting. You must tell me more about it next time we meet.' She felt like a femme fatale as she said it. But surely there was nothing whorish in merely suggesting that they might meet again?

'Yes. I could tell you all about my second meeting with the police.'

She'd been wondering how she could ask him if they'd been back, and here he was offering her the information on a plate. It was easy really, when you were a woman. And in no way was she being a harlot here. She quite liked young Jamie, and she was merely exploiting the charms she had been given. Not God-given: she didn't believe in all that stuff. But the natural attributes which came with being a young and healthy and not entirely unattractive woman. She smiled at herself in the mirror and flicked a strand of yellow hair away over her forehead. The new lipstick had been a good choice. Putty in her hands, Jamie Norris would be, when she put on the war paint. Discreet war paint, of course – or was that an oxymoron? She said, 'I've got another lecture to give yet. But we could meet this evening, if you like.' You didn't give straight lectures nowadays, but most people were impressed by the word.

Jamie smiled at his phone, scarcely able to believe this. 'I would like that, yes.' She'd taken the initiative, when he'd been wondering how to ask her. He could hardly believe it had happened. 'Shall we meet in a pub? Go for a drink together? Or would you rather—'

'I'll come to your place. If that's all right.'

'If you wish. It's not much of a pad, mind. I'm hoping to get myself something better when—'

'It's private. That's the important thing. We don't want other people poking their noses into our business, do we?'

'No, we don't.' His mind was reeling at the prospect of what that business might be.

'We don't want those intrusive fuzz prying into everything

we do. We want our private lives to be free of their intrusions, don't we?'

'Yes, we do. One hundred per cent free.' He wondered feverishly what she was proposing. This was a young woman with the best mind he'd ever encountered. He hadn't a lot of evidence yet to support that, but he was sure that it was so: the heady perfume of infatuation raises the beloved to new heights of intellect. And a mind like that in a body like that! This was Hollywood, not Brunton, but he'd take it. Seize it with both hands, in fact! He gave her his address and detailed instructions of how to find it. She mustn't get lost. Nothing must go wrong now. 'If we can agree a time I'll open the door myself. We don't want you to be vetted by my dragon of a landlady, do we?'

She giggled. 'All right. Eight o'clock on the dot. You keep Mrs Danvers away and I'll come straight into your stately home!'

Jane Preston put down the phone and looked at herself critically in the mirror. Not bad, really. Quite good enough for innocent Jamie Norris. It was surprising what you could achieve when you really put your mind to it.

SEVENTEEN

Sharon Burgess watched the police car drive up to the front of the house, then turn and park ready for its exit. She wondered what the next half hour would bring for her, but she made no effort to conceal herself. Her blank, unrevealing face was evident at the window of the lounge as she watched the CID officers leave the car and walk to her front door. I have nothing to hide, her stance told them.

The maid answered the door within a couple of seconds of their ring. She led them into the huge lounge, where the house-owner turned from the window to meet them as they were ushered into the room. She was erect and dignified and her grey eyes studied her visitors without embarrassment or fear. There was no evidence of a facelift or any other cosmetic surgery here, but her skin was good and her face had fewer lines than a woman of sixty-seven would normally carry. Her hair was more grey than gold nowadays, but the blend was effective; there was not a hair out of place in the short-cut style.

She indicated the wide sofa where they should sit and said without consulting them, 'We'll have that coffee now, Mrs Waterson, please.' A woman perfectly secure in her own luxurious home and with nothing to fear from the world outside it. She sat in the chair she had positioned precisely before they came and smoothed her simple but expensive blue woollen dress over her knees. 'I trust your enquiries are progressing as you would wish, Detective Chief Inspector Peach.'

'We have made some progress, Mrs Burgess. My chief would no doubt say that is a blanket term which covers a multitude of sins.'

'And I suppose he might well be right. But equally, he might be wrong: you might mean what you say quite literally. I didn't mention the case to Mr Tucker when I saw him over the weekend. I thought he wouldn't want to be bothered with silly questions from the public.'

'I'm sure you're right, Mrs Burgess. About Chief Superintendent Tucker, I mean. But I'm sure any questions you put would have been well-informed rather than silly. And you're scarcely just a member of the public. You're much closer to the centre of this case than that.'

The verbal fencing had begun from the start, she thought. She should have known from their earlier meeting that this man wouldn't back off. And she should have known that he wouldn't be inhibited by her mention of that pompous twit Thomas Bulstrode Tucker, whom Frank had always disliked. She was sorry that she'd ventured that cheap shot now. She poured the coffee when it came, taking particular care over the requirements of the ominous figure of Detective Sergeant Northcott. In her narrow social circle, she had little contact with black men and was absurdly concerned that she should now show no trace of prejudice. The Crown Derby cup and saucer looked ridiculously small in those large, careful hands.

Peach accepted his coffee eagerly and bit into one of the excellent home-made ginger cookies which accompanied it. Better the sweet snacks of the high gentry than the uncertainties of the police canteen. He nodded his approval and said, 'We know a lot more about Alfred Norbury than when we last spoke to you.'

Sharon nodded and sipped her coffee. 'That's progress, I suppose.'

'We also know a lot more about the people who were closest to him on the day before he died.'

'I suppose that again must represent progress. I am not experienced in these things, but I imagine that by now you must be very experienced.' She offered the plate of cookies again and smiled as Peach took another and complimented her upon their quality. He said, 'It took our expert some time to get into Mr Norbury's computer. He had some very interesting files there. Including one on you, Mrs Burgess.'

Sharon didn't flinch at all. She nodded slowly. She'd been prepared for this; every elegant inch of her emphasized that. 'Alfred was a waspish man. Talented, but waspish. I don't imagine that the files he kept on me or anyone else would be notable for their generosity.'

'You're now claiming a detailed knowledge of his character. You told us on Friday that you didn't know him well.'

'You didn't have to know Alfred well to realize that he was waspish. I think I also told you that he was articulate and stimulating. You asked me for my impressions of Norbury and I gave them to you.' She finished her coffee and set her cup and saucer down deliberately on the tray, as if it was important to her to show them how very steady her hands were.

Peach watched her and took his time. He held the key cards here and he would make them tell by delivering them with deliberation. People wanted things over quickly, once they realized that you had the advantage. Therefore you could only gain by deliberation. 'What we found in the computer file Mr Norbury had compiled on you indicates that you have had much closer dealings with him in the past than you revealed to us on Friday.'

'That is correct. My previous dealings with Mr Norbury were a source of embarrassment and considerable pain to me and to others. I chose to keep them private when we spoke on Friday because of that. They had nothing to do with his death.'

'Do you expect me simply to accept that assurance from you?'

She paused and gave the matter thought. She was an intelligent woman and she was vain enough to want them to see that. 'No. I've never been involved in a murder enquiry before and I wasn't aware of the rules. My natural inclination was to protect my private life from the public gaze. When you now force me to consider the issue from your point of view, I see that you cannot afford to take anything at face value. I assume that other people involved in your investigation are being examined as pitilessly as I am.'

Peach gave her a grim smile. 'I can assure you of that. We are not without pity, but we have to be thorough. Mr Norbury's file on you goes back a little over twelve years and contains detailed material from that time.'

'Yes. I've no idea where he got his information from. Like senior policemen, he didn't reveal his sources.'

Peach gave the slightest of nods, acknowledging her terse little joke at his expense with the tiniest movement of his lips. 'Mr Norbury saw fit to inform you of your husband's infidelity.'

'He not only informed me. He provided detailed chapter and verse, in case I should doubt him.'

'Mr Burgess's infidelity was with Enid Frott.'

'Yes. She was Frank's PA at the time. It's a cliché of adultery, isn't it? Boss's secretary flashing her elegant legs and removing her fancy knickers, whilst the stupid wife at home knows nothing of it and understands even less.' Her face was ugly with pain and for a moment she was back in the anguish of Norbury's revelations.

Peach said, 'I know this must seem an unwarranted intrusion into your private life and that of a husband who is no longer with us. I can assure you that we are interested in these events only in so far as they may have a bearing on the murder of Alfred Norbury on Monday last.'

'Which they don't. But I appreciate that you need to be convinced of that.'

'Thank you. I need to have a clear picture of events which took place a decade and more ago. Had you any idea that your husband was conducting a relationship with Ms Frott before Alfred Norbury's revelations?'

'No. You may think I was very stupid, because Frank was an attractive man, even though he was much older than me. And he was the head of a successful and continually expanding firm, which meant that he had power, the ultimate aphrodisiac. But he wasn't a serial adulterer, so I wasn't perpetually on the lookout for infidelity, as some wives are. I suppose that with what you see of life, you would say I was naive. I was quite unprepared for what Norbury revealed to me. It was under the guise of friendship, of course – he was sad that I should have to suffer, but I had the right to know – all of that and similar rubbish.'

Her bitterness rasped out in these last phrases. Peach waited for a moment to see if she would go further, then said, 'Exactly how were you made aware of your husband's affair with Enid Frott?'

She glanced up into his face, her features hard with interest. 'That's what it was, an affair! Frank tried to convince me that it was something much grander, that he was going to leave home and set up house with Enid. I held firm and said that he had obligations to his family and that he would never get away from those. I and his children would remain with him, even as he aged and died in lonely luxury with his new love.'

She was looking out of the window as she spoke, down the long garden of the house where she had lived and loved and suffered, remembering the man who had excited her passion and was now dead. Peach reminded her of his question. 'I asked how it was that Norbury chose to make you aware of this problem in your life.'

She smiled sourly at that anodyne phrase. 'Have you spoken with Enid Frott about this?'

'We spoke with Ms Frott yesterday, yes. Now I am asking you.'

'She told you the truth, I expect. She's an honest woman, Enid. And she's no more a serial adulterer than Frank was. Oh, I'm not saying she's lived like a nun; I'm sure she's had her moments. But Frank was the only serious love in her life, as he was in mine. I couldn't have been as objective as that about her ten years ago! When I was fighting for my husband and for the rest of my life, I thought of her as a Jezebel who was maliciously destroying my marriage, but I can see her point of view ten years on. We're not so very different from each other, really. They say men go for the same woman again when they stray, don't they?' She snapped herself back to the present. 'Sorry, I'm still not answering your question, am I? What was it again?'

'There are certain indications in the file Alfred Norbury kept about the way he planned to let you know about your husband's affair. We'd like to hear how that came about from you.'

'It was typical Alfred. He told the wife of the senior sales manager at Burgess Electronics about what was going on in confidence. But he knew that she was a great gossip who would never be able to keep a confidence to herself. She chatted to others and it got back to me within a couple of weeks at the most. Alfred Norbury was all contrite and concerned for me, but he'd known exactly what he was about. He liked to do things in roundabout and indirect ways. It gave him a kick and emphasized how clever he was to all and sundry.'

'And how did Enid Frott react to this?'

'I don't know that, do I? I imagine she was as furious as I was at Alfred's actions, but we weren't in touch at the time!

I'm sure she hated my guts almost as much I hated hers. I wouldn't even have fought with her if the prize had been different. But Frank was worth fighting over.'

Peach looked at her evenly for seconds on end, trying to decide what, if anything, she was still holding back. Then he said evenly, 'I never knew your husband, except by reputation. He seems to me to have been a very lucky man, to have a woman like you willing to fight for him.'

Sharon smiled wryly. 'And Enid. She had class, Enid. I didn't think so at the time, but I've come to realize that since.'

'I see. The relationship between the two of you is one of the more remarkable things in this strange case.'

'Time heals, they say. And I was the winner in our contest. It's easier to be magnanimous, when you're the winner.'

'Nevertheless, it seems to me remarkable that you should be even on speaking terms, let alone initiating a book club together.'

'I suppose it is. Perhaps I've given you the wrong impression. We're not close friends. In fact, we hadn't seen each other for years until Frank's funeral a couple of months ago. I rang her up and insisted that she should come to the wake, as she was the only other woman who had been really important in Frank's life. I think she appreciated that. We chatted at the reception afterwards and she told me about her book club notion. I thought it was a good idea, especially for me, with acres of time to fill as a new widow. I rang her up and prodded her into action. We met here and got things moving.'

'Including the mutual decision to invite along Alfred Norbury. That seems to me the most remarkable thing of all.'

'It was Enid who invited him. But she ran it past me and I approved.'

'And why on earth did you do that?'

Sharon knew where this was going now. But it was a question which couldn't be avoided. 'Female curiosity? I think we were both intrigued to see whether Alfred would come, after what he'd done to both of us in the past. Of course, he always maintained that he hadn't wished me to find out about Frank and Enid, but all three of us knew exactly what the score was. He turned up as bold as brass, of course: that was Alfred. And he brought his latest project with him. Jamie

Norris seems a pleasant young man who's keen on books and
writing, but believe me he's well rid of Alfred Norbury,
whether he realizes it or not.'

'So curiosity was your only reason for including Norbury in
the group? You wanted to see whether he would come?'

'It wasn't just that. I meant everything I said about Alfred
being an intelligent and stimulating companion. He was very
bright: too bright for his own and other people's good at times.
He was a mischief-maker, but never dull. The ideal person to
get things going in a new group where everyone is shy.'

'And that overrode all your reservations about him?' Peach's
eyebrows arched impossibly high towards the bald pate.

Sharon responded by raising her own brows coquettishly, the
way she had done with Frank forty years ago. 'What other reason
could there possibly be, Detective Chief Inspector Peach?'

Peach smiled back at her. He was in danger of developing
an affection for this oldest and least likely of his suspects. He
reminded himself austerely that he might be sitting in the luxurious home of a cold-blooded murderer. 'Mr Norbury was shot
through the head on the day after the first meeting of your book
club, Mrs Burgess. Any investigating officer would have to
consider the possibility that you or Ms Frott, or perhaps both
of you in combination, invited along an old enemy so as to
accord yourself opportunities for revenge. And that one of you,
or both of you in concert, then took the very first opportunity
that was offered, after he furnished you with the information
that he always carried a pistol in his car. A pistol, incidentally,
which you surprisingly failed to mention before being reminded
of it when we spoke on Friday.'

'It's an intriguing scenario. It unfortunately has no basis in
fact.'

'So you both assure me. Policemen are suspicious creatures:
they like to have something more tangible than assurances. We
are in fact in possession of one very tangible item which our
forensic boys have found most interesting. You were kind
enough to offer our forensic officers a DNA sample on Thursday.'

'Yes. I was anxious to assist the police in the pursuit of their
enquiries.' She allowed herself a smile as she produced the
familiar phrase.

'In common with the other five people who attended your Monday-night book club meeting with Mr Norbury. All model citizens, all willing to help.' The ironic smile on his very different face mirrored hers exactly. 'Forensic examination of the car has now revealed a dark blue leather glove beneath the front passenger seat. Our forensic scientists say their tests indicate that this glove was recently worn by you, Mrs Burgess.'

She was shaken, but determined not to concede. 'That's impossible. I haven't been in that car. Certainly not in the last ten years, anyway.'

'Forensic science is very exact and completely reliable. Courts of law accept its findings without question.'

'I haven't been in that classic car of Alfred's. That glove must have got there by some other means. Perhaps Alfred took it for some reason of his own. It's the sort of mischief which entertained him.'

'It's difficult to think of a purpose for such a theft. Unless he knew that he was going to be shot, he could scarcely have perpetrated much mischief by the use of your glove.'

'You may be right. But I can't think of any other way in which that glove could have got there. I certainly haven't been in that car.'

'Then I can only advise you to give the matter further thought. I am quite sure that it is indeed your glove, if forensic analysis has established that.'

Sharon looked at him hard for a moment, seemingly checking whether he would yield anything further. Then she said quietly, 'If I'd shot Alfred, I'd have made pretty sure that I had an alibi.'

He resisted the thought that this competent woman would probably have done just that. 'Not always possible, though, is it?' He stood up, signifying to Northcott and Sharon Burgess that the interview was almost concluded. Then he walked across to the window and looked down on the police Mondeo below it at the top of the house's long drive. 'You witnessed our arrival here today?'

'Yes. You arrived exactly when you'd said you would. I think you saw me at the window.'

'We did indeed. Can you recall the make of car we came in?'

She looked puzzled as she tried to follow his train of thought.

'No. I probably couldn't have told you anything beyond the colour, even at the time. I'm pretty hopeless with cars.'

'Really? That's rather interesting. When we last spoke, you knew not only the make but the model of the car in which Alfred Norbury was murdered. That was after you'd omitted to mention the pistol you knew he carried there.'

There were cars parked tightly on the concrete in front of the house, with barely room for a person to pass between them to reach the front entrance. Jane Preston hesitated at the battered green door, looking at the grubby notice beside it which gave the names of the residents in the various bedsits within the terraced house.

The pause was enough for the door to open silently before her, as if her presence alone had excited some mysterious hidden switch. Jamie Norris smiled anxiously at her from the doorway. 'You come most carefully upon your hour,' he said nervously. And then, because she didn't respond, he added, 'like the ghost in *Hamlet*, you see.'

'I think it was the sentry actually,' Jane said, 'when he came to relieve his mate on the battlements in the first scene. But it scarcely matters, does it?' She followed him up the narrow stairs with the threadbare carpet and cursed herself for correcting him. It had got her off on the wrong foot and there had been no real need for it.

The room when she reached it was better than she had expected it to be. She had prepared herself for filth, and here all was clean. She had prepared herself for disorganization, but here all was tidy. She had prepared herself for obsolete clothes, and here was Jamie Norris in a brand-new yellow shirt and jeans in the latest fashion. She had prepared herself for lust, and here was a man full of courtly politeness. This project might be more difficult than she had anticipated.

He had a bottle of New Zealand chardonnay and two glasses on the table, across which he had spread an immaculate white napkin. 'I don't do tablecloths,' he said, as he indicated where she should sit.

'That's the most original chat-up line I've heard for some time,' said Jane. She'd put a skirt on for him. She tugged it modestly towards her knees as she sat down. She knew now that this was going to be more complicated than she'd expected. Good thing she'd allotted plenty of time to it. She accepted the glass of wine and was glad to see that he'd given himself a generous one. Wine always helped things along and sometimes it accelerated them agreeably. He was quite a personable young man and she was going to enjoy this.

Jane sought desperately for words which wouldn't sound entirely false. She was used to men making the running. She was used to having to hold men back, to slow things down so that she could keep control of the situation. She was glad to see that Jamie Norris sat down on the sofa where he had installed her, not on the small armchair beside it. But he sat as far away as he could, almost comically so. 'You'll fall off the end there if you're not careful!' she said, sliding her thigh as far towards him as she judged a well-brought-up girl could safely do.

He grinned but could not speak. Instead he took a hasty gulp of his wine and moved two inches away from his end of the sofa. She crossed her legs, exposing a decent portion of her lower thigh. His sudden intake of breath was probably quite flattering, she thought. But she mustn't force things. This was definitely going to take longer than she'd thought. She took his right hand in her left one as she raised her wine glass with her right. 'Glad you told me you weren't involved sexually with Alfred,' she said happily. 'We wouldn't have known quite where we were, if you hadn't said that, would we?'

'There was nothing sexual between me and Alfred and there never would have been,' said Jamie Norris firmly. 'I made that absolutely clear to him.' He squeezed her small hand a little. How delicate and feminine and desirable it seemed, within his larger and coarser one! He moved his fingers on to her slim, smooth wrist, left them there for a few seconds, and then stroked her forearm daringly.

Jane put her wine glass down carefully on the table, turned her clear blue eyes directly upon Jamie's brown ones and let her mouth slide softly into a smile. Then she kissed him, full upon the lips, but chastely. No tongues; not yet. She moved both hands around his back and felt his shoulder blades, sharp and desirable beneath the smooth cotton shirt. She held the kiss for a full twenty seconds, then released him slowly, reluctantly. 'That was nice!' she murmured in his ear.

Jamie was not quite sure that this was happening. He kept his arm round her shoulders and said the only thing that came into his head. 'The pigs asked me about Alfred. I told them I was definitely not gay!'

It was scarcely a chat-up line, but she giggled at it and stroked the inside of his thigh. She thought of handling the bit that would prove he wasn't gay, but then decided she'd better not push things along too quickly. This was exactly the opposite of the way it normally was with men, when they went straight for what they wanted and she had to put the brakes on. Rather nice, really, even if a little disconcerting. She'd have found this really enjoyable, if she hadn't had her other agenda.

But even that was under way. He'd introduced the police, when she'd been wondering how she was going to do that herself. She eased away from him a little and said, 'Did it go all right when the fuzz came to see you again? Tell me all about it. I might not shake quite so much with fear about them then!'

'I'm sure you've nothing to fear at all!' said Jamie stoutly. 'They came to see me at work this time. It was a bit embarrassing, because the manager wanted to know what it was all about and everything they'd said.'

'Everyone's like that. Murder has a sickly glamour, and this one's all over the papers and the telly. You become a minor celebrity and a source of interest just by being close to it. You should probably be pleased to be involved, really – unless you killed poor old Alfred, of course!'

Her laugh tinkled round the room and Jamie tried to join in. He didn't get beyond what he was sure was a rather sickly grin. 'I didn't do it. And neither did you. We should try to forget about it.'

He put his arms round her, a little clumsily, taking the initiative for the first time. The embrace grew more confident as he took control, scarcely believing that this wonderful woman was assisting, not resisting. The nagging thought that he was out of his class here was thrust to the back of his brain now, almost gone. He slid his hand cautiously under the green sweater, felt the smooth skin there. His brain told him that this must be simply skin as other skin, flesh as other flesh, but his heart told him that this was more special flesh than any he had stroked before. And then he was stroking those breasts which, when he had first seen them a week ago, had been so magnificent, so unattainable, feeling the nipples harden beneath his fingers. She murmured 'Jamie!' urgently into his ear and sought out his member with those slim, feminine, surprisingly confident fingers.

He wasn't sure how many seconds passed before they separated gently, reluctantly. He looked into those very blue eyes from no more than a few inches for a long time, conscious of nothing but their sparkle and the soft smile beneath them. He wasn't sure how many more seconds passed before she pulled a little further away from him and said, 'I wasn't expecting this.'

'Neither was I.' He grinned involuntarily: she couldn't know how absolutely true that was.

'You must think I'm an easy lay!'

He was silent at that. He knew he should say something to refute it, but the words wouldn't come. His mind was reeling with the future delights which the phrase had promised him. He must do nothing, absolutely nothing, to affect the progress of this wonderful and unlikely happening. Take it easy, his mind said. Force nothing. It's all going wonderfully well without your assistance. Just let it happen spontaneously, as it's been happening so far. Play along. It's going to happen, so long as you don't say anything to derail this train of passion. Say anything you like so long as you think it's what Jane will welcome. He said breathlessly, 'They weren't bad. The fuzz, I mean. They seemed quite understanding, really, compared with the pigs I've met in the past.'

He shouldn't have said that. He didn't want her to know about the past. But she didn't take it up as he feared she would. Instead, she crossed those legs he had lately been stroking, picked up her glass, and said, 'Tell me about it, Jamie.'

He'd nothing to lose by telling her almost all of it, he reckoned. It would only reinforce how strongly he felt about her. 'They pressed me very strongly about my relationship with Alfred, especially in the week before his death. I told them that

I didn't particularly like being paraded as his protégé, but I had to be fair to Alfred. He'd been very good to me, very generous. He'd helped me with my writing. He didn't pull any punches, when he thought something was trite or second-hand. But it's no use being thin-skinned if you want to improve as a writer.' He could hear Alfred saying that. The dead man seemed uncannily close at this moment, and that stopped Jamie's tongue.

Jane said softly, 'You're a very fair-minded man, Jamie. You sound to me very generous yourself, in your assessment of Alfred and what he did for you.'

'I hope I am, because he genuinely helped me. I might show you something I've written, in a little while. I've been trying to write something about you.'

'How flattering! I'd love to see it and I'd feel privileged. But you must take the decision, when you feel that the moment is right for you to show it to me. What else did you tell them about Alfred?'

'Well, they questioned me very hard about whether there'd been any sexual relationship, and how much pressure for that there'd been from him. I said emphatically that there'd never been any question of a sexual relationship as far as I was concerned. But you should be very cautious with that DCI Peach if he comes back to question you again. He's a shrewd bugger and he doesn't let you get away with anything. But he did seem to accept that I was strictly heterosexual.' Jamie stopped for a moment and risked a soft stroke of her breast from outside the sweater. He received a reassuring smile. 'But Peach pressed me very hard about Alfred and what he wanted from me. I had to admit that it seemed he wanted to bed me and that I'd had to tell him in no uncertain terms that I wasn't up for that.'

'And did the two of them accept that?'

'I think they did.' He leaned over and stroked the softness at the top of her arm.

Jane kissed him softly. 'You don't have to convince me you're straight! But did they believe you?'

'Who knows? They're paid to believe everyone's lying to them, aren't they? I think they accepted what I said. But they made me admit I'd lied to them when I spoke to them the first time, last Thursday.'

She frowned. Jamie thought it was quite the most beguiling creasing of the forehead he had ever seen. 'That's not a good thing, is it? What did you have to put right with them?'

'I told them on Thursday that I hadn't seen Alfred after our book club meeting on Monday night. Today I had to confess that I'd been round to see him on Tuesday afternoon after I'd finished work at Tesco. Someone had seen me, I think.'

She frowned again, looking very concerned for him. 'I don't like that. Probably makes you the last person known to have seen Alfred alive.'

Jamie gave her a bleak little smile. 'That's what they said. I'd gone round to Alfred's place because I wanted to make it absolutely clear to him that I was straight and he'd no chance of bedding me.'

'And did the police believe that?'

'I don't know. They don't give much away, those two. Still, it doesn't seem to matter much, now that you're here.'

He reached out for her and she kissed him and held him tight for a long moment. She let go of him reluctantly, holding his face close to hers still. 'Perhaps we could help each other.'

'How could we do that?' Any sort of alliance with this enchanting creature must surely be a fine thing. It would prolong their association and bring them even closer.

'I'm not sure. I'll have to give it some thought. You're distracting me at the moment. You're making me think of more urgent and much more desirable things!' She seized his manhood, making him gasp with pleasure and anticipation. He had not thought that such an ethereal creature could be so uncomplicated and so direct. He would amend his sonnet now – put in some reference to carnal joys, which he had not dared to include earlier. She slid her hands under the yellow shirt and up his back and whispered into his ear, 'I'm a shameless hussy, aren't I? I don't seem able to help myself, with you!'

He was glad he'd put clean sheets on his bed today. They were in it ten minutes later. There was an hour of uninhibited joy and then she told him that, what the hell, she would stay the night. There wasn't much sleep during the next few hours, but it had never been more worth the forfeit.

It was when they lay on their backs, exhausted, with her head resting upon his arm, that Jane came up with her suggestion. 'I don't like you being in the frame for this killing, Jamie. Especially not now, when we're as close as this.' They both smiled at the ceiling on that thought. 'You need an alibi for the time of the murder. It wouldn't do me any harm to have one, either. I don't think they see me as a serious suspect, but it would be nice to be finished with them and their questioning and free to get on with the rest of my life.'

'What are you thinking of? I don't want anything that would put you in any danger.'

'Oh, I don't see why it would do that. I was thinking that we could simply say that we were together in the early evening of last Tuesday. That would give us both an alibi for the time of the death and get you off the hook. I don't like you being the last person known to have seen the victim alive.'

'I don't think I could let you do that, Jane. Not on my behalf.'

'Oh, I don't think there'd be much risk in it. And it's not just on your behalf. There'd be advantages for me, too, as I said.'

He didn't say a word, but turned on to his side and held her softly against him, hoping that she could feel gratitude seeping through his very skin. Jane Preston was altogether the most fascinating person he had ever met.

EIGHTEEN

Most people wouldn't have noticed the difference, but CID officers are trained and encouraged to observe all sorts of things. The places where people live are of special interest, for they sometimes reveal things which the occupants wish to conceal. When they had been here on Friday afternoon, Dick Fosdyke's three-year-old flat had struck them as warm, comfortable, and completely characterless.

Now, less than four days later, it had significant additions. There was a framed colour print of Malham Cove on the wall; Dick had cycled and walked there as an adolescent. There were two different pictures of his children. In the one on top of the television, they were scarcely more than toddlers. In the later one on the sideboard, when they were ten and eight, they were smiling cheerfully at his camera. Small additions, but significant. Despite his divorce, Fosdyke was trying to give the image of the family man, dull but unthreatening, above all conventional – the last person who would get himself involved in the hatred and violence which went with murder.

He ushered them in, installed them upon his sofa, tried very hard to seem casual and unthreatened by this second CID visit. 'I want to help, of course, even though Alfred Norbury was no great friend of mine. But I don't think I'll be able to offer you anything that's useful.' Fosdyke was the picture of concerned citizenship. Or a caricature of it, depending on your view of him.

DCI Peach was in no doubt what his view was. 'You'll need to prove to us that you wish to help, Mr Fosdyke. So far you have been obstructive. We're cynical men: the job makes us like that. You have reinforced our scepticism.'

Dick looked shocked. In fact, he wasn't surprised by this uncompromising beginning. Ernie Ainsworth had rung him and told him about the visit of DS Northcott and DC Murphy and what he'd had to tell them at his house in Bolton. Dick looked at Clyde Northcott now, but found those ebony features as unrevealing as ever.

Percy Peach caught the hint of nervousness and seized upon it immediately. 'You weren't in the restaurant at the White Hart at the time of Mr Norbury's murder.'

'Apparently not, no. I made a mistake about the time.'

'You didn't make a mistake, Mr Fosdyke. You deliberately attempted to deceive us. You persuaded Mr Ernest Ainsworth to lie on your behalf. That is a very serious offence. It may make him an accessory after the fact, if we choose to bring a charge of murder against you.'

'You won't be doing that. I didn't kill Alfred Norbury.' He flicked a hand quickly back over his straight, very black hair.

'Then why did you lie to us so consistently when you spoke to us on Friday?'

'I wouldn't say I lied. I may have concealed a few things.'

'You told us direct lies, Mr Fosdyke. You claimed that you and Alfred Norbury "didn't know each other well enough to be friends or enemies". You said that you "knew of him" because of his reputation as a local character, and when asked exactly how well you knew him, you told us "not well at all". I consider this direct lying; I think a jury in a criminal court would do so, if we finish this case by putting that issue before them.'

'All right. It's a fair cop – that seems the appropriate expression. I had previous with Alfred Norbury and I didn't want you to know about it. I should have thought it was obvious why.'

'I think you'd better tell us now why you consider it so obvious that you should give us pretty well the direct opposite of the truth when we are investigating murder. You're an intelligent man, Mr Fosdyke. Which suggests to me that you wouldn't feed us a string of porkies without having something very serious to conceal from us. DS Northcott and I have been discussing exactly what that might be.'

'Surely it's obvious, as I said?'

'Not to us, it isn't. DS Northcott and I are just unimaginative coppers who tend to go for the facts. The facts look very unpromising for you, Mr Fosdyke.'

'I pretended I'd hardly known Norbury before that Monday night because I knew it would look bad if I gave you a detailed history and you realized that we'd had a serious falling-out. With the man lying dead in the morgue, it would have given me an obvious motive for putting him there. I looked at who else had been at that book club meeting and found that there were three women. I thought you wouldn't rate them likely candidates for shooting a man through the head. Why hand the police a ready-made arrest on a plate, I thought.'

'Because you'd settled the score with your old enemy? Because it was inevitable that even slow-witted plods like us would eventually unearth your past history and nail the crime on you?'

Fosdyke gave a grisly smile. 'I was the slow-witted one, I suppose, to think I could get away with telling you that I hardly knew Norbury. I realized after we'd spoken on Friday that you were bound to go away and check what I'd said. Perhaps I realized even when you were with me that I wouldn't get away with it. That's why I came up with the Ernie Ainsworth story – I knew he owed me a favour and I thought this was the time to call it in.'

Northcott looked up from his notes. 'People tend to back off pretty quickly, when they realize that they're likely to be asked to perjure themselves during a murder investigation. It's a big frightener, murder.'

'Yes. I don't blame Ernie for backing down. Especially with you leaning on him.' He ran his eyes from top to toe over Clyde's formidable frame and nodded quietly, in what was presumably some sort of compliment. 'We did actually eat together at the White Hart last Tuesday night, you know. It was just not at the time when Norbury was being killed. I think Ernie might actually have been there at that time, but I wasn't. I brought my presence forward a bit, to give myself an alibi. I should have known it wouldn't work.'

'You should indeed. You've increased the suspicion falling on you, rather than diminished it. People who lie to us invariably do that. We've learned a little about your previous dealings with Mr Norbury, as you now say you expected us to do. I think it's high time we had the full story from you.'

Dick put his face into his hands for a moment, shutting out Peach's alert, insistent face. He needed to concentrate. But he realized that he didn't know just how much they knew and how much he could hold back. He'd just admitted to deliberate attempts to deceive them and to persuading Ernie Ainsworth to lie on his behalf. He couldn't afford to be caught out again. 'We worked together. We worked for the *Daily Mail*. I was full-time; Alfred was freelance, but getting a lot of work. He reviewed books – most of the fiction and some of the historical stuff. I was billed as arts correspondent. I reviewed all the major exhibitions and commented on competitions like the Turner Prize. I also had a regular cartoon in the paper. I enjoyed the work and I was earning good money.'

'But Alfred Norbury changed all that.'

They knew, then. Knew the important stuff, anyway. 'I should have realized that I was in a dangerous situation with Alfred. Success always made him envious. He said he liked to see people jumping hurdles. In fact he liked to see them falling flat on their faces, in as much mud as possible.'

'So when he saw things going well for you, he didn't like it?'

'That's putting it mildly. And I wasn't prepared for what he did: I'd seen only the better side of him until that point. He could be very helpful, when you were making your way. He knew a lot of powerful people in the arts world and he had words with them on my behalf. As long as I was his discovery, the bright young man whom he had spotted and was helping along, I was fine. That sounds silly, because he was only six years older than I was. But when you're twenty-eight, that seems quite a difference, and certainly Alfred always seemed vastly more experienced and worldly-wise than I was.'

Peach's normally very mobile features remained totally impassive, so that Fosdyke had no idea whether or not he was accepting this. 'So what did Norbury do to disturb the smooth progress of your career?'

'Small things at first. People in the world of art and the world of books were suddenly more reserved and less helpful to me. I realized that where once Alfred had been putting in good words for me behind the scenes, he was now doing exactly the opposite. Eventually the editor of the paper wasn't passing me the assignments which I had once been given. When I realized what was going on and tackled Alfred about it, he shrugged it aside. A week later I found he was attempting to destroy my marriage.'

'In what way?'

Dick flicked his hair again, that sudden gesture of disquiet which he was scarcely aware of in himself. 'Not many news-papermen are saints, Chief Inspector. I was sleeping around a bit. Not serious, earth-shattering affairs. Opportunist, I suppose. Stupid and selfish – oh, I've been through the self-examination and self-recrimination stuff many times. I found that my wife was suddenly asking about my activities and where I'd been at certain times. It didn't take me long to work out who her informant was. When I confronted Norbury, he went all senten-tious and said that she had a right to know and he was bringing me to my senses. He did that all right. I lost my job at the *Daily Mail* and I've been freelance ever since. Alison and I patched things up and the marriage struggled on for several years, but it was the beginning of the end.'

Peach looked round at the small, comfortable flat and at the pictures of Fosdyke's children which had appeared there since his last visit. 'You've picked your life up since then.'

Dick allowed himself a bitter smile. 'Sort of. I'm earning again, though life as a freelance is always rather precarious. But I think that I've now managed to acquire a certain reputa-tion as a cartoonist. I earn decent money, even if there's not a lot left over after my monthly payments to Alison. I've got a reasonable life going again, I suppose.'

'So why tangle again with the man who'd destroyed every-thing, according to the account you've just given to us?'

Dick had known this would come, just as he'd known that he must now try to make his explanation as convincing as he possibly could. 'I can't fully explain that, even to myself. I thought of pulling out, when I found Norbury was to be a member of the book club. But then I thought that I wasn't going to let that sod dictate the way I lived my life.' He looked at Peach, but found no clue in the round, impassive face as to whether he was convincing him. 'I suppose there was also a certain vanity: I wanted to show Alfred that I'd made a new and successful life, with demanding work and interesting friends, despite what he'd done to me ten years ago. And perhaps there was also a certain curiosity. I wanted to see how Norbury would react to me after all this time, especially in the presence of others who did not know our history.'

Peach nodded slowly, his first visible reaction in many minutes. 'And what were your first thoughts when you saw him at that initial book club meeting?'

'He was as bold as brass, for a start. It didn't seem at all embarrassing to him meeting me again, even though we both knew what he'd done to me. He wanted to take over the conversation as he'd always done and to tell other people what they should be thinking. He also had a young man in tow. Jamie Norris. He seemed a pleasant, intelligent lad from what I saw of him. I suspect he's mid-twenties, but I'd say he's younger than his years. And just the kind of candidate to become an Alfred Norbury protégé. I made a note on that Monday night that I was going to take the first opportunity to warn Jamie Norris about Norbury. Alfred would help him along, be very kind to him at first, but he'd have his own agenda. Don't trust the sod as far as you can throw him, I was going to tell young Jamie. I don't need to do that now.'

Peach nodded, allowing those mobile black eyebrows to dance a little for the first time. 'You said earlier that you didn't think we'd consider the three women who were present at that first book club meeting as likely candidates for murder. The other member of that group was the nice lad who was a protégé of Norbury's and beholden to him, you thought. He doesn't seem a very likely suspect for us either, does he? Which leaves you, Mr Fosdyke. A man who has now confessed to the murderous hate which is often the prelude to a killing. A man who tried to sell us a clumsily contrived alibi. A man who contrived a meeting with a murder victim so as to allow himself the opportunity for long-sought revenge.'

'I didn't kill Norbury.'

Peach now gave him a huge and disconcerting beam. 'You're the only convincing suspect, on your own admission. We don't often get that, do we, DS Northcott? A man setting himself up for us as our prime suspect?'

'It's unique in my experience, sir. But it shows admirable frankness in a member of the public. I think we should encourage it, sir. Publicise it, perhaps, after the arrest – try to establish a trend.'

Fosdyke almost snarled at them. 'I didn't shoot Norbury. I'd have been tempted, given the opportunity, but I'm not your killer.'

Peach's black eyebrows arched impossibly high beneath the bald pate. 'You gave yourself the opportunity, Mr Fosdyke, when you joined that book club. And Alfred Norbury practically suggested the method to you, when he volunteered the information that he carried a loaded pistol in his car.'

'And I knew his car – he'd had that Triumph Stag as long as I'd known him – and I now have no alibi for the time he was killed. But the onus of proof is still on you, DCI Peach, and you won't be able to meet it.'

Dick spoke with all the confidence he could muster, but his adversary looked singularly unimpressed. 'We're now certain that Alfred Norbury was shot at quarter to seven on Tuesday the twenty-first of January. Killed within ten minutes' walk of the White Hart, where you presented yourself, according to independent witnesses, at around seven o'clock. Where do you now claim to have been at quarter to seven?'

'Walking from here to the White Hart. I didn't take the car because I wanted to be free to drink as much as I wished with my old friend.'

'Whom you'd agreed to meet there to provide yourself with a sort of alibi for the murder you'd already planned.'

'Whom I'd agreed to meet to enjoy a pleasant evening together and reminisce about old times. You'll find it difficult to prove it otherwise, DCI Peach.'

'We'll find the proof, if it's needed, Mr Fosdyke. Perhaps this is the time for you to consult a good criminal defence lawyer.'

Enid Frott thought long and hard before inviting Sharon Burgess for coffee. She still wasn't sure about their relationship. How could you be? What rules could there possibly be for the association of a wife and the mistress who had almost destroyed her marriage?'

That was years ago, of course, and time heals most things.

But surely not this? Surely armed neutrality was the nearest she and Sharon should get to any sort of relationship? And now there was murder. Murder of a man both of them had hated; murder of a man who had been crucial in the agonies both of them had endured a decade and more ago. Enid was sure now that both of them had wished Alfred Norbury dead. Why had she invited him to join the book club? Why had Sharon taken up her suggestion of a book club so eagerly and pushed it along, when it might otherwise have been one of those good ideas that never found a practical outlet?

Her life seemed at present to be dominated by a series of questions, to none of which she could provide a satisfactory answer. It was as though Alfred Norbury was taunting her from beyond the grave, amusing himself with her pain now as he had done so thoroughly in life. As the time of this meeting she had arranged approached, she agonized over yet another question. Was Sharon Burgess the right person to meet now, in view of their history? Wasn't a conversation with Sharon likely to leave her further confused rather than clear her mind? Would the police, who seemed to discover everything which went on among them, get to know of this meeting? And if they did, how would they interpret her action in arranging it?

She was thoroughly regretting her initiative by the time Sharon Burgess arrived. The simple electronic chime sounded in her ears like the knell of doom. Enid painted a welcoming smile across her lips and opened the door of the flat. 'Good of you to come, Sharon. I thought we should have a talk.'

'I'm glad you did. You probably think I've got plenty of people to talk to at Pendle View, but the family aren't around and you don't talk to the people who work for you about things like this. I feel as isolated as you are. Sorry, that sounds rather rude. I didn't mean it to be.'

Enid smiled wanly. 'There's no need to apologize. Perhaps it's being involved in a murder enquiry that puts us on edge. Because we are involved, you know: we're suspects, and it's not a good feeling. I think we feel we can only really talk about it to other people who are in it as deeply as we are.'

Sharon wondered if Enid suspected her, if she'd brought her here to quiz her with a view to making her incriminate herself.

Had she heard about the glove in Alfred's Triumph Stag? The police wouldn't have told her, but all kinds of information seemed to be flying around the town in the feverish atmosphere that had built up during the last week. She accepted the offer of coffee because that would give her time to think and perhaps to prepare herself for whatever it was that Enid Frott wanted of her.

She'd never been here until that fateful Monday-night meeting of the book club, and she'd been much too preoccupied with the other people there to give much attention to her surroundings. Enid's ground-floor flat was a strange mixture, but one which worked well. The flat had the large rooms and long, simple windows of the original Georgian house, but the comfort and elegance of a modern flat. Part of its appeal was no doubt due to Enid, who as she would have expected had made the most of the place. The furnishings and decoration were minimalist, with every piece no doubt chosen carefully to make the maximum effect within the whole.

Enid was only four years younger than her, which meant that she must be sixty-three now. But the style she had gone for and brought off here was that of a much younger person. Sharon herself would never have dared to attempt it, even if it had been her taste, which it was not. It was easier to bring off these effects, she supposed, when you had no children or grandchildren to bring their appealing chaos into the rooms where you lived. Or was she just being bitchy? She wasn't generally bitchy, but you could surely make an exception of your husband's mistress.

When Enid brought in the coffee, it was almost as if she read these thoughts. She said rather abruptly as she set the tray on the low table, 'Frank was never here, you know. The house is old, but the conversion to four flats was only undertaken three years ago.'

Sharon smiled, acknowledging that the daring introduction of Frank had been well meant. She accepted her coffee, said nothing during the several seconds the two women took to arrange themselves in sofa and armchair, then came back quietly with, 'He was a good man, Frank.'

'Yes. He had a conscience.' Enid stared hard at her coffee

as she summoned her courage. 'He did the right thing in the end.'

Sharon tried not to show her surprise. She was shocked as much at herself as at Enid for letting the conversation run this way. 'Perhaps he did. Which of us knows, in the end? We fight for what we have. Monogamy may not be the most natural arrangement for mankind. It certainly isn't the easiest.'

'We shan't have Alfred Norbury around to complicate the rest of our lives.'

'No. I'm surprised how glad I am that someone's put paid to him.'

Enid wondered if this was a genuine thought, or simply Sharon's assertion that she hadn't committed this crime. 'I'm glad too. Seeing him again reminded me how bitterly I felt about him all those years ago.'

Sharon smiled '"All those years". Ten years doesn't seem much, when you reach your sixties.'

'That's true. Perhaps I never really ceased hating him. Perhaps it was seeing him again that brought it back to the surface.'

'Are you telling me that you killed him?' Sharon delivered it with a smile, to conceal the real enquiry behind it.

'No. But then I wouldn't be, even if I'd shot the bugger, would I?'

Sharon grinned, feeling a welcome relaxation of the tension. 'He was a bugger, wasn't he? Quite literally, I suppose. I'm sure he had sexual plans for that young man he brought along to the book club meeting: I could tell by the way he glanced at him from time to time.' She stretched her legs, glancing at the calf leather on her blue, elegant shoes. 'In the old days, I used to think of Alfred as a likeable rascal, shading into rogue, but he was worse than that, wasn't he?'

'He was, yes. Much worse. When they're up to no good, it's always the intelligent ones who are the worst. I'd say he was highly intelligent and highly dangerous. Like a lot of other people, I didn't realize that at the time when he was damaging me.'

Sharon suddenly looked hard at the woman who had brought her here. 'You've fired a few pistols in your time, I seem to remember.'

Enid refused to take offence. 'I used to be a member of the Brunton Small Arms Club, yes. Thirty years ago and more. And in case you wish to throw this in too, I was quite a good shot. I won the odd prize, in those days. My then boyfriend was a member of the club, and quite proud of me. That was long before I became Frank's PA. But I should point out that whoever shot Alfred had no need of any arms expertise. I gather the killer simply put the pistol close to his temple and pulled the trigger. You don't need any previous experience to do that.'

'But at least the thought of handling a pistol wouldn't inhibit you. I've always been terrified of the whole business of firearms. I don't believe I could bring myself to handle a pistol.'

'Oh, I'm sure you could, if you were bent on murder.' This was the kind of barbed exchange they'd enjoyed at Sharon's big house on the hill, Enid thought, when they were setting up the book club, before any of this had happened. And she was in danger of enjoying it now, as she'd enjoyed it then.

Perhaps Sharon Burgess felt something of the same odd, irrelevant excitement. But she now switched the subject away from the two of them again. 'Do you think that Jamie Norris might have killed him? If he didn't want to be bedded and Alfred was too persistent, I mean?'

She's ruling herself out again, Enid thought. But ruling out me as well: perhaps I'm being ultra-sensitive. 'He might well have done, I suppose. When I was as young and as inexperienced as he still seems to be, I'd have panicked if Alfred Norbury had been digging his sexual claws into me. Speaking of youngsters, what about that bright young woman you brought along? I liked her.'

'Jane Preston? Oh, I think Jane can look after herself. I don't think she'd panic, even if Alfred set his sights upon her – I always used to wonder if he was bisexual, you know. But with her looks and her figure, she must by now be well used to handling male attention, welcome or unwelcome. I've seen her in action at my evening class. She's a highly competent teacher, but she also keeps people at a distance easily enough, when she wants to. She's a bright girl: I expect she's late twenties, but anyone that age is a girl to me now.'

'And me.' Enid was wondering now quite why she'd brought

Sharon Burgess here. Frank was a bond between them, however unlikely that seemed. Strange how a man who was now dead and whom she hadn't seen for many years previously could still be so strong a presence for the two women he had loved. She'd been vaguely hoping the two of them could help each other in some way with the police, but she'd realized as soon as Sharon had come into her flat that she was wrong. She said thoughtfully, 'Do you think either of those young ones could have killed Alfred?'

'You've obviously been looking for a killer, as I have.' Sharon smiled grimly, aware that what she was going to say was narrowing the field, transferring suspicion back to the woman in front of her – and to herself, of course. 'I don't really see either of those two killing Alfred – unless Jamie panicked in the face of sexual advances, as we thought he might have done. Jane wouldn't have lost her head like that, and I can't see any other reason for her to have killed Alfred.'

Neither of these women who were bound so unusually together could know that DCI Peach was on his way at that moment to speak with Ms Preston about exactly why she might have killed Alfred Norbury.

NINETEEN

'**R**eport to me at midday.' The order from Tommy Bloody Tucker was stark and uncompromising. Percy Peach didn't like it, but he'd been half-expecting it. His afternoon appointment wasn't until two-thirty, so he couldn't say it was inconvenient. Better attend and take whatever fun he could from the meeting.

'It's a week today since this happened, Peach. Are you close to an arrest?'

'We have made progress, sir. Research into the backgrounds of those involved has thrown up several possibilities.'

'Possibilities, Peach? I want action. Drastic action. As far as I'm concerned, possibilities are just gobbledegook.'

'I bow to your superior experience in that field, sir.'

Tucker looked puzzled and even more vacant than usual, but one had to be an expert of Percy's calibre to note the difference. 'There are important people involved in this case, Peach. You need to tread carefully.'

'At the same time as taking drastic action? I see, sir. Mrs Sharon Burgess is one of our leading suspects.'

'Of Burgess Electronics? Involved, but surely not a suspect, Peach. She is a friend of mine.'

'That doesn't automatically exclude people from suspicion, sir. Our murder victim caused Mrs Burgess much pain some years ago. She has told us that he came near to breaking up her marriage. She also claims she has never been in Mr Norbury's car in the last few years, but a glove worn quite recently by her was found beneath the passenger seat of that car. She has so far failed to provide us with a satisfactory explanation for that.'

Tucker wore his baffled-goldfish look now and Peach felt rewarded. 'I suppose you have questioned her thoroughly.'

'I've done that, sir. Perhaps it needs your expertise. Would you like me to get her into our smallest interview room and shine an arc lamp into her face whilst you grill her, sir? I know you hail from a more brutal age of policing, but I'm sure—'

'You will treat Mrs Burgess with proper courtesy, Peach. And don't allow that black bagman of yours to go terrifying her. Do you hear?'

'I hear, sir. I admire the way you keep your inclination towards violence under such strict control. I presume you will not wish to put the thumbscrews on Ms Enid Frott. She makes no secret of the fact that she is the late Frank Burgess's former PA and mistress, who also had good reason to hate Mr Norbury.'

A bright thought flooded suddenly into Tucker's face, making him look for a moment almost intelligent. 'This won't be a woman, you know. It was a shooting.'

'I see, sir. I don't think we can simply rule out all women. The weapon was provided ready to hand by Alfred Norbury, who advertised its presence in his car to the five people he met on the night before his death. And the pistol was simply held close to the side of his head and fired: no expertise or previous firearms experience was needed.'

Tuckers lips set sullenly. 'This will be a man, Peach. You mark my words.'

'I always do that, sir. They have given me much food for thought over the years. We have a man in the frame who was just six years younger than Norbury and was a former work colleague of his. He is a political and sports cartoonist who operates freelance and is doing rather well. However, he claims he lost his full-time post with the *Daily Mail* some years ago because of the treachery of Alfred Norbury, who also severely damaged his marriage – Mr Fosdyke is now divorced. He contrived a false alibi for the time of the murder, which we have now exposed.'

'Well, there you are, then. Bring him in. Charge him and get him behind bars. Furnish me with the details and I'll arrange a media briefing.' Tucker's eyes shone with the missionary light which always blazed in them with the prospect of good publicity.

'We need proof to arrest him, sir. He hasn't yet confessed.'

'Break him down, Peach. He sounds to me like your man. But you've also got a young thug on your list too, haven't you? This Jamie Norris fellow. No regular employment for years.'

'No, sir. He has ambitions to be a writer, sir.'

'Well, there you are, then. I'm surprised you haven't got the idle young sod locked away by now.' Tucker seemed to see no lack of logic in offering his DCI two very different candidates for arrest. All part of the necessary bollocking process, as far as Thomas Bulstrode Tucker was concerned.

'Mr Norris was something of a protégé of the dead man. It seems possible that Alfred Norbury had sexual designs upon him which were not reciprocated.'

Tommy Bloody Tucker was triumphant. 'Dissolute, you see. This yobbo has been a drain on the state whilst he farted about pretending to write, and now turns out to be a pooftah as well. A pooftah who's fallen out with his bedmate and ends up by shooting him! Happens all the time nowadays, this sort of thing.' The Chief Superintendent's noble features tightened into a prim disdain.

'A commendably forthright attitude, sir. I'm sure it will be received sympathetically at your media conference. In view of your certainty, it seems hardly worth mentioning our fifth suspect, but I shall do so in the interests of comprehensiveness. In addition to Mrs Burgess and Ms Frott, a much younger woman was also present at that meeting on the eve of Mr Norbury's death. She goes by the name of Jane Preston, sir. She is a lecturer in English Literature at the University of Central Lancashire. Perhaps seen by Mr Norbury as an intellectual challenge, but that hardly gives her a motive for murder. However, we have discovered—'

'She is obviously as unlikely a candidate as the other two women, Peach. Don't waste my time any further. I have given you the informed overview that you demanded of me. I now expect action.' Tommy Bloody Tucker jutted his jaw at his most heroic angle and dismissed his junior from his presence.

The toad in the hole was much better than usual in the police canteen. A new chef had started this week and he was male. Percy held his peace on that, listening with interest to the comments on the food from his female colleagues. Then he locked himself in his office and did his homework. He had no idea what to expect during the afternoon. Blank denial? An assertion that the most extreme of actions had in this case been justified? Silence and a blunt challenge to prove what he alleged?

He was determined to be prepared for whatever he met. He called Clyde Northcott into his office, made sure that the big man thought as he did. Having checked that his DS was as well briefed as he was, he went down to the police Mondeo with firm resolve. Most of the men and women who worked with him thought Percy Peach never felt pressure, and he did everything he could to foster that impression. But there were occasions when he needed his privacy and a period of solitude to summon his resolve. This had been one of them.

Northcott drove and neither of them spoke much on the ten-mile journey to the University of Central Lancashire. He could have brought Jane Preston in to the station and interviewed her there. He could have talked to her with others able to observe from outside the room because of the modern technology. He hadn't quite come to terms with the one-way glass wall yet: sometimes he thought that the knowledge that he was being observed by people he couldn't see from beyond the glass disturbed him more than it did his subjects.

He also had an instinct that on this occasion the subject might speak more freely in her own surroundings.

Jane Preston certainly seemed quite relaxed as she collected them from the reception area. She commented on the latest developments on the campus as she led them a considerable distance to the tutorial room which had her name displayed clearly upon its door. 'We won't be disturbed. I've no classes for the rest of the day. Not that I'm anticipating this will take as long as that!' Her little giggle might have been a sign of nervousness, or mere social unease. She'd never entertained senior policemen in her room before. And never would again, she hoped.

Peach gave her one of his enigmatic smiles. They usually made people nervous – especially younger people like this one, who had no criminal background and weren't used to his approach. He sat in the chair usually occupied by a nervous student who was here to discuss an essay and said, 'You don't look like a serious criminal. But I learned long ago not to trust appearances.'

Jane smiled back at him and decided not to react to that. She was aware that her fair colouring was against her here. Her naturally blonde hair and clear blue eyes had brought her many advantages over the years, but her fair skin could be a disadvantage when she was nervous. You blushed more easily than people with sallow skins – not that she expected to blush much here. But you also tended to turn more obviously pale when you were nervous or when something shocked you. The blood seemed to leave your face more visibly than it did with darker-skinned people. She glanced at Detective Sergeant Clyde Northcott, sitting with the smoothly polished countenance of an African god beside his chief, and thought how little trouble he must have with his skin when it came to concealing feelings.

Peached sighed. 'You told us on Saturday that you had no long-standing grievance against Alfred Norbury.'

Jane gave him a wide smile. 'I hadn't met him before that Monday-night meeting of our book club.'

Peach stretched his legs in front of him and looked at the shine on his shoes, almost regretfully, it seemed. 'Perhaps not. You knew a lot about him, though, didn't you?'

'It was Mrs Burgess who persuaded me to go along to the book club. I didn't really want to join anything like that, but she convinced me that it might be fun.'

'Yes. I can picture you acting out your reluctance to join. I should think you were quite good at it. You seem to have a talent for deception.'

'I think you're trying hard to be offensive. Is this part of your technique, Chief Inspector? I can't think that I've done anything to merit your hostility.'

'How long have you been calling yourself Jane Preston?'

She looked blank; did it rather well, she thought. Pale skin was at least excellent for looking blank. 'As long as I've been alive, I suppose. Certainly as long as I can remember.'

'You lie well. I've seen a lot of liars over the years, but you're certainly as good as most.' His voice hardened. 'We know that you are Eleanor Garside. Usually known as Ellie. Universally known as Ellie, in your native Penrith.'

'Jane Preston was for professional reasons.' She kept her face straight, with that slight, enigmatic smile playing about the corners of her mouth. Behind it, she was frantically trying to think of how there could be any professional advantage for her in her change of name.

'You didn't change your name by deed poll. That is why it took us longer to unearth your deception.'

'It's not illegal. I used Preston when I applied for the post here. Everyone here knows me as Jane Preston. If the bureaucrats had chosen to check my qualifications, they'd have found they were in my original name, but they rarely do that. Jane has always been my second name. I decided to use it. I've grown quite used to it now.'

Peach stood up without taking his eyes from her face. He took the single step which was all he needed and picked up the photograph which had been facing her on her desk. It was another copy of the colour photograph of her and her brother she kept in the house. It had been taken eighteen years ago, when she was still a child and Adam was a foot taller than her. Peach looked at it for a moment, then set it carefully back on her desk exactly where it had been, looking at her sympathetically as he did so.

He sounded almost reluctant as he said, 'Why did you tell me those lies about being a solitary child when we spoke on Saturday? Why did you try to give us the impression that you were an only child?'

She couldn't think of any reason. He seemed so calm, so certain, that it seemed scarcely worth the effort of trying to contest things. But he might be merely probing, trying to build on a little knowledge to secure further revelations from her. She forced a smile. 'I don't know why I did that. It was silly, really. You were pressing me about Penrith and how I grew up there and why I didn't go back there very much. It just came out with the rest of what I was telling you. There was a difference of six years between my brother and me. I suppose I felt like an only child sometimes, especially after Adam had grown up and gone away.'

'But you were very close, weren't you, you and Adam?'

It was the first time he had used the name and she felt almost violated. Adam was hers. She didn't want other people bandying his name about. She felt the first crack in her voice as she said, 'Yes. We were very close.' She was sure she'd gone pale now, that the blood had drained from her face with his mention of Adam. 'He looked after me, Adam did. At home, at school, when we played with other children. Even in the house. If he felt Mum and Dad were being hard on me, he always spoke up for me.'

'You missed him when he grew up and moved away.'

'Yes. It felt as if I was alone for the first time. Dad and I were never as close as some fathers and daughters. It was Adam I always looked to for guidance and help. Both of us knew that.'

'I expect you missed him even more after he died. Even though you've grown up and made a career for yourself since then.'

She looked straight ahead, speaking more to herself than her visitors now. 'I still miss Adam. I'll never stop missing him. Even though I feel better, now that he's been avenged.'

It was the first admission, the first acknowledgement that she wasn't going to go on fighting them. As if marking a change of mood or introducing a different movement in music, Clyde Northcott took over the questioning. His voice was basso profundo, but not threatening. It was smooth, emollient, persuasive. 'Adam died eight years ago, didn't he?'

'He did, yes. We took him home to Penrith to burn him.' Her face twisted suddenly with the pain of the memory, but then in two seconds was clear and blank again.

'Do you want to tell us about that death, Ellie?'

She looked at Clyde sharply when he used that name, then glanced down at her desk and smiled. He was quite fit, really, this big black policeman. Dangerous, perhaps, but she'd always liked a bit of danger. Adam had warned her about that. Adam should be here now to talk to her about DS Northcott. Perhaps he'd have told her she was a big girl now and should be able to look after herself. Lots of other people had told her that, but she'd never felt it herself. Professionally she was independent, yes, but not in her private life. Not until last Tuesday, anyway, when she'd finally put things to rights. She said, 'Alfred Norbury killed Adam, you know. Killed him as surely as if he'd put a knife through his heart.'

'But that wasn't the official verdict, was it, Ellie?'

The big black man knew. He knew and he was sympathetic. He probably understood exactly why she'd had to do it. She smiled at him. 'They said it was suicide. "Suicide whilst the balance of the mind was disturbed", they said. Mum said they were trying to be kind. But being kind wasn't going to bring Adam back, was it?'

'No, it wasn't, Ellie. Tell us how you think Alfred Norbury killed him, please.'

She was glad he was calling her Ellie now. It brought a kind of relief to her, when she heard her name spoken in that soft, impossibly deep voice. Like a lullaby singing you to sleep. 'Alfred Norbury took Adam up like a new hobby, just a fortnight after my brother came to live in Brunton. Nine years ago, that was. I was only eighteen and still in the sixth form.'

'So you knew nothing about what was going on here.'

'No. I'd never set foot in Brunton then. But I could tell things were going wrong for Adam just by speaking to him on the phone. He had his degree from Cambridge and he knew lots of things. But he didn't know enough about life to beware of Norbury.' She spoke the name like a curse, as no doubt it was to her. 'Adam was a research assistant at Manchester University who was living here with one of his university friends. He wasn't earning much, but there was talk of a full-time teaching post at the end of the year. Norbury got him work writing reviews of books. He helped him with short stories. He lured him into bed. That was Adam's mistake.' She was almost as anguished in admitting a flaw in her beloved brother as she had been at the thought of Norbury's villainy. 'Adam knew immediately that it was a mistake, but Alfred Norbury wouldn't let him go. He threatened him with all kinds of things. He said Adam had no idea how vicious he could turn if he didn't get his way. The Coroner's Court said it was suicide, but it was Norbury who killed Adam. As surely as . . . well, as surely as . . .'

'As surely as you killed Alfred Norbury himself last Tuesday evening, Ellie.'

'That's right, yes. Adam can rest in peace now, can't he?'

She looked up for the first time at Northcott, who gave her a grave smile and the smallest of nods. 'You said earlier that you changed your name when you applied for the teaching post here.'

She looked now at the wall lined with books in her tutorial room, as if she needed to remind herself where she was. 'Yes. Jane's my second name – I told you. I thought I'd use that and change from Garside to Preston. I needed to get near to Norbury without him suspecting who I was, you see. And he never did, until I told him in the car last Tuesday. I shot him immediately after I'd told him. I was glad he knew who I was and why he was dying.' She spoke as calmly as if she had delivered a birthday present rather than death.

Northcott let her words hang in the quiet room for a few seconds before he said, 'You'd been planning to kill him for a long time, hadn't you, Ellie?'

She didn't answer him directly. Instead, she said unexpectedly, 'I thought you were on to me on Saturday, when you asked why I'd chosen to come here without any promotion being involved. It was to get as near as I could to Alfred Norbury without being spotted. I'd known I was going to kill him ever since we burnt Adam.'

It was the second time she had used that harsh expression. Perhaps she had needed to keep the literal truth before her, to fire her mind towards her revenge. Clyde Northcott smiled at her now, as if he had followed all of this and considered it wholly understandable. He said quietly, 'It took you a little while to get your opportunity, didn't it, Ellie?'

'Oh, not very long really. I'd have been prepared to wait much longer. It seemed like fate when I found he was going to attend the book club. I'd almost said no to Sharon Burgess when she asked me to join, but I decided to give it a go because I knew Norbury was part of the Brunton literary set. Then a couple of days later Sharon rang me to run the names of the group past me for my approval and I found that Norbury was to be one of them. So that was fate, wasn't it?'

'Everything seemed to be working out well for you.'

'It was, wasn't it? And then when we met for the first time Alfred Norbury boasted about having that pistol in his old car. It was almost as if some force outside this world was organizing things for me.' She cast her eyes speculatively towards the ceiling, and both of them thought she was going to mention Adam again. But then she shook her head firmly and said, 'But I don't believe in that sort of thing. Perhaps this death was some sort of poetic justice. That would appeal to me more.'

She looked interrogatively at Northcott then, as if convincing him of this was far more important than any admission of murder. He nodded and said, 'I expect it was you who put Mrs Burgess's glove under the passenger seat in that car, wasn't it, Ellie?'

'It was. Yes. She'd left it behind after my evening class on the nineteenth-century novel. I'd kept it carefully to return it to her, but then when I got the opportunity to shoot Norbury I thought it would confuse things if I left it in his car. I wouldn't have allowed her to suffer, you know. If you'd arrested her for murder, I'd have come forward and said I put that glove there.'

'Yes, I expect you would have done that, Ellie.' She would indeed, Clyde thought. When it came to the reckoning, Ellie Garside, aka Jane Preston, wouldn't have allowed anyone else to take what she saw as the credit for this wholly merited death. 'We're going to arrest you now, Ellie. You realize that, don't you?'

'Yes. People will understand, when they hear about it.'

She was perfectly serene as Peach, who had not spoken now for what seemed a long time, stepped forward and pronounced the words of arrest. Clyde Northcott wondered what a good defence counsel would make of her reasons for this death, how much the eventual sentence would be mitigated by the reasons she had for killing Alfred Norbury. He was glad that he would not be involved in any way in those decisions.

They didn't handcuff her, after she assured them that she would make no attempt to escape. She held herself very upright as she accompanied them through noisy crowds of students, who had no idea of the drama which was being enacted within their midst. Peach drove the car back to the station and the cells at Brunton. Their murderer sat straight-backed in the rear of the vehicle beside the vigilant Clyde Northcott, with both of them thinking of what might have been if she had never seen or heard of Alfred Norbury.